安徽省高等学校"十四五"规划教材
安徽省一流本科教材建设项目成果

新活力英语翻译系列教材

英汉翻译教程

主　编：赵从义　张　艳　高福猛
副主编：姚　强　宋仕振　李珍莉
　　　　李晓宁　李梦瑞
编　者：彭云清　王宥鑫　孙晓霞
　　　　王雨奇

北京师范大学出版集团
BEIJING NORMAL UNIVERSITY PUBLISHING GROUP
安徽大学出版社

图书在版编目（CIP）数据

英汉翻译教程 / 赵从义，张艳，高福猛主编 .— 合肥：安徽大学出版社，2023.4
新活力英语翻译系列教材 / 朱玉斌总主编
ISBN 978-7-5664-2555-3

I. ①英… II. ①赵… ②张… ③高… III. ①英语—翻译—高等学校—教材 IV. ① H315.9

中国版本图书馆 CIP 数据核字（2022）第 258275 号

英汉翻译教程
Yinghan Fanyi Jiaocheng

赵从义　张　艳　高福猛　主编

出版发行：	北京师范大学出版集团 安 徽 大 学 出 版 社 （安徽省合肥市肥西路 3 号　邮编 230039） www.bnupg.com www.ahupress.com.cn
印　　刷：	安徽利民印务有限公司
经　　销：	全国新华书店
开　　本：	787 mm × 1092 mm　1/16
印　　张：	20.5
字　　数：	573 千字
版　　次：	2023 年 4 月第 1 版
印　　次：	2023 年 4 月第 1 次印刷
定　　价：	72.00 元

ISBN 978-7-5664-2555-3

策划编辑：李　雪		装帧设计：李　军　孟献辉	
责任编辑：李　雪		美术编辑：李　军	
责任校对：高婷婷		责任印制：赵明炎	

版权所有　侵权必究

反盗版、侵权举报电话：0551-65106311
外埠邮购电话：0551-65107716
本书如有印装质量问题，请与印制管理部联系调换。
印制管理部电话：0551-65106311

前言

本书简明地介绍了翻译的基本理论知识，通过英汉两种语言的对比和大量译例，阐释了英汉翻译的一系列常用方法和技巧。本书是为普通高校英语专业和翻译专业本科学生编写的英汉翻译教程，也适合翻译爱好者自学使用。

本书分为上下册，共六章。各章节后配有翻译练习，以便学生通过实践熟悉翻译技巧、提高翻译能力。

本书主要特色如下：

一、批判性地保留了传统翻译教学的增、减、拆、合等翻译方法和技巧，在翻译学习的入门阶段，用词句的翻译来解释一些基本的现象和规律。

二、设置了常见文体翻译章节，引导学生将翻译学习从词句层面扩展到段落篇章层面。

三、每一章节除了理论概述、技巧讲解，还包括翻译实例评析，让学生意识到译文篇章中语句连贯的重要性，并从经典译例中吸取经验。

四、注重精讲多练，翻译练习力求编排科学，灵活多变，体现实用性、针对性和可操作性，尽可能地选用内容较新的材料，以激发学生的学习兴趣。

本书参考了国内外近年来出版的许多相关著作和刊物，从中精心挑选了一些练习和例句，有的出处列在书后的参考书目中，有的因种种原因未能一一列出，在此一并表示衷心的感谢。

由于编者经验和水平有限，且时间仓促，书中难免有疏漏和不尽如人意之处，恳请使用本书的师生和其他读者不吝批评指正。

编写组
2023 年 2 月

目 录

第一章　翻译概述 ………………………………………… 1
- 第一节　翻译的定义 …………………………………… 2
- 第二节　翻译的标准 …………………………………… 3
- 第三节　翻译的过程 …………………………………… 5
- 第四节　翻译的方法 …………………………………… 11
- 第五节　译者的素养 …………………………………… 14

第二章　英汉语言对比 …………………………………… 17
- 第一节　英汉语言宏观对比 …………………………… 18
- 第二节　英汉语言微观对比 …………………………… 37

第三章　翻译基本技巧 …………………………………… 53
- 第一节　词义的选择 …………………………………… 54
- 第二节　词类转换 ……………………………………… 62
- 第三节　增词法 ………………………………………… 69
- 第四节　减词法 ………………………………………… 74
- 第五节　重译法 ………………………………………… 80
- 第六节　正反、反正译法 ……………………………… 86
- 第七节　被动语态的译法 ……………………………… 98
- 第八节　分译合译法 …………………………………… 106

第四章　从句的翻译 …… 119
第一节　名词性从句的翻译 …… 120
第二节　定语从句的翻译 …… 128
第三节　状语从句的翻译 …… 137

第五章　长句的翻译 …… 145
第一节　顺译法 …… 147
第二节　分译法 …… 155
第三节　逆译法 …… 162
第四节　综合法 …… 169

第六章　常见文体的翻译 …… 177
第一节　文学文体的翻译 …… 179
第二节　广告文体的翻译 …… 198
第三节　新闻文体的翻译 …… 215
第四节　商务文体的翻译 …… 231
第五节　科技文体的翻译 …… 251

参考答案 …… 271

附录一　全国翻译专业资格（水平）考试介绍 …… 311

附录二　全国翻译专业资格（水平）考试
　　　　　英语笔译三级考试大纲（2020版） …… 315

参考书目 …… 317

第一章
翻译概述

第一节 翻译的定义

人类自从有了语言交流，翻译活动就与之形影不离。据史书记载，中国在周代就有专门司职翻译的官员。如《礼记·王制》中齐心记载："五方之民，言语不通，嗜欲不同。达其志，通其欲，东方曰寄，南方曰象，西方曰狄鞮，北方曰译。"文中的"寄""象""狄鞮"和"译"等均为从事翻译的官员。由此可见，翻译这种语言活动是人们互相交流沟通的桥梁。古今中外的很多翻译家都对翻译有过不同的阐释。

我国唐朝的贾公彦在《义疏》中把翻译界定为："译即易，谓换易言语使相解也。"宋代的法云在《翻译名义集》中提出："夫翻译者，谓翻梵天之语，转成汉地之言。音虽似别，义则大同。"

当代学者张培基认为："翻译是运用一种语言把另一种语言所表达的思想内容准确而完整地重新表达出来的语言活动。"孙致礼指出："翻译是把一种语言表达的意义用另一种语言表达出来，已达到沟通思想情感、传播文化知识、促进社会文明，特别是推动译语文化兴旺昌盛的目的。"许钧则认为："翻译是以符号转换为手段，意义再生为任务的一项跨文化的交际活动。"

英国语言学家和翻译理论家卡特福德认为："翻译是用一种语言中的对等文本材料去替代另一种语言中的文本材料。"苏联语言学家巴尔胡达罗夫在《语言与翻译》中指出："翻译是把一种语言的言语产物，在保持内容也就是意义不变的情况下，改变为另一种语言产物的过程。"美国翻译理论家奈达认为："所谓翻译，是指在译语中用最切近而又最自然的对等语再现源语的信息，首先是就意义而言，其次是就风格而言。"英国翻译理论家纽马克认为："翻译就是按照作者的创作意图把一篇文章的意思用另一种语言描述出来的过程。"

各种中外辞书也给出了关于翻译的定义：

把一种语言文字的意义用另一种语言文字表达出来。(《辞海》)

把一种语言文字的意义用另一种语言文字表达出来（也指方言与民族共同语、方言与方言、古代语与现代语之间一种用另一种表达）；把代表语言文字的符号或数码用语言文字表达出来。(《现代汉语词典》)

翻译是按社会认知需要、在具有不同规则的符号系统之间传递信息的语言文化活动。(《译学词典》)

The process of translating words or text from one language into another. (*The New Oxford*

Dictionary of English, 1998)

Translating is the art of recomposing a work in another language without losing its original flavor. (Columbia Encyclopedia)

关于翻译的定义还有很多，这里不再一一列举。从上述定义中可以看出：

1. 翻译本质上是一种语际转换活动，涉及两种不同的语言，即把源语转化为目的语的过程。

2. 翻译的根本目的在于完整、准确、流畅地传递原文信息。

3. 翻译还涉及两种语言背后的社会文化因素，是两个拥有不同文化背景的民族进行沟通的桥梁。

因此，我们认为：翻译是以传递信息为目标的一种跨语言、跨文化、跨符号的交际活动。

第二节　翻译的标准

方梦之在《译学词典》中将翻译的标准定义为："翻译活动必须遵循的准绳，是衡量译文质量的尺度，是翻译工作者不断努力以期达到的目标。"对于翻译的标准，古今中外的翻译家们有着不同的观点，可谓仁者见仁，智者见智。

三国时期的高僧支谦就在《法句经序》中提出了"因循本旨，不加文饰"的观点；东晋的道安提出"案本而传，不令有损言游字"的看法；唐代高僧玄奘也提出了"既需求真，又需喻俗"的翻译标准。这些都是他们在佛经翻译中的心得体会。而在我国最受推崇的当属严复在《天演论》首卷《译例言》中提出的"信、达、雅"三字标准：

"译事三难：信、达、雅。求其信，已大难矣。顾信矣，不达，虽译，尤不译也，则达尚焉……至原文辞理本深，难于共喻，则当前后引衬，以显其意。凡此经营，皆以为达；为达，即所以为信也。"

其中，"信"强调的是译文必须忠实于原文；"达"强调的是译文应该通俗易懂；而"雅"在严复所处的时代指的是译文应该使用汉代以前的文风，现在一般指译文要有与原文相当的文采。

此外，英国翻译理论家泰特勒在《论翻译的原则》一书中提出了著名的翻译三原则：

1. 译作应完全复写出原作的思想。
2. 译作的风格和手法应与原作属于同一性质。
3. 译作应与原作同样流畅。

由此可见，泰特勒的翻译三原则与严复的"信、达、雅"有着异曲同工之妙。

此后，中西方很多学者和翻译家结合翻译实践，对翻译标准提出了独特的见解。国内有鲁迅的"宁信而不顺"，傅雷的"神似"说，钱钟书的"化境"论，刘重德的"信达切"以及辜正坤提出的"翻译标准多元互补论"。在西方，有美国翻译理论家奈达提出的以"等效原则"为基础的动态对等，强调"接受者和信息之间的关系应该和源语接受者和原文信息之间存在的关系相同"。英国翻译理论家纽马克提出的"交际翻译与语义翻译"，莱斯、弗米尔和诺德的"功能目的"翻译标准等。

从以上列举的翻译标准中可以看出，很难得出一个放之四海而皆准的结论。不过，在我国翻译界，大多数学者都能接受"忠实"和"通顺"的翻译标准。当代翻译理论家张培基在其所著的《英汉翻译教程》中提出了这两项标准，对翻译初学者来说，这也是最重要的两项基本要求。书中指出：

> 所谓忠实，首先是指忠实于原作的内容。译者必须把原作的内容完整地表达出来，不得任意篡改、歪曲、遗漏或增删原文内容。内容通常指作品中所叙述的事实，说明的事理，描写的景物以及作者在叙述、说明和描写过程中所反映的思想、观点、立场和所流露的感情。

> 忠实还指保持原作的风格——即原作的民族风格、时代风格、语体风格、作者个人的语言风格等。译者对原作的风格不能任意破坏和改变，不能以译者的风格代替原作的风格。

> 所谓通顺，即指译文语言必须通顺易懂，符合规范。译文必须是明白晓畅的现代语言……

前文中玄奘提出的"既需求真，又需喻俗"，与"忠实、通顺"颇有异曲同工之妙；而奈达在关于翻译的定义中所提到的 closest 和 natural 似乎也可以理解为"忠实、通顺"。

教育部颁布的《高等学校英语专业高年级教学大纲》中也规定，英译汉、汉译英的评分标准分为"忠实"和"通顺"两项。前者指"原文的信息全部传达，语气和文体风格与原文相一致"，后者则要求"断句恰当，句式正确，选词妥帖，段落之间、句子之间呼应自然（英译汉）"。以百分比来衡量，其中"忠实"占 60%，"通顺"占 40%。

总之，"忠实"与"通顺"互相依存，好的译文往往两者兼顾。要达到这个基本要求就必须抓住原文真正的含义，但不能受原文结构形式的束缚。现举几例略加说明：

例 1　There are books and books.

原译：有好些本书。

本例句型虽然简单，但两个 books 意思并不同，若译为"好些本书"，则流于形式，与原意相差太大。例如：

There are teachers and teachers. = There are good teachers and bad teachers. (*A University Grammar of English*)

There are shopkeepers and shopkeepers. = Some shopkeepers do their business honestly while others do not. (*English Idioms and How to Use Them*)

从上面两例中可以看出，用 and 来连接两个相同的词表示同一事物有不同性质。有趣的是，台湾省著名作家李敖的《坐牢家爸爸给女儿的八十封信》中有一篇《打老虎秘诀》，其中有一句话：Those who go tiger hunting should remember that there are tigers and tigers. 这意思并不是"打老虎要记着老虎多得很"，而是"打老虎要记着老虎有各式各样的——有好打的，有难打的"。

所以例 1 可改译为：书有种种，好坏不一。也直接体现了"忠实"对于译文的重要性。

例 2　Louisa (a peasant girl): As you have come to my house, I feel greatly honored.

原译：路易莎（一位农家姑娘）：光临寒舍，蓬荜生辉！

改译：路易莎（一位农家姑娘）：您到俺家来，真是贵客临门。

原译固然用词讲究，文采斐然，但对于一位农家姑娘来说语气有些过于正式，与原作的风格也显得有些格格不入。考虑到人物的身份，改译后的版本更为得当。

例 3　The history of a tree from the time it starts in the forest until the boards which it yields are used, would form an interesting and, in many instances, an exciting story.

原译：树的历史开始于森林中，直到生产为木板后被使用为止，成为一个有趣且有许多事例的激动人心的故事。

改译：一棵树，从它在森林中生长起直到被制成木板使用为止，这段历史会构成一个饶有趣味的故事，在很多情况下这个故事十分激动人心。

原译机械地对应英文语序，层次不清，语言生硬。如果按照逻辑关系分为两层意思：树的历史的起止时间和树的历史如何不平凡，那么译文可以达成"忠实"和"通顺"的一致。

第三节　翻译的过程

翻译的过程是准确理解原文并创造性地用另一种语言再现原文信息和风格的过程。奈达把翻译的过程分为四个阶段：1. 源语文本的分析；2. 源语到目的语的转换；3. 目的语的重构；4. 译文读者的代表检验译文。而张培基在《英汉翻译教程》中将翻译过程分为理解、表达和校核三个阶段。在翻译实践中，理解是基础，只有准确理解，方能译出佳作；表达是关键，是对理解的再现；而校核是改进，是对理解和表达的进一步深化。

一、理解阶段

方梦之在《译学词典》中将理解定义为："指弄懂源语的种种含义，是译者认识事物之间联系的本质与规律的一种思维活动。"对原文的理解覆盖词义、语法结构、背景知识、文化因素等各个方面。理解既要从大处着眼，注意整体和全貌，又需从小处入手，关注局部和细节。

（一）确定词义

英语词语的意义丰富，一词多义现象非常普遍，是理解过程中最大的"拦路虎"，所以辨义应为翻译之本。正如英国哲学家维特根斯坦所言："The meaning of a word is in the use of it." 任何语言现象都不是孤立存在的，也绝不能断章取义地去理解。例如：

例 1　You have to slow down now. There is a *sleeping policeman*.

译文 1：你要减速才行。前面有个隐身警察。

译文 2：你要减速才行，前面有个路障。

此例中的两种译文均有错误。sleeping policeman 既不是"隐身警察"，也不是"路障"。英文中表示"路障"的单词为 roadblock。而 sleeping policeman 意为：A bump in the road intended to cause traffic to reduce speed. 见于英式英语，而美式英语中多用 speed bump，两者都相当于中文里的"减速带"。另外，原译文从逻辑方面也经不起推敲，"隐身警察"又如何能够看见？"路障"也多指为了检查而设置的障碍物。建议改译为：你得开慢点儿，前面有减速带。

例 2　The meeting starts at ten o'clock *sharp* and finishes sometime between eleven-thirty and twelve, depending on the agenda.

按照议程，会议将于 10 点整开始，11:30~12:00 结束。

上例中的 sharp 也容易出现误译，在句中用作副词，意思是：used after an expression for a time of day to mean "exactly or precisely"，表示"……点整"或"准时"。

（二）习惯用法

在英汉翻译中，译者对于一些惯用语或固定词组也要多加小心，切忌望文生义，否则译文必将"南辕北辙"。例如：

例 3　*The name of the game* is controlling the population.

原译：游戏的名称是控制人口。

上例中的 the name of the game 意为：一项活动的主要目的或最重要的方面。按字面意思硬译会令读者困惑不已。

改译：问题的关键在于控制人口。

例 4　Stoves, sofas, refrigerators, sinks, carpets. **You name it**, and you could find it idling curbside, waiting to be evacuated by men in dump trucks.

不管是炉子、沙发、冰箱、还是洗涤槽和地毯，只要你能点出名字，都可以在马路边找得到，它就随随便便地躺在那里，等着开垃圾车的人运走。

不少人将 You name it 译为"你给他们起名字"或"你呼叫他们"。其实原文意在总结，不管有多少东西，只要你能想得到或叫得出名字，就一定可以找到。这种情况对于初学翻译的人来说绝非罕见，当引以为戒。

此外，英语中有许多习语从表面上看与汉语的某些说法高度相似，实则差异颇大，在翻译实践中要高度警惕这类"假朋友"，切忌因望文生义、不求甚解而造成误译。例如：

原文	误译 / 正解
busboy	公汽售票员 / 餐馆勤杂工
mad doctor	发疯的医生 / 精神病科医生
eleventh hour	十一点 / 紧要关头
busybody	大忙人 / 好事之徒
Indian summer	印度的夏日 / 愉快宁静的晚年
Greek gift	希腊礼物 / 害人的礼物
to pull one's leg	拖后腿 / 戏弄某人

（三）分析句法结构

王力先生曾经指出："就句子的结构而论，西洋语言是法治的，中国语言是人治的。"所谓"法治"，即句子的形式会严格受到语法的制约。在翻译实践中，对原文进行句法结构分析是准确理解的关键。

例 5　New machines or techniques are not merely a product, but a source of creative ideas.

原译：新的机器、新的技术不仅是一种产品，而且是创造性思想的源泉。

上面译文之所以错误，是因为对原文句法结构分析不够透彻。

改译：新的机器、新的技术不仅是创造性思想的结晶，而且是创造性思想的源泉。

例 6　① There are several reasons　② why Kissinger no longer appears to be　③ the magician the world press had made him out to be, ④ an illusion which he failed to discourage ⑤ because, as he would admit himself, ⑥ he has a tendency toward megalomania.

面对上面的这个长句，如果没有梳理清楚各部分之间的语法关系，就无法把握原文的意思，并译出理想的译文。为方便理解，在各部分前加上了序号。其中①和②是整体概括，③和④是具体事实，⑤和⑥是解释原因。根据句意可对语序进行调整：③④⑤⑥②①。

译文：全世界的报界曾经把基辛格渲染成一个魔术师般的人物，他也没有阻止报界去制造这种错误印象。因为正如他自己承认的，他有一种自大狂的倾向。而现在他已失去了这种魔力，这里面有几个原因。

（四）理顺逻辑关系

当语法手段无法奏效时，尤其是面对容易产生歧义的内容，往往需要借助逻辑手段，来推理某个词或者短语的意思。

例 7　Clare stood still, and inclined his face towards hers.

"Oh, *Tessy*!" he exclaimed.

The girl's cheeks burned to the **breeze**, and she could not look into his eyes for the emotion. (Hardy: Tess, Ch. 23)

上例选自英国作家托马斯·哈代的小说《德伯家的苔丝》，描绘了苔丝和克莱尔见面的场景。有人曾将 breeze 译为微风，整句译为：苔丝姑娘的面颊在微风中烧得发烫，情感荡漾，不敢再看他的眼睛了。然而根据上文，克莱尔将脸颊贴近苔丝，咫尺之遥呼喊着她的名字，breeze 未必是自然界的微风。若是凉风习习，脸颊何以发烫？所以此处的 breeze 应理解为克莱尔嘴中呼出的热气。

试译：克莱尔站住了脚，把脸贴向苔丝的脸。

"哦，苔丝！"他失声嚷道。

苔丝感到了他嘴里呼出的气息，脸上给烧得火辣辣的，她心摇神荡，不敢再盯着克莱尔的眼睛了。

例 8　North Korea's official media said scientists in the country had invented an alcoholic drink that does not cause hangovers. It is said to be made of a type of ginseng and glutinous rice. Implausible claims are a North Korean **staple**.

朝鲜官方媒体称该国科学家已研制出了不会导致宿醉的酒。据说这种混合酒由糯米制成，并加入了高丽参。

本例中的 staple 是理解中的难点，有同学曾将其译为：

A. 有不靠谱的传言说这种酒精饮料是用一种主食做的。

B. 有不靠谱的传言说朝鲜人用这种酒精饮料当主食。

根据和朝鲜相关的一些背景知识，用酒精饮料作为主食可信度确实不高。而详查词典之后会发现，staple 还可以指某事的"主要内容或主要部分"。

试译：不过夸大其辞是朝鲜的一贯作风。

从上两例中可以看出，一名合格的译者要能从字里行间理顺原文中存在的逻辑关系。

（五）熟悉背景知识

在理解阶段，译者还应该尽量多查阅原作的背景知识，以及相关的专门知识。此外还需关注文化方面的差异，避免出现文化误读。

例 9   Then he was off to Columbia Business School, where he found his ***Rosetta Stone*** of investing. (Roger Lowenstein: *An Unassuming Billionaire*)

后来他进了哥伦比亚商学院，在那里找到了自己的投资指南。

Rosetta Stone 指在埃及出土的古代石碑，意为"提供线索"，在句中喻指"帮助了解难题的事物"。

例 10   In order to win the election, he took the voters by an ***October Surprise***.

为了争夺选民，他制造了一次"十月惊变"。

[注] 美国总统候选人通常在大选前夕（一般在十月份）采取意外行动，或惊人之举，以提高自己的知名度或是打击对手，争取选民的支持，堪称最后的杀手锏。

译者采取直译加注的方式，阐释了原文的背景知识，更方便读者理解，不失为一种应对良策。

总而言之，准确充分地理解原文是翻译实践必要的前提和保障。

二、表达阶段

如果对原文的理解准确，那么表达便成为影响译文质量的关键。这主要取决于译者对于目的语的语言修养。译文应该保证通顺易懂，符合目的语的表达习惯，而不必过分拘泥于原文字面或句子结构。同时要注意表达充分，兼顾原文风格，不要随意删减或添枝加叶。

例 11   Thank you for your letter conveying congratulations to me on the award of the Who's Who honor.

原译：感谢你的转达了我进入"名人录"荣誉册的祝贺的信。

改译：本人有幸被选入"名人录"，你来信向我表达祝贺，特此致信感谢。

余光中先生曾在《中文的常态与变态》一文中指出："白话文一用到形容词，似乎就离不开'的',简直无'的'不成句了。"原译"的的不休",读来颇感累赘。而中文习惯于先交代背景,层层铺垫,重心靠后,有种"水到渠成"之感。改译将原文切分为3个小句,灵活添加动词,读来一气呵成,方为中文的"常态"。

例 12　He was but a man with many grey hairs, with a heavy burden of responsibility, of thoughts and worries.

原译:他已是长了许多灰发、肩负责任、心中充满思考和忧虑的人。

改译:他已是鬓发斑白,肩负重任,思绪万千,焦虑满怀。

改译充分考虑到汉语表达的特点,运用四字格结构,既言简意赅,又体现了节奏感。

例 13　But this arms race strained the government's principles as well as its budgets.

但是这场军备竞赛使政府的原则无法自圆其说,也使其预算捉襟见肘。

原文中的 strain 搭配能力较强,后跟 principle 和 budget 两个宾语。译文灵活拆分,根据汉语的习惯选择更合理的搭配,读来简洁地道。

例 14　Across the street on the side of a house was painted a giant woman with a five-foot smile and long blond hair, holding out a giant bottle.

原译:街对面房子的墙上有一幅大型广告画——一位肩披金色长发的女郎,笑容满面,手里举着一个大瓶子。

上面的译文与原文基本上亦步亦趋,没有考虑读者观察事物的角度和叙事顺序,可以根据由近到远、从整体到局部的原则加以调整。

改译:街对面有一座房子,临街的墙上有一副巨型广告画,画中一位金发女郎笑容可掬,手中举着一个大瓶子。

上述几例均可体现表达对译文质量高低的重要性,至于如何提高表达能力,可以参阅本书关于翻译方法和翻译技巧的章节。

三、校核阶段

本阶段是对理解和表达的进一步深化,可以进一步核实原文内容,对译文语言进行推敲润色。如果想确保译文符合"忠实""通顺"的标准,这是不可或缺的一个环节。译文完成后,至少应该校对两遍方能定稿,第一遍重在校对内容,第二遍重在润饰文字。如时间允许,对照原文再通读一遍译文会更为稳妥。一般来说,译者要特别留意以下几方面:

1. 是否存在段落、句子或关键词等的漏译;
2. 对原文理解是否有误;

3. 译文中是否有措辞不当之处或错别字；

4. 译文语句是否有不通顺之处，比如"欧式汉语"；

5. 格式和标点符号是否符合规范。

第四节　翻译的方法

《译学词典》将翻译方法与策略定义为："译者根据一定的翻译任务和要求，为达到特定目的而采取的具体途径、策略、手法和技巧。"提到翻译的具体策略和方法，必然会涉及翻译研究中的两对名词：直译和意译；归化和异化。

一、直译和意译

无论在我国还是在西方翻译界，"直译和意译"的话题一直是争论的焦点，各种流派众说纷纭，莫衷一是。事实上，直译与意译只是两种常用的翻译策略，各有长处，译者也不应采取非此即彼的态度。

（一）直译法

张培基等人认为："所谓直译，就是在语言条件许可时，在译文中既保留原文的内容，又保持原文的形式——特别指保持原文的比喻、形象和民族、地方色彩等。但直译不是死译或者硬译。"一般说来，如果英汉语言在形式上基本相同，原文中的比喻或形象也可以为目的语读者所接受，便可使用直译法。例如：

cold war 冷战　　　　　　　hot line 热线

Hot-selling books 畅销书　　　black market 黑市

pillar industry 支柱产业　　　Blood is thicker than water. 血浓于水

例 1　我们要再次敦促英方，不要再在香港问题上*指手画脚，煽风点火*。

We again urge it to stop *finger-pointing* and *fanning the flames* on the Hong Kong issue.

例 2　The Senate Foreign Relations Committee today *extended the olive branch* to the Clinton Government by pleading for cooperation in developing foreign policy.

参议院外交委员会今天向克林顿政府*伸出了橄榄枝*，要求在制定外交政策上开展合作。

（二）意译法

范仲英认为："意译则从意义出发，只要求将原文大意表达出来，不注意细节，译文自然流畅即可。意译不注意原作形式，包括句法结构、用词、比喻以及其他修辞手段。

但意译并不意味着可以将内容随意删改，或添枝加叶。"当原文与译文形式无法兼容时，译者就需要"不破不立"，采用符合目的语的表达手段，力求做到保留原文的意蕴。

例 3　I talked to him with brutal frankness.

译文 1：我同他谈话用粗暴的坦率。（逐词翻译）

译文 2：我同他谈话时，使用了令人不快的真诚的语言。（直译）

译文 3：我对他讲的话，虽然逆耳，但是忠言。（意译）

例 4　His irritation could not withstand the silent beauty of the night.

译文 1：他的烦恼不能承受夜晚宁静的美丽。（逐词翻译）

译文 2：他的烦恼经不起这宁静的良宵美景的感染。（直译）

译文 3：面对这宁静的良宵美景，他的烦恼不禁涣然冰释了。（意译）

例 5　Watch out for Harlow, he's full of Mickey mouse ideas.

译文 1：要小心哈洛，他满脑子都是米老鼠的想法。（直译）

译文 2：要提防着点哈洛，他满脑子歪门邪道。（意译）

由于英汉两种语言的差别很大，完全的直译和意译都是不可能的，只能说某种译法更趋向于直译或者意译。两者之间并非泾渭分明，而是互为补充，相辅相成。直译有助于保留原文的格调并引进新鲜、生动的词语、句法结构和表达方法，从而使目的语不断丰富、日益完善。而意译则便于调和原文与译文形式上的矛盾，使译文通顺流畅，符合目的语的语法规范和表达习惯。需要强调的是，直译不是死译或硬译，不是生搬硬套，逐字照译。意译不是任意增删，不是胡译或乱译。

一般来说，翻译法律、科技、学术和政论文献时，要求更准确地再现原文的字面意思，因此更适用直译；而翻译文学作品，如诗歌、散文、小说等可更趋向于意译。用陆殿扬教授的话来总结："能直译就尽量直译，不能直译就采取意译。"译者要善于把两者结合起来，用以解决翻译实践中的问题。

二、归化和异化

1813 年，德国古典语言学家、翻译理论家施莱尔马赫在《论翻译的方法》中提出：翻译的途径"只有两种：一种是尽可能让作者安居不动，而引导读者去接近作者；另一种是尽可能让读者安居不动，而引导作者去接近读者。""读者接近作者"指译者以保持原文作者所有的表达方式来传达原文内容；"作者接近读者"指译者使用译文读者习惯的表达方式传达原文内容。

美国翻译理论家韦努蒂于 1995 年在《译者的隐形》一书中提出了异化法和归化法。

异化和归化可以看作直译和意译的概念延伸，但又不完全等同于直译和意译。直译和意译所关注的核心问题是如何在语言层面处理形式和意义；而异化和归化则突破了语言因素的局限，将视野扩展到了语言、文化和美学等因素。异化和归化作为两种主要的翻译策略历来是翻译界争论的焦点之一。

（一）归化法

归化策略以目的语读者为中心，恪守目的语的语言文化传统，采用读者耳熟能详的表达方式，把一种文化中的异质成分转化为另一种文化中人们所熟知的内容，使读者读来轻松自然，降低了理解的难度。比如英语和汉语中的许多成语和习语，虽然找不到完全对应的说法，但内涵一致的情况比比皆是。用归化策略翻译这些成语、惯用语，不仅地道、生动，还易于被读者理解。但遗憾的是有时也会失去了解、欣赏和借鉴其他国家和民族文化的意义。例如：

as timid as a hare 胆小如鼠　　　as stubborn as a mule 犟得像牛

seek a hare in a hen's nest 缘木求鱼　　as dumb as an oyster 守口如瓶

lead a dog's life 过着牛马一样的生活　　cry up wine and sell vinegar 挂羊头卖狗肉

kill the goose that lays the golden eggs 杀鸡取卵

drink like a fish 牛饮

Once the wife of a person, always the wife of a person.

嫁鸡随鸡，嫁狗随狗。

例 6　A girl who was her father's **little flower** had to marry off as early as possible to enhance her value.

一个父亲爱如**掌上明珠**的姑娘，为了抬高身价，不得不尽早出嫁。

例 7　High buildings and large mansions *are springing up like mushrooms* in China.

在中国，高楼大厦犹如**雨后春笋**般涌现。

（二）异化法

异化策略指译者在翻译过程中迁就原文作者，设法保留原文语言及文化特征，带给目的语读者异国情调。这种策略能把一种文化和语言中的信息以近乎保持其本来面目的方式传递给另一种文化及语言，有利于两种异质文化和语言的相互交流、渗透和融合。比如中国读者现在已经对"武装到牙齿"（armed to the teeth）、"象牙塔"（ivory tower）等表达方式习以为常。

例 8　to kill two birds with one stone

译文 1：一石二鸟（异化）

译文 2：一箭双雕、一举两得（归化）

例 9　All roads lead to Rome.

译文 1：条条大路通罗马（异化）

译文 2：殊途同归（归化）

例 10　Unless you've an ace up your sleeve, we are dished.

译文 1：除非你袖中藏有王牌，否则我们就输定了。（异化）

译文 2：除非你有锦囊妙计，否则我们就输定了。（归化）

译者在翻译的过程中，自始至终面临着异化与归化的选择。通过选择，在作者和读者之间找到一个"融会点"。这个"融会点"绝不是一成不变的"居中点"，它有时距离作者近一些，有时距离读者近一些。但无论更接近哪一方，都必须恪守一条原则：接近作者时，不能距离读者太远；接近读者时，又不能距离作者太远。换言之，异化时不妨碍译文的通顺易懂，归化时不改变原作的"风味"，特别是不能导致"文化错乱"。

第五节　译者的素养

作为翻译活动的主体，译者在作者与读者、原作与译文、源语文化与译语文化之间架起了一座桥梁。译文质量的高低在很大程度上取决于译者自身的素养和经验。要想成为一名合格的译者，必须满足以下几个基本条件。

一、扎实的语言功底

一名称职的译者必须熟练掌握母语和目的语。对于英汉翻译来说，译者就是要具备扎实的中英文功底。英语水平高可以保证理解准确；汉语水平高则是表达的必要条件。

二、广博的知识面

吕叔湘先生在《翻译工作与"杂学"》中指出翻译工作者需要很多的"杂学"。所谓"杂学"，就是字典不能帮忙的那些个东西：上至天文，下至地理，人情风俗，俚语方言，历史上的事件，小说里的人物，五花八门，无以名之，名之以"杂学"。所以除了双语能力，译者还应熟悉母语和目的语国家的历史和文化等方面的背景知识。正如奈达所说："For truly successful translating, biculturalism is even more important than bilingualism, since words only have meanings in terms of cultures in which they function." 此外，翻译活动会涉及政治、经济、法律、科技、商贸、建筑等各个方面内容，如果不具备一定的专业知识，很难顺利完成翻译任务。请一名英语师范专业的同学翻译一份科技资料，可能会勉为其难。若没有经过系统学习相关理论和知识，译文不够严谨，甚至会造成经济损失和生产事故。这绝不是危言耸听，而恰恰体现了"术业有专攻"的道理。

三、翻译理论与技巧

译者还需要熟悉翻译理论以及常用的翻译方法和技巧。有些译者对翻译理论不屑一顾，认为不懂理论一样可以进行实践，这种看法有失偏颇。不能否认有些翻译理论确实较为抽象，但适当了解基本的翻译理论，有助于译者在实践中全面思考，把握大局。而翻译技巧是翻译家们多年的经验积累，对个人的翻译实践有颇多益处。

四、善于利用各种工具

个人的知识和经验总是有限的，而在翻译实践中译者不可避免地会遇到各种问题。俗话说："工欲善其事，必先利其器。"身处信息化时代，除了传统的纸质词典、百科全书，还有浩如烟海的电子和网络资源供译者使用，要注重提高自己搜索信息的能力。此外，译者还应关注人工智能、计算机辅助翻译等方面的研究进展，熟悉各种翻译软件，加强团队合作，提升工作效率。

五、严谨的工作态度

自古译事多艰辛，严复曾经说过："一名之立，旬月踟蹰。"前面提到的几点对于译者固然重要，但严谨的工作态度也不可或缺。在翻译过程中要认真细心，一丝不苟。此外，如果想在翻译领域中立足，译者还需要具有良好的职业道德。

课后练习

一、翻译下列句子，注意"忠实"和"通顺"的原则。

1. I believe the speech was needlessly stubborn.

2. Jobs and work do much more than most of us realize to provide happiness and contentment.

3. The only concession he made to the climate was to wear a white dinner jacket.

4. But the next century we'll be able to alter our DNA radically, encoding our visions and vanities while conducting new life-forms.

5. He had a disconcerting habit of expressing contradictory ideas in rapid succession.

二、翻译下列短语或句子，注意运用直译法或意译法。

1. to trim the sail to the wind

2. Too many cooks spoil the broth.

3. to bring down the house

4. Every bean has its black.

5. to go on a wild goose chase

三、翻译下列短语，注意使用归化法或异化法。

1. live a dog's life

2. seek a hare in hen's nest

3. new wine in old bottles

4. a trump card

5. ivory tower

第二章
英汉语言对比

英语和汉语隶属于不同的语系，英语属于印欧体系，而汉语属于汉藏体系。通过对英汉两种语言进行对比，可以促进对两种语言的研究。美国著名语言学家和翻译学家奈达曾指出，翻译就是在目标语中寻找和源语信息尽可能接近的、自然的对等话语（Nida & Taber, 1969）。就英汉翻译而言，要想做好翻译，首先要对两种语言有深刻的了解和把握，才能自如地将两种语言进行转换，寻找到最合适的对等语。同时重视英汉语言对比可以提高学生跨语言、跨文化意识，在翻译过程中能够更加游刃有余地处理因两种语言差异而带来的种种翻译问题。

英汉语言对比属于语言学的一个分支，近些年来英汉语言的研究出现了理论和方法多元化的局面。根据索绪尔对微观语言学和宏观语言学的划分，英汉语言对比可分为两大类：微观研究和宏观研究（周振峰，2010）。本章主要从宏观和微观两个角度对英汉两种语言进行对比分析。

第一节　英汉语言宏观对比

本节主要是从语言结构及文化差异两个层面对英汉两种语言进行宏观对比。

一、英汉语言结构

英汉语言结构在宏观层面的差异主要体现在以下几点：静态与动态，抽象与具体，物称与人称，直接与间接。

（一）静态与动态

英语中多倾向于使用名词，而动词被弱化，语言表达整体呈静态。汉语中多倾向于使用动词，因而汉语整体呈动态。

英语的静态化趋向主要有以下表现：

第一，英语中名词化现象较为普遍。名词化主要指用名词来表达原本属于动词（或形容词）所表达的概念，如用抽象名词来表达动作、行为、变化、状态、品质、情感等概念（连淑能，1993）。使用名词的优势在于表达可以更为简洁灵活。英语中名词化结构的运用在科普文本、专业领域中尤其明显。例如：

例 1　Rectification of fault is achieved by insertion of a wedge.

嵌入一个楔子就可以纠正误差。

根据译文，这句话同样可以表述为"You can rectify the fault if you can insert a wedge."。但是人称以及动词的重复使用会显得句子繁琐且不够专业，名词化的应用更能传达科学性。

例 2　The originality of these buildings lies in the application of advanced building techniques.

这些建筑的创新之处在于使用了先进的建筑技术。

例 3　The abuse of basic human rights in their own country in violation of the agreement reached at Helsinki earned them the condemnation of freedom-loving people everywhere.

他们违反在赫尔辛基达成的协议，在国内侵犯基本人权，因此受到了各地热爱自由的人们的谴责。

例 4　Most economists acknowledge this trading system as one of the greatest contributors to the world's rapid recovery from the desolation of the Second World War.

很多经济学家都认为这种贸易体制为世界经济从二战的颓废中复苏起到很大作用。

例 5　Studies serve for delight, for ornament, and for ability.

读书足以怡情，足以增彩，足以长才。

第二，英语中常用名词表示施事者，传达行为和动作。比如英文中的后缀 -or、-er 等，不仅可以表示职业，在句中同样可以表示动作性。这些和动词组合派生出来的名词和其修饰成分也可以构成静态结构。而汉语则不同，汉语中"……者（员、家）"（如教师、医护人员、作家）一般表示人的职业和身份，如果想要表示相应的动作则用动词。

例 6　I'm not a good piano player.

我钢琴弹得不好。

英文中想传递出"我的钢琴水平如何"可以在句中使用 piano player 这一表述职业的名词，再用相应的形容词进行修饰，而中文则一般用动词直接进行表述。

例 7　He was a clever man; a pleasant companion; a careless student; with a great propensity for running into debt, and a partiality for the tavern. (*Vanity Fair*)

他是个聪明人，很好相处，可是学习不肯用功；他老是东挪西借，又喜欢上酒馆喝酒。

上述例子中用多个表示身份的名词来描述人物，对其进行定位，但是人物描写往往需要语言生动，若简单直译成名词则过于平淡，趋向于人物介绍，体现不出文学作品的特征，而汉语中的动词更能活灵活现地刻画出人物的性格特征。

例 8　When he catches a glimpse of a potential antagonist, his instinct is to win him over with charm and humor.

只要一发现有可能反对他的人，他就本能地要用魅力和风趣将这些人争取过来。

例9　She was essentially a photographer of New York and its environs.

她基本上拍摄纽约及其周边地区。

例10　He is co-author, with Andrew Blowers, of *The international Politics of Nuclear Waste*.

他与安德鲁·布洛尔斯合著了《透过核废料看国际政治》。

第三，英文中常用同源的形容词或副词表达出动词的含义。英文具有严格的语法规则，一个句子中只能出现一个谓语动词，且英文中最常用的一些动词都属于弱势动词。所谓"弱势动词"，指动作意味较弱，缺乏动态感的动词，一般包括 be 动词及其各种形式，以及 have, become, feel, go, come, get 等（连淑能，1993）。在这种情况下英语需要借助其他的词类如形容词、副词、介词等应用广泛的词来表达一些动词所想表达的概念。例如：

例11　I am doubtful whether he is still alive.

我怀疑他是否还活着。

例12　Scientists are confident that all matters are indestructible.

科学家们深信，所有的物质都是不灭的。

英文中有些表示情绪、思想情感的形容词本身就带有动作性的色彩，如 thankful, afraid, sad, angry 等，这类词汇常与 be 动词等弱势动词连用，凸显了英文静态的语言特征。而中文中表达情绪情感一般用动词表示。例如：

例13　I'm afraid Mr. Brown is out, but he'll be in soon.

恐怕布朗先生出去了，但是他很快就会回来。

英文中往往用副词表示位置、去向等，如 down, out, away, 而汉语中往往用动词表述此类含义。

例14　Down with the old, up with the new.

破旧立新。

综上，英语虽然语法规则严谨，比如动词只能充当谓语，但是其他词类（名词、形容词、副词等）功能强大，可以表达动词的概念，因此英语为静态语言。而汉语中动词占优势，为动态语言。汉语的动态化趋向主要有以下表现：

第一，汉语中经常动词连用。汉语中主要包括以下句式：连动式、兼语式、把字式、被字式等，句式较为灵活，可以互相套用，一句话中也可以使用多个动词。

例15　伯父家盖房，想用它垒山墙。

My uncle had wanted to use it for the gable.

例16　我被老师叫到办公室去做检讨。

I was called to the office by the teacher to make a self-criticism.

例 17　要把控制人口、节约资源、保护环境放在重要的位置上。

Population control, the conservation of resources and environmental protection should be put in an important place.

例 18　唐朝始于618年，终于907年，是中国历史上最灿烂的时期。

The Tang Dynasty, which was from 618 to 907, is the most splendid period in Chinese history.

第二，汉语中动词可以充当句子各种成分。不像英语中动词有时态、语态、单复数各方面的限制。汉语中动词使用非常方便，也体现了汉语动态化的特点。

例 19　他们喜欢乘火车旅行。（作宾语）

They enjoy travelling by train.

例 20　了解过去有助于了解现在，了解现在有助于预知未来。（作主语、宾语）

An acquaintance of the past is helpful to the acquaintance of the present, which is in turn helpful to the prediction of the future.

例 21　解决问题的最好方法是进行调查研究。（作定语、表语）

The best way to solve the problem is to conduct investigations.

第三，汉语中动词可以重叠使用。汉语中善用叠词、对偶、排比，以增强语言的感染力，给读者以画面感。

例 22　说说笑笑，跑跑跳跳，孩子们过得十分愉快。

Talking and laughing, running and jumping, the children have a good time.

例 23　细娃盼过年，大人盼开春。

Little children look forward to the arrival of lunar New Year, adults to that of spring.

例 24　我们谈到自己，谈到前途，谈到旅程，谈到天气，谈到彼此的情况——谈到一切，只是不谈我们的男女主人。

We talked of ourselves, of our prospects, of the journey, of the weather, of each other—of everything but our host and hostess.

基于上述对比分析，可见英译汉的过程也是一个由静态向动态转换的过程。因此为使译文更符合目标语的表达习惯，更加通顺，在英汉翻译的过程中，英语的名词、介词、形容词、副词等需要根据情况转换成汉语中的动词。

> 翻译实践

翻译下列句子，注意思考英汉语言结构的差异。

1. The university was the making of him.

2. His words were suggestive of his determination to finish the tough job.

3. Horticulture furnishes the setting for many recreational events, from picnics in the outdoors living area of a home to the tough turf of a football field.

4. …and in every step of his swift, mechanical march, and in every pause of his resolute observation, there is one and the same expression of perfect egotism, perfect independence and self-confidence, and conviction of the world's having been made for flies.

（二）抽象与具体

从语言表达方式上来看，英文具有用词抽象化的特点，而汉语倾向于用词具体化，常用实的词汇去表达虚的概念。

英文表达抽象化，究其原因有以下几点：

第一，英文中多用名词，英语的名词化往往导致表达的抽象化。英文中有丰富的词缀文化，尤其是名词后缀，动词和后缀的结合构成抽象名词。如表示性质、状态、行为的后缀有：-ment, -ity, -sion, -tion, -enced 等等。表示主义、学说、行为的有 -ism。此类抽象名词被广泛应用于英文中各种文体，如新闻、法律、商务文件等。如：

例 25　We should by no means neglect the <u>evaporation</u> of water.

我们绝不能忽视水的<u>蒸发作用</u>。

例 26　No one is satisfied with her <u>favoritism</u> in her work.

对她工作中表现出的<u>徇私做法</u>，所有人都感到不满意。

例 27　The signs of the times point to the necessity of the <u>modification</u> of the system of <u>administration</u>.

<u>管理体制</u>需要<u>改革</u>，这已经越来越清楚了。

例 28　There seems to have been an absence of attempts at <u>conciliation</u> between rival sects.

对立的派别似乎从来就没有试图去谋求<u>和解</u>。

第二，从思维方式来看，西方思维传统注重科学、理性，重视分析、实证，因而必然注重逻辑。而逻辑论证会借助判断推理等方式对思维对象进行间接的、概括的加工处理，因此具有抽象性的特点（连淑能，2002）。此种思维方式折射到英语语言上也是如此。而中国的思维方式是将思想理论和道理蕴含于具体的事物和物象当中，用一种形象具体的方式来表达抽象的事物。如：

例 29　The absence of intelligence is an indication of satisfactory developments.

没有消息即表明有令人满意的进展。

例 30　It was nearly midnight and eerily dark all round here.

夜深了，到处是一片黑黝黝的怪影。

例 31　Science is a method that ignores religion, race, nationality, economics, morality, and ethics.

科学是一种忽略宗教、种族、民族、经济、道德和伦理的方法。

第三，英语中虚化手段丰富，除了用抽象名词，还可以用介词和介词短语表示虚泛的概念。如：

例 32　Government of the people, by the people, for the people shall not perish from the earth.

这个民有、民治、民享的国家将不会从地球上消失。

例 33　I understand he is in for a job in the company.

我知道他在申请公司的一个职位。

例 34　I thought she had stopped crying, but now she is at it again.

我原以为她已经不哭了，谁知她现在又哭了起来。

汉语中用词具体，抽象名词较少，如"性"（重要性、必要性）、"化"（现代化、全球化）、"主义"（英雄主义、社会主义）等，而且虚化手段有限。因此，在英汉互译过程中一般需要将英文中的抽象表达译成汉语中具体化的表达，具体可以参照下列几种方法。

第一，汉语中动词的应用。英文中有大量的抽象名词表示行为动作的概念和内涵，若将其直译成中文相对应的名词，则译文晦涩难懂，翻译腔明显。因此，汉语需要充分发挥其动词优势，以具体表抽象。例如：

例 35　These problems defy easy classification.

这些问题难以归类。

例 36　After the receptionist gathers room-query data, the next step is also to check the availability of the required type of room.

在接待员收集客房查询信息之后，下一步往往是检查所需类型的房间是否可以入住。

例 37　Laser is one of the most sensational developments in recent years, because of its applicability to many fields of science and its adaptability to practical uses.

激光可以应用于许多科学领域，又适合于各种实际用途，因此成为近年来轰动一时的科学成就之一。

例 38 The landscape is delightful, a <u>combination</u> of tropical and mountainous Africa.

这里风景优美迷人，<u>综合了</u>赤道非洲和山区非洲的景色。

第二，汉语中范畴词的应用。所谓"范畴词"，指用来表示行为、现象、属性等概念所属的范畴，是汉语中较为常用的特指手段（连淑能，1993）。在英译汉实践过程中，使用汉语范畴词可以使英文中抽象的概念具体化，语义更加明确。示例如下：

例 39 His <u>arrogance</u> sent him into isolation and helplessness.

他的<u>傲慢态度</u>使他孤立无援。

例 40 He spoke with <u>firmness</u>, but his face was very sad and his eyes at times were dim.

他讲话时<u>态度坚定</u>，但面带愁容，时而眼神黯淡。

例 41 The pharmacologists are making a careful study of the <u>allergy</u> of this new medicine.

药理学家们正在认真研究这种新药的<u>过敏反应</u>。

例 42 The sight of his native place called back his <u>childhood</u>.

见到自己的故乡，他想起了<u>童年的情景</u>。

第三，汉语中形象性词语的应用。汉语语言文化博大精深，有很多四字成语、习语、谚语、歇后语等，这类词汇不仅生动形象还能达到一定的修辞效果，可以用来翻译英文中的抽象词汇，同样，汉译英时，也应关注英语抽象化的特点。如：

例 43 <u>蒙在鼓里</u> be kept in dark

<u>丢盔弃甲</u> throw away everything

<u>深思熟虑</u> careful consideration

Feed on fancies <u>画饼充饥</u>

Total exhaustion <u>精疲力竭</u>

Lack of perseverance <u>三天打鱼，两天晒网</u>

例 44 Wisdom <u>prepares for the worst</u>, but folly <u>leaves the worst for the day it comes</u>.

聪明人<u>未雨绸缪</u>，愚蠢者<u>临渴掘井</u>。

例 45 He waited for her arrival with <u>a frenzied agitation</u>.

他等着她来，急得像<u>热锅上的蚂蚁</u>。

例 46 他这一阵心头如同<u>十五个吊桶打水，七上八下</u>，老是宁静不下来。

His mind was <u>in a turmoil</u> these days and he was quite unable to think straight.

由于文化传统和历史等因素，英文擅用抽象概念表达具体事物，中文擅用具体事物表达抽象概念。但是还有一种特殊情况，英文中同样有些俚语内含具体形象或事物，在这种情况下，为了实现译文的忠实准确，往往在英译汉时需要对其进行抽象化的处理，这就要求译者要准确分析原文及其文字背后蕴含的文化。

例 47 Please don't wake up a sleeping dog.

请不要惹是生非。

例 48 Tim is a rolling stone. I don't think he can go far.

蒂姆是个见异思迁的人，我想他不会有太大的出息。

例 49 Tom was practically on his knees but she still refused.

汤姆几乎是苦苦哀求，但她还是拒绝了。

翻译实践

翻译下列句子，注意思考英汉语言结构的差异。

1. It is essential to strengthen the national defense.

2. Both we and the Chinese approached that first opening toward each other with caution, uncertainty, and even trepidation.

3. The theme is characterized by three distinctions: reflecting the needs of our age, being original in concept and having universal significance.

4. The new generation is always better than the previous one.

（三）物称与人称

英语偏重于逻辑和科学，注重事物的客观性，重视客体以及客观世界的研究，在语言表达上常用物称作主语，以此陈述客观事实。这些非人称表达常用于论文著作、公文、通知等书面语中，确保研究和信息的客观性、科学性。而汉语文化注重主体思维，讲究以人为中心，从人的角度去看待描述事物，因此汉语常用人称作主语，即便在没有人称的情况下，也多使用无主句。关于这一区别，拟从以下两个方面进行分析。

第一，英语多用抽象名词和无生命的事物作主语，注重以客观的方式阐述事实，汉语使用人称作主语，强调的是人的状态和反应。如：

例 50 An idea suddenly struck me.

我突然想到一个主意。

例 51 Excitement deprived me of all power of utterance.

我兴奋得什么话也说不出来。

例 52 His new book hits off the American temperament with amazing insight.

他在新作中对美国人性格的描写可谓洞察秋毫。

例 53 With the growing use of the Internet, one could be fooled into thinking the odds of success in finding that elusive, top-performing trade partner will be increased.

随着互联网的不断普及，<u>人们</u>可能会产生错觉，误认为寻找那些难以寻觅的最佳贸易伙伴的几率将会增加。

例 54　<u>The invitation</u> to me from the British Broadcasting Corporation was to present the development of science in a series of television programmes.

<u>英国广播公司</u>邀请我通过一套电视节目来表现科学的发展过程。

在上述例子中，英文中的主语均为表示抽象概念、思想情感的客体，但是中文译文均选择了以人或比较确定的事物作主语，如此更加符合汉语的表达习惯。反之，汉译英过程中也应注意人称和非人称的转换。如：

例 55　一看到那棵大树，<u>我</u>便想起了童年的情景。

<u>The sight</u> of big tree always reminds me of my childhood.

例 56　恕<u>我</u>孤陋寡闻，对此关系一无所知。

<u>My total ignorance</u> of the connection must plead my apology.

例 57　<u>小梅</u>心地善良，性情温和，对她朋友这种没有心肝的行为实在看不顺眼。

<u>Xiaomei's kindly and gentle nature</u> could not but revolt at her friend's callous behavior.

第二，英文中常用非人称代词"it"或 there be 结构作主语，具有物称倾向。汉语中没有类似结构或表达，因此多用人称或采用无主句结构。代词"it"作主语，在句中有着不同的作用。

1. it 在句中代替真正的主语。

例 58　<u>It</u> is my hope that world peace will really be achieved.

<u>我</u>希望世界和平能够真正实现。

例 59　<u>It</u> is doubtful whether he will have an opportunity.

他是否有机会还很难说。

例 60　<u>It</u> happens that the moon completes one revolution in one month.

<u>月球</u>公转一周恰巧是一个月。

例 61　<u>It</u> is said that hundreds of thousands of chemical compounds can be made from petroleum.

<u>据说</u>，能从石油中提取出几十万种化合物。

2. it 在句中无实际含义，常用于表示一般情况、自然现象、时间、空间、距离、度量等，此为英语中的习惯用法。

例 62　<u>It's</u> only half an hour's walk to the ferry.

只要走半个钟头就可以到轮渡。

例 63　It is going to be windy tomorrow according to the weather broadcast.

根据天气预报，明天将有风。

例 64　It is all pitch dark in the depth of the sea, yet life abounds there just as well.

海洋深处一片漆黑，可是照样有大量的生命存在。

3. it 在句中作形式主语，其后加被强调成分，和先行词 that, which 构成强调句型。在翻译中为了突出原文的强调意味，译文中可使用"正是""才""就"等字眼。

例 65　It is in the hour of trial that a man finds his true profession.

人总是在面临考验的关头，才发现自己的专长。（强调状语）

例 66　It is only the presence of force which can this normal state.

只有施加压力，才能改变这种正常状态。（强调主语）

例 67　It is oxygen that our body needs every second.（强调宾语）

人体时刻不能缺少的就是氧气。

此外，除了非人称代词 it，there be 句型也具有物称倾向，同样汉语中采用人称或客观事物作主语，或采用无主句结构。

例 68　There are many women who want to see this moving film.

许多女性想看这部感人的电影。

例 69　In 1958, there was a strike participated in by 5000 workers.

1958 年，5000 名工人参加了一次罢工。

例 70　There are not any perfect conductors.

没有绝对完善的导体。

● 翻译实践

翻译下列句子，注意思考英汉语言结构的差异。

1. The alarm began to take the entire possession of him.

2. It has been noted with concern that the stock of books in the library has been declining alarmingly.

3. It is not our view that the substance or the tone of his remarks this morning will contribute to creating a lasting peace in the Middle East.

4. Second, we deepened reform and opening-up and invigorated economic and social development.

5. We have continued to give the central stage in reform to streamlining administration and delegating more powers to lower-level governments and to society in general while improving regulation.

二、英汉文化差异

文化是语言生存发展的土壤，语言是文化的载体，是文化传播的工具。翻译不是简单地从一种语言转化成另一种语言的过程，翻译是一个创造性的实践活动。英汉翻译的背后涉及两种语言所处的文化背景，由于中西方不同的文化体系，英汉两种语言的表达也有所差异，因此翻译过程中，译者也要充分考虑到语言所处的文化语境。以下将从自然环境、宗教信仰、观念习俗、俚语典故四个方面探讨英汉文化差异及其在语言上的反映。

（一）自然环境

地域环境的差异会对文化产生影响，而语言承载着不同国家和民族的文化。因此在英汉互译时，译者应首先注意到语言中不同地域环境折射的文化差异及其背后隐含意义。

例 71　Shall I compare thee to a summer's day? —William Shakespeare

我能否将你比作夏日璀璨？——威廉·莎士比亚

该句诗歌出自莎士比亚的十四行诗 *Sonnet 18*，诗中作者以夏日的美好来表达自己对心爱之人的赞美。众所周知，英国夏日气候舒适，温暖宜人，而中国的夏日大都是酷暑炎热。因此此处需要读者结合中英两国不同自然环境才能联想到诗歌背后的内涵，体会到作者对爱人的深切情感。

例 72　*Ode to the West Wind*— Shelley

《西风颂》——雪莱

例 73　It's warm wind, the west wind, full of birds' cries. —John Masefield

那是一种温暖的风，西风吹时，万鸟争鸣。——曼斯菲尔德

由于地理位置的差异，来自极地的东风给英国带去的是寒冷，而中国的东风则是春的使者，因此"东风"的概念在中英两种文化中截然不同。中文中常用东风指代春天、希望等美好的事物，如"东风报春""万事俱备，只欠东风"等。而在英国，"西风"代表了春天的来临，因此文学家们会在作品中对西风进行赞颂，如上述例子中，雪莱讴歌西风，全诗表达了对春的期盼以及对革命力量的颂扬。英国著名桂冠诗人曼斯菲尔德在《西风歌》中表达了对故土春天的怀念。

除此之外，自然环境造成中英语言文化差异的例子比比皆是。《论语》有云，"岁寒，

然后知松柏之后凋也"，于是中文中松树柏树成了不畏艰难、坚强不屈的代名词，也是坚贞品格的象征，而在西方文化中松树和柏树并无特殊的文化内涵。《诗经》有云："昔我往矣，杨柳依依。今我来思，雨雪霏霏。"文中"柳"寓意"留"，古人常折柳送别，表达离别的不舍之情。而在英文中柳树只是一种普通植物。反之，英文中某些植物也有其独特的文化内涵。Palm（棕榈树）象征胜利，lily（百合花）象征着纯洁；ivy（常春藤）四季常青，被誉为永恒生命的象征。

由此可见，包括天气、植物等在内的自然环境会被赋予独特的文化含义，从而引起语言上的差异。

翻译实践

翻译下列词组，注意思考词汇背后的文化内涵。

1. take the wind out of sb's sails
2. sound in wind and limb
3. extremely proud of one's success
4. one's face shines with pleasure
5. spring up like mushrooms
6. drink like a fish

（二）宗教信仰

中西方在宗教信仰方面差异明显，因此英汉语言中有不少宗教方面的特色词汇。从中国历史来看，道教、佛教对语言的影响较大，如"涅槃""解脱""劫""因缘际会""临时抱佛脚""不看僧面看佛面"等文化词汇。西方国家主要信仰基督教，很多具有特定内涵的文化词汇和耶稣基督、《圣经》等息息相关，如 forbidden fruit(禁果)，a covenant of salt(不可背弃的盟约)，the salt of the earth (社会中坚力量)，go to hell(下地狱去吧)，rule with rod of iron(高压统治)等。

例 74　God helps those who help themselves.

译文 1：上帝帮助自助的人。

译文 2：自助者，天助之。

西方国家信仰基督，崇尚上帝的力量。中国人一般用"天"来指代苍天、老天爷，这里的内涵等同于西方文化中的上帝。这里两种译文分别采用了归化和异化的翻译策略。

例 75　Every man must bear his own cross.

人人都得背负自己的十字架。

十字架在基督教中有着特殊的含义，是基督信仰的标志。《圣经》记载，耶稣基督为了救赎全人类的罪，被钉死在十字架上，因此十字架象征着上帝对世人的爱与救赎。上述译文中采用异化的翻译策略，将"十字架"直译了出来。

例 76　John can be relied on. He eats no fish and plays the game.

约翰可以信赖，他既忠诚，又守规矩。

一些句子中蕴含的宗教文化和典故很难为大众所了解，因此在翻译时可采用意译的方法。上述例子中如直译则为"约翰可以信赖，他不吃鱼，而且玩游戏"。此话意思不通，而且理解有误，需要结合宗教背景知识进行解读。结合英国宗教斗争的历史，罗马天主教规定教徒斋日可以吃鱼，而新教教徒则用不吃鱼的举动表示，忠于新教。因此 eat no fish 可理解为忠诚。

例 77　临时抱佛脚。

Seek help at the last moment.

中文中"临时抱佛脚"原意为年老信佛，以求保佑，有临渴掘井之意。后用来形容遇事毫无准备，临时才设法应付。翻译时为使意义更加明了，未直译出宗教色彩词汇，直接采用了释义的方法。类似例子如："道高一尺，魔高一丈"（The more illumination, the more temptation）。

例 78　谋事在人，成事在天。

译文 1：Man proposes, heaven disposes.（杨宪益，戴乃迭译）

译文 2：Man proposes, God disposes.（David Hawks 译）

关于《红楼梦》英译本中此句话的翻译，不同译本译法不一。由于不同的宗教文化背景，杨戴夫妇将句中的"天"译为 heaven，中国传统的道教文化和佛教文化中强调"上天"的力量。而英国汉学家霍克斯将"天"译为"God"，也就对应西方文化中对于上帝力量的尊崇。

例 79　He was already three score and ten.

他已至古稀之年。

例 80　David and Jonathan 管鲍之交（意为密友）

例 81　A Job's comforter 约伯的安慰者（意为安慰）

例 82　A wrong active person achieves salvation as soon as he gives up evil.

放下屠刀，立地成佛。

宗教信仰对语言词汇产生了一定的影响，因此译者在翻译时应考虑到不同文化背景下宗教的影响，从而采用合适的翻译方法，准确地传达原文之意。

> 翻译实践

翻译下列句子。

1. He is the seventh son of a seventh son in the family.
2. The woman in charge of the accounts department is an absolute dragon.
3. I was made the scapegoat, but it was the others who started the fire.
4. The joke you told us is as old as Adam, but I still think it's funny.

（三）观念习俗

英汉观念习俗的差异表现在多个方面。比如在对待不同动物时，中英文化态度有所区别。中国传统文化中"狗"是一种比较卑微的动物，和狗相关的词汇习语大多为贬义，如"狗仗人势""狗急跳墙""狗眼看人低""丧家犬""狗咬吕洞宾，不识好人心""虎落平阳被犬欺"，等等。而在英语文化中，狗被看作忠诚的象征，从习语中也可看出人们对狗的赞扬。如"a lucky dog"（幸运儿），"top dog"（优胜者，领军人物）等。

中国传统文化中"蝠"字音同"福"，因此"蝙蝠"被看作吉祥、健康的象征。但是在英语文化中，"蝙蝠"被视为一种邪恶的动物，常常和罪恶以及黑暗势力联系在一起。如"vampire bat"（吸血蝠），"as blind as a bat"（有眼无珠，鼠目寸光），"have bats in the belfry"（异想天开，不切实际的想法）等。

在中国文化中老虎被誉为"百兽之王"，人们对其有着敬畏、崇敬之情，反映到语言中"老虎"具有了多样的文化含义，中文中有很多表达老虎"威猛、威严"之意的习语，如"龙腾虎跃""气吞万里如虎""将门虎子""生龙活虎""藏龙卧虎"等。而在英美文化中"狮子"（lion）被看作百兽之王，其形象相当于我国的虎，反而英文中虎的文化含义较少。英文中较多关于 lion 的习语，如 The British Lion 指代英国，lion-hearted（勇敢的），play oneself in the lion's mouth（置身虎穴），come in like a lion go out like a lamb（虎头蛇尾）等。汉语中的"拦路虎"翻译成英文为"a lion in the way"，"虎穴"则译为"lion's mouth"。

英汉观念习俗还体现在人们对于颜色的认知上。人们对于颜色的不同理解也反映了中西方文化的差异。比如，红色在中西文化中都有喜庆和欢乐氛围之意。西方国家把一些节假日，如圣诞节称为 red-letter days（喜庆的日子），paint the town red（狂欢痛饮），roll out the red carpet for sb. (隆重欢迎某人）。在中国传统文化中，人们一般用红色表示喜事，如"满堂红"（success in every field）、"开门红"（Get off to a good start）、"红运"谐音鸿运（good luck）等。除此之外，在西方国家红色还有战争、暴力、死亡、流血之意，红色代表着血腥。如 a red battle（血战），have red hands（杀人犯），英国发生火灾用 red ruin 表示，危险信号用 red light 表示。在英语文化中红色还可表示亏损，如 red figure、in the red、red ink、red balance 都可表示赤字、亏损。

黄色在中国传统文化中曾是帝王专用的色彩，具有至高无上、崇高之意。如"黄袍加身""黄马褂"。中国文化中讲究吉利，一般大事的操办皆会挑一个诸事皆宜的日子，即"黄道吉日"。而英语将紫色誉为皇家王权的象征，寓意为高贵、地位、王位。相关俗语有：be born in the purple（出身王室），to marry into the purple（与皇室联姻），a purple airway（皇家专用飞机跑道）。在英文中，黄色具有贬义，一般表示怯懦、卑鄙，如：a yellow belly（胆小鬼），yellow looks（尖酸多疑的神情），be yellow with jealousy（嫉妒）等。

因此，译者应提高对中西方不同观念习俗的认识，在翻译过程中，不仅实现语言的转换，更应该传达出语言背后的文化底蕴，实现跨文化翻译的目标。

● 翻译实践

翻译下列词组。

1. green back

2. white elephant

3. plenty fish in the sea

4. be beaten black and blue

5. change horse in the midstream

（四）俚语典故

中华文化博大精深，中文中的很多习语源自于古书典籍，神话、传说以及寓言、故事等各种题材。如"说曹操曹操到""夸父逐日""嫦娥奔月""守株待兔"等，这些习语带有中国特有的文化色彩，在英文中无法找到完全对等的翻译。因此，译者在翻译此类习语时，应考虑译文中是否应保留中国传统文化内涵，或是只需达到形式上的对等。

而英文中许多俚语典故源自于古希腊、古罗马文化，了解相关神话故事及文化有助于正确翻译这些俚语及其背后含义。如：

例 83　the golden apple of discord 斗争的根源

希腊神话中纷争女神厄里斯未被邀请参加珀琉斯国王和海洋女神的婚礼，因此，她将刻有"最美丽的女人"字样的金苹果扔到婚礼现场的众女神当中，引起了女神们之间的争端，间接导致了持续十年的特洛伊战争。

关于希腊神话中的典故还有很多，如 Hang by a thread 千钧一发；Pandora's box 潘多拉魔盒——灾难、祸害的根源；Achilles' heel 阿喀琉斯之踵——致命弱点；The Trojan horse 特洛伊木马——隐藏的危险、木马病毒；The sword of Damocles 达摩克利斯之剑——时刻存在的危险；Gordian Knot 戈尔迪之结——难题，等等。关于此类俚语典故的翻译，译者要考虑到目标语读者的文化水平及需求，从而决定用归化还是异化的翻译策略，或者适当选取直译加注解的方式进行翻译，切忌望文生义。

英语中包含大量俚语，除具有典型文化色彩的俚语之外，还有部分俚语也需要译者查阅相关资料，根据上下文语境准确理解俚语的确切含义，借助中文中俚语、俗语或成语等形式对其进行翻译。如：

例 84　I put my ass on the line for you. I know you'll do the same for me someday.

我为你两肋插刀，我知道有朝一日你也会为我这么做。

例 85　Grace is always correcting other people. She thinks she is just a know-it-all.

格雷斯总是在纠正别人，她觉得自己是一个万事通。

例 86　That team was not very good. We beat the pants off them. The final score was 21∶3.

那个球队真差，我们最终以 21∶3 的比分把他们打得落花流水。

例 87　I have let the cat out of the bag already, Mr. Corthell, and I might as well tell the whole thing now.

我已经泄露了秘密，科塞先生，干脆现在就把全部的情况都告诉你吧。

英汉语言中俚语典故的差异还表现在中英两种语言有时可以用不同的词汇传达同一种概念。如：

例 88　crocodile tears

译文 1：鳄鱼的眼泪

译文 2：猫哭耗子假慈悲

例 89　In the land of the blind, the one-eyed man is king.

译文 1：盲眼圈中，独眼称雄。

译文 2：山中无老虎，猴子称霸王。

例 90　to kill two birds with one stone

译文 1：一石二鸟

译文 2：一箭双雕

针对语言中的文化因素，翻译时译者应根据具体情况采用不同的翻译策略和方法，如归化、异化；直译、意译、直译加注解等。示例如下：

例 91　俗话说："杀人不过头点地。"

译文 1：Remember the proverb "A murder can only lose his head".（杨宪益译）

译文 2：You know what the proverb says: "He who checks a moment's rage shall calm and carefree end his days."（霍克斯译）

关于此句谚语，两位译者采取了截然不同的翻译方法。杨宪益采用了直译法，译文简洁明了，传达了原文的含义；而霍克斯采用了归化译法，使译文读者更能清楚地了解原文的内涵。

例 92　由于"平均主义"和"大锅饭"的分配机制制约，使人的劳动量与其所分配到的劳动成果没有直接的联系，即劳动与物质利益相脱节。

Under the "big rice pot" distribution system, characterized by a "leveled-off" standard (unequal work for equal pay), people's income had nothing to do with their contribution.

此句译文中并未将原文中"平均主义"直译成英文中的 egalitarianism，因为在英文中，egalitarianism 一词意为"平等，平等主义"，代表的是积极的含义，而在原文中"平均主义"代表的是一种不良的分配方式，因此翻译时不可直接选取目标语中的对应词，需考虑到文化差异。

● 翻译实践

翻译下列词组或句子。

1. a black sheep

2. to cast pearls before swine

3. to fish in the air

4. Van Gogh's ear for music

5. Better late than never.

6. Don't count your chickens before they hatch.

● 课后练习

一、词语翻译

1. 一贫如洗

2. 付诸东流

3. 皇天不负有心人

4. 说曹操，曹操到

5. 心有余而力不足

二、句子翻译

1. The problem of possible genetic damage to human population from radiation exposures including those resulting from the fallouts from testing of atomic weapons has properly claimed much popular attention in recent years.

2. But now it is realized that supplies of some of them are limited, and it is even possible to give a reasonable estimate of their "expectation of life", the time it will take to exhaust all known sources and reserves of these materials.

3. The land cracked and the springs dried up and the cattle listlessly nibbled dry twigs.

4. But the real boom in franchising began in the late 1950s, with the proliferation of hotels and motels like Holiday Inn and fast-food establishments like Baskin-Robbins, and Dunkin, Donuts.

5. You have got to have faith up your sleeve, otherwise you won't succeed.

三、段落翻译

1. Terrorism is the common enemy of humanity, and the target of joint action by the international community. Terrorist forces, by means of violence, sabotage and intimidation, pose a serious threat to world peace and security by scorning human rights, slaughtering innocent people, endangering public security, and creating fear and panic in society. The infiltration and spread of extremism is a hotbed for violence and terror, constituting a direct threat to human rights. The Chinese government stands firmly against all forms of terrorism and extremism, and is relentless in striking hard, in accordance with the law, at any conduct advocating terrorism and extremism and any action that involves organizing, planning and carrying out terrorist activities, or infringing upon citizens' human rights.

2. 杭州是南宋的都城，位于大运河南端和"鱼米之乡"。最令人心驰神往的景观莫过于西湖，一个人工浅水湖。中国历史上一些伟大的诗人，如9世纪的白居易、11世纪的苏东坡都为西湖的改造与创新做出了不小的贡献。这两位诗人在担任杭州地方官时，曾主持修建了海塘、堤坝、堤道、桥梁，并重建了寺庙与宝塔。

四、篇章翻译

1. You hear it all along the river. You hear it, loud and strong, from the rowers as they urge the junk with its high stern, the mast lashed alongside, down the swift running stream. You hear it from the trackers, a more breathless chant, as they pull desperately against the current, half a dozen of them perhaps if they are taking up a small wooden ship, a couple of hundred if they

are hauling a splendid junk, its square sail set, over a rapid. On the junk, a man stands amidships beating a drum incessantly to guide their efforts, and they pull with all their strength, like men possessed, bent double; and sometimes in the extremity of their travail they crawl on the ground, on all fours, like the beasts of the field. They strain, strain fiercely, against the pitiless might of the stream. The leader goes up and down the line and when he sees one who is not putting all his will into the task he brings down his split bamboo on the naked back. Each one must do his utmost or the labor of all is vain. And still they sing a vehement, eager chant, the chant of the turbulent waters. I do not know words can describe what there is in it of effort. It serves to express the straining heart, the breaking muscles, and at the same time the indomitable spirit of man which overcomes the pitiless force of nature. Though the rope may part and the great junk swing back, in the end the rapid will be passed; and at the close of the weary day there is the hearty meal...

  2. Through decades of efforts, the number of rural poor has markedly dropped and the poverty headcount ratio has seen a continuous decrease. Solid steps have been taken to eliminate regional poverty, and the working conditions and living standards of the rural poor have notably improved, which created a stronger sense of gain for the people, indicating decisive progress has been made in the fight against poverty. According to World Bank estimates, over the past 40 years, the number of people in China living on less than US$1.9 a day (international poverty line) has dropped by more than 850 million—this represents 70 percent of the total world figure. The number of rural poor fell from 770 million in 1978 to 30.46 million in 2017 when calculated in accordance with China's current poverty line, with the incidence of poverty dropping from 97.5 percent to 3.1 percent. More than 10 million people rose and remained above the poverty level every year from 2012 to 2017. With the highest number of people moving out of poverty, China was the first developing country to realize the UN Millennium Development Goal for poverty reduction. Poverty reduction is the most telling evidence of China's progress in human rights.

第二节　英汉语言微观对比

本节主要从词汇和句法两个层面对英汉两种语言进行微观对比。英汉词汇对比拟从词义对等、一词多义、词汇空缺和词义冲突四个方面进行分析。英汉句法对比主要从主动与被动、复杂与简约、形合与意合、替代与重复四个方面进行分析。

一、英汉词汇对比

从语法角度来看，词是句子中可以独立使用的最小的语言单位。正确理解英汉词汇中的差异有助于译者更好地在目标语中选取恰当词汇进行翻译。

（一）词义对等

语言是人们进行沟通交流的表达方式，因此不同语言之间具有一定的相似性。每一种语言里都会有很多词汇用来描述客观世界，表达人们的观念或想法。因此英汉语言中很多词汇的词义可以做到完全对等。词义完全对等的词汇在翻译中较为简单，译者只需要在目标语当中找到源语的对等词即可。这种词义对等现象一般发生在科技词汇、术语以及日常事物的翻译中，如：European Union 欧盟；the Middle East Crisis 中东危机；book 书本；bridge 桥梁。

另外，随着全球化步伐的加快，各国之间交流日益加深，很多源自英文的词汇也能通过直译、音译等方法找到合适的汉语译文，并为广大公众所接受。如：Bluetooth 蓝牙；laser 激光；radar 雷达；Coca cola 可口可乐；gene 基因。

翻译实践

翻译下列词汇。

1. bonsai
2. cheongsam
3. coolie
4. IChing
5. cumshaw

（二）一词多义

奈达在其著作 *Toward a Science of Translating* 中首次提出动态对等概念，指出动态对等指从语义到语体，在接受语中用"最切近的自然对等语"再现源语信息，其检验标准在于译文读者与原文读者对所接收的信息能否作出基本一致的反应。由于翻译涉及两种截然不同的语言，而每一种语言都有自己的表达方式，在表述内容时所用词汇往往并非一一对应，因此会出现一词多义的现象。因此在翻译过程中译者需要结合不同语境正确理解原文的词义，做到正确选词。

英文中部分单词在不同语境中有不同含义。如 cell 一词为半科技词汇，在不同学科有不同的释义：cell 一般释义为"小房间""牢房"，在生物相关学科中可译为"细胞"，在物理相关学科中可译为"电池"，具体到大气科学领域，cell 译为"单体"。科普文中往往涉及许多半科技词汇，这类词汇有其普通释义，但具体到某一专业领域则有其专业释义。由于科普文本注重传达信息，因此译者要对原文内容进行准确理解才能正确翻译。

再如：build 一词为普通词汇，在不同语境下含义也有不同：

build a house 盖房子　　　build a bridge 架桥　　　build a dam 筑坝

build a ship 造船　　　　build an answer 思考作答　　build a fire 生火

build one's confidence 树立信心

试比较以下几个例句。

1. He bought a chair at the furniture store.

2. Please address the chair.

3. He will chair the meeting.

4. He was appointed to the chair of philosophy at the university.

在这里，根据语法标记我们可以判断出，句 1、2、4 中 chair 为名词，句 3 中 chair 为动词。再根据句子语境可得出结论：句 1 中 furniture store 表明，这里 chair 应译为"椅子"；句 2 中 address 意为"向某人致辞，说话"，因此这里 chair 应译为"主席"；句 3 中 chair 为动词，加上与 meeting 搭配，译为"主持"；句 4 中 chair 为名词，根据下文语境中出现 philosophy，chair 应译为"大学中的职位"，the chair of philosophy 意为"哲学系主任"。

同样，中文中某个词在不同语境中往往表达含义也会不一样。试分析下列一组词汇：青山、青天、青布。中文中有"绿水青山"一词，在这里"青山"指的是长满绿色植物的山，因此译为 green hills；"青天"一词指的是蓝天，因此译为 blue sky；"青布"在中文中实际上指的是黑色的布，因此译为 black cloth。

再如"大"字的翻译，"大城市"可以译为 big city / major city；"大雨"译为 heavy rain；"大志"指"远大的志向"可译为 great ambition；"大道理"译为 general (major) principle。

翻译实践

翻译下列词组。

1. a good Christian
2. a good parent
3. a good child
4. a good wife
5. a good husband

（三）词义空缺

由于不同国家生活环境、宗教信仰、风俗习惯及文化背景等方面存在差异，有时一种语言之中的特有词汇很难在另外一种语言中找到与之相对应的对等词，即词汇空缺现象。在这种情况下，译者可以根据语境或结合相关文化背景，采取归化或者异化的翻译策略以及音译、意译、释义等翻译方法对此类词汇进行处理。

如英文中有个单词 pumpkin-eater，该单词源自一首童谣："Peter, Peter, pumpkin eater, had a wife and couldn't keep her"，根据单词的出处，我们可以将该词汇意译为"养不活老婆的人"。再如"swan song"，在英文中 swan 一词用来指才华横溢的诗人，因此，"swan song"——"天鹅的绝唱"用来指作家或音乐家最后的作品。

同样，中文中有很多中国特色文化词汇，在英文中很难找到相应的对等词，也会造成词汇空缺现象。如"嫦娥""玉皇大帝""王母""玉兔"等，对于此类中国特色神话或传说中的"经典形象或人物"，在翻译时译者可以采取音译或意译的方法。如"嫦娥"可以直接翻译成"Chang'e"或者"goddess in the moon / lady in the moon"。除此之外，在翻译中国古代习俗文化或者历史典故相关的特色词时，为使读者更加清楚了解其文化内涵，译者也可采用释译的方法，如"裹足"一词，源自中国古代乃至近代的一种文化，即将女子的双脚用布帛缠裹起来，使其变成"三寸金莲"，因此，该词可以译成"bound feet (a vile feudal practice which crippled women both physically and spiritually)"。

翻译实践

翻译下列词汇。

1. the New Testament
2. Gerrymander
3. 红烧狮子头

4. 佛跳墙

5. 鸳鸯火锅

（四）词义冲突

在翻译的过程中，译者应该从目标语当中找到和原文相对应的对等语，而非同一语，这就意味着译者在再现源语信息的时候，要考虑两种语言中某些词汇意义是否一致，当词汇意义不一致时，就产生了词义冲突现象。词汇意义可以分为两个方面：指称意义和联想意义。"指称意义"指的是用词汇来描述某一客观事物、某一思想概念时语言所获得的意义，是语言之外、由社会场合所引起的意义。"联想意义"指的是人们在使用语言时附加给语言的意义，是语言以外、社会行为方面的意义，一般指文化方面的东西。指称意义较为客观，而联想意义较为主观（谭载喜，2002）。这里提及的词义冲突现象一般有两种。

第一种是词汇的指称意义相符而联想意义不符造成的词义冲突现象。比如英汉语言中的数字文化。在汉语文化中人们往往更崇尚偶数，认为其是吉祥如意的象征，中国人喜欢"六"，认为"六六大顺"，而在英文中，six 没有此种寓意。再如中文中"二"，有成双成对之意，但是在英美文化中对应的 two 被看作邪恶的根源，是一个不吉利的数字，因此两者虽指称意义一致，但联想意义不符。另外关于自然现象或者自然界的某些事物，中西方文化中的同样词汇代表了不同的意义。如汉语中"西风"一词，代表的寒冷干燥的冬风，有凄凉之意，古诗有云："古道西风瘦马，夕阳西下，断肠人在天涯。"而在英文中 west wind 代表的是送来希望的春风，往往受到文学家的赞颂，如雪莱的《西风颂》 *Ode to the West Wind*。汉文化中"喜鹊"是祥瑞的象征，还有"灵鹊报喜"一说，而在英美文化中 magpie 是不祥之兆，还可用来比喻"爱嚼舌根之人"。

第二种是词汇的指称意义和联想意义都不符的词义冲突现象。比如汉语中的"龙"指传说中的一种神异动物，是权威吉祥的象征，在中国古代"龙"被看作帝王的象征，如"真龙天子"，中国人自称"龙的传人"，龙在中国文化中具有极高的地位，如"卧虎藏龙""龙马精神"等，反映了龙的正面文化内涵。而在西方文化中，"龙"指一种会喷火的怪物，被认为邪恶的象征，如在英国著名叙事长诗 *Beowulf* 中描述了主人公 Beowulf 与恶魔 fire dragon（火龙）斗争的故事。《圣经》中将和上帝作对的撒旦称为 the great dragon。

在遇到词义冲突现象时，译者不应一味追求词汇在形式上的对等，而应该正确理解词汇背后传达的文化释义，从而选择正确的译文。

二、英汉句法对比

微观角度的英汉句法对比拟从主动与被动、复杂与简约、形合与意合、替代与重复四个方面进行分析。

（一）主动与被动

英文多用被动句，中文多用主动句（连淑能，1993）。被动语态在英文中使用更为普遍，尤其在科技、新闻等正式文体中。英文被动语态的使用可以给人以客观公正之感，并不涉及当事人对于事件的主观臆断或评价，同时可避免句子成分冗余。中文中被字句使用大多表示主语遭受到了不愉快的事情或者不公正的对待，但是随着语言的发展变化，汉语中被字句的使用范围扩大，但相较于英语来说，使用范围和频率依旧不如英语。

1. 中文中有时虽然表达被动的意义，但是经常采取主动的形式，即"主动形式，被动意义"。在这种情况下，英文一般采用被动句进行翻译。例如：

例 1　股息可以在宣布之后从公司已经实现的或未支付的利润中支付，或从利润中拨出的董事会认为已经不需要的任何储备金中提取，或不等额支付。

Dividends <u>may be declared</u> and <u>paid out</u> of profits of the Company, realized or unrealized, or from any reserve set aside from profits which the Directors determine is no longer needed, or not in the same amount.

此句话中，中文虽然表述的是被动的意义，但是这里不能直译成"股息被宣布，被支付"，应采用更加符合中文表达方式的主动句，而英文中可以直接将被动的意味翻译出来。

例 2　困难<u>克服了</u>，工作<u>完成了</u>，问题也<u>解决了</u>。

The difficulties <u>have been overcome</u>; the work <u>has been finished</u> and the problem <u>solved</u>.

例 3　<u>发送</u>至任何成员的通知均可由公司专人送达或寄送至该成员登记在成员登记簿上的地址，或其他为此目的而<u>提供</u>的地址。

A notice may <u>be given</u> by the Company the any Member either by delivering it to such Member in person or by sending it to such Member's address in the Register of Members or to such other address <u>given</u> for the purpose.

上述例 2、例 3 两个例子中，强调的是受事者，而非施事者。因此在这里可以直接译为被动语态，无需考虑"谁"克服了困难、完成了工作、发送了通知。

2. 中文多无主句，或句中省略主语，在这种情况下无需指明施事者，英文直接使用被动语态即可准确传达句子含义。例如：

例 4　要制造飞机，就必须仔细考虑空气阻力的问题。

Air resistance must be given into careful consideration when the aircraft is to be manufactured.

例 5　注意看看信的地址是否写对了。

Care should be taken to see that the letter is properly addressed.

例 6　Individualized tuition and assessment are carried on to help the students.

继续实施个性化收费和评估以帮助学生。

3. 中文除无主句之外，常在句中使用泛指主语，如"人们""有人""大家"等。在这种情况下，英文一般多用被动或用 it 来作形式主语。如：

例 7　人们普遍认为……

It is generally considered that…

例 8　众所周知，中国人在两千多年前就发明了指南针。

It is well known that the compass was invented in China more than two thousand years ago.

例 9　A woman was heard moaning after midnight.

有人深夜听见一名女子在呻吟。

例 10　Although little is known about how hypnosis works, it has been made use of in medical treatment.

尽管人们对催眠术知之甚少，但是该技术已经用于临床治疗。

4. 中文把字句是较为常见的一种句型，它更为强调动作的发出者以及动作的结果，因此英文的被动句有时也可翻译成中文中的把字句，两种句型可以互相转换。示例如下：

例 11　凡是做功，都是把能量从一种形式转换成另一种形式。

Whenever work is being done, energy is being converted from one form into another.

例 12　Metals are deliberately mixed to produce hundreds of new substances.

有意识地把各种金属混合在一起，可以产生数百种新物质。

● 翻译实践

翻译下列句子，注意句中语态的转换。

1. A small step has been taken in the direction of a national agency with the creation of Canadian Coordinating Office for Health Technology Assessment, funded by Ottawa and the provinces.

2. A total of 8,440 new post offices have been built in towns and townships, with the result

that every township-level unit has a post office and every village has access to postal services.

3. It has been found that people at first can suddenly become sensitive to a certain a smell when they are exposed to it often enough.

4. It is flattering to believe that their ideas are too profound to be expressed so clearly that all who run may read, and naturally it does not occur to such writes that the fault is with their own minds, which have not the faculty of precise reflection.

5. Meanwhile, the theft of information about some 40 million credit-card accounts in America disclosed on June 17th, overshadowed a hugely important decision a day earlier by America's Federal Trade Commission (FTC) that puts corporate America on notice that regulators will act if firms fail to provide adequate data security.

（二）复杂与简约

英文句式结构较为复杂，中文句式结构较为简约。英文多用从属结构，从句种类繁多，如名词性从句、定语从句、状语从句等。除此之外，还有各种修饰成分，如同位语、插入语、独立成分等，再加上各种连接手段，英文句式是树式结构，句子主干虽短，但起修饰作用的旁枝末节较多。相较而言，汉语多采用流水记事法，为竹节式结构（连淑能，1993）。汉语多流水小短句，句式简约，尤其多借助标点符号，将句子切分开，简洁明了，言简意赅。此外，中文擅用四字格短语，简短有力。因此，由于中英文句式的差异，译者在英译中时首先要分析英文句式结构，划分意群，切分句子，必要时可适当调整句子语序。示例如下：

例 13　In the doorway lay at least twelve umbrellas of all sizes and colors.

门口放着一堆雨伞，少说也有十二把，五颜六色，大小不一。

例 14　Can you answer a question which I want to ask and which is puzzling me?

我有一个问题弄不懂，想请教你，你可以为我答疑解惑吗？

例 15　Translation is first a science, which entails the knowledge and verification of the facts and the language that describe them—here, what is wrong, mistakes of truth, can be identified.

首先，翻译是一门科学，它需要知识，需要核对事实的能力，需要懂得描述这些事实的语言。翻译中，对于错误的内容、错误的事实，应该加以鉴别。

例 16　Social science is that branch of intellectual enquiry which seeks to study humans and their endeavors in the same reasoned, orderly, systematic, and dispassionate manner that natural scientists use for the study of natural phenomena.

社会科学是知识探索的一个分支，它试图用相同的、有道理的、有序的、有系统的以及冷静的方式来研究人类及其行为，而自然科学家却用这种方式来研究自然现象。

例 17　I was seized with sadness as I thought of how the ancient city had been separated during the Second World War and now might be destroyed by an impending riot.

我一想到这座古老的城市在第二次世界大战中得以幸免，而现在遭到即将来临的暴乱的破坏，不禁悲从中来。

例 18　Many man-made substances are replacing certain natural materials because either the quantity of the natural product cannot meet our ever-increasing requirement, or, more often, because the physical properties of the synthetic substance, which is the common name for man-made materials, have been chosen, and even emphasized, so that it would be of the greatest use in the fields in which it is to be applied.

人造材料通称为合成材料。许多人造材料正在代替某些天然材料，这或者是由于天然材料的数量不能满足日益增长的需要，或者往往是由于人们选择了合成材料的一些物理性质并加以突出而造成的，因此，合成材料在拟用的领域中将具有极大的用途。

科技文本中为清楚表达某些概念或意义，多用长难句，句子结构中也会借助各种从句、连接词。而汉语句式结构较松散，很少用连接词，但是句意层次分明。在上述例子中，译文中进行合理断句，拆分句子结构，对句子进行重组，用简洁的汉语短句有效传达了原文长句的意思。

另外，汉语的小短句在翻译成英语时，译者需考虑短句之间的逻辑关系，借助连接词或者从句将其组合成长句。如：

例 19　因为距离远又缺乏交通工具，所以农村社会是与外界隔绝的。这种隔绝状态因通讯工具不足而变得更加严重了。

The isolation of the rural world because of distance and the lack of transport facilities is compounded by the paucity of the information media.

例 20　顷刻之间，滚滚的浊水像堵墙一般压了下来，一股脑儿连人带车都给冲走了。这情景，直到现在还印在我的脑海里。

The image of a sudden wall of dark water carrying the man and his car away in an instant is still imprinted on my mind.

例 21　他这时已是将近六旬的人，一表人才，高个儿，眉清目秀，头发又多又黑略带花白，恰好衬出他那堂堂的仪表。

He was at this time in his late fifties, a tall, elegant man with good features and thick dark hair only sufficiently greying to add to the distinction to his appearance.

另外，英文多用倒装结构，词序较为灵活，词序倒装现象较为常见。一般倒装句可以起到强调作用或者加强语气。而汉语书面语中词序一般较为固定，词序的变化会导致语义不通或者语义发生变化。

1. 英文若表示时间、地点、方向的副词、副词短语或介词短语置于句首，则句子需要完全倒装，即将谓语部分移至主语前面。此类词汇如：here, there, down, up, in, out, then 等。如：

例 22　There stands a great temple on the top of that mountain.

那座山的山顶上有一座巨大的寺庙。

例 23　In my heart was desire to live more dangerously.

在我心中，渴望一种更加惊险的生活。

2. 表示否定意义的副词或连词置于句首时，英文句式需要部分倒装。如：little, seldom, hardly, rarely, scarcely, by no means, on no condition, in no case 等。

例 24　Never shall I do the same things again.

我再也不会做同样的事情了。

例 25　Under no circumstances should we yield to difficulty.

我们在任何情况下都不应向困难屈服。

3. only 修饰状语置于句首时，句子需要部分倒装。如：

例 26　Only by reading extensively can you widen your horizons.

只有通过广泛阅读，才能拓宽视野。

4. if 虚拟条件句中，若含有 had/were/should 则可以省略 if，将 had/were/should 提前，构成部分倒装结构。如：

例 27　Were it to rain, the crops would be saved.

要是下雨的话，庄稼就有救了。

例 28　Had you work harder, you would have succeeded.

如果你再努下力的话，你就会取得成功。

5. as, though 引导的让步状语从句中，可以使用部分倒装结构。如：

例 29　尽管他还是孩子，他已经能够独立生活了。

Child as he was, he was able to stand on his own feet.

例 30　尽管暴风雪很大，但是我们继续赶路。

Terrible as the storm was, we continued our way.

6. 英文感叹句型中常用倒装结构。如：

例 31　What a beautiful voice you have!

你的嗓音多么好听啊！

7. 表示祝愿的句型中多用倒装结构。如：

例 32　Long live the People's Republic of China!

中华人民共和国万岁！

例 33　May you live a long and happy life!

祝你幸福长寿！

除了语法方面的需要，英文中的倒装还可以出于修辞的需要，如诗歌等文学作品中较为常见的韵律倒装现象。如：

例 34　Good friend for Jesus' sake, forbear

To dig the dust enclosed here,

<u>Blessed</u> be he that spares these stones

And <u>curst</u> be he that moves my bones. (William Shakespeare)

好朋友呀，看在耶稣的份上，请你住手

别来挖掘这块土丘

那肯保存这几块石头的，但愿他添福添寿

那要来打扰我骸骨的，但愿他挨骂挨咒。——莎士比亚墓志铭

这段英文墓志铭中为了压尾韵，在句中运用了倒装结构，使得句子对仗工整。

翻译实践

翻译下列句子，注意中英文句式结构的转换。

1. Odd though it sounds, cosmic inflation is a scientifically plausible consequence of some respected ideas in elementary-particle physics, and many astrophysicists have been convinced for the better part of a decade that it is true.

2. Americans no longer expect public figures whether in speech or in writing to command the English with skill and gift. Nor do they aspire to such command themselves.

3. The company, a major energy supplier in New England, provoked justified outrage in Vermont last week when it announced it was reneging on a longstanding commitment to abide by the strict nuclear regulations.

4. Considering the quality of this year's selection of companies and the outstanding response

we have been receiving from our Chinese and European sponsors and partners throughout the organization of this multicultural event, I am confident this conference will be again a great success for all of us and will keep on setting the standard for ICT innovation dialogue between China and Europe.

(三) 形合与意合

英文属于形合语言，而中文属于意合语言。"形合注重的是显性接应（overt cohesion），以形显义；意合注重的是隐形连贯（overt coherence）以意统形"（龚光明，2004）。所谓的形合指的是，句子内部词组之间或者分句之间使用语言形式手段（如关联词）连接，从而表达句子的语法意义和逻辑关系。所谓意合指的是，句子内部词组之间或者分句之间不用语言形式手段进行连接，主要通过词语或者分句的含义传达句中的语法意义和逻辑关系。这里的语言连接手段主要指的是英文中的各类连接词，如连词（and, but, however, while, until, if, unless, before）、关系代词（which, that, who）、关系副词（when, where, why, how）、介词（in, on, at, about, through, inside）等。英文注重句子结构的完整性，连接词的使用较为频繁，而中文恰恰相反，注重意合。例如：

例35 It had been a fine golden autumn, a lovely farewell to those who would lose their youth, and some of them their lives, before the leaves turned again in a peacetime fall.

那是个天气晴朗，金秋可爱的秋天，美好的秋色为那些青年们送别。待到战后和平时期，黄叶纷飞的秋天再度来临时，当日的青年已经失去了青春，有的丧失了生命。

例36 It was what sentimentalists, who deal in very big words, call a yearning after the deal, and simply means that women are not satisfied until they have husbands and children on whom they may centre affections, which are spent elsewhere, as it were, in small change.

一般情感主义者，喜欢用大字眼称之为对于理想爱情的渴望。换言之，他们认为女人的情感平时只能零星发泄，必须有了丈夫和孩子，情感收聚起来有了归宿，自己才能得到满足。

例37 Power can be transmitted over a great distance with practically negligible loss if it is carried by an electric current.

电源可以把动力传送到很远的地方，其消耗几乎可以忽略不计。

例38 The present onslaught of vehicles poses a serious threat to urban life and pedestrian peace of mind.

当前车辆横冲直撞，严重地威胁着城市生活，路上行人无不提心吊胆。

上述例子中，英文句子较长且在句中运用了多种连接手段，如关系代词、关系副词、并列连词、介词等用来连接分句，而译文主要采用了意合法，省译了这些连接词，通过切分断句，达到了译文的流畅。

在汉译英的过程中，往往需要译者思考句中含的逻辑关系，从而增译恰当的连词或者运用从句等连接手段，使译文符合英文的行文规范。例如：

例39　我多次劝他放弃一些不现实的想法，他对此置若罔闻。

<u>Though</u> I have persuaded him for times to give up some unrealistic ideas, he always turns a deaf ear to what I have said.

例40　上梁不正，下梁歪。

<u>If</u> the upper beam is not straight, the lower ones will go aslant.

例41　不到黄河心不死。

<u>Until</u> all is over, ambition never dies.

英文形合与中文意合的特点可以追溯到中英文化逻辑思维的差异。中国人更注重具体，西方人更注重逻辑；这种思维方式的差异折射到语言上就是汉语更加注重意合，英语注重形合。因此译者在翻译的过程中要学会转换思维，使译文更符合目标语的表达习惯。

● **翻译实践**

翻译下列句子，注意中英文句式结构的转换。

1. This was an intelligently organized and fervent meeting in a packed Town Hall, with Mr. Strong in the chair.

2. The slightly porous nature of the surface of the oxide film allows it to be colored with either organic or inorganic dyes.

3. She said with perfect truth, that "it must be delightful to have a brother" and easily got the pity of tender-hearted Amelia, for being along in the world, an orphan without friends or kindred. (*Vanity Fair*)

4. There is nothing more disappointing to hostess who has gone to a lot of trouble or expense than to have her guest so interested in talking politics or business with her husband that he fails to notice the flavor of the coffee, the lightness of the cake, or the attractiveness of the house, which may be her chief interest and pride.

（四）替代与重复

在上下文句意连贯方面，英文多用替换，中文多用重复。英文多用替代的形式来代替句中或者上文中已经出现过的内容，以避免句中出现重复。替代的主要形式包括名词性替代（如第三人称代词、指示性代词、关系代词、不定代词等）、动词性替代（如 do, do it, do that, do so 等）和分句性替代（如 so, not, if so, if not, as 等）（连淑能，1993）。

例 42　He hated failure, he had conquered <u>it</u> all his life, risen above <u>it</u>, and despised <u>it</u> in others.

他讨厌<u>失败</u>，他一生中曾战胜<u>失败</u>，超越<u>失败</u>，并且藐视别人的<u>失败</u>。

例 43　Translation from English into Chinese is not easy as <u>that</u> from English into French.

<u>英译汉</u>不如<u>英译法</u>容易。

例 44　We have advocated the principle of peaceful co-existence, <u>which</u> is now growing more and more popular in the world.

我们提倡和平共处的<u>原则</u>，这项<u>原则</u>目前在世界上已经越来越得人心了。

例 45　You don't want to lag behind. <u>Neither does she.</u>

你<u>不愿意落后</u>，她也<u>不愿意落后</u>。

相较于英语，汉语多用重复，重复包括重叠、排比、反复等修辞手法，通过这些修辞手法的应用，汉语可以达到一种均衡美和韵律美，也可为文章增加文采。如中文中常用各种形式的叠词（亮晶晶、白茫茫、吵吵嚷嚷、熙熙攘攘、杨柳依依、风雨潇潇）。叠词表达是汉语中一大语言特色，可以使语言表达更为生动活泼。因此，在英译汉时，译者应考虑到汉语的表达习惯，适当应用叠词，通过重复，以增强译文的感染力。如：

例 46　The road was packed with a <u>noisy</u> crowd of <u>men and women</u>, who were selling and buying <u>all kinds of things</u>.

路上挤满了<u>男男女女</u>，他们<u>熙熙攘攘</u>，正在买卖<u>各种各样</u>的东西。

例 47　Walking <u>up and down</u> the <u>empty</u> room, he <u>stopped here and there</u> to <u>touch or look</u>.

房间<u>空空荡荡</u>，他<u>走来走去</u>，这儿<u>停停</u>，那儿<u>停停</u>，<u>东摸摸</u>，<u>西瞧瞧</u>。

例 48　老年人<u>如</u>夕照，少年人<u>如</u>朝阳；老年人<u>如</u>瘠牛，少年人<u>如</u>乳虎；老年人<u>如</u>僧，少年人<u>如</u>侠；老年人<u>如</u>字典，少年人<u>如</u>戏文；老年人<u>如</u>鸦片烟，少年人<u>如</u>白兰地酒；老年人<u>如</u>别行星之陨石，少年人<u>如</u>大海洋之珊瑚岛；老年人<u>如</u>埃及沙漠之金字塔，少年人<u>如</u>西伯利亚之铁路；老年人<u>如</u>秋后之柳，少年人<u>如</u>春间之草……

The old man <u>is like</u> the setting sun; the young man, the morning sun. The old man <u>is like</u> a lean ox; the young man, a cub tiger. The old man <u>is like</u> a monk; the young man, a knight. The old man <u>is like</u> a dictionary; the young man, the text of a play. The old man <u>is like</u> opium; the young, brandy. The old man <u>is like</u> a shooting star; the young man, a coral island. The old man <u>is like</u> the pyramid of Egypt; the young man, the Siberian railroad. The old man <u>is like</u> the willow after autumn; the young man, the grass in spring...

英文虽多用替代，忌讳重复，但在英文中同样存在平行结构，英文的平行结构类似于汉语中的排比，在面对此类句子的翻译时，译者应该保留原文的形式，以准确传达出原文的气势和文学色彩。如：

例 49 It was the best of times, it was the worst of times; it was the age of wisdom, it was the age of foolishness; it was the epoch of belief, it was the epoch of incredulity; it was the season of light, it was the season of darkness; it was the spring of hope, it was the winter of despair; we had everything before us, we had nothing before us; we were all going direct to heaven, we were all going direct to the other way. (Charles Dickens: *A Tale of Two Cities*)

这是最好的时代，这是最坏的时代；这是智慧的年代，这是愚蠢的年代；这是信仰的时期，这是怀疑的时期；这是光明的季节，这是黑暗的季节；这是希望之春，这也是绝望之冬；我们面前万物皆有，我们面前一无所有；我们正走向天堂，我们也正直下地狱。（查尔斯·狄更斯《双城记》）

● 翻译实践

翻译下列句子，注意中英文句式结构的转换。

1. People believe that American team will win the football game. Peter thinks so, but I believe not.

2. Reading exercises one's eyes; speaking, one's tongue; while writing, one's mind.

3. Association with the good can only produce good. With the wicked, evil.

4. Crafty men contemn studies, simple men admire them and wise men use them.

5. Histories makes men wise; poets witty; the mathematics subtle; natural philosophy deep; moral grave; logic and rhetoric able to contend.

● 课后练习

一、句子翻译

1. She fell asleep.

2. The city fell to the enemy.

3. Don't walk along the top of the wall; you might fall.

4. Her face fell when I told her the news.

5. Interest rates fell sharply last week.

6. A prayer was said in memory of those who fell in the war.

7. We should work for common security in a spirit of democracy, inclusiveness, cooperation and win-win progress. The internal affairs of a country should be handled independently by the country itself, and the international affairs should be dealt with collectively through consultation by all countries.

8. The threshold of complexity beyond which this phenomenon occurs has already been crossed by many existing systems, including some compiling and computer operating system.

9. Histories make men wise; poets witty; the mathematics subtle; natural philosophy deep; moral grave; logic and rhetoric able to contend.

10. We crossed the Yangtze and arrived at the station, where I bought a ticket while he saw to my luggage. At the sight of his back tears started to my eyes, but I wiped them hastily so that neither he nor anyone else might see them.

二、段落翻译

1. Navigation satellite systems are the common wealth of the development of mankind and also a space infrastructure which can provide all-time precise time and space information. They promote the development of emerging industrial clusters that are technology-and knowledge-intensive with huge growth potentials and sound comprehensive benefits, thus becoming critical support for national security, economic and social development, and increasingly improve the people's production and living activities.

2. 卫星导航系统是全球性公共资源，多系统兼容与互操作已成为发展趋势。中国始终秉持和践行"中国的北斗，世界的北斗"的发展理念，服务"一带一路"建设发展，积极推进北斗系统国际合作。与其他卫星导航系统携手，与各个国家、地区和国际组织一起，共同推动全球卫星导航事业发展，让北斗系统更好地服务全球、造福人类。

三、篇章翻译

1. Over the past year, Chinese diplomacy has been fruitful. President Xi Jinping and other state leaders visited many countries and attended major international events, including the G20 Leaders Summit, the BRICS Leaders Meeting, the Shanghai Cooperation Organization Summit, the East Asian leaders' meetings on cooperation, the Asia-Europe Meeting, the Annual Meeting of the New Champions 2014 in Tianjin, and the World Economic Forum annual meeting 2015 in Davos, Switzerland. China hosted the 22nd APEC Economic Leaders Meeting, the Fourth Summit of the Conference on Interaction and Confidence Building Measures in Asia, and

the Boao Forum for Asia. China has been participating actively in establishing multilateral mechanisms and writing international rules. We have made steady progress in developing relations with other major countries, entered a new phase in neighborhood diplomacy, and made new headway in our cooperation with other developing countries. Notable progress has been made in conducting economic diplomacy. Progress has been made in pursuing the Silk Road Economic Belt and 21st Century Maritime Silk Road initiatives; preparations have been made for establishing the Asian Infrastructure Investment Bank, and the Silk Road Fund has been set up. China is engaging in more exchanges and cooperation with other countries, and is increasingly recognized as a major responsible country on the international stage.

2. China is a multi-ethnic country with a vast territory and a long history covering thousands of years. It boasts of abundant tourist resources, with beautiful natural landscapes, numerous scenic spots and historic sites, and a rich splendid culture. Since the introduction of the reform and opening policy, China's economy has seen sustained growth at an annual average rate of nearly 10 percent. There has been vigorous development in its various public undertakings and marked improvement in the people's lives. All this has laid a solid foundation for a boom in the tourist sector. China now enjoys political stability, economic development and a prosperous market. The Chinese government sticks to the reform and opening policy and vigorously develops relations with other countries. These have created favorable conditions for the development of tourism. The Chinese government attaches great importance to the development of tourism and regards tourism as the top priority of its tertiary industry. It has made unremitting efforts to tap its tourist resources, improve its tourist facilities and upgrade its service quality, which have effectively promoted the rapid development of international and domestic tourism. With the improvement of the living standard of the Chinese people, the number of Chinese traveling abroad has gradually increased with each passing year, injecting new vitality to the development of world tourism.

第三章
翻译基本技巧

语言和思维密不可分。英汉思维方式的差异外显的是完全不同的句法结构。因此在英汉翻译实践中遇到的具体麻烦，需要翻译技巧的辅佐，从微观层面指导翻译过程。常见的翻译技巧有词义的选择，词类转换，增词法，减词法，重译法，正反、反正译法，被动语态的译法，分译、合译法等。基本翻译技巧的熟练运用不仅能有效减少汉译版本的翻译痕迹，而且可以最大限度地实现"功能对等"。

第一节 词义的选择

词是语言中具备音、义、形，可以独立使用的最小单位，在英译汉的过程中，如何针对原文原句的词义恰当地选择合适的汉语词义是保证译文质量的前提和基础。

一、根据词类来确定词义

英汉两种语言体系里的很多词汇都有一词多类的现象，即同一个词往往分属几个不同的词类，拥有不同的词义，例如 round 这个单词，作为形容词可翻译为"圆的，肥胖的"，作为介词却理解为"在……周围"。值得一提的是，英语有十大词类：名词，冠词，代词，数词，形容词，副词，动词，介词，连词和感叹词。因此在实际翻译中，首先要判定这个词在整句话中扮演什么词性，然后再确定其词义，甚至同一种词性的同一个单词在不同的场合下也扮演着不同的中文意义，这就是词汇的复杂之处。如 right 这个单词：

例 1　I tend to view that he is right.

我倾向于认为他是对的。

例 2　The toes of his right foot felt odd.

他的右脚趾头感觉不舒服。

例 3　They have no rights as a UK citizen.

他们没有英国公民该享有的权利。

例 4　I will make a commitment with you right now.

我要马上跟你把租约敲定。

再看 stand 这个单词，不仅仅只有动词这一种词性，更不只是"站起来"的意思：

例 5　I twisted my ankle, and I couldn't stand up.

我的脚踝扭伤，简直无法站起来。

例 6　She is funny, but I can't stand her.

她滑稽，但我却无法忍受她。

例 7　He set up a stand on the market.

他在市场上设了个摊位。

例 8　You have to know where to stand for a good viewpoint.

你得知道站在哪里观察角度比较理想。

Home 是一词多义的典型：

例 9　I will see her home tonight.

今晚我送她回家。

例 10　India is the home of elephants.

印度是大象的繁殖地。

例 11　He is at home with the classics.

他精通古典文学。

例 12　Maternity home costs in America have gone up sharply.

美国妇产医院收费已经急剧上涨。

例 13　Much is produced here for home market.

这里为国内市场生产了许多产品。

二、根据语境来确定词义

上下文也就是语境，即语言的使用环境。每一个微小词语的表述都要受到语境的限制，先拿汉语词汇来举个简单例子吧，说到"去世"，有"寿终正寝"，有"命归黄泉"，有"咽气"，也有"翘辫子"之说，这些或文雅，或通俗，或粗野的表达取决于整个语境。

在英汉翻译中，如何准确地理解原文很大程度上会受到语境的影响和制约。从微观角度来说，译者必须根据源语语境提供的信息，正确理解原文中每个词语的确切含义，使译文更忠实贴切，理解无偏差。

先举个简单例子，比如英文形容词 heavy，和它有关的搭配不胜枚举，我们耳熟能详的有 heavy clouds，heavy wine，前者翻译为厚云，后者翻译为烈酒，这种现象就要归结于语境了。在此将 heavy 的所有常见搭配做个总结，以备读者拿来使用。

heavy frost 浓霜　　　　　　heavy news 悲痛的消息

heavy crops 丰收　　　　　　heavy heart 忧郁的心

heavy road 泥泞的路　　　　heavy fire 猛烈的炮火

heavy sea 波涛汹涌的海　　　heavy bread 没有发好的面包

heavy load 重载　　　　　　heavy traffic 拥挤的交通
heavy reader 冗长的读物　　heavy smoker 烟瘾大的人

再来感受一下英文单词于不同的句子环境下所外化出来的不同词义：

He is the last man to come. 他是最后来的。

He is the last person for such a job. 他最不配做这份工作。

He should be the last man to blame. 怎么也不该怪他。

This is the last place where I expected to meet you. 我怎么也没料到会在这个地方见到你。

如上文的 last 一词，在四种句子环境下分别折射出了不同的含义，确保正确地理解和表达才能够消除歧义，符合汉语习惯。

又如动词 work，如果上下文不同，汉语习惯搭配也不一样，翻译时应该选择不同的词义来表达。

例 14　I think your suggestion will work.

我想你的建议行得通。

例 15　The new treatment works like magic.

新疗法疗效神奇。

例 16　My watch doesn't work.

我的表不走了。

例 17　The sea works high.

海浪汹涌起伏。

例 18　She worked her way to the front.

她好不容易才挤到前面。

例 19　The root of the pine tree worked down between the stones.

松树的树根在石缝间扎根下去。

例 20　The new regulation is working well.

新规定执行得很顺利。

通常情况下，语境会从三个方面制约词义，即语言语境、情景语境和文化语境，这也是语言学家胡壮麟对语境的分类。下文将分别对这些概念进行阐述。

（一）语言语境对词义的影响

在英文词汇的大家庭里，几乎没有一个词语只有单独的一个意义，字典里也不可能列出一个词语的所有意义，单词的具体意义往往依赖于其寄存的词组、句子，或者语篇，这些语言环境会赋予一个单词相应的内涵。比如 good 一词，根本意思是"好的，优秀

的",但是放在不同的语言环境里,会被外化成不同的表述:

a piece of good news 一个好新闻　　　a good boy 一个有规矩的孩子
a good man 一个善良的人　　　　　　have a good time 玩得愉快
good to see you 很高兴能见到你　　　a good table 饕餮盛宴

从褒贬的角度来看,大部分的单词属于中性词,不像 good 的褒义色彩这么明显,也不像诸如 bad 此类显然是贬义词,因此译者必须仔细研读整个语言环境,反复推敲上下文,确定出最符合原文感情色彩的汉语词汇,从而实现翻译的风格对等。

来看看下面两个单词 aggressive 和 talkative 在不同的句子环境里所折射出的不同内涵:

例 21　It is an aggressive war.

这是一场侵略性战争。

例 22　Mark is an aggressive young leader.

马克是一个颇有进取心的年轻领导。

例 23　The boy's aggressive character disturbs his mother.

小男孩爱打人的习性使他妈妈特别困扰。

例 24　Not any roommate likes her because she is too talkative.

因为她太长舌了,室友们都不喜欢她。

例 25　She is in a talkative mood.

她滔滔不绝,话兴正浓。

上述例句表明,语言语境可以改变一个单词的情感属性,使字典里笼统、抽象的概念更有了烟火气。正如著名的英国语言学家 Firth 曾说过的,任何一个词用在不同的语境中都是一个新词。相较于情景语境和文化语境,语言语境所承载的东西更少,所以理解起来也更为浅显,在此不作赘述。

(二)情景语境对词义的影响

何为情景语境?和语言语境不同,它更多的是指产生语言活动的环境,包括时间、空间和交际活动的参与者。费罗姆金和罗德曼在《语言导论》中说:"语言不是文人学士、辞书编纂者制定的一种抽象物,它有坚实宽厚的基础,它产生于人类世世代代的劳动、需求、交往、娱乐、情爱和志趣"。在语言材料中,作者和读者常常不自觉地调动诸如时间、地点、对象、背景等知识来叙述或论证说理。因此,在实际的翻译过程中译者应该充分关注情景语境对语篇的暗示作用。

情景语境对于理解原文同样重要,一旦脱离对情景的分析和把握,翻译就会有失偏颇。例如,莎士比亚在《哈姆雷特》中有一句非常经典的对白:To be or not to be, this is the question. 当时的情景语境是：哈姆雷特的父亲原本是丹麦国王，被他叔叔克劳狄斯毒害夺取王位，并且娶了他的母亲，哈姆雷特内心极为矛盾、彷徨。他想为父亲报仇，但因为自己势单力薄而犹豫不决，所以较合适的翻译是："生存还是毁灭，这是个问题。"

但是如果语境改变了，对句子的翻译就要做出一定的调整。比如：The college entrance examination is coming. The time is not much. To be or not to be, this is the question. 因为这里主要是讲高考已经来临，所剩时间不多。这里翻译成"坚持还是放弃，这是个问题"更合适。

又如 Tomorrow morning at dawn I am to be picked up from the castle and driven to the camp (journey time: approximately one hour) where I am to be received by the Commandant, Rudolf Hoess. 该句选自当年纳粹德国的外交部次长马丁·卢瑟对奥斯维辛集中营的巡视笔记。故事发生在1943年7月4日，他代表外交部去奥斯维辛集中营作一次全程检查，此句告诉我们他第二天的行程安排，考虑到原文的特定情景，他的目的地 the camp，不是"露营地"，而是"集中营"，此外，根据上下文来判断，pick up 意思是"搭乘"。所以综合情景语境来考虑，此句话译为：明日拂晓我将从这里乘车去奥斯维辛集中营（行程约1小时）。在那里，我将由司令官鲁道夫·霍斯接待。

（三）文化语境对词义的影响

文化语境是指言语行为发生时所处的社会文化背景。语言是文化的组成部分，也是文化的载体。翻译不仅是语言活动，还是跨文化的交流，这就要求译文要准确地表达出原文的内容、文化特点和风格，还要满足特定文化背景下译文读者的阅读习惯和要求。如果在翻译时只是从字、词、句的层面去考虑而忽略了文化语境，翻译出来的作品就无法准确地传递原作的信息。因此，翻译与文化语境息息相关。小到每个单词的处理，只有顺应文化语境，才能对等地传递出相应的文化信息。本部分选取美国作家海明威的经典传世之作《老人与海》中译本里的一些例句分析体现各方面的文化语境对词义选择的影响。

例 26　They spread apart after they were out of the mouth of the harbor and each one headed for the part of the ocean where he hoped to find fish.

它们一出港口就分散开来，每一条都驶向指望能找到鱼的那片海面。

这句话的译文体现了翻译与社会文化语境的顺应。The mouth of harbor 可直译为"港湾的嘴巴"，但是这种翻译方式不符合中文的逻辑和表达，因此将 mouth 理解为一个地方的开口部分，翻译为港口而不是嘴巴。采用这样的翻译方式使中国读者更容易明白作者想要表达的意思。

例 27　He always thought of the sea as la mar which is what people call her in Spanish when they love her.

他每想到海洋，总是叫她海娘子，这是人们对海洋抱有好感时的称呼。

这句话选自于张爱玲的译本，体现了翻译与生态文化语境的顺应。源语中 la mar 在西班牙文化中是神秘女孩的意思，张爱玲在处理 la mar 这个词时就结合了中国文化的特色，翻译为"海娘子"。根据句子语境可以判断出 la mar 是用来形容海洋。渔夫将海洋比作女孩子，体现出了渔夫对海洋的好感。将 la mar 译为海娘子即能准确地传达渔夫对海洋的感情，符合中文的表达方式，又能够提高中国读者的接受度。这样做能使译文更加准确且生动形象。

例 28　Why did they make birds so delicate and fine as those sea swallows when the ocean can be so cruel?

既然海洋这样残暴，为什么像海燕那样的鸟儿生来就如此柔弱和纤巧？

这句话的译文体现了翻译与宗教文化语境的顺应。结合整个句子意思，可以推断出这句话中的 they 指的是鸟儿的造物者。原著中主人公圣地亚哥是古巴人，他信仰宗教，相信世间万物都是由造物者创造的。在这句话的译文中，译者没有直接将 they 翻译为造物者或者是天神，而是用"生来"一词来暗含这一层含义，准确地表达出了像海燕那样的鸟儿从来到世上的那天起就是柔弱的。

例 29　… And you nearly were killed when I brought the fish in too green and he nearly tore the boat to pieces.

……我把一条活蹦乱跳的鱼拖上船去，它差一点把船撞得粉碎，你也差一点因此送了命。

这句话也体现了翻译与社会文化语境的顺应。在这句话中，译者将 the fish in too green 翻译为"一条活蹦乱跳的鱼"。

Green 在英文文化中不仅有"绿色"这一含义，还用来形容事物生机盎然，充满活力。假如在译文中将 green 直接翻译为绿色，会误导读者想当然地认为"我"带来的是一条颜色很绿的鱼，所以在此处必须将 green 意译为"活蹦乱跳"才能准确地传达出源语的意义。

在了解语境的基础上处理单个词义，从而能够更好地宏观把握语篇，为译者升华其翻译能力提供了新的思路和启发，打开了一扇新世界的大门。

三、通过引申确定词义

字典里给"引申"下的定义是"从本来的意义生出一个新的意义来"。例如"白"这个词本来指"白色",后来引申出"空白"义,这便是从"白色"义生出了一个新的意义"空白"。翻译中的所谓词义引申,是指在一个源语词所具有的基本词义的基础上,进一步加以引申,选择比较恰当的目的语词来表达,使原文的思想表现得更加准确,译文更加流畅。很多情况下,针对同一种实物或者思想,英汉两种语言会根据自己的语系特点和表达习惯给出不对等的词汇,因此译者必须透过语言表象,抓住内在实质,摆脱原文表层的束缚,在"虚"与"实"之间进行词义的引申。

(一)抽象化引申

英语中表示具体意义的词往往可用来表示事物的一种属性或一个概念,翻译时可将具体意义引申为某种属性或者抽象概念。

例 30　Every life has its roses and thorns.

每一种生活都有它的甜和苦。

例 31　They have their smiles and tears.

他们有他们的欢乐与悲哀。

例 32　The pen is mightier than the sword.

智慧胜过武力。

例 33　I was not one to let my heart rule my head.

我不是一个让情感凌驾于理智之上的人。

例 34　He gave up the sword for the plough.

他解甲归农了。

例 35　There is a mixture of the tiger and the ape in the character of the imperialists.

帝国主义者的性格既残暴又狡猾。

英语中还有很多的固定短语采用的是具体化的意象,中译时也需要做出抽象化引申,解释出其本质含义。在此列举出一些典型例子:

例 36　I was practically on my knees but he still refused.

我几乎是苦苦哀求,但他依然拒绝。

例 37　He is a rolling stone. I don't think he can go far.

他是个见异思迁的人,我想他不会有多大出息。

例 38　I will break my neck to get this done by Friday, but I can't promise for sure.

我一定要尽最大努力在周五之前完成此事,但我不能说定。

例 39　By this means she cast in a bone between the wife and the husband.

她用这种手段离间这对夫妻。

上述例句可以看出，在英译汉的过程中，信息往往不是完全对等的，很多时候找不到与源语一一对应的词汇，如果一味地生搬硬套，字对字翻译，会造成译文的晦涩难懂，不合乎逻辑，所以译者要对一部分的单词做抽象化处理。

（二）具体化引申

抽象的词义也能引申为具体化。所谓具体化引申就是使用代表抽象概念的词来表现一种具体事物，尤其是英语中有些单词在特定的上下文里，其含义是清晰的，但译成汉语时如果不进行具体化处理，就很容易造成歧义。下面通过一些例句做出详细说明：

例 40　The car in front of me stalled and I missed the green.

前面的车停了，我错过了绿灯。

例 41　The administration was free from corruption.

这届政府没有腐败现象。

例 42　Human will can overpower natural forces.

人定胜天。

英语中还有个值得一提的现象叫转喻，比如以人名代替其作品，也可以理解为具体化引申。

例 43　I have read Shakespeare, Mark Twain, and Tolstoy.

我读了莎士比亚、马克·吐温和托尔斯泰的作品。

课后练习

一、翻译下列句子，注意划线单词的词义。

1. He was tall and straight and clear-eyed and dark.

2. The accounts are straight.

3. Put your room straight.

4. She keeps straight.

5. There are a lot of problems we need to get straight.

6. This is a very straight place.

7. My relationship with him was up and down.

8. Both musically and lyrically it is effective.

9. I have to watch every penny because of poverty.

10. He is a great man for doing dirty jobs.

11. He had lived all his life in desert where every cupful of water might be a matter of life

and death.

12. It is easy for girls to engage in self-critical conversations, and once it <u>starts</u> there's often pressure for you to join in.

13. "<u>You chicken!</u>" he cried, looking at William with contempt.

14. <u>Words once reserved for restroom walls</u> are now common stuff in films, plays, books and even on television.

15. The behavior that they <u>bow to</u> the billionaire looks very disgusting.

16. Please don't <u>wake a sleeping dog</u>.

17. He thinks by all his fast talking and flattery he can <u>pull the wool over her eyes</u>, but she isn't deceived.

18. He is the <u>admiration</u> of all the school.

19. <u>Beauty</u> lies in lover's eyes.

20. As a kid, he was the <u>despair</u> of all teachers.

21. Very soon, he became a <u>national phenomenon</u>.

第二节　词类转换

　　词类转换作为最实用的翻译技巧之一，是指翻译过程中为了使译文符合目的语的表达习惯而适当调整和转换原文中的英语词性，避免出现翻译腔。具体来说，英译汉实践中的词类转换主要分为以下几种。

一、名词转换为动词

　　名词和动词作为词类范畴里重要的两大类，它们之间的转换无处不在。尤其是英语语法偏爱名词，句子多呈静态结构，汉语语法以动词为主，动态句子占多数，因此英译汉实践中名词转换为动词频率最高。

　　例 1　In China, there is a lot of <u>emphasis</u> on politeness.

　　译文：在中国，人们非常注重礼貌。

　　分析：本句中进行词类转换的对象是 emphasis，原意为名词"要点，重点"，倘若不改变词性，继续译为名词，那么整个句子呈现出来就是"在中国，人们把重点放在礼貌上"，翻译腔过重，读起来相当拗口，进行词类转换之后，译为动词"注重"，整句话变得言简意赅，琅琅上口。

例 2　The sight and sound of jet planes filled me with special longing.

译文：看到喷气式飞机，听到隆隆的机声，让我特别神往。

分析：本句中需要转换的名词 sight 和 sound，这两个是含有动作性意味的名词，表面看来是"视觉"和"声音"，用来修饰飞机，变成"喷气式飞机的视觉和声音"，完全不符合中文的表达逻辑，所以需要翻译出它们隐含的动作，也就是"看"和"听"，变成动态感十足的句子，符合中文句式的美感。

接下来再欣赏几组名词转换动词的英译汉句式：

例 3　Too much exposure to TV programs will do harm to the eyesight of kids.

小孩子过多地看电视会大大损伤视力。

例 4　He gave the strange woman a quick glance.

他快速地瞥了一眼那个奇怪的女士。

例 5　The old man was the forgiver of the young man's past wrong doings.

老人宽恕了年轻人过去所做的坏事。

例 6　She had a good knowledge of computer games.

她精通电脑游戏。

例 7　The next news bulletin made no mention of the demonstration.

下面一条新闻没提到游行。

二、形容词转换为动词

英语中表示情感，欲望，知觉等心理活动的形容词放在系动词后面作表语时，可译为动词，常见的有 familiar, delighted, thankful, grateful, confident, anxious, cautious, discouraged, doubtful, ignorant, frustrated, ashamed 等。例如：

例 8　They are very much concerned about the future of their country.

他们非常关心国家的前途。

原句中 concerned 作为形容词意为"担忧的，牵挂的"，位于 be 动词的后面作表语修饰 future，直译的话为"担忧的未来"，明显搭配不当，改为动词"担忧，关心"之后，译文就变成"关心国家未来"，动宾词组使表达流畅自然。

例 9　I am grateful to you for your kindness.

我感激你的善意帮忙。

本句中的 grateful 是形容词性，原意为"感谢的"，如果直译，整句话译为"我感谢的你的善意帮助"，语义完全混乱，不知所云，必须进行词类转换，调整为动词"感谢，感激",语句通畅,表达自然。

类似的形容词转换为动词句式数不胜数:

例 10　Doctors have said that they are not sure they can save his life.

医生说他们不敢肯定能否救得了他的命。

例 11　They are quite content with the data obtained from the experiment.

他们满足于在实验中获得的数据。

例 12　It is impossible to live in a society and be independent of society.

生于社会,不能脱离社会。

例 13　His career is stormy.

他的事业充满曲折。

例 14　Tom is frustrated at the escaping of Jerry.

杰瑞逃跑了,汤姆十分受挫。

三、介词和副词转换为动词

英语中很多介词或者某些形式上与介词相同的副词,皆可以译为汉语动词,举一些实例作为说明:

例 15　I am all for your opinion.

我完全赞同你的意见。

例 16　We are inside two marriages.

我们正在观察两对夫妻。

例 17　Millions of the people in the mountainous areas are finally off poverty.

千百万山区人终于摆脱了贫困。

例 18　The manager let the experts in and others out.

经理让专家进来,让其他人出去。

例 19　We are a week ahead of the schedule.

我们比原计划提前了一周。

例 20　She opened the window to let the fresh air in.

她打开窗户,让新鲜空气进来。

例 21　He is up and down.

他已经起床下楼去了。

上述 8 个例句中,前面 4 个属于介词转换为动词,后面 4 个看似介词,实则是副词对动词的转换。

四、动词转换为名词

英语中有些动词，特别是名词派生的动词，在汉语中很难找到对等的动词，翻译时往往将这类动词转换为汉语的名词。例如：

例 22　The ten-year-old girl <u>behaves</u> as if she were an adult.

这个十岁小女孩的举止俨然一副成年人的样子。

例 23　As the war progressed, he would <u>symbolize</u> their frustrations, the embodiment of all evils.

随着战争的进行，他成了他们受挫的象征，成了一切坏事的化身。

例 24　Round-the-clock service <u>features</u> this store.

日夜服务是这家商店的特色。

例 25　The camel is <u>characterized</u> by the ability to go for long periods without water.

骆驼的特点是能够长期行走而不喝水。

例 26　He <u>impressed</u> me as a man of great charm.

他给我的印象是他相当有魅力。

上述五句原文中的动词如果不做转变，会导致翻译效果欠佳，比如第四句中的 characterized，原意为动词"以……为特点"，硬译出来就是"骆驼以长期行走而不喝水为特点"，读起来异常别扭，所以适时的变通非常有必要。

五、形容词转换为名词

英语中的形容词转换为汉语中的名词一般有两种情况，一种是形容词前面有定冠词 the 的时候需要转换为名词；另一种是表示事物特征的形容词用作表语时可以转换为名词。

例 27　They did their best to help the <u>sick</u> and the <u>wound</u>.

他们尽了最大的努力帮助病号和伤员。

Sick 和 wound 两个形容词前面都加了定冠词 "the"，代表了一类人，翻译出来名词为所有的"伤员"和"病号"。

例 28　Computers are more <u>flexible</u>, and can do a greater variety of jobs.

计算机的灵活性比较大，因此能做更多种不同的工作。

原句中 flexible 是形容词"灵活的"，位于 be 动词的后面，属于典型的表语结构，翻译成汉语为计算机的"灵活性"，非常符合中国人的表达习惯。

下文是一些类似的实例赏析：

例 29　Stevenson was eloquent and elegant, but very soft.

史蒂文森有口才，有风度，但很软弱。

例 30　We should try every means to build a school for the blind and the deaf.

我们应该想尽一切办法为聋哑人创办一所学校。

例 31　The new contract would be good for ten years.

新条约的有效期为十年。

例 32　The man is armed and dangerous.

这人有枪，是危险人物。

六、副词转换为名词

英语中有些副词，尤其是以 -ly 为结尾的副词，通常需要译为名词才符合汉语的表达方式。例如：

例 33　He is physically weak but mentally strong.

他身体虽弱，但思想健全。

例 34　It is officially announced that Paris is invited to the meeting.

官方宣布，巴黎应邀出席会议。

例 35　They have not done so well ideologically, however, as organizationally.

但是，他们的思想工作没有他们的组织工作做得好。

七、名词转换为形容词

英语中有两种名词一般在译成汉语时需要转换为形容词，分别是形容词派生的名词和某些名词加不定冠词作表语时。举例说明如下：

例 36　Independent thinking is an absolute necessity in study.

学习中的独立思考是绝对必需的。

例 37　The blockade during the period was a success.

封锁很成功。

八、副词转换为形容词

英语中的副词比汉语中的副词用得更广泛，许多英语副词都可以转换为汉语形容词，尤其是当动词被转换成名词时，修饰该动词的副词相应地就被转变成形容词。例如：

例 38　Earthquakes are <u>closely</u> related to faulting.

地震与地层断裂有着密切的关系。

例 39　She chirped, blinking her eyes <u>happily</u>.

她叽叽喳喳地叫着，两眼闪烁着快乐的光芒。

例 40　The sun affects <u>tremendously</u> both the mind and body of a man.

太阳对人的身体和精神都有极大的影响。

九、形容词转换为副词

副词可以转换为形容词，同样的，英语中的名词被转换为汉语动词时，修饰该名词的形容词可译作汉语副词。例如：

例 41　On weekends, they usually give the classroom a <u>thorough</u> cleaning.

他们通常会在周末把教室彻底地打扫一番。

例 42　At last, he whispered a <u>hurried</u> good-bye to his host and darted toward the door.

最后，他匆匆地向主人轻声道别，飞快走到门口。

例 43　We place highest value on our <u>friendly</u> relations with developing countries.

我们非常珍视同发展中国家的友好关系。

十、名词和动词转换为副词

作为最后一种常见的词类转换，值得一提的是，英语中的两大主流词性，即名词和动词，也经常被转换为汉语副词使用，听上去似乎很费解，通过例句展现就很浅显易懂了。

例 44　The new mayor earned some appreciation by the <u>courtesy</u> of coming to visit the city poor.

新市长有礼貌地前来慰问城市贫民，获得了他们的一些好感。

例 45　Only after they had done hundreds of <u>experiments</u> they <u>succeeded</u> in solving the problem.

在做了数百次试验后，他们才成功地解决了这一问题。

上述两个例句分别是名词和动词与副词的转换，由此可见，副词在汉语中也是扮演着举足轻重的地位，使表达更为生动传神。

综上所述，词类转换是英汉翻译实践中最普遍的策略，但译者并不能肆意而为之，必须遵循两种语言的规律和逻辑。因此，学习者们应该在实践中不断摸索，观察并总结其技巧，进而提高翻译水平。

课后练习

一、翻译下列句子，注意划线部分的词类转换。

1. She is a very hard worker.

2. He is still recovering from his operation.

3. She is a compulsive reader of romances.

4. I can't teach you French. I think my little brother is a better teacher.

5. Rockets have found application for the exploration of the universe.

6. If you don't go online every day, you will be ignorant of the developments both at home and abroad.

7. She was very anxious about her mother's health.

8. Salt is soluble in water.

9. We should never be content with our current achievement.

10. As his leg was broken, he lay in bed for a month.

11. It is against the local regulations to sell cigarettes to children under 18 years old.

12. After a long wait, I finally got a cab, but the traffic was moving at a snail's pace.

13. The voices had toned away to mere whisperings.

14. The computer behaves well.

15. A well-dressed man, who looked and talked like an American, went into the car.

16. The design aims at automatic operation, easy regulation, simple maintenance and high productivity.

17. X is used in mathematics for the unknown in equation.

18. They showed a sympathetic understanding of our problem.

19. The wounded have been sent to the hospital.

20. We should think globally.

21. This is where you were wrong.

22. Eating an apple every day makes you healthy physically.

23. The road show last Friday was quite a success.

24. We provide a variety of ladies' scarves.

25. Exchange of ideas is a vital necessity.

26. This love story impressed me very <u>deeply</u>.

27. <u>Hopefully</u>, it will be done early next month.

28. The accident is <u>closely</u> related to his careless driving.

29. This is <u>sheer</u> nonsense.

30. A successful scientist must be a <u>good</u> observer.

31. The trade has a <u>tremendous</u> increase to the advantage of both countries.

32. I had the <u>fortune</u> to meet him.

33. We must serve our clients <u>heart and soul</u>.

34. I <u>succeeded</u> in persuading him.

二、翻译下列段落，注意使用词类转换法。

Golden Wedding Anniversary

A couple was celebrating their golden wedding anniversary. Their domestic tranquility had long been the talk of the town. A local newspaper reporter was inquiring as to the secret of their long and happy marriage. "Well, it dates back to our honeymoon," explained the man. "We visited the Grand Canyon and took a trip down to the bottom of the canyon by pack mule. We hadn't gone too far when my wife's mule stumbled. My wife quietly said, 'That's once.'"

第三节　增词法

增词法，顾名思义，就是在翻译时增加一些词使原文的思想内容更忠实通顺。使用增词法不是随意地添油加醋，其目的是更加准确和完整地再现原文的内容，所以应该增加原文中虽无其词而有其意的一些词。

一、意义上或修辞的需要

（一）增加动词

根据意义上的需要，可以在名词前后适当增加动词。

例 1　In every Chinese city, we got into the streets, shops, parks, theatres and restaurants.

在中国，我们每到一个城市就<u>逛</u>大街，<u>逛</u>商店，<u>游</u>公园，<u>看</u>演出，<u>吃</u>名菜。

例 2　Everything was on a larger scale on him, the highs were higher, the lows lower.

他总是喜欢夸大事实，高的<u>说得</u>更高，低的<u>说得</u>更低。

例 3　In this year's World Cup, players will be whacking around the latest in soccer ball technology.

在今年的世界杯足球赛上，球员们将会踢一种用最新技术<u>制造</u>的足球。

例 4　He dismissed the meeting without a closing speech.

他没有<u>发表</u>闭幕演讲就结束了会议。

（二）增加名词

1. 在不及物动词后面增加名词

英语中有些动词在当作不及物动词使用时，宾语实际上是隐含在动词后面的，译成汉语时往往需要把它表达出来。

例 5　Mary washed for a living after her husband died of cancer.

玛丽在丈夫患癌去世后，就靠洗<u>衣服</u>维持生活。

例 6　Day after day he came to his work—sweeping, scrubbing, and cleaning.

他每天来干活——扫地，擦<u>地板</u>，打扫<u>房间</u>。

2. 在形容词前面增加名词

例 7　The old lady was wrinkled and black, with scant gray hair.

那个老太太满脸皱纹，<u>皮肤</u>很黑，头发灰白稀疏。

例 8　This typewriter is indeed cheap and fine.

这台打印机真是<u>价廉物美</u>。

3. 在抽象名词后增加名词

某些由动词或者形容词派生出来的抽象名词，翻译时可根据上下文在其后面增添适当的名词，使译文更合乎规范。

例 9　They wanted to ease the tension in the Middle East.

他们试图缓解中东的<u>紧张局势</u>。

例 10　After all preparations are made, our meeting will begin.

一切<u>准备工作</u>就绪以后，会议就开始了。

4. 在具体名词后面增加名词

当具体名词表达一种抽象概念时，译文中也常根据上下文增加一些适当的名词。

例 11　He felt the patriot rise within his breast.

他感到一种爱国<u>热情</u>在胸中激荡。

例 12　He allowed the father to be overruled by the judge, and declared his own son guilty.

他让法官的<u>职责</u>战胜父子的<u>私情</u>，而判决他儿子有罪。

（三）增加形容词

根据原文的上下文，有些动词在一定场合可以增加适当的形容词。

例 13　When I watched Ronaldo's moves, our goal seemed pretty hopeless.

当我看到罗纳尔多在场上<u>灵活地</u>奔跑时，感觉我们要进球是没什么希望了。

例 14　America has been a melting pot since its beginnings.

美国建国以来一直是个<u>民族的</u>大熔炉。

例 15　The war made a man of him.

战争把他锻炼成一个<u>堂堂的</u>男子汉。

（四）增加副词

根据原文的上下文，有些动词在一定场合可增加适当的副词，才能更贴切地表达原意。

例 16　Time droops in decay, like a candle burnt out.

时间<u>一点一点地</u>逝去，犹如蜡烛慢慢燃尽。

例 17　The crowds melted away.

人群<u>渐渐地</u>散开了。

例 18　As he sat down and began talking, words poured out.

他一坐下来就讲开了，<u>滔滔不绝地</u>讲个没完。

（五）增加表示名词复数的词

1. 增加重叠词表示复数

例 19　Flowers bloom all over the yard.

<u>朵朵</u>鲜花开满庭院。

例 20　There were rows of houses which he had never seen before.

<u>一排排</u>的房子都是他从来没有见过的。

2. 增加副词或其他词表示复数

例 21　The lion is the king of animals.

狮子是<u>百兽</u>之王。

例 22　The mountains began to throw their long blue shadows over the valley.

<u>群</u>山已在山谷中开始投下蔚蓝色长影。

（六）增加时态隐含的词

1. 强调时间概念

例 23　I had never thought I'd be happy to find myself considered unimportant. But this time I was.

以往我从未想过，当我发觉人们认为我无足轻重时，我会感到高兴。但这次情况确实如此。

2. 强调时间对比

例 24　I was, and remain, grateful for the part he played in my release.

我的获释是他成全的，对此我过去很感激，现在依然很感激。

（七）增加语态隐含的词

例 25　People all sympathized with her as she was married to a rich man and she loved a laborer on the farm.

人们都很同情她，因为她被迫嫁了个有钱人，而她爱着的是一个农场工人。

（八）增加语气助词

例 26　As for me, I didn't agree from the very beginning.

我呢，一开始就不赞成。

例 27　Don't take it seriously. I'm just making fun of you.

不要认真嘛！我只不过是开个玩笑罢了！

（九）增加承上启下的词

例 28　Yes, I like Chinese food. Lots of people do these days, sort of the fashion.

不错，我喜欢中国菜。现在很多人喜欢中国菜，这种情况算是有点赶时髦吧。

例 29　For mistakes had been made, bad ones.

因为已经犯了很多错误，而且还是很糟糕的错误。

二、根据句法上的需要增词

（一）增补原文回答句中的省略部分

例 30　—Is this your book?

　　　　—Yes, it is. (Yes, it is mine.)

　　　　—这是你的书吗？

　　　　—是我的。

例 31　—Which do you like better, green or red?

　　　　—Neither. (Neither green nor red.)

　　　　—你喜欢哪一种颜色，绿色还是红色？

　　　　—都不喜欢。（红色和绿色都不喜欢）

（二）增补原文原句中省略的动词

例 32　He remembered the incident, as did his wife.

他记得这件事情，他的妻子也<u>记得</u>（这件事情）。

例 33　Reading makes a full man, talking a ready man, writing an exact man.

读书使人充实，交谈<u>使人</u>敏捷，写作<u>使人</u>严谨。

（三）增补原文比较句中省略的部分

例 34　Better be wise by the defeat of others than by your own.

(**It is better to be wise** by the defeat of others than **to be wise by the defeat of** your own.)

从别人的失败中汲取教训比从自己的失败中<u>汲取教训</u>更好。

例 35　The footmen were as ready to serve her as they were their own mistress.

(The footmen were as ready to serve her as they were **ready to serve** their own mistress.)

仆人们愿意服侍她，就像<u>愿意服侍</u>他们的女主人一样。

（四）增补原文含蓄条件句中的省略部分

例 36　But without Adolf Hitler, there almost certainly would never have been a Third Reich.

然而<u>如果</u>没有阿道夫·希特勒，那就几乎肯定不会有第三帝国。

例 37　A book, tight shut, is but a block of paper.

一本书，<u>如果</u>紧紧合上而不读，只是一叠废纸。

● 三、语境的需要

这里的语境更多的是强调之前提到过的文化语境，也就是句子背后所隐藏的文化背景信息。

例 38　She gave me a bright and amicable flash of her white teeth.

她嫣然一笑，<u>明眸皓齿</u>。

西方人认为露齿大笑是一种美，所以英文有个单词叫 grin，表示露齿而笑，译为汉语后，如果依然用"那个女孩露齿大笑"，不符合中国人含蓄的审美，所以需要用优美的东方词汇适当增译一下。

例 39　The blond boy crossed himself nervously.

那个金发小男孩紧张地在胸前画着十字，<u>祈求上帝保佑</u>。

课后练习

一、请把下列句子译为中文，注意使用增词法。

1. I fell madly in love with her, and she with me.

2. The daily newspaper guides, educates and encourages the masses.

3. Ignorance is the mother of fear as well as of admiration.

4. He stretched his legs which were scattered with scars.

5. Was there a faint noise? What was it?

6. Lung cancer, diagnosed early, can be successfully treated by surgery.

7. Inflation was and still is NO.1 problem for the country.

8. The English language is in very good shape, and it is changing in its own undiscoverable way.

9. The virus may survive weeks and months.

10. Surely the noise of the machine won't disturb your rest, Jack?

11. Do what you like!

二、段落翻译

请将下列段落译为中文，注意使用增词法。

If you are hungry, what do you do? Grab a piece of your favorite meal and stay quiet after that? Just like your stomach, even your mind is hungry. But it never lets you know, because you keep it busy thinking about your dream lover, favorite star and many such absurd things. So it silently began to pay careful attention to your needs and never let itself grow. When mind loosens its freedom to grow, creativity gets a full stop.

第四节　减词法

由于汉语表达的简洁性，英译汉时需要采取减词法这一策略，同增词法类似，减词也不能任意而为之，需要遵守一定的原则。一般来讲，省去的词必须是在译文中可有可无的，或者是其含义已经包含在译文上下文的语境中。

一、句法的需要

从语法角度考虑，汉语中没有冠词，连词、介词、代词（尤其是关系代词和人称代词)、关系副词等出现频率也远远少于英语。所以，上述词类在汉译时往往省略，省略后的语法和语义反而更简洁。

（一）省略代词

在英语中代词的使用十分普遍，在一篇英语文章中，人称代词，反身代词，物主代词等各种代词会占到很大的比例，并且多用来充当主语。然而，代词在汉语中的地位却比较尴尬，可借用现代汉语学家王力先生的一句话形容就是"若要明白，不如名词复说；若要简洁，不如索性不用"。英译汉必须要考虑到这种差异，省译不必要的介词。

1. 为避免重复，代词做主语的英文句子翻译成汉语时采用无主句，实则主语就是前面的代词。

例 1 He was thin and haggard and he looked miserable.

他消瘦而憔悴，看上去痛苦不堪的样子。

例 2 But it's the way I am, and try as I might, I haven't been able to change it.

这就是真实的我，尽管已经尝试着去改变，但我还是没能做到。

2. 表示泛指的人称代词做主语时，汉译时往往省略，翻译为无主句。

例 3 One can never be too careful in one's work.

工作越细心越好。

例 4 As you come into the room, you'll see a piano.

一进房间门就能看到一架钢琴。

例 5 He who made the mistake should have the courage to admit.

犯了错误就要有勇气承认。

3. 英语中做宾语的代词，翻译时也要省略。

例 6 Linda will not be jealous, or if she is, she will not show it.

琳达不会嫉妒的，即便嫉妒，她也不会表现出来。

例 7 Please take off the old picture and throw it away.

请把那幅旧画摘下来扔掉。

4. 英语中只要涉及某人的或者和某人有关的，都会使用到相对应的物主代词，汉译时需要省略。

例 8 Her dark hair waved untidy across her broad forehead, her face was short, her upper lip short, showing a glint of teeth, her brows were straight and dark, her lashes long and dark, her nose straight.

她的黑发蓬松地飘拂在宽宽的前额，脸是短短的，上唇也是短短的，露出明亮的牙齿，眉毛又黑又直，睫毛又黑又长，鼻子挺拔。

例 9　He entered the room, his coat covered with snow and his nose red with cold.

他走进房间，大衣上满是雪，鼻子因为太冷而冻得通红。

5. Yourself, myself, himself, themselves 等这些反身代词汉译时也常常要省略。

例 10　Scientists have to train themselves to use their brain efficiently.

科学家必须锻炼高效用脑。

例 11　The teacher had a deep breath to keep herself calm.

老师深吸一口气，尽量保持平静。

6. 提到代词，必须要讲一下 it。作为代词的代表，it 用法颇多，可以指天气，可以指时间，可以作形式主语和形式宾语，也可以引导强调句型等。无论如何，译成汉语时"it"一般也作省略处理。

例 12　It was very sunny the day I met her.

我初遇她那天是个晴朗的日子。

例 13　The coin makes it easy to have the decision.

抛硬币做决定让事情变得简单多了。

例 14　It is only shallow people who judge by appearance.

只有浅薄者才会以貌取人。

（二）省略连词

中国传统哲学思维注重"天人合一"，而西方民族强调"主客分离"，表现在语言上就是汉语重意合，英语重形合。展现在句子层面就是汉语依靠暗含的意义组织句内的逻辑关系，不一定需要连接词，英语句子成分组成严密，主从句脉络清晰。因此英译汉时必定要考虑到这一点，该省略的连词就要省略，才能符合汉语的意合特点。

例 15　The gap between the rich and the poor is the product of complex forces, and won't be fixed overnight.

贫富差距是多种因素的产物，不可能一夜之间消除。

例 16　He didn't sleep much, but when he did, he dreamed of a beautiful princess, splendid castles, and gold and silver.

他没睡多久，一入梦便是沉鱼落雁的公主，富丽堂皇的城堡，金山银山。

例 17　Practically all substances expand when heated and contract when cooled.

事实上一切物质都是热胀冷缩的。

例 18　As the desert is like a sea, so is the camel like a ship.

沙漠似海，骆驼似舟。

（三）省略冠词

英语中的冠词虽然只有三个 a，an，the，却不容小觑，它们用途广泛，用法复杂。冠词的作用一般是语法需要和表达某种实际意义，如果仅仅是语法需要，不用来表达实际意义的冠词，汉译时可以省略。

例 19　The Confucius became the first individual to initiate a private school.

孔子开创了中国历史上的私学。

例 20　Things of a kind come together; people of a mind fall into the same group.

物以类聚，人以群分。

例 21　We should improve the ranks of our teachers.

必须加强教师队伍建设。

值得注意的是，在某些特定情况下，冠词的翻译不能省略：

1. 不定冠词表示"一""每一""同一"时，例如：

例 22　He stared at me without saying a word.

他瞪着我，一言不发。

2. 定冠词强调"这""那"时，例如：

例 23　How do you like the story?

你觉得这个故事怎么样？

（四）省略介词

英语中存在大量的介词，除了本书之前提到过的介词汉译时可以转换为其他词性，还有一大部分的介词是需要省译的，尤其是表示时间和地点的介词。

例 24　Rumors had already spread along the streets and lanes.

各种流言传遍了大街小巷。

例 25　Models from all fields should be publicized.

应当宣传各个领域的先进模范人物。

例 26　Regarding marriage, I have my own way.

我有我自己的婚姻观。

但是动词后面的介词一般不能省略。

例 27　The cat hid in the tree.

那只猫躲在了树上。

例 28　An ancient castle stood on the edge of the cliff.

一座古老的城堡矗立在悬崖边。

（五）省略动词

众所周知，尽管英语中很多动词都是充当谓语，连接主语和宾语，实则它们的语法作用强于词汇意义，所以汉译时可以省略；另外，连系动词是用来连接主语和表语的，如果表语是名词，通常需要把连系动词翻译出来，例如 We are a family 汉译为"我们是一家人"。但当表语是副词，形容词或者介词短语时，原句的连系动词应该省译。

例 29　The developing countries <u>cover</u> vast territories, <u>encompass</u> a large population and abound in natural resources.

发展中国家领土广阔，人口众多，自然资源丰富。

例 30　When the pressure <u>gets</u> low, the boiling point <u>becomes</u> low.

气压低，沸点就低。

● 二、修辞的需要

了解翻译的人都知道，把句子的每一个部分叠加起来，并不等于原句的全部意义，英汉两种语言无论是在思维方式还是表达习惯上都大为不同，从修辞的角度来说，原句中一些次要的部分需要舍弃，这样不仅不会影响原句原意的传达，而且中文译文读起来不会那么佶屈聱牙。举个例子来讲，going too far is as bad as not going far enough，这个英文表达字面意思理解是"走太远和走得不够远一样不好"，语义上确实说得通，但是考虑到修辞的美感，我们完全可以把它译为一个成语叫"过犹不及"。这就是修辞性减词的精髓所在。

例 31　Her dark eyes made little reflected stars. She was looking at him as she was always looking at him when she awakened.

她那双乌黑的双眸就像亮晶晶的星星在闪烁，他平时醒来的时候，她也是这样望着他。

原句中有两处 she was looking at him 的表达，如果不做省译，修辞上相当繁琐赘余。

例 32　With a part of the proceeds of his plan of piracy, he carried on a subtle system of corruption.

他利用一部分不义之财，上下打点，疏通关系。

原句前半部分直译是"利用他掠夺计划的一部分钱"，啰嗦冗长；his plan of 省译，proceeds of piracy 译为"不义之财"，更能显示出他利用不正当手段贿赂别人。

● 课后练习

一、翻译下列句子，注意使用减词法。

1. He who has never reached the Great Wall is not a true man.

2. It was a cold, dark day, the sky overcast.

3. The city has a dense manufacturing population.

4. If you confer a benefit, never remember it; if you receive one, remember it always.

5. They had ground him beneath their heel, they had taken the best of him, they had murdered his father, they had broken and wrecked his wife, and they had crushed his whole family.

6. The true joy of joys is the joy that joys in the joy of others.

7. Never trouble yourself with trouble till trouble troubles you.

8. He was arrested, convicted and sentenced to prison.

9. There was no snow, the leaves were gone from the trees, and the grass was dead.

10. Part-time waitress applicants who had worked at a job would receive preference over those who had not.

11. She hesitated for a minute and stood still while a tear or two splashed on the worn red carpet.

12. I knew the train was coming as I had seen the passengers swam into the platform.

13. We are looking forward with interest to your reply.

14. The government has put the new coins into circulation, but only a small number of people have ever seen them.

15. The fox may grow grey, but never good.

二、翻译下列段落，注意使用减词法。

The words "winner" and "loser" have many meanings. When we refer to a person as a winner, we do not mean one who makes someone else lose. To us, a winner is one who responds authentically by being credible, trustworthy, responsive, and genuine, both as an individual and as a member of a society.

第五节 重译法

重译法是指为了使表达更加明确，在译文中适当地重现原文出现过的词语；或者为了凸显某些内容，进一步加强语气以收到更好的修辞效果。通常情况下，为了避免单调乏味，英语往往行文简洁，尽量不重复表达，会借助同义词，近义词或者反义词来表示。相反，汉语的一个显著特点就是重复多，在很多场合下，有些词语只有不断重复，语义才能明确，表达才能流畅。因此，为了力求汉语译文实现信达雅，英译汉需要使用重译法。一般来讲，重译法有三个目的：明确译文；加强语气；生动文字。

一、译文明确的需要

重译法最直接的目的就是为了忠实于原文，不得不重复某些词语，准确再现原文的意义，使译文表达更明确。

（一）重复动词

1. 英语句子中经常用一个谓语动词连接几个宾语或者表语，汉译时要重复这个动词。

例 1　Are you glad or sad?

你是开心呢，还是难过呢？

例 2　Cars travel much more quickly than buses do.

小汽车跑得比大巴车跑得快多了。

例 3　His wife kept dining in his ears about his carelessness, his idleness, and the ruin he was bringing on his family.

他妻子在他耳边不停地絮叨，说他粗心，说他愚蠢，说一家人都毁在他身上。

2. 英语句子里不及物动词后有介词时，在除第一次以外的再次或者多次出现，往往只用介词而省略动词，汉译时要重复这个动词。

例 4　I no longer look for fame, for position, for money, just to be a free man.

我不再追寻名利、追寻地位、追寻金钱，只想要自由。

例 5　They talked about themselves, about the journey, about the future, about everything.

他们聊了他们自己，聊了旅途，聊了未来，聊了很多很多。

（二）重复名词

1. 重复原句中做宾语的名词

例 6　Employees are very reluctant to postpone or cancel the trip abroad.

员工非常不乐意推迟国外旅游或者取消国外旅游。

例 7　You have to learn to analyze and solve problems.

你必须学会分析问题，解决问题。

2. 重复原句中做表语的名词

例 8　He became an oil baron—all by himself.

他成为一个石油大王——一个白手起家的石油大王。

例 9　Vivian is your teacher as much as she is mine.

薇薇安既是你的老师，也是我的老师。

例 10　Taking care of parents is your duty as well as your elder brother's.

赡养父母是你的责任，也是你哥哥的责任。

3. 重复原句中介词前面省略的名词

例 11　This guy often got into argument with his colleagues or with the boss.

这个人经常和他的同事们争吵，或者和老板争吵。

例 12　The story of Jean is a story of groans and tears, of poor families destroyed by the capitalist.

基恩的故事是一个充满哀鸣与泪水的故事，是资本家摧残贫苦家庭的故事。

例 13　The doctor will get more practice out of her mother than out of hundreds of ordinary patients.

医生从她母亲那里得到的实践，比他从成百上千个普通病人身上得到的实践还多。

例 14　Ignorance is the mother of fear as well as of jealousy.

无知是恐惧的根源，也是嫉妒的根源。

4. 重复定语从句中做先行词的名词

例 15　I went to visit the American writer who wrote a number of books about China.

我去拜访了这位美国作家。这位美国作家写了很多关于中国的书。

例 16　The touching story happened in 2008, when Wenchuan was suffering from the massive earthquake.

这个感人的故事发生在2008年，2008年那个时候汶川正遭受大地震的破坏。

例 17　I admire this professor who is very knowledgeable.

我很欣赏这位教授，这位教授学识非常渊博。

例 18　I picked up the garbage which was thrown away by the tourist.

我把垃圾捡了起来，垃圾是游客扔的。

（三）重复代词

1. 英语中的代词使用特别频繁，汉语一般不会多用代词，防止造成指代不明的现象。所以汉译时除了适当地将原文中的一些代词直译外，还需要将某些代词所指代的名词重复译出，以便读者更清晰明了地理解译文。

例 19　A big nation has its problems; a small nation its advantages.

大国有大国的问题；小国有小国的优势。

例 20　I hope the discussion can be cancelled, for it will only waste time.

我希望取消讨论，因为讨论只会浪费时间。

例 21　He hated failure; he had conquered it all his life, risen about it, despised it in others.

他讨厌失败，他一生中曾战胜失败，超越失败，并蔑视别人的失败。

2. 英语经常使用形容词性的物主代词 my, his, their 等，或者名词性的物主代词 mine, yours, hers, theirs 等代替句子中做主语的名词，汉译时可以重复其代词所代替的名词以明确语义。

例 22　Each person has his behavior.

每个人有每个人的行为方式。

例 23　The old vagrant believes that poverty has its advantage.

那个老流浪汉认为穷也有穷的好处。

例 24　The Confucius believes that every student has his talent.

孔子认为，每个学生有每个学生的天资。

3. 英语中的关系代词或者关系副词 whenever, wherever, whoever 等，汉译时也需要使用重复法。

例 25　Come to see me whenever you are free.

你什么时候有空，就什么时候来找我。

例 26　Wherever severe oppression existed, there would be revolution.

哪里有压迫，哪里就有反抗。

例 27　You may take whichever will interest you best.

哪一个你最感兴趣，就拿哪一个吧。

4. 英语中 some…, others… 或者 some…and others… 的句型汉译时，主语往往是重复形式的"的"字结构，有时也可以用"一些……，一些……"或者"有的……，有的……"的句型。

例 28　Holiday is coming, some went shopping and others went home.

假期来了，逛商场的逛商场去了，回家的回家去了。

（假期来了，一些人逛商场去了，一些人回家去了。）

例 29　After graduation, some hunted a job and others started a business.

大学毕业后，找工作的找工作去了，创业的创业去了。

（大学毕业后，有的找工作去了，有的创业去了。）

二、加强语气的需要

任何一种语言都有一个共性，即为了强调而多次重复使用某些词语，显然加强了语气效果。英语也不例外，英语原文中用到的重复性关键词汉译时也要保留，否则会弱化原文语气，达不到译语读者读译文和源语读者读原文同样的感受。

例 30　Blood must atone for blood.

血债要用血来还。

例 31　He wandered about in the chill rain, thinking and thinking, brooding and brooding.

他在凄风惨雨中荡来荡去，想了又想，盘算了又盘算。

例 32　Be polite to all neighbors, above all, to old people.

对邻居要有礼貌，尤其是对老年人要有礼貌。

例 33　Year after year and century after century the moon goes through its cycle.

一年又一年，一个世纪又一个世纪，月亮盈亏变化，周而复始。

三、文字生动的需要

中国现代翻译家傅雷在讲到翻译理论时提出"传神"二字，要领悟和感受原文的字句风色，使译文在行文上也栩栩如生，这就要求译者适时地重复一些词句，增添译文的生动色彩。

（一）运用叠词

叠词是汉语中特别常用的一种修辞手法，尤其是 AABB 式的重叠词组。英译汉时译者可适当采用这种手段使译文通顺达意，生动传神。

例 34　Her daughter wrote her homework very neatly.

她女儿的家庭作业写得干干净净。

例 35　The so-called famous singer was greeted by only very slight and very scattering ripples of hand-clapping from the audience.

这位所谓的著名歌手收到的欢迎只有几下轻轻的、稀稀拉拉的掌声。

例 36　I had been completely honest in my replies, withholding nothing.

我的回答完全是坦坦荡荡，不藏不掖。

例 37　Eating and drinking, my younger sister passed through her holiday.

我妹妹吃吃喝喝地过完了她的假期。

例 38　The kid is always in rags as if he were an orphan.

这个孩子整天穿得破破烂烂，像个孤儿似的。

（二）运用两个四字格

汉语中有大量的四字格，这也是汉语的一大特色，四字格起到锦上添花的作用，增加了文字的美感。因此汉译时可以充分利用汉语的这一大优势，酌情重复使用两个同义或者近义的四字格。

例 39　Something about the rumor had been too much publicity.

谣言已经弄得满城风雨，人尽皆知了。

例 40　This decision, in her opinion, is absolutely fair.

在她看来，这次决定绝对是公开公正，公平合理的。

例 41　Her elegant disposition set her apart from other participants.

她温文尔雅，秀丽端庄的气质显得她与别的参会者截然不同。

例 42　As a popular president, he speaks appropriately.

作为一位民众喜爱的总统，他讲话总是恰如其分，恰到好处。

（三）运用对偶四字词组

在汉语的大量四字格里，有一些是结构相同，平仄相对的，前后两个词语往往具有相同或者相似的含义，这种对偶成语看起来整齐美观，实则也是一种重复强调，例如"漫山遍野，聪明伶俐，钟灵毓秀，慈眉善目"等，英译汉保留这种对偶结构可使译文读起来节奏铿锵，琅琅上口。

例 43　The apartment is in chaos after the whole night party.

整夜的狂欢聚会之后，公寓里一片乌烟瘴气。

例 44　His elderly parents could expect only ingratitude from the rich son.

他年迈的父母从有钱的儿子那里得来的只有忘恩负义。

例 45　Our country is enjoying a period of peace and prosperity.

我们国家正值繁荣昌盛，国泰民安之际。

例 46　If it is a time of triumph for the many, it is a painful period for the few.

多数人兴高采烈之时，也是少数人伤心失意之日。

值得注意的是，重译法也不可盲目使用，毕竟过度重复会造成译文单调乏味，啰嗦累赘。译者需要在充分考虑原文的基础上，灵活使用重译法，才能使译文通顺流畅，准确生动。

课后练习

一、翻译下列句子，注意使用重译法。

1. A large family has its weak points.

2. It is easier to vent anger at a stranger, particularly a faceless voice on the phone.

3. Although you are admitted, you still have defects, and very big ones.

4. You may be whatever you resolve to be. Determine to be something in the world, and you will be something.

5. Gentlemen may cry peace, peace—but there is no peace.

6. After a person died, people forgot his face, then his name.

7. You can find doctors and doctors in the big city.

8. This has been our position—but not theirs.

9. The blow hurt not only his hands but his shoulder too.

10. He was proficient both as a flyer and as a navigator.

11. His careless behavior annoyed his immediate boss.

12. A group of noisy children tumbled out of the bus.

13. The stamp collector is said to have a unique stamp.

14. He told us a very vivid story about his life in Africa.

15. She would like to express her sincere gratitude to the old couple who adopted her.

16. All the afternoon, he wore a dreamy appearance.

二、翻译下列段落，注意使用重译法。

Our life is nothing more than our time. To kill time is therefore a form of suicide. We are shocked when we think of death, and we spare no pains, no trouble, and no expense to preserve life. But we are too often indifferent to the loss of an hour or of a day, forgetting that our life is the sum total of the days and of the hours we live. A day or an hour wasted is therefore so much life forfeited. Our life is a brief span measuring some seventy or eighty years in all. But nearly one third of this has to be spent in sleep; some years have to be spent over our meals; some in making journeys on land and voyages by sea; some in merrymaking; some in watching over the sickbeds of our nearest and dearest relatives. Now if all these years were to be reduced from the term over which our life extends, we shall find about twenty or thirty years at our disposal for active work. Whoever remembers this can never willingly waste a single moment of his life.

第六节　正反、反正译法

　　正反、反正译法是翻译中最常见、最重要的技巧之一。英语的否定表达是一个常见又复杂的问题，有些英语句子形式上是肯定的而含义上是否定的，有些形式上是否定的而含义上是肯定的。因此在英汉翻译过程中，有些从正面表达的词或句子，译文可从反面表达，即正说反译；而有些从反面表达的词或句子，译文需从正面陈述，即反说正译。究其原因，是由于英、汉民族的思维方式和表达方式具有较大差异。同一想法，同一概念，一个民族会从正面表达其逻辑，而另一民族则会自然地从反面加以说明。根据"忠实"与"通顺"的原则，恰如其分地运用正反、反正译法是十分必要的。

一、正反译法

　　正反译法是指英文表达从形式上看是肯定的，但其内容带有否定意义。也就是说，英文中既未出现带有否定意义的词，如 no, not, none, nothing, nobody, neither 或 barely, rarely, hardly 等，也未出现带有否定词缀的词，如 de-, dis-, in-, ir- 或 -less 等。但其陈述的内容却是否定的，而且有时其否定语气还很强。因此在译成汉语时应根据其深层含义译成相应的否定形式，需要使用正反译法的情况通常包括动词、名词、副词、形容词、介词、连接词和一些固定短语。

　　（一）动词的反译
　　英语中有部分动词带有否定含义，有些是本身自带的明显否定，有些是语境中暗含的否定，正译这些动词是无法展现其否定含义的，所以可以考虑反译法。需要反译的动词可分为否定性动词和否定性的动词词组。
　　1. 否定性动词
　　有些英语动词形式上是肯定的，却含有否定的意义，汉译时需要再现出其否定意味，如 lack, ignore, refuse, defy, stop, forbid, miss, disagree 等词。
　　例 1　He always <u>avoids</u> accepting others' kindness.
　　他从不接受别人的好心帮忙。
　　例 2　The conclusion <u>disagreed</u> with the fact we had looked for.

结论和我们所查找的事实不一致。

例 3　I regret to learn that you have <u>failed</u> in the examination.

很遗憾你没能通过考试。

例 4　The car <u>refused</u> to start on the road.

车子在半路上发动不起来了。

例 5　I'm afraid that you will <u>miss</u> the professor's class.

恐怕你赶不上教授的课了。

例 6　The specification <u>lacks</u> details.

这份说明书不够详细。

例 7　Time <u>rejects</u> me to finish my talk.

时间不允许我把话说完。

2. 否定性的动词词组

有些动词和介词、副词搭配构成的固定动词词组本身看似肯定，实则也蕴含否定意思，汉译时也要反译。

例 8　I would like to <u>warn</u> you <u>against</u> discouragement.

我想告诫你们千万不要灰心。

例 9　To preserve the fiction he <u>restrained from</u> blaming his son until all the guests left.

为了不漏破绽，他强忍着不责骂自己的儿子，直到所有的客人都离开。

例 10　I beg to <u>differ from</u> you on the opinion.

恕我与你的看法不敢苟同。

例 11　Her sudden arrival <u>prevented</u> him <u>from</u> going out.

她的突然造访，使他不能外出了。

● 课后练习

翻译下列句子，注意划线部分动词（词组）的反译。

1. Such a chance was <u>denied</u> to me.

2. He <u>washed</u> his hands of gambling not long ago.

3. Do you know why she is always trying to <u>avoid</u> you?

4. The traffic police <u>prohibit</u> cyclists <u>from</u> riding on the sidewalk.

5. The newspaper <u>refused</u> to <u>keep</u> the facts <u>from</u> the public.

（二）名词的反译

英语中有些名词反译比正译更能加强其语气效果，所以也采用反译法处理。

例 12　There was complete <u>absence</u> of information on the oil deposit in that country.

关于该国的石油储备情况，人们一无所知。

例 13　Short of time has required the <u>omission</u> of some countries.

由于时间不够，没能访问有些国家。

例 14　Politeness is not always the sign of wisdom but the <u>want</u> of it always leaves room for the suspicion of folly.

尽管有礼貌并不一定标志着此人有智慧，但无礼貌总会使人怀疑其愚蠢。

例 15　He did it just out of <u>ignorance</u>.

他做了此事只是出于无知。

例 16　Her <u>abstraction</u> was not because of the tea party.

她那心不在焉的神情并不是因为茶话会。

例 17　His <u>hesitation</u> leads to his failure.

他的不果断导致了他的失败。

课后练习

翻译下列句子，注意划线部分名词的反译。

1. A <u>lack</u> of awareness of cultural differences or local customs can create problems.

2. Darkness is the <u>absence</u> of light.

3. There is a <u>lack</u> of water supply here.

4. Memories of the past filled her mind to the <u>exclusion</u> of anything else.

5. All international disputes should be settled through negotiations and <u>avoidance</u> of any armed conflicts.

（三）副词的反译

英语中有些副词的翻译也建议使用反译法，比如大家耳熟能详的 too...to... 结构译为"太……而不……"，很多其他副词或者副词短语也是如此。

例 18　The news is <u>too</u> good <u>to</u> be true.

这消息太好了，我都不敢相信。

例 19　The earth is <u>too</u> dry for crops <u>to</u> grow.

土地太干了，农作物无法生长。

例 20　They may safely do so.

他们这样做万无一失。

例 21　He dived into the water fully clothed and rescued the children.

他衣服都没脱就跳入水中，将孩子们救了上来。

● **课后练习**

翻译下列句子，注意划线部分副词的反译。

1. The boy was doing his homework very carelessly.

2. Slowly he took out of tools and began to make a desk.

3. She said idly: "Well, what does it matter?"

4. This summer is predictably hotter.

5. He has become understandably restless.

（四）形容词或形容词短语的反译

由于语言体系和表达习惯的差异，英语中有些形容词和形容词词组看似肯定，可能包含否定的意义，所以汉译时可以根据汉语的表述方式稍作调整，采用反译法更为直截了当。

例 22　This official document would be an integral part of the contract.

这份正式文件将是合同内容不可或缺的一部分。

例 23　The child is still awkward with his chopsticks.

这孩子还是不太会用筷子。

例 24　The explanation is pretty thin.

这个解释一点也站不住脚。

例 25　How could you marry a guy dead to shame?

你怎么会和一个如此不知廉耻的家伙结婚了呢？

例 26　Graduates were reluctant to leave the campus which was full of good memories.

毕业生不愿意离开这个充满美好记忆的校园。

例 27　The terrible COVID-19 makes global economy situation bleak.

可怕的新冠病毒使全球经济环境十分不景气。

● 课后练习

翻译下列句子，注意划线部分形容词或形容词短语的反译。

1. My father would be the <u>last</u> man to scold me.

2. Parents are often <u>blind</u> to their children's merits.

3. They were watching the <u>fluid</u> situation with concern.

4. For old people, modern pop music <u>is inferior to</u> traditional music.

5. The company's failure was due to <u>bad</u> management.

6. His key was <u>lost</u>.

7. She felt <u>miserable</u> in her stomach.

（五）介词或介词短语的反译

像 out of, beyond, beneath, against, except, in spite of, without 等常见的介词或者介词短语只要在上下文语境里表示超过一定限度或者能力时，往往含有否定的意义，翻译时可译为否定句。

例 28　It was <u>beyond</u> human's power to conquer the disasters from nature.

人类没有能力战胜大自然带来的种种灾难。

例 29　It is undeniable that men who are habitually <u>behind</u> time will be habitually <u>behind</u> success.

不可否认的是，经常不守时的人往往也不会成功。

例 30　What you have said is <u>above</u> me.

你所讲的话我听不懂。

例 31　The soldiers would fight to death <u>before</u> their surrender.

士兵们宁可战死，也决不投降。

例 32　He was <u>at loss</u> for a word to express his gratitude.

他一时找不到恰当的字眼来表达他的感激之情。

例 33　The authorities used quiet persuasion <u>instead of</u> the big stick.

政府心平气和地劝说，而不是施加压力。

例 34　Their demands go <u>beyond</u> all reasons.

他们的要求毫无道理。

> 课后练习

翻译下列句子，注意划线部分介词的反译。

1. Those who are under 18 years old are not admitted to get married.

2. My achievements are beneath mention.

3. The speaker was speaking over my head.

4. He managed to get promoted within two years.

5. Unless there is any other business, we can end the meeting.

6. Before he could stop me, I had taken the words out of my mouth.

（六）连接词的反译

众所周知英语中有很多连词，部分连词和词组如 until, not…until, before, since, no more than, no less than, rather than, other than, would as soon…as 等这些其实都蕴藏着否定的含义，汉译时也常常使用反译法。

例 35　I will do it before I forget it.

趁着我还没忘记，要赶紧把它做了。

例 36　I will stay here until my mom arrives.

妈妈不来，我就不走。

例 37　I won't stop shouting until you let me go.

你不放我走，我就会一直喊叫。

例 38　The demands seemed less than reasonable.

这些要求似乎不近情理。

例 39　The result is quite other than what you expected.

结果与你所期望的完全不同。

例 40　My friend would as soon go home for lunch as have something to eat in the street.

我朋友宁肯回家吃饭也不愿在大街上吃东西。

例 41　Most people will be fleeing cold and hunger rather than fighting.

大部分人会因为饥寒交迫逃亡，而不是战争。

例 42　It is no less than blackmail to ask for such a high price.

开这么高的价格，简直是在敲竹杠。

● 课后练习

翻译下列句子，注意划线部分连接词的反译。

1. I had not realized he is a foreigner until he began to speak.

2. His behavior is more than I can understand.

3. She would sooner try a tenth time than give up.

4. Rather than doing her a favor, her boyfriend is in the way here.

5. His family seems more generous than hospitable.

（七）固定短语的反译

随着语言的发展和使用，有些固定的英文短语结构（其中包括一些俚语）已经被约定俗成地翻译为否定句，渐渐地变成一种思维方式，这也是反译法的一种体现。

例 43　This Chinese restaurant in London was anything but satisfactory.

伦敦的这家中餐厅让人太不满意了。

例 44　I was at a loss to understand what my tutor said.

我无法领会导师所讲的话。

例 45　The decision has to come.

决定尚未做出。

例 46　The critic had something of a case.

批评家也并非全然没有道理。

例 47　Let sleeping dog lie.

不要惹是生非。

例 48　Seeing is believing.

百闻不如一见。

例 49　Keep off the grass.

请勿践踏草坪。

● 课后练习

翻译下列句子，注意固定短语（或者俚语）的反译。

1. Wet paint!

2. His article is full of pretty phrases.

3. There are many energy resources in store.

4. Admission by invitation only.

5. The line of the horizon was clear and hard against the sky, and in one particular quarter it showed black against a silvery climbing phosphorescence that grew and grew. At last, over the rim of the waiting earth the moon lifted with slow majesty till it swung clear of the horizon and rode off, free of moorings; and once more they began to see surfaces—meadows wide-spread, and quiet gardens, and the river itself from bank to bank, all softly disclosed, all washed clean of mystery and terror, all radiant again as by day, but with a difference that was tremendous. Their old haunts greeted them again in other raiment, as if they had slipped away and put on this pure new apparel and come quietly back, smiling as they shyly waited to see if they would be recognized again under it.

二、反正译法

正如正说反译一样，反说正译法只是进行了逻辑转换，即由肯定到否定变成了由否定到肯定，源语中否定的表达转换成目的语中肯定的表达，这种技巧也就是我们平时所讲的"形否意肯"，实则也是为了尊重目的语读者的习惯，符合汉语的表达习惯以及修辞和语气的要求。一般来讲，需要使用反说正译法的词类（一般为派生词）包括一些动词，名词，形容词，副词和介词短语。

需要注意的是，所谓的反面表达主要是指在英语用了 no, not, never, none 或者带有 anti-, de-, dis-, im-, in-, un-, -less, ir-, non- 等词缀的词，在汉语用了"不""无""非""没（有）""未""否"等的字词，这时候，如果原文从反面表达的动词，名词，形容词，副词和介词短语，译文正面表达更能确切表达原文思想内容，更符合语言习惯，那么需把原文的否定译成汉语的肯定式。

接下来列个表格以明确示范：

Conversion of English Words with Negative Prefixes or Suffixes into Affirmative Forms

Words	Negative Form	Affirmative Form
incomplete	不完全的	残缺的
unasked	未经邀请的	自告奋勇的
unprecedented	前所未有的	空前的
dislike	不喜欢	反感、讨厌
disbelief	不相信	怀疑
undisguised	无伪装的	公然、公开的

（一）否定动词的正译

英语中用作反面表达的动词如果加了否定前缀，在译文中可以从正面表达，比如 dislike, disappear, disagree, disapprove, unload, uncover, unblock 等。

例 50　We disagreed over what should be done.

对于应该怎么做我们的意见存在分歧。

例 51　Why do you dislike her so much?

你为什么会如此讨厌她？

例 52　These beautiful birds are fast disappearing.

这些漂亮的鸟类濒临灭绝了。

例 53　When we got home and were unloading the car, I could hardly believe my eyes when my brother took a dog out of the car.

到家后，当我们正在把行李从车上往下卸的时候，我弟弟从车里拿出一只小狗，我简直不敢相信自己的眼睛。

例 54　It took internal whistling-blowing and investigative journalism to uncover the rot.

是内部检举和调查性报道揭露了这一腐败事实。

例 55　The doubt was still unsolved after his repeated explanation.

虽然他一再解释，疑虑依然存在。

例 56　South Africa has unshackled its trade, restructured its rickety banks and tightened its fiscal belt.

南非开放了贸易，整顿了自己摇摇欲坠的银行，紧缩了财政开支。

● 课后练习

翻译下列句子，注意划线部分否定动词的正译。

1. This problem is still unsolved.

2. He disobeyed his mother and hung out with guys.

3. She always disapproved of adopting that poor orphan.

4. "Don't unstring your shoes, Kevin," she said.

5. The theme of this topic is to unriddle the social values issues today.

（二）否定名词的正译

英语中用作反面表达的名词如果加了否定前缀，在译文中可以从正面表达，比如 unemployment, impatience, disbelief, unhappiness, disadvantage, disappointment 等。

例 57　He expressed a strong disappointment to his students' performance.

他对学生们的表现表示强烈的失望。

例 58　He was thrown into unemployment when the factory closed, and now he is living on the unemployment compensation.

工厂倒闭后他就失业了，现在他靠失业救济金度日。

例 59　The government has worked out new plans for disarmament.

政府已经制定出了裁军的新方案。

例 60　In general, she could accept the family life in all its crowded inadequacy.

通常情况下，她还是能够忍受她那拥挤寒碜的家庭生活。

例 61　Global deforestation and the use of fossil fuels accelerate the trend of global warming.

全球性的毁林以及化石燃料的使用加剧了全球变暖的趋势。

例 62　It was said that someone had sown discord among them.

据说有人在他们中间挑拨离间。

● 课后练习

翻译下列句子，注意划线部分否定名词的正译。

1. The dishonesty of the city officials was exposed by the newspaper.
2. Born into postwar uncertainties in 1946, he grew up with a sense of vocation.
3. Genetic engineering is a disrespect of life.
4. There was a hint of incredibility in her voice.
5. The government has declared war on illiteracy.
6. Spielberg is known as the master of disquiet.

（三）否定形容词的正译

同样的，加了否定前缀或者否定后缀的形容词，也可以采用反说正译法表示强调，类似的形容词不计其数，有 unhappy, unusual, untouchable, uncommon, impatient, impossible, impolite, irregular, irresponsible, non-essential, misleading, careless 等。

例 63　I like that painting best because it is the most unusual.

我最喜欢那幅画，因为它最别具一格。

例 64　He returned home with a hopeless face.

他带着绝望的表情回家了。

例 65　He was a sort of <u>indecisive</u> person and always capricious.

他这个人优柔寡断，而且总是反复无常。

例 66　The structure has an <u>indefinite</u> life.

这是一座永久性的建筑物。

例 67　Increasingly rapid and <u>inexpensive</u> transport and communication will pose a threat to national cuisine.

越来越便捷又便宜的交通运输业会给民族烹饪带来威胁。

例 68　The family's subsequent financial struggles left an <u>irreversible</u> impression on him.

一家人全都在为经济问题苦苦挣扎，这给他留下了永难磨灭的印象。

课后练习

翻译下列句子，注意划线部分否定形容词的正译。

1. All the articles are <u>untouchable</u> in the museum.

2. It was an acute <u>uncomfortable</u> journey back to London.

3. I just felt <u>incredible</u> relief.

4. The old man is <u>toothless</u>.

5. It was slightly <u>inconsiderate</u> for Linda to say something like this.

6. But the fear of being <u>penniless</u> again never left him.

（四）否定副词的正译

英语中很多显形的否定词都是副词，比如 never, hardly, seldom, rarely, scarcely 等，也有一些带前缀后缀的否定性形容词加 -ly 之后变成的副词，比如 emotionlessly, unusually, dishonorably, noiselessly 等，这些词汉译时也可大胆地采用正译法，以保证译文的流畅和通顺。

例 69　He said it is <u>not hard</u> to understand why.

他说其原因很容易理解。

例 70　I never <u>lose</u> sight of that dream.

我一直把那份理想铭记于心。

例 71　Suddenly he saw a dim yellow light moving <u>noiselessly</u> towards him from the far end of a long lane.

突然，他看到有一盏昏黄的灯正从巷道的深处静静地朝他移动过来。

例 72　Many agreed that the prime minister had in effect resigned <u>dishonorably</u>.

许多人认为首相辞职其实是很丢脸的。

例 73　He answered journalists' sharp questions unassumingly.

他非常谦逊地回答记者各种尖锐的问题。

例 74　She uncannily resembled her dead sister.

她和她死去的姐姐出奇地相似。

课后练习

翻译下列句子，注意否定副词的正译。

1. We must never stop taking an optimistic view of life.

2. He stood there motionlessly, being at a loss what to say.

3. He drummed his fingers on the table impatiently.

4. She was eating irregularly, steadily losing weight.

5. He had scarcely put the phone down when the doorbell rang.

6. It never rains but it pours.

（五）习惯用法和固定搭配的正译

英语中存在一些形式上是否定的习惯用法和固定搭配，例如 no one but...，never without...，nothing else, none the less 等，但其表达的内容是肯定的，含有这些短语的句子译成汉语时大多从正面表达。

例 75　No one but a great philosopher could solve such a question.

只有大思想家才能解决这样的问题。

例 76　After her call, I could think of nothing else all day.

接过她的电话后，我整天脑子里想的全是这件事。

例 77　There is nothing like mineral water to quench one's thirst.

矿泉水是最解渴的饮料。

例 78　He is old, none the less he works like a young man.

他虽然老了，但干起活来还是像个年轻人。

例 79　To be or not to be, that's a question.

生存还是毁灭，这是值得思考的问题。

例 80　You cannot be too careful to cross the street.

过马路时你千万要加倍小心。

第七节　被动语态的译法

被动语态作为一种常见的语法现象，在英语中占有相当重要的一席之地，其范围极其广泛。凡是不必说出行为者，不愿说出行为者，无从说出行为者，行为者在上下文中自明或者便于连贯上下文等，往往都会使用被动语态。汉语中也有被动句，但它的表现形式非常多样化，不一定局限于"被"字，这也是汉语"意合"和英语"形合"的外在表现之一，值得一提的是，汉语被动语态的使用范围远远小于英语被动语态的使用范围。本节将通过四个部分详细阐述如何汉译英语中的被动语态。

一、直接译为"被"字句

如果原文被动句重在强调被表述的动作，译为汉语时应继续译为被动效果明显的"被"字句，正式的文体都会保留这种被动句，一般都有强调被动动作的语用意味，从翻译方法的角度来看，这就是按照原文句型进行直译。

例 1　Visitors to New Zealand are often charmed by its beautiful scenery.

来到新西兰的游客常常被它美丽的风景所陶醉。

例 2　The Harry Potter series of novels have already been translated into many languages.

《哈利·波特》系列小说已经被译成了多种语言。

例 3　His passport was confiscated by the police.

他的护照被警方没收了。

例 4　The spaceship will be totally controlled by an on-board electronic computer.

这艘宇宙飞船将完全由机载电子计算机控制。

例 5　The plan is going to be examined first by the research group.

计划将先由研究小组加以研究。

例 6　Every single member of that first party had been captured by Spanish Frontier police and put into a concentration camp.

第一批的所有人都被西班牙边防警察逮捕并关进了集中营。

例 7　The Gettysburg Address by Abraham Lincoln was recognized as a literary masterpiece for its simple and graceful prose style.

林肯的葛底斯堡演讲被世人公认为是文学巨作，其文风简洁优美。

● 课后练习

将下列英文被动句直接译为"被"字句。

1. He was looked down upon by all his friends.

2. The company was forbidden from using false advertising.

3. The poor child was beaten black and blue.

4. He was sent to the front.

5. The famous hotel had been particularly destroyed by the big fire.

6. Vitamin C is destroyed when it is over heated.

7. I was caught in the downpour.

● 二、译为变体"被"字句

除了"被"字以外，汉语中表示被动意义的标志还有很多，例如"挨，叫，让，使，遭到，受到，得以，加以，有待，使得，予以，为……所……，以……而……"等表达被动意义的词和词组，这种表示被动但没有出现"被"字出现的句式称为"变体被动句"。汉语被动语态的用词和结构比英语更加灵活，如果感觉"被"字结构使用过多，或者明确说出施动者不妥，或者叙述角度不当，就可以采用"被"字以外的表现形式。

例 8　The American trade delegation was given a hearty welcome.

美国贸易代表团受到热烈的欢迎。

例 9　Our clothes were soaked with sweat.

我们的衣服被汗水浸透了。

例 10　Your car was towed away by a truck.

你的车让一辆大卡车拖走了。

例 11　He was released soon after detention.

他在受到拘留之后不久就获释了。

例 12　David was given a prize at the closing ceremony.

大卫在闭幕式上得了奖。

例 13　Farmers were hit by a natural disaster last autumn.

农民去年秋天遭灾了。

例 14　It must be dealt with at the appropriate time with appropriate means.

这件事必须在适当的时候用适当的手段予以解决。

例 15　I was so impressed by these words that I used them later for a Christmas card.

我被这些话深深感动，后来我就把它们写在圣诞卡上。

课后练习

将下列英文被动句译为变体"被"字句。

1. Television keeps us informed about current events at home and abroad.

2. Those who perform deeds of merit will be rewarded.

3. Translation techniques should be paid enough attention to.

4. He was set upon by two masked men.

5. Mistakes must not be covered up, but be exposed before you can correct.

6. Granny Zhao was forced by fail circumstances to enter a knitting mill in Shanghai as a child laborer at the age of twelve.

三、译为主动句

基于英汉两种语言在被动语态上的差异，很多英语被动句需要处理成汉语的主动句，即"受动者 + be done by + 施动者"变为"施动者（受动者）+ 主动式谓语 + 受动者（施动者）"，采用这种方式来化解英文的被动语态，可以避免翻译痕迹过重造成的翻译腔，使译文更加地道流畅。将被动句汉译为主动句一般包含以下六种形式：

（一）保留原句主语

当被动句的主语是句子陈述的中心，翻译时可以把原来的主语保留下来作为译文的主语继续使用。

例 16　Love can't be forced.

爱情不能强求。

例 17　Illness must be correctly diagnosed before they can be treated with medicine.

疾病必须先确诊，再用药。

例 18　Poets are born, but orators are made.

诗人是天生的，但演说家是后天的。

例 19　The hardest work was assigned to the strongest laborers.

最艰苦的工作分配给了最强壮的劳工。

例 20　The sense of inferiority that he acquired in his youth has never been totally eradicated.

他在青少年时期留下的自卑感还没有完全消除。

例 21　Our book has been translated into many foreign languages.

我们的书籍已经被译为多国版本。

例 22　The decision to attack was not taken lightly.

进攻的决定不是轻易做出的。

例 23　His pride must be pinched.

他的这股傲气应该打压下去。

（二）把 by 短语译为主语

英语中带 by 短语的被动语态都是为了突出动作的执行者，是句子的逻辑主语，也是作者要强调的对象。汉译时，by 介词短语可以很自然地被转移为译文的主语，达到简洁通顺的效果。

例 24　Rivers are controlled by dams.

拦河大坝把河流控制住了。

例 25　At least two liters of water are required daily by a normal individual.

一个正常人每天至少要摄入两升的水。

例 26　An honorary degree was conferred on him by Cambridge University in 2020.

剑桥大学于 2020 年授予了他荣誉学位。

例 27　She was upset by the whole matter.

整个事情弄得她心烦意乱。

例 28　The restaurant was being cleaned by cleaners.

清洁工正在打扫餐厅。

例 29　His rage was soon calmed down by the rustic peace.

乡村的宁静使他的怒气平息下来了。

例 30　The compass was invented by Chinese people four thousand years ago.

中国人在四千年前就发明了指南针。

例 31　The novel "A Dream of Red Mansions" has been translated into many foreign languages by lots of translators.

许多翻译家已经把小说《红楼梦》翻译成了多种语言。

（三）补充施动者

英语中有些被动句主要用来陈述事实情况或者强调行动本身，由于动作的施动者不是特别重要或者完全不需要交代，常常会被省略，但汉译时考虑到句子的完整性和表达的通畅性，需要补充施动者，一般被补充的施动者是泛指性的主语，比如"我们""大家""人们""有人"等。这类的被动结构一般就是"it + 被动语态 + that..."，其中it是形式主语，that引导的是主语从句。从翻译技巧的角度分析，这种情况其实也是本章前部分所提及的增补译法。

例32　It is universally accepted that fruits should be cleaned before eating.

大家都认为水果食用前应该清洗。

例33　It must be pointed out that such a mistake should not be repeated.

必须有人指出，这样的错误不能再犯。

例34　It is believed that an increasing number of people in China will be moving out of the city to live in the country.

人们相信，越来越多的中国人将离开城市搬到郊区去住。

例35　It is known to all that smoking does harm to our health.

众所周知，抽烟对健康有害。

例36　It is hoped that you will be back after you complete your Ph.D. in the USA.

大家都希望你在美国博士毕业后能够回国。

例37　It is said that the new president is going to pay a visit to the refugee camp.

有人说新总统将要去慰问难民营。

例38　It is known that the earth turns around the sun.

众所周知地球围绕太阳转。

（四）译为无主句

英语中大量表示观点、告诫、态度、号召、要求等的被动句，在实际应用中会被汉译为无主句，这类例句的数量也是非常可观，随处可见。

例39　Smoking is not permitted in the theatre.

本剧院禁止吸烟。

例40　The inspection was conducted last week.

上星期已经做过检查。

例41　Attention has been paid to the new measures to prevent corrosion.

已经注意到要采取新的防腐措施。

例42　If there is no petrol, diesel oil can be used instead.

如果没有汽油，可用柴油来代替。

例43　The specifics of the project shall be discussed before the contract is awarded.

这个项目的各种细节将在签订合同之前详细讨论。

例 44　The nuclear death that threatens us all has to be and can be stopped by the efforts of all.

威胁我们全人类的核毁灭必须加以制止，而且通过共同的努力能够得到制止。

例 45　Some pictures were hung on the wall.

墙上挂了一些画。

（五）译为无被动词但包含被动的结构

汉语句子不拘泥于形式，有些英语被动句也可转换成比较自由的汉语句子，即字里行间不带表被动意义的标志性词语，看上去好像是主动句，但实际上包含被动意义，这样的汉语句子的被动意义是通过其主谓成分表达的逻辑意义关系来确定的。

例 46　A new student is kept on probation for one semester.

新学生要见习一个学期。

例 47　He was assassinated in a theatre last night.

他昨晚在一家剧院遇刺身亡。

例 48　Solution to the problem was ultimately found.

问题的解决方法终于找到了。

例 49　Robin, you are wanted on the phone.

罗宾，你有电话。

例 50　His leg was broken in an accident.

他的腿在一次事故中摔断了。

例 51　Most of the questions have been settled satisfactorily, and only a few questions of secondary importance remain to be discussed.

多数问题已经圆满解决，只剩下几个次要问题有待讨论。

例 52　Don't be alarmed if your newborn fails to be startled by loud noises or fails to turn toward sound.

如果你的新生儿听到响声并不吃惊，或者没有把头转向发出声音的方向，不必慌张。

（六）更换主语译为主动句

为了避免翻译腔，有时可以采用灵活的汉译法，即从原句中或者从其深层概念里挑选一个合适的名词概念作为译文的主语，代替原句的主语，把被动句变为主动句。这种现象其实恰恰证明了汉语句式的灵活多变性。

例 53　The findings of the court will be published on Friday.

法庭将在星期五公布调查结果。

例 54　A tremendous weight has been lifted from my mind.

我心里一个沉重的担子放下了。

例 55　He was laughed at by his friends.

朋友们都笑话他。

例 56　English was spoken in Britain, the USA and some other countries.

讲英语的国家有英国、美国和其他一些国家。

例 57　I was struck by how thoroughly engaged they were—and how I envied them.

他们那种聚精会神的样子深深打动了我——我真羡慕他们。

例 58　When the meal is finished, the guests put their napkins on the table and rise.

客人们吃完饭后把餐巾放在桌子上并站起身来。

例 59　The monkeys were given sweet potatoes by scientists who wanted to attract them to the shore of an island.

科学家们给猴子白薯，想把他们引到海岛的岸边。

课后练习

一、将下列英文被动句译为中文主动句。

1. The ground was covered with pieces of paper, cigarette-end, empty bottles and rusty tins.

2. The old man lives in a very old town which is surrounded by beautiful woods.

3. Football is played all over the world.

4. When he went into the laboratory, the teacher was followed by a silent procession of students.

5. It is expected that this project will draw on overseas experience.

6. It is well known that the number of people has been increasing.

7. Our former differences were forgotten.

8. Smokers must be warned that doctors have reached the conclusion that smoking increases the possibility of lung cancer.

9. Attention must be paid to safety in handling radioactive materials.

10. The unpleasant noise must be immediately put to an end.

11. Accordingly, Reagan's proposals were rejected by the Congress and the allies.

（四）译为汉语判断句

英语中有一部分的被动句是用来表明客观存在的情况，也就是说，这些句子中的被动语态不是强调动作本身，而是强调某一个事实或者行为的存在。汉译时可以采用判断句的句式"……是……的"来处理。这种汉语里的判断句在语义上含有被动的意义，效果对等于英语句子中的被动语态。

例 60　The suggestion was put forward by my tutor.

这个建议是我的导师提出的。

例 61　Printing was introduced to Europe from China.

印刷术是由中国传入欧洲的。

例 62　The song was composed by the outstanding musician.

这首歌是由那个杰出的音乐家谱写的。

例 63　The life of that COVID-19 patient was saved by all dedicated doctors.

那个新冠患者的生命是所有无私奉献的医生挽救的。

例 64　History is made by the people.

历史是人民创造的。

例 65　The tree was cut down by a lumberjack with an axe last week.

这棵树是一个伐木工上周用斧头砍倒的。

综上所述，被动语态在英语中属于使用频率很高的表达形式，译为汉语的方法也十分灵活多变。语言的终极目的是为了有效地沟通与交流，所以翻译时不能过于死板，逐字翻译，一定要结合上下文的语境灵活把握，才能处理出符合译语表达习惯，通顺流畅的句子。

● 课后练习

一、将下列英文被动句译为中文的判断句。

1. Water is considered essential for the evolution of life.

2. These books were lent to me by my friend.

3. The Statue of Liberty was presented to the United States of America in the 19th century by the people of France.

4. Rainbows are formed when sunlight passes through small drops of water in the sky.

5. They are ordered to do this.

6. Arranged marriages provide a good example both of how prospective lovers are brought

together and how cultural values and practices limit the choice of partners.

二、翻译下列段落，注意被动语态。

As oil **is found** deep in the ground its presence **cannot be determined** by a study of the surface. Consequently, a geological survey of the underground rock structure **must be carried out**. If it **is thought** that the rocks in a certain area contain oil, a "drilling rig" **is assembled**. The most obvious part of a drilling rig **is called** "a derrick". It **is used** to lifting section of pipe, which **are lowered** into the hole **made** by the drill. As the hole **is being drilled**, a steel pipe **is pushed** down to prevent the sides from falling in. If oil **is struck**, a cover **is firmly fixed** to the top of the pipe and the oil **is allowed** to escape through a serious of valves.

第八节　分译合译法

一、分译法

为了更准确形象地展现分译法的效果，请看下列两个例句使用分译法前后的译文比较：

例 1　This season witnessed an ominous dawning of one day.

分译前：这个季节看见了某一天的不详破晓。

分译后：在这个季节，某一天黎明时分的景象是个不祥之兆。

例 2　I put on my clothes by the light of a half-moon just setting, where rays streamed through the narrow window near my bed.

分译前：我趁着正要落下去的半个月亮穿上衣服，月光从床边狭窄的窗子照射了进来。

分译后：半轮残月渐渐西坠，月光透过床边一扇狭窄的窗子照射进来，我趁着月光穿上衣服。

（一）词语的分译

英语句子中有些单词逐字翻译时很难处理，因为其词义呈"综合性"状态，即一个单词集合了几个语义成分，汉译时找不到合适的对等词，很难将其词义一次性全部表达出来。在这种情况之下，需要采用分译法，即"扩散型"的方式分译原词，将其语义成分附着到几个不同的词语上。

（1）名词的分译

例3　The price limits its production.

它价格昂贵，限制了批量生产。

例4　The inside of each tent depended on the personality of its occupants.

每个帐篷内怎样布置，还要看使用者的性格了。

例5　The dust, the uproar and the growing dark threw everything into chaos.

烟尘滚滚，人声嘈杂，夜色渐深，一切都陷入混乱之中。

例6　He wrote three books in the first two years, a record never touched before.

他头两年写了三本书，打破了以往的记录。

例7　The military is forbidden to kill the vessel, a relatively easy task.

军方未获批准击毁这艘潜艇，虽然要击毁这艘潜艇并不费事。

例8　Energy can neither be created nor destroyed, a universally accepted law.

人们既不能创造也不能消灭能量，这是一条普遍公认的规律。

（2）动词的分译

例9　Love has been considered priceless.

人们已经认识到，爱是无价的。

例10　The maximum demand for electricity today is expected to double within a decade.

可以预料，目前对电的最大需求量在十年内可望增加一倍。

例11　We recognize that China's long-term modernization program understandably and necessarily emphasizes economic growth.

我们意识到，中国的长期现代化建设以发展经济为重点，这是可以理解的，也是必要的。

例12　She inspected the table for dust with her finger.

她用手指抹抹桌子，看看有没有灰尘。

例13　It is universally acknowledged that trees are indispensable to humans.

全世界都知道，树木对人类来说十分重要。

例14　We can notice the qualities of their living have gone from bad to worse.

我们可以发现，他们的生活质量已经每况愈下。

（3）形容词的分译

例15　It is understandable for him to go abroad.

他去国外了，这可以理解。

例 16　He has been pursued by a most astonishing luckiness year by year.

他每年都被幸运眷顾，这的确令人惊叹不已。

例 17　My neighbor was in a clear minority.

我的邻居是少数民族，这是明摆着的事实。

例 18　On behalf of all of your American guests, I wish to thank you for the incomparable hospitality.

我谨代表你们所有的美国客人向你们表示感谢，感谢你们的盛情款待，这种盛情是无可比拟的。

例 19　That city was the most identifiable trouble place.

那座城市是个麻烦的地方，这是大家很容易看出来的。

例 20　You are talking delightful nonsense.

你虽然信口胡扯，倒也蛮有情趣。

（4）副词的分译

例 21　Jerry quickly ordered everyone to put on life jackets, and tried unsuccessfully to put out the fire.

杰瑞立刻让大家穿上救生衣，并且奋力扑火，但并没有成功。

例 22　Surprisingly Turkey defeated England in European Football Championship.

土耳其竟然在欧洲足球锦标赛上击败了英格兰，真是令人大吃一惊。

例 23　I tried vainly to persuade him to change his mind.

我试图说服他改变主意，但我失败了。

例 24　The time could have been more profitably spent on making a detailed investigation.

如果当初把时间花在细致的调查研究上，益处就更多了。

例 25　The senior leaders' departure could curiously help the two parties sink an age-long party feud.

老一代领导人的离去竟然使这两个政党陷入了长久的党政之间的不和，这确实让人百思不得其解。

例 26　Jordan cannot politely turn down the invitation to an Arab foreign ministers conference.

约旦如果拒绝接受阿拉伯外长会议的邀请，这在礼貌上也说不过去。

课后练习

一、翻译下列句子，注意划线词语的分译。

1. I always <u>avoid</u> the temptation to think about that matter.

2. The small village boasts <u>a beautiful lake</u>.

3. Their <u>wealth</u> enabled them to do everything.

4. She was <u>pardonably</u> proud of her wonderful cooking.

5. Radio waves have been <u>considered</u> radiant energy.

6. <u>The bitter weather</u> had driven everyone indoors.

7. The computer can give Jack the <u>right</u> lesson for her, neither too fast nor too slow.

（二）短语的分译

短语的分译比单词的分译更为常见，是指把原文中的某一个短语译为句子，使原文的一个句子分译成两个或两个以上的句子。英语中能分译的短语主要包括分词短语，动词不定式短语，介词短语和名词短语。

（1）分词短语的分译

例 27　We were at home in the home of the village, <u>moving confidently without fear</u>.

我们在村民家里时就像在自己家一样，<u>行动时心里踏实，无忧无虑</u>。

例 28　He sat with his hands cupping his chin, <u>staring at a corner of the bedroom</u>.

他坐在那里双手托着下巴，<u>眼睛凝视着卧室的一角</u>。

例 29　<u>Known to human beings for recent years</u>, eco-balance is closely related to every creature.

生态平衡与每种生物息息相关，<u>最近这些年人类更加了解这个事实</u>。

例 30　She lay reclined on a sofa by the fireside, <u>her darlings surrounding her</u>.

她斜靠在炉边的沙发上，<u>心爱的儿女都围在她身边</u>。

例 31　There are many kinds of atoms, <u>differing in both mass and properties</u>.

原子的种类很多，<u>其质量与性质各不相同</u>。

例 32　<u>Sympathizing with the peasant uprisings</u>, he praised the peasant leaders.

<u>因为他同情农民起义</u>，所以他赞扬农民领袖。

（2）动词不定式短语的分译

例 33　Einstein's theory of relatively is too difficult <u>for the average mind to understand</u>.

爱因斯坦的相对论太难，<u>一般人无法理解</u>。

例 34　To be allowed to speak out is one of the democratic principles to be observed.

允许别人讲话，这是一个应该遵循的民主原则。

例 35　He made a long speech, only to show his ignorance of the subject.

他讲了一大段话，反而暴露了他对这一内容的无知。

例 36　To reach an agreement, some compromise is needed for both parties.

为了达成一致，双方需要稍微折中一下。

例 37　Not to miss any word, he sat in the front row and his head thrust forward.

他坐在最前排，伸长脖子，唯恐听漏一词。

（3）介词短语的分译

例 38　The factory was already spreading fame for its products.

这个工厂产品质量过硬，这点已经远近闻名了。

例 39　She made tea for us in a most agreeable manner.

她为我们泡茶，态度殷勤。

例 40　With the increase of production the living condition of the common people is becoming better and better.

随着生产的增加，普通人民的生活条件变得越来越好了。

例 41　He was not to be moved either by advice or entreaties.

别人劝说也好，恳求也罢，他都无动于衷。

例 42　With all its disadvantages this design is considered to be one of the best.

尽管还有种种不足，这个设计依然被认为是最好之一。

例 43　We cannot see it for the fog.

由于有雾，我们看不清它。

例 44　The coast road is closed due to the bad weather.

由于天气恶劣，滨海公路暂时封闭。

例 45　The team has worked for ten months for the treatment of this disease.

为了治疗这种疾病，团队已经连续工作十个月了。

（4）名词短语的分译

例 46　His irritation could not withstand the silent beauty of the night.

面对这宁静的良宵美景，他的烦恼不禁烟消云散了。

例 47　Energy can neither be created nor destroyed, a universally accepted law.

能量既不能被创造也不能被毁灭，这是一条公认的规律。

The school forbade students to have a part-time job, <u>a rather difficult task</u>.

学校禁止学生从事兼职工作，尽管要做到这一点是相当困难的。

例 48　<u>A lot of naked animals</u> who attach such great importance to staying alive that they claw their neighbors to death are just for the privilege.

都是些赤裸裸的畜生，把生命看得如此重要，为了自己能活下去，可以把邻居活活弄死。

例 49　He was six feet one inch tall, <u>weighed 185 pounds</u> and had incredible speed and power.

他高六英尺一英寸，体重185磅，速度奇快，力气大得惊人。

例 50　<u>His youthful indifference to studies</u> and <u>his unwillingness to think of a non-sports career</u> caught up with him.

他年轻时对学业漫不经心，又一直不愿意考虑运动员之外的职业，这一切终于给他带来了不幸。

● 课后练习

翻译下列句子，注意划线部分的分译。

1. They were very frank and candid with each other <u>in a relaxed way</u>.

2. She arrived in London <u>at a ripe moment internationally</u>.

3. Throughout his life, Benjamin Franklin continued his education, <u>learning from human contacts as well as from books</u>.

4. <u>The lecture having begun</u>, he left his seat so quietly that no one complained his leaving disturbed the speaker.

5. <u>His weariness and the increasing heat</u> determined him to sit down in the first convenient shade.

6. The foreign visitors watched <u>in a fascinated manner</u> the tournament held in Beijing.

（三）句子的分译

英语句子结构复杂，层层嵌套，汉译时最忌逐字翻译，应当整体把握，排兵布阵，重新分译。句子的分译是指把原文的从句译成分句，或者把一个句子拆开，译成两个或两个以上的句子，以及在翻译复杂句的过程中增加分句或句子的数量。在此按照英语句子结构的三大类别——解析分译法的使用。此外，对于这三种句式杂糅的复杂结构也要引起注意，必须根据具体情况、意群的分布等进行灵活处理，恰当切分，使译文层次清晰，意义明朗。

（1）简单句的分译

例 51　He began to prepare his lessons with a dictionary.

他拿本字典，开始准备功课。

例 52　The good tidings filled the whole nation with joy.

捷报传来，举国欢腾。

例 53　His absence of mind during the driving nearly caused an accident.

他开车时心不在焉，差点出车祸。

例 54　Increased cooperation with China is in the interests of the United States.

同中国加强合作，符合美国的利益。

例 55　Her wisdom enables her to do everything.

她有智慧，什么事都能成功。

例 56　Daybreak comes with thick mist and drizzle.

破晓时分，大雾弥漫，细雨蒙蒙。

（2）并列句的分译

例 57　The half-moon streamed through the narrow window of my room and I put on my clothes by the light of it.

残月透过狭窄的窗户流淌下来，我借着月光披上了衣服。

例 58　The city boosts many growing commercial opportunities so it enjoys a wide-spread fame.

这个城市经商机会越来越多，名声也日益远扬。

例 59　The young group should care for the elderly or they will be criticized morally.

年轻人应该多关照长者，否则会受到道德谴责。

例 60　He failed to observe the safety regulations and it resulted in an accident to the machinery.

他没有遵守安全规章，导致机器出了故障。

（3）主从句的分译

例 61　There are many wonderful stories to tell about the places I visited and the people I met.

我访问过不少地方，遇到过一些人，要谈起来，奇妙的事情多着呢。（定语从句的分译）

例 62 Liquid water changes to vapor, which is called evaporating.

液态水变成蒸汽，这叫蒸发。（定语从句的分译）

例 63 All this had come to an end in 1905 when the medical mission was dissolved and several of Mother's colleagues were killed in the uprising.

1905年，这一切都宣告结束了。在一次暴动中，妈妈的几个同事牺牲了，医疗队也解散了。（定语从句的分译）

例 64 Nothing is hard in this world for anyone if he dares to scale the height.

世上无难事，只要肯攀登。（条件状语从句的分译）

例 65 Because the young man frequently came to the lady's house, he was regarded as the mistress's lover.

这个小伙子经常来太太家，因此别人都以为他是这女主人的情人。（原因状语从句的分译）

例 66 What can be easily seen in his poems are his imagery and originality, power and range.

他的诗作形象生动，独具一格，气势磅礴，题材广泛，这是显而易见的。（主语从句的分译）

例 67 I had a great honor of seeing our president when he visited my hometown last year.

去年主席访问我们的家乡时，我有幸见到了他。（时间状语从句的分译）

例 68 Dr. Bethune set to work at once although he was very tired on his arrival.

白求恩大夫到达时虽然很疲惫了，但他仍然立即投入了工作。（让步状语从句的分译）

例 69 The librarians have compiled a card-index catalogue so that they can afford facilities for reference.

为了便于参考，图书馆馆员们编制了索引目录卡。

（4）复杂结构的分译

例 70 It was mostly he who talked and he seemed afraid to stop for fear she'd ask him to leave her by herself.

大部分时间都是他在讲话。他似乎害怕停下来，生怕话一停，她就会请他离开。

例 71 During the nineteenth century, she argues, the concept of the "useful" child who contributed to the family economy gave way gradually to the present day notion of the "useless" child who, though producing no income, and indeed extremely costly to his parents, is yet considered emotionally "priceless".

她指出，给家庭经济做出贡献的孩子才"有用"的概念是19世纪的概念，现在已经慢慢改变了，今天提到那些没有挣取收入甚至还要花销很多的"无用"孩子，仍然在情感上被认为是无价的。

英汉思维之差异表现在语言层面就是语序结构不同，要在这种矛盾中找到平衡点，分译法就显得尤为重要。综合本节内容所述，分译法也要遵循两个原则：当分则分，但也不可硬行拆分，否则适得其反；正确把握分割点，严格按照汉语的表达习惯组织句子，否则会造成译文结构紊乱，不知所云。

● 课后练习

翻译下列句子，注意使用分译法。

1. Poor acoustics spoilt the performance.

2. We saw many signs of occupation while strolling along a street past a major concentration of the huts not far away from the Central Avenue.

3. The way of instruction in the teaching of mathematics is generally traditional, with teachers presenting formal lectures and students taking notes.

4. This land, which once barred the way of weary travelers, now has become a land for winter and summer vacations, a land of magic and wonder.

5. She used to relate how she met in Italy an elderly gentleman who was looking very sad and she inquired the reason of his melancholy and he said that he had just parted from his two grandchildren.

翻译下列段落，注意使用分译法。

A fundamental shift is occurring in the world economy. We are moving rapidly away from a world in which national economies were relatively self-contained entities, isolated from each other by barriers to cross-border trade and investment; by distance, time zones, and language; and by national differences in government regulation, culture, and business systems. And we are moving toward a world in which barriers to cross-border trade and investment are tumbling; perceived distance is shrinking due to advances in transportation and telecommunications technology; material culture is starting to look similar the world over; and national economies are merging into an interdependent global economic system. The process by which this is occurring is commonly referred to as globalization.

二、合译法

合译法主要体现在句子层面，是指把两个或者两个以上的简单句、复合句或复杂句合并翻译成一个句子。合译时需要省掉一些重复的词语或者句子成分，或者增加一些语义蕴含的成分，使译文紧凑、流畅，更加符合汉语表达习惯。

（一）简单句的合译

简单句的合译分为两种情况：第一，两个或两个以上的简单句拥有相同或相关的主语，而汉语不习惯重复主语，也不常用代词代替主语，因此汉译时要把重复过几次的相同或相关主语的句子合并成一句话；第二，当几个简单句之间存在一定的逻辑关系时，也需要增加相应的连接词进行合译。

例 72　He had been ill in bed for years. He died in loneliness finally.

他卧病在床很多年之后孤独地去世了。

例 73　Nicole was a quiet guy. He usually didn't let his face show his feelings.

尼克性格很安静，不轻易将喜怒哀乐挂在脸上。

例 74　The novel is of no great literary merit. It is merely a pot-boiler.

这部小说纯属胡编乱造，没有什么文学价值。

例 75　I was slow to understand the deep grievance of women in ancient times. This was because I had envied them as a child.

我迟迟未能理解古代女子的痛楚，因为小时候我曾很羡慕她们。

例 76　Young people don't hesitate to attempt one thing after another. Eager to experiment, they welcome new ideas. They are restless, alive and never satisfied. They seek perfection.

年轻人总是不停地探索，渴求实践，乐于接受新的思想，充满活力，永不满足，尽善尽美。

例 77　It was half past twelve. My grandma was watching eagerly outside the door to see me home.

已经十二点半了，我奶奶焦急地望着门外等我回家。

例 78　Confucius was a believer in moral action and in what we today call human development. He advocates the establishment of harmony within social order.

孔子信仰道德的行为，信仰我们今天所讲的人的发展，提倡在社会秩序内建立和谐。

（二）复合句的合译

复合句的合译在翻译实践中极为常见。一般而言，复合句中的两个句子之间的语意关联都非常密切，不可分割，从句部分都是对主句的解释说明，补述总结等，此时为了完整系统地表达出原意，可把原句中的各独立分句杂糅整合后译出，译文效果会更佳。

例 79　His father had a small business in the city of Pisa which is in the north of Italy near the sea.（定语从句的合译）

他父亲在意大利北部近海的比萨开小铺。

例 80　He was very clean and his mind was open.（并列句的合译）

他为人单纯坦率。

例 81　The weather in London is always changeable, where it rains sometimes, it is fine sometimes, and more often it is foggy.（地点状语从句的合译）

伦敦的天气总是让人捉摸不透，有时下雨，有时大晴天，而且经常大雾茫茫。

例 82　I was wandering when I saw a notice outside a college.（时间状语从句的合译）

我闲逛时看到一所大学门口贴着一张告示。

例 83　The moment they saw the guard, the children ran away from the orchard.（时间状语从句的合译）

孩子们一看到保安就赶紧从果园里跑开了。

例 84　He saw in front that haggard white-haired old man, whose eyes flashed red with fury.（定语从句的合译）

他看见前面那个憔悴的白发老人眼睛里闪烁着愤怒的红光。

例 85　The judge said that it was difficult to comprehend why the police acted so in this matter.

法官很难理解警察这么做的动机。

（三）复杂句的合译

对于英语复杂句的处理，大多数情况下采用分译法，摆脱源语语序和句子形式的约束，从而符合汉语"意合"语言的特点，但在一些特殊文体中，汉语也会表现出形合的一面，比如科技文和政论文，合译处理会显得语句较为正式，更加符合文体特征。值得一提的是，在这个过程中也会使用到顺译法，逆译法，增词法，词类转换等策略，所以复杂句的合译被称为翻译技巧的综合使用。

例 86　Aluminum remained unknown until the nineteenth century, because nowhere in nature is it found free, owing to its always being combined with other elements, most commonly with oxygen, for which it has a strong affinity.

铝总是跟其他元素结合在一起，最普遍的是跟氧结合；因为铝跟氧有很强的亲和力，

由于这个原因,在自然界找不到游离状态的铝。所以,铝直到19世纪才被人发现。(逆译法)

The simple fact shows that the more of the force of friction is got rid of, the farther will the ball travel, and we are led to infer that, if all the impeding forces of gravitation and resistance could be removed, there is no reason why the ball, once in motion, should ever stop.

这个简单事实证明,摩擦力减少得越多,球会滚得越远,由此我们可以推论出:如果一切起阻碍作用的引力和阻力能够消失的话,就没有理由认为处于运动中的球还会停下来。(顺译法,增词法)

课后练习

翻译下列段落,注意综合使用本章的翻译技巧。

There is more agreement on the kinds of behavior referred to by the term "intelligence" than there is on how to interpret or classify them. But it is generally agreed that a person of high intelligence is one who can grasp ideas, readily make distinctions, reason logically, and make use of verbal and mathematical symbols in solving problems. An intelligence test is a rough measure of a child's capacity for learning particularly for learning the kinds of things required in school. It does not measure character, social adjustment, physical endurance, manual skills, or artistic abilities. It is not supposed to—it was not designed for such purposes. To criticize it for such failure is roughly comparable to criticizing a thermometer for not measuring wind velocity. Now since the assessment of intelligence is a comparative matter we must be sure that the scale with which we are comparing our subjects provides a "valid" or "fair" comparison.

第四章
从句的翻译

英语中的从句主要是指名词性从句、定语从句和状语从句，每种从句在英汉表达上都有很大的不同，对从句的翻译也是翻译中的一个难点。名词性从句的翻译主要探讨英语中起名词作用的从句，如主语从句、宾语从句、表语从句和同位语从句。定语从句的翻译，分析英语定语从句的特点，提出相应的译法。状语从句的翻译，阐述英语状语从句的特点，强调状语从句的翻译要符合汉语的意合特点，可采用多种手段来翻译。

第一节　名词性从句的翻译

名词性从句是指在句子中起名词作用的从句，由关系代词或关系副词引导，可作主语、宾语、表语或同位语，因此英语中的名词性从句主要包括主语从句、宾语从句、表语从句和同位语从句等四种从句。句子中含有名词性从句时，其信息量会更大，语义更深刻，结构更复杂。翻译时，可采用原序法、逆序法和转换法等，译为相应的汉语。

一、主语从句的翻译

主语从句是指那些在句子中作主语的从句，一般由 that, what, whatever, whoever, who 和 which 等引导，放在句首。汉译时，可用原序法，即按照主语从句在原文中的顺序翻译，先译主语从句，后译主语。有时，根据汉语行文的需要，也可采用逆序法，把主语从句移至后面。如：

例 1　What Jack told me was not true.

杰克告诉我的事不是真的。

例 2　Whatever Mark Twin saw and heard on his trip gave him a very deep impression.

马克·吐温此行所见所闻给他留下了深刻的印象。

例 3　That mass is the measure of the inertia of a body has been established.

已经确定，质量是衡量物体惯性的量度。

例 4　Whether an organism is a plant or an animal sometimes taxes the brain of a biologist.

一种生物究竟是植物还是动物，有时会让生物学家颇伤脑筋。

例 5　How and when human language developed and whether animals such as chimpanzees and gorillas can develop a more elaborate system of communication are issues at present being researched, but as yet little understood.

人类的语言是如何发展起来的，是什么时候形成的，诸如黑猩猩和大猩猩一类的动物是否会形成一种更加复杂的交流系统，都是现阶段人们研究的课题，但对此人们都知之甚

少。(主语从句)

例 6　How well the prediction will be validated by later performance depends upon the amount, reliability, and appropriateness of the information used and on the skill and wisdom with which it is interpreted.

这些预测能在多大程度上被后来的成绩所证实取决于所使用的信息量、可靠性和适合程度，并取决于对信息作出解释的技能和智慧。

例 7　From the end of the Second World War until very recently, it was generally accepted in Britain that the State should provide a full range of free educational facilities from nursery schools to universities.

从第二次世界大战结束直到最近，英国人普遍接受这样一个观点，即：国家应该提供从幼儿园到大学的全方位的免费教育设施。

主语从句也常用形式主语 it 来代替，构成 It is...that... 的结构，真正的主语由 that 引导，置于后面，避免句子头重脚轻。翻译时，可以把真正的主语放在原来的位置，但要省略形式主语 it；也可以把真正的主语译在句子的前面。如：

例 8　It doesn't make much difference whether she attends the class or not.

她是否来上课没有多大关系。

例 9　It is strange that the top one student failed the exam.

真奇怪，这个尖子生考试没及格。

例 10　It seemed incredible that she should have lied to us.

她居然对我们说谎，这真是不可思议。

例 11　It is often said that wide reading is the best alternative course of action but even here it is necessary to make some kind of selection.

人们常说，大量阅读是可供选择的最佳方案，但即使在这一方面，也需要某些选择。

例 12　It is also important that the coolant be equally distributed on both sides of the wheel.

让冷却液均匀地分布在砂轮两侧，这一点很重要。

二、宾语从句的翻译

名词性从句作宾语时，该从句就是宾语从句。一般是由 that, what, whether, how, if 等引导的宾语从句，也有由 it 作形式宾语的宾语从句，翻译时略有不同。由 that, how, when, what, which, why, whether, if 等引起的宾语从句，翻译成汉语时，一般不需要改变它在原句中的顺序，顺译即可，但是要注意这些连接词的翻译，如：that 可省略不译有时可译为说，或用冒号代替，how 译为怎么样、多么，when 译为什么时候，what 译为什么，什么情况，which 译为哪个，why 译为为什么，whether 和 if 译为是否。根据行文的需要，有的宾语从句也可采用逆序法，把从句译在句首，主句紧跟其后。如：

例 13　I told him that because of his wrong decision, I have to give up the plan.

我告诉他，由于他的错误决定，我不得不放弃这一计划。

例 14　I heard it said that Mary had gone abroad.

听说玛丽已经出国了。(it 不需要翻译)

例 15　A simple experiment shows whether or not air does not have weight.

空气是否有重量，一个简单的实验就可以证明。

例 16　I made it clear to them that they must hand in their papers before class was over.

我向他们讲清楚了的，他们必须在课结束前交卷。

例 17　We all know that cigarette smoking is hazardous to health and that alcohol abuse can kill.

我们都知道吸烟对健康有害，我们也知道酗酒会危及人的生命。

例 18　I told him how appealing I found the offer.

我告诉他，这机会对我有着多么大的吸引力。

It 作形式宾语的句子，that 所引导的宾语从句一般可按英语原句的顺序翻译；it 一般可以不译。例如：

例 19　Nutritional experiments have made it evident that vitamins are indispensable for one's health.

营养实验证明，维生素是人们的健康所必需的。

例 20　I made it clear to them that they must hand in their papers before 10 o'clock in the morning.

我向他们讲清楚了，他们必须在上午10点之前交卷。

例 21　He believes that the highly mobile American society leaves individuals with feelings of rootlessness, isolation, indifference to community welfare, and shallow personal relationships.

他认为，流动性很大的美国社会留给个人的感觉是没有根基、孤立、对社会福利漠不关心和个人关系淡漠。(宾语从句)

it 作形式宾语的句子，当主句部分表示"感到……，认为……"时，可以将 that 引导的宾语从句提到句子最前面翻译。例如：

例 22　I regard it as a shame that I was blamed by my teacher.

遭到老师的批评，我感到很丢人。

例 23　We consider it absolutely right that we should try our best to achieve a greater success.

我们应该努力去获得更大的成功，这样做是十分正确的。

三、表语从句的翻译

表语从句是位于主句的联系动词后面、充当主句主语的表语的从句，它也是由 that，what，why，how，when，where，whether 等连词和关联词引导的。一般来讲，可以先译主句，后译从句。如：

例 24　This is what he hopes to do.

这就是他希望做的。

例 25　The problem is which experiment we should do first.

问题是我们应该先做哪一个试验。

例 26　The problem is whether he has signed the contract.

问题是他是否已经在合同上签了字。

例 27　What he emphasized again and again was that no matter how difficult it might be, they should never retreat even for an inch.

他再三强调的就是，不管多困难，绝不后退半步。

例 28　One difficulty is that almost all of what is called behavioral science continues to trace behavior to states of mind, feelings, traits of character, human nature, and so on.

难题之一在于，所谓的行为科学还都是从心态、情感、性格特征、人性等方面去寻找行为的根源。

例 29　The question is how people can find an effective way to store the sun's heat.

问题在于，人们怎样才能找到一种有效的方式来储存太阳的热量。

四、同位语从句的翻译

同位语从句主要是用来对名词作进一步的解释，说明名词的具体内容。能接同位语从句的名词主要有：belief（相信），fact（事实），hope（希望），idea（想法，观点），doubt（怀疑），news（新闻，消息），rumor（传闻），conclusion（结论），evidence（证据），suggestion（建议），problem（问题），order（命令），answer（回答），decision（决定），discovery（发现），explanation（解释），information（消息），opinion（意见，观点），truth（真理，事实），

promise（承诺），thought（思想），statement（声明），possibility（可能）等。同位语从句的翻译要复杂一些，可用顺序法、转换法、逆序法等。

一般来说，翻译同位语从句时，可以保持原来的语序，将同位语从句直接翻译在主句后面。例如：

例 30 Einstein came to the conclusion that the maximum speed possible in the universe is that of light.

爱因斯坦得出的结论是，宇宙中的最大速度是光速。

例 31 As an obedient son, he had accepted his father's decision that he was to be a doctor, though the prospect didn't interest him at all.

作为一个孝顺的儿子，他接受了父亲的决定，要当个医生，虽然他对这样的前途毫无兴趣可言。

有些同位语从句在翻译时可以放到所修饰的名词前面，构成类似定语的结构或者独立成句。例如：

例 31 But I knew I couldn't trust him. There was the possibility that he was a political swindler.

但我知道不能轻信他。他是政治骗子的可能性还是存在的。

例 32 It does not alter the fact that he is the man responsible for the delay.

延迟应由他负责，这个事实是改变不了的。

有些同位语从句在翻译时，可以采取顺译法，放在所修饰名词的后面，但是中间经常使用冒号、破折号等标点符号，或者使用"这样""这一""即"等字眼。例如：

例 33 But considering realistically, we had to face the fact that our prospects were less than good.

但是现实地考虑一下，我们不得不正视这样一个事实：我们的前景并不好。

例 34 Not long ago, the scientists made an exciting discovery that this kind of waste material could be turned into plastics.

不久之前，科学家们有了一个令人振奋的发现——可以把这种废物转变成塑料。

在翻译有些同位语从句时，需要改变原文的同位语结构，用汉语的无主句或其他方式译出。例如：

例 35 An order has been given that the researchers who are now in the Skylab should be sent back.

已下命令将现在在航天实验室里的研究人员送回来。

例 36   Even the most precisely conducted experiments offer no hope that the result can be obtained without any error.

即使是最精确的实验，也没有希望获得无任何误差的实验结果。

例 37   An excellent, all-round student with a congenial personality, Miss Ruel is a promising candidate for WOW, an international scholarship program for outstanding women around the world.

鲁尔小姐是一个全面发展的学生，品学兼优，堪称前程无量的 WOW 候选人；所谓 WOW，乃是为世界各国杰出妇女而设的一个国际性的奖学金。

例 38   This is the source of our confidence-the knowledge that God calls on us to shape an uncertain destiny.

这就是我们自信的来源——认识到上帝呼唤我们在前途不明的情况下掌握自己的命运。

例 39   He is now faced with an important decision-a decision that can affect his entire future.

译文：他现在正面临着一个重大的决策，这个决策将影响他的整个前程。

例 40   All of these arrangements were a prelude to the ball, the hostess's ultimate prize.

所有这一切安排仅仅是这次舞会的序曲，舞会才是女主人的最终目的。

● 课后练习

一、翻译下列句子，其中注意名词性从句的翻译。

1. Part of the immune reaction against AIDS or any virus is that the lymph nodes enlarge.

2. The takeaway point from this is that we don't know for sure whether cheating is worse now than in the past.

3. An excellent, all-round student with a congenial personality, Miss Rose is a promising candidate for WOW, an international scholarship program for outstanding women around the world.

4. Literally hundreds of heart-warming stories unfolded in every corner of the country-stories of neighbor helping neighbor, of young helping old, of rich helping poor.

5. Dying patients, especially those who are easiest to mislead and most often kept in the dark, can then not make decisions about the end of life: about whether or not they should enter a hospital, or have surgery; about where and with whom they should spend their remaining time; about how they should bring their affairs to a close and leave.

6. These individuals and organizations engaged in bribery to decide who would televise games, where games would be held, and who would run the organization overseeing organized soccer worldwide.

7. We don't know if cheating in sports is more prevalent today than in the past, but institutional corruption appears to be a growing problem in sport organization, most of which lack formally enforced mandates to be transparent or accountable.

8. It is a matter of common experience that bodies are lighter in water than they are in air.

9. It is often said that wide reading is the best alternative course of action but even here it is necessary to make some kind of selection.

10. It was evident that to answer the letter he needed something more than goodwill, ink, and paper.

11. Parents are required by law to see that their children receive full-time education, at school or elsewhere, between the age of 5 and 16 in England, Scotland and Wales and 4 and 16 in Northern Ireland.

12. He said that part of the problem was that when it set the targets, the European Union was trying desperately to solve the problem of rising transportation emissions.

13. It is virtually impossible to imagine that universities, hospitals, large businesses or even science and technology could have come into being without cities to support them.

14. Nutritional experiments have made it evident that vitamins are indispensable for one's growth and health.

15. The most important part of any therapy is not what you understand or what you talk about, but what you do.

16. What matters is whether you have tried to finish the task.

17. That he once came to China made all the people present very excited.

18. The reason why he didn't attend the meeting was that he had been caught in a traffic jam.

19. That is how he deals with it, which made me worried.

20. Doctors gradually realized that the environment in the hospital is important to the recovery of diseases.

21. The difficulty lies in the fact that attitudes towards the population growth vary from country to country.

22. There is no doubt that the government will take measures to prevent the COVID-19 from spreading.

23. It is reported that so far more than 100 children have died in the flood.

24. What is the most important thing for us to do is to protect the wild animals which are being threatened with extinction.

25. The suggestion that teachers should be further-educated has been discussed.

二、翻译下面的段落，注意其中的名词性从句的翻译。

1. It is frequently said that computers solve problems only because they are "programmed" to do so. They can only do what men have them do. One must remember that human beings also can only do what they are "programmed" to do. Our genes "program" us and our potentialities are limited by that "program". Our "program" is so much more enormously complex, though, that we might like to define "thinking" in terms of our creativity in literature, art, science and technology. In that sense, computers certainly can't think.

2. To be truly happy is a question of how we begin and not of how we end, of what we want and not of what we have. An aspiration is a joy forever, a possession as solid as a landed estate, a fortune which we can never exhaust and which gives us year by year a revenue of pleasurable activity. To have many of these is to be spiritually rich. Life is only a very dull and ill-directed theater unless we have some interests in the piece; and to those who have neither art nor science, the world is a mere arrangement of colors, or a rough footway where they may break their shins. It is in virtue of his own desires and curiosities that any man continues to exist with even patience, that he is charmed by the look of things and people, and that he wakens every morning with a renewed appetite for work and pleasure. Desire and curiosity are the two eyes through which he sees the world in the most enchanting colors; it is they that make women beautiful or fossils interesting; and the man may squander his estate and come to beggary, but if he keeps these two amulets he is still rich in the possibilities of pleasure.

第二节 定语从句的翻译

一、定语从句定义及分类

定语从句，也称关系从句、形容词性从句，是指一类由关系词（relative word）引导的从句，因为这类从句的句法功能多是做定语，所以曾被称为定语从句（attributive clause），这类从句除了可以做定语之外，还可以充当状语等其他成分，所以现代语言学多使用"关系从句"这一术语。

在英语中，定语从句主要通过关系代名词法构成。关系从句的句法功能主要是充当定语。在英语中，关系从句通常位于它所修饰的词（组）之后。被关系从句修饰的词（组）叫做先行词（antecedent），引导关系从句的词称为关系词，关系词指代先行词并在关系从句中充当一定的成分。如在 This is the movie which interests me 一句中，先行词为 movie，而关系词 which 指代先行词 movie 并在关系子句中充当主语。

定语从句的分类：关系从句有限制性关系从句和非限制性关系从句之分。限制性关系从句起限定作用，修饰特定的名词或名词短语；而非限制性关系从句只起补充说明某种信息的作用。例如：

例 1　The government which promises to cut taxes will be popular.（限制性关系从句，指任何一个减税的政府）

例 2　The government, which promises to cut taxes, will be popular.（非限制性关系从句，指本政府）

例 3　The boys who wanted to play football were disappointed when it rained.
渴望踢足球的孩子们因下雨而感到失望。

例 4　The boys, who wanted to play football, were disappointed when it rained.
孩子们本来想踢足球，下雨使他们失望。

但是需要注意的是，有无逗号并非判断限定性与非限定性的唯一标准，也有一些例外发生。如：

例 5　Will you buy me a magazine that I can read on the journey?
你能给我买本杂志吗？我好在路上读读。

例 6　Nature, which Emerson says "is loved by what is best in us", is all about us.
爱默生说的"被人类至善至美之心所爱的自然"，就环绕在我们周围。

二、定语从句的翻译方法

定语从句是英语中使用得最频繁的从句之一，也是给英语的句子理解带来严重干扰的因素之一。英语定语从句为右开放型，和汉语的定语不同，英语中，除一个或几个并列的形容词、名词或代词作定语一般要放在所修饰的词前面外，短语定语和定语从句均后置；而汉语的定语一般前置，无论这个定语是词还是短语，而定语往往不是很长。定语从句是由关系代词或关系副词引导的从句，一般是对某一名词进行修饰和限定。被修饰词通常称为先行词，而定语从句位于先行词后。在翻译定语从句时，我们不能只从语法关系上去把握定语从句，还要从语用功能上去把握它。定语从句不能简单地翻译为"……的"这种前置字结构，从翻译的角度来看，可把英语的定语从句分为限制性定语从句和非限制性定语从句。下面将讨论集中常见的翻译定语从句的方法。

（一）前置法

一些具有"区别""分类"和"限定"等语用功能的定语从句在译为汉语时被直接译到所修饰词的前面作定语，从而将英语的复合句译成汉语简单句。把英语的定语从句译成带"的"字的定语词组放在前面，这种译法既适用于限制性定语从句，又适用于非限制性定语从句，一些较短的具有描述性的非限制性定语从句也可采用前置法，但没有限制性定语从句使用得普遍。

限制性定语从句主要对先行词起限制作用，与先行词关系密切，无论从结构上还是意义上都是全局必不可少的，不用逗号把它们和先行词分开，可译成"……的"句式。如：

例 7　My friend always comes on those days when I am busy.

我的朋友总是在我忙的日子时候来。

例 8　Usually the things we dream of, then work and struggle for, are what we value most.

我们梦寐以求后来又为之努力的东西，往往是我们最珍惜的东西。

例 9　He had many of the qualities of leadership that people admire.

他具有人们所崇尚的领袖人物的诸多品质。

例 10　There is a definite odor that I am not familiar with.

肯定有股我不熟悉的怪味道。

例 11　This is the cat that killed the rat that ate the cake.

这就是那只捕杀了偷吃了蛋糕的老鼠的猫。

例 12　There will come a day when people all over the world will live a happy life under the sun of socialism.

全世界人民在社会主义阳光下过幸福生活的一天是会到来的。

例13 The sun, which had hidden all day, now came out in all its splendor.

那个整天躲在云层里的太阳，现在又光芒四射地露面了。

例14 But his laugh, which was very infectious, broke the silence.

但他的富有感染力的笑声打破了静默。

对于较长的定语，可以首先译出定语从句前的主句，然后重复先行词，再把定语从句译成定语置于被重复的先行词之前。如：

例15 They are striving for the ideal which is close to the heart of every Chinese and for which, in the past, many Chinese have laid down their lives.

译文1：他们正在为实现一个理想而努力，这个理想是每个中国人所珍爱的，在过去，许多中国人曾为了这个理想而牺牲了自己的生命。

译文2：他们正努力去实现那个理想，那个每一位中国人珍藏于心中的理想，那个许许多多中国人曾为之献出了生命的理想。

例16 They would have had to live the rest of their lives under the stigma that he had recklessly precipitated an action which wrecked the Summit Conference and conceivably could have launched a nuclear war.

译文1：他们可能已不得不蒙着一种臭名而终其余生，这个臭名就是：他曾贸然采取了一项行动，这项行动破坏了最高级会谈，并且可以设想，还可能已触发一场核战争。

译文2：他们的余生很可能得蒙上耻辱，因为他曾贸然促成过一项既破坏了最高级会谈又差点引发一场核战争的行动。

例17 Kissinger and his small group of aides toured the Forbidden City, where the Chinese emperors had once lived in lofty splendor.

译文1：基辛格和他的小组随从参观了故宫，从前的中国皇帝曾在这故宫过着奢华显赫的生活。

译文2：基辛格和他的小组随行人员参观了故宫，那座历代中国皇帝养尊处优的宫殿。

（二）后置法

如果定语从句结构复杂，译成汉语前置定语显得太长，不符合汉语表达习惯，则往往可将定语从句译成后置的并列分句，放置于原来它所修饰词的后面。翻译时可以用三种方法来处理。

1. 译成并列分句，重复英语先行词

例18 Stratford is the native place of Shakespeare I have longed for.

斯特拉福特镇是莎士比亚的故乡，是我向往的地方。

例19 I told the story to John, who told it to his brother.

我把这件事告诉了约翰，约翰又告诉了他的弟弟。

例20 World War II was, however, more complex than World War I, which was a collision among the imperialist powers over the spoils of markets, resources and territories.

第一次世界大战是帝国主义列强之间争夺市场、资源和领土的冲突，而第二次世界大战却比第一次复杂。

例21 He's written a book whose name I've totally forgotten.

他写了本书，但书名我完全忘了。

例22 The grammar school legally could only teach the classical subjects for which they had been founded.

按规定文法学校只能讲授古典学科，这些学校的办学宗旨本来就是如此。

例23 A writer—in fact every one of us in life—needs that loving—mother force from which all creation flows.

一个作家——实际上生活中的每个人——都需要慈母的力量，它是一切创作的源泉。

2. 译成并列分句，省略先行词

例24 It is he who received the letter that announced the death of your uncle.

是他接到那封信，说你的叔叔去世了。

例25 He saw in front that haggard white-haired old man, whose eyes flashed red with fury.

他看见前面那个憔悴的白发老人，眼睛里愤怒地闪着红光。

例26 She is a movie star who is going into business now.

她是个电影明星，目前正在经商。

3. 译成状语从句

英语中有些定语从句，兼有状语从句的职能，在逻辑上与主句有状语关系，说明原因、结果、目的、让步、假设、时间等关系，翻译时应善于从原文的字里行间发现这些逻辑上的关系，然后译成汉语中相应的偏正复合句。例如，英语中不少非限制性定语从句主要说明主句或主句某一部分所表达的结果或产生的原因，而非起限制作用，因而可以译为汉语的原因状语从句。因而，英语中的部分定语从句也可以译成表条件，表让步，表时间的状语从句等。

例 27　You must learn the lesson which is very important in your life.

你必须要吸取教训，因为它对你的生活很重要。（表原因）

例 28　The ambassador was giving a dinner for a few people whom he wished especially to talk to or to hear from.

大使只宴请了几个人，因为他特别想和这些人谈谈，听听他们的意见。（表原因）

例 29　She also said I was fun, bright and could do anything I put my mind to.

她说我很风趣，很聪明，只要用心什么事情都能做成。（表条件）

例 30　He decided to take this difficult course, which has made him extremely busy during the summer.

他决定修这门很难的课，结果他整个夏天都很忙。（表结果）

例 31　He insisted on building another house which he had no use for.

他坚持再造一栋房子，尽管他并不需要。（表让步）

例 32　The coming of the time at which all the shares of a listed company should be circulated on the stock market indicates that the Chinese stock market enters an era of healthy development.

当上市公司的所有股票都必须在股市流通时，中国股市就进入了一个健康发展的时期。（表时间）

例 33　She had deceived him to save him—to put him off with something in which he should be able to rest.

她为了解救他而欺骗了他——使他有所寄托，这样他就放心了。（表目的）

例 34　My uncle, who will be 70 tomorrow, is still a keen sportsman.

我的伯父，虽然明天就 70 岁了，仍然热爱运动。（表让步）

例 35　There was something original, independent, and heroic about the plan that pleased all of them.

这个方案富于创造性，独出心裁，很有魄力，所以他们都很喜欢。（表原因）

（三）融合法

融合法是指翻译时把主句和定语从句融合在一起译成一个简单句。由于限制性定语从句与主句关系较紧密，所以融合法多用于翻译限制性定语从句，尤其是 there be 结构带有定语从句的句型。在含有定语从句的复合句中，当主句仅起结构上的作用时，本身的语义并不突出，而定语从句反而在意义上突出了全句的重点，在译为汉语时采用融合法，把定语从句译为谓语，或者兼语式或连动式的一部分。例如：

例 36　There were men in that crowd who had stood there every day for a month.

在那群人中，有些人每天站在那里，站了一个月。

例 37　We used a plane of which almost every part carried some indication of national identity.

我们驾驶的飞机几乎每一个部件都有国籍的某些标志。

例 38　There have been good results in the experiment that have given him great encouragement.

实验中良好的结果给了他莫大的鼓励。

在上面的例子中，主句为 there be 句型，并未表达主要语义。句子的主要语义体现在定语从句中，因而，定语从句译为了谓语。再如：

例 39　We have a social and political system which differs in many respects from your own.

我们的社会和政治制度在许多方面与你们的不同。

兼语式是汉语中的一种特殊句式。当定语从句中的先行词在定语从句中充当主语或宾语，即先行词在逻辑上与定语从句中的动词构成主谓或动宾关系时，有时可以把英语中含有此类定语从句的主从复合句译为汉语中的兼语式，以使译文更加简洁、紧凑。例如：

例 40　There are many people who want to see the film.

许多人要看这部电影。

例 41　I need someone who can instruct me in my English study.

我需要一个人来指导我学习英语。

在上面的例子中，我们在翻译时把 who 省略了，把英语定语从句译成了汉语典型的兼语式句子。再如：

例 42　When I passed by, I saw a man who was quarreling with his wife.

我经过时，看到一位男士和他的妻子正在吵架。

此外，为了行文方便，当定语从句中的主语，从句中的动词是相继发生时，可以在英译汉时把主句和从句中的动词连起来翻译，译为汉语中的连动式，这样可以使句子更加连贯，符合汉语的表达习惯。例如：

例 43　We will send the boy to Britain, where he can receive a better education.

我们要把这个孩子送到英国，接受更好的教育。

在上面的例子中，主句中的"送到英国"与从句中的"接受更好的教育"是相继发生的，因而被译成汉语中的连动式。

● 课后练习

一、翻译下列句子，其中注意定语从句的翻译。

1. The results, which have just been reported to Britain's Medical Research Council, show that some of the divers who were apparently healthy had areas of brain damage similar to those found in stroke victims.

2. Many individual American states—notably California with whose Governor I signed a bilateral agreement on this subject last year—are setting targets for reducing emissions and taking far-reaching action to achieve them.

3. We believe that it is a serious responsibility of your government to insure that weapons which you have provided to Cuba are not employed to interfere with this surveillance which is so important to us all in obtaining reliable information on which improvements in the situation can be based.

4. Then we are faced with a choice between using technology to provide and fulfill needs which have hitherto been regarded as unnecessary or, on the other hand, using technology to reduce the number of hours of work which a man must do in order to earn a given standard of living.

5. If she had long lost the blue-eyed, flower-like charm, the cool slim purity of face and form, the apple-blossom coloring which had so swiftly and so oddly affected Ashurst twenty-six years ago, she was still at forty-three a comely and faithful companion, whose cheeks were faintly mottled, and whose grey-eyes had acquired a certain fullness.

6. He is on a path typical for someone who attended college without getting a four-year degree.

7. Apple may well be the only technical company on the planet that would dare compare itself to Picasso.

8. Ivana Trump, the first wife of President Donald Trump, is writing a memoir that will focus on the couple's three children.

9. A pessimist is one who makes difficulties of his opportunities; an optimist is one who makes opportunities of his difficulties.

10. The conditions that determine what will be raised in an area include climate, water supply, and terrain.

11. It was one of those days that the peasant fishermen on this tributary of the Amazon River dream about.

12. He had great success in football which made him an idol in the eyes of every football player.

13. The serviceman will send the washing machine to the repair shop, where it will be checked and repaired.

14. It was a Shanghai scholar who was then traveling in London who came up with the perfect translation "Ke Kou Ke Le" for Coca-Cola in a name search competition in the 1930s. The Chinese characters, which means "delicious and happy", were an instant hit, and it has become one of the most popular brand names in Chinese ever since.

15. One was a violent thunderstorm, the worst I had ever seen, which obscured my objective.

16. The school system of reaching for A's underlies the country's culture, which emphasizes the chase for economic excellence where wealth and status are must-haves.

17. The strange fact about radiation is that it can harm without causing pain, which is the warning signal we expect from injuries.

18. But we are much less conscious of the extent to which work provides the cultural life that can make the difference between a full or an empty life.

19. This will be an epoch-making revolution in China's social productive forces which will lay down the material foundation for the socialist and communist mode of production.

20. He runs a firm of handymen which helps with everything from fixing curtain rods to stopping a dripping tap. His employees mainly come from the generation of 50-somethings who have a lifetime if handyman experience doing stuff for friends and family.

21. Many flowers which once grew only in china are now found everywhere in the world.

22. The good time that they had together is gone forever.

23. The horrible virus, which was spreading in many cities, has now been contained.

24. Anyone who breaks the rules is to be punished.

25. She lives in a building on whose roof there is a beautiful garden.

26. Of all the factors affecting agricultural production, the weather is the one that influences farmers most.

27. Yesterday at the shopping center, I met the professor whom I met at a party.

28. People will always remember the time when Hong Kong and Macao returned to our

motherland.

29. He who has never tasted what is bitter does not know what is sweet.

30. His laughter, which was infectious, broke the silence.

二、翻译下面的段落，注意其中定语从句的翻译。

1. A Chinese saying goes like that: You're not a true man if you fail to reach the Great wall and no visit to Beijing is complete if you miss eating Beijing Roast Duck. As a famous and delicious food with a long history, Beijing Roast Duck is an excellent choice if you want to know more about Chinese cuisine, culture and customs. There is one point which you need to pay attention to, that is, the best seasons of eating it are spring, autumn and winter. The hot roast duck will be brought on the dining table by the chef where he will slice it into more than 100 thin flakes, and each of them is covered with crispy skin. The terrific taste will make it unforgettable in your life!

2. By comparison, living in my overpriced city apartment, walking to work past putrid sacks of street garbage, paying usurious taxes to local and state governments I generally abhor, am rated middle class. This causes me to wonder, do the measurement make sense? Are we measuring only that which easily measured—the numbers on the money chart—and ignoring values more central to the good life?

For my sons there is of course the rural bounty of fresh-grown vegetables, line-caught fish and the shared riches of neighbors' orchards and gardens. There is the unpaid baby-sitter for whose children my daughter-in-law baby-sits in return, and neighbors who barter their skills and labor. But more than that, how do you measure serenity? Sense of self?

I don't want to idealize life in small places. There are times when the outside world intrudes brutally, as when the cost of gasoline goes up or developers cast their eyes on untouched farmland; there are cruelties, there is intolerance, and there are all the many vices and meannesses in small places that exist in large cities. Furthermore, it is harder to ignore them when they cannot be banished psychologically to another part of town or excused as the whims of alien groups—when they have to be acknowledged as "part of us".

第三节 状语从句的翻译

一、状语从句的翻译方法

根据句法功能,英语有时间、原因、条件、让步、目的、结果等状语从句,他们最大的特点是使用连接性词语,清楚表达了各自不同的功能。也正是因为有了连词,所以从句在句中的位置才比较灵活,可以放在主句的前面,也可以放在主句的后面。由于受到西方语言的影响,汉语越来越多地采用这样的逻辑关联词,如,"因为……所以""不但……而且"等。尽管如此,汉语复合句仍然遵循意合组织原则:先主后次、先原因后结果、先条件后结果、先目的后结果等,许多状语分句不用连接词引导。翻译英语状语从句时,要根据汉语的特点组织译文,同时针对不同的从句采用不同的方法,使译文更加符合汉语的表达习惯。下面是一些常见的英语状语从句的译法:

(一)时间状语从句

When, whenever, as, before, after, until, since, while, once, each time 等,译成相应的状语从句(即当……时,……时)。

例 1 While she spoke, the tears were running down.

她说话时,泪水直流。

例 2 When the history of the Nixon administration is finally written, the chances are that his Chinese policy will stand out as a model of common sense and good diplomacy.

当尼克松政府的历史盖棺定论时,他的对华政策可能成为理智行事和外交有方的杰出典范。

例 3 Please turn off the light when you leave the room.

离屋时请关电灯。

另外,When 引导的时间状语从句除了译为"当……时",还可以译为"在……之后""若""一旦""如果"等。

例 4 When our high level language program is fed into the machine, the compiler translates it into machine code so that it can be followed by the computer.

高级语言程序输入计算机之后,编译程序就把它译成机器代码,以便计算机执行。

例 5 When a foundation is laid in poor soil, it is necessary to excavate to a greater depth than normal to reach a solid base.

若将基础建在地基土层较差的地方，其基坑的深度必须大于常规深度，以使基础落于较坚实的地基上。

例6 Insurance companies are obliged to cover the cost of everything insured when it is lost or damaged during the valid period of insurance.

一切有保险的东西，如在有效保险期内丢失或受损，保险公司都要赔偿其成本。

（二）表示原因的状语从句

because, since, as, now that, seeing that, considering that, for the reason that, in that, in as much as 按照汉语的逻辑顺序，先因后果。

例7 The crops failed because the season was dry.

因为气候干旱，作物歉收。

例8 Because we are both prepared to proceed on the basis of equality and mutual respect, we meet at a moment when we can make peaceful cooperation a reality.

由于我们双方都准备在平等互敬的基础上行事，所以我们在此刻会晤就能够使和平合作成为现实。

受英语句法的影响，有时先果后因也可以。如：

例9 She could get away with anything, because she looked such a baby.

她怎么捣蛋都没事，因为她看上去简直还像是个娃娃模样。

例10 The strike leaders were alarmed when I told them what had happened as the reporter was unfriendly.

当我把发生的事情讲给罢工领导人听时，他们吓了一跳，因为这位记者是不友好的。

其他情况：偏正复句。

例11 Because he was convinced of the accuracy of this fact, he stuck to his opinion.

他深信这件事正确可靠，因此坚持己见。

例12 Pure iron is not used in industry because it is too soft.

纯铁太软，所以不用在工业上。

例13 The perspiration embarrasses him slightly because the dampness on his brow and chin makes him look more tenser than he really is.

额头和下巴上出的汗使他看起来比他实际上更加紧张，因而出汗常使他感到有点困窘。

例14 He was not only surprised but, to start with, extremely suspicious, as he had every reason to be.

他不但惊讶而且首先是十分怀疑,他这样感觉是完全有理由的。

(三) 表示地点的状语从句

由 where 或 wherever 引导的从句,可以分为两种情况,一是表示地点的状语从句,二是表示条件的状语从句。

表示地点:

例 15　We should go where we are needed.

我们应该到需要我们的地方去。

例 16　This is where Chinese immigrants once landed by boat.

这就是中国移民曾经乘船登陆的地方。

例 17　Wuhan lies where the Changjiang River and the Han Jiang River meet.

武汉位于长江与汉江交汇处。

例 18　You say English is the most important. This is where I don't agree.

表示条件:

例 19　Businesses may only hire foreign workers where an American cannot be found.

在找不到美国人的情况下企业才可以雇用外国工人。

例 20　I find it difficult to be objective where he's concerned.

只要涉及他,我就难以做到保持客观。

例 21　The question we ask today is not whether our government is too big or too small, but whether it works, whether it helps families find jobs at a decent wage, care they can afford, a retirement that is dignified. Where the answer is yes, we intend to move forward. Where the answer is no, programs will end.

今天,我们的问题不在于政府的大小,而在于政府能否起作用、能否帮助每个家庭找到薪水合适的工作、能否提供他们可以负担得起的医疗保障并让他们体面地退休。哪个方案能给予肯定的答案,我们就推进哪个方案。哪个方案给予的答案是否定的,我们就选择终止。

(四) 表示条件的状语分句

有 if, as long as, unless, in case, providing that, provided, should, suppose that, on condition that, in the event that 等引导的句子,例如:

例 22　They can't go through any city! If they lay over, it's got to be in a special garage.

他们不能穿过任何城市!如果途中要停留,就得进专门的车库。

例 23　If the government survives the confidence vote, its next crucial test will come in a direct Bundestag vote on the treaties May 4.

译文 1：假设政府经过信任投票而保全下来的话，它的下一个决定性的考验将是 5 月 4 日在联邦议院就条约举行的直接投票。

译文 2：如果政府在信任投票中幸存下来，它的下一个关键考验将是 5 月 4 日联邦议院对这些条约的直接投票。

（五）让步状语从句

有 although, though, even if, even though, as, while, whether, notwithstanding, no matter how, no matter whether, no matter what, no matter when 等引导的句子，例如：

例 24　Although he seems hearty and outgoing in public, Mr. Cooks is a withdrawn, introverted man.

虽然库克斯在公共场合是热情而开朗的，但他却是一个孤僻的、性格内向的人。

例 25　At Paris, they were sheltered by the French members, because although the Comet line started in Belgium, it was very much a combined Belgium-French effort.

在巴黎，就由法国成员来掩护他们；因为，尽管彗星路线是在比利时开创的，但在很大程度上它是比利时人和法国人的共同事业。

例 26　The threat of death does not depress him, even though he has become the No. 1 villain to them.

即使他在他们心目中成了第一号坏蛋，死亡的威胁也不会使他消沉。

例 27　While this is true of some, it is not true of all.

虽然有一部分是如此，但不见得全部如此。

例 28　While I grant his honesty, I suspect his memory.

虽然我对他的诚实没有异议，但我对他的记忆力却感到怀疑。

例 29　I still think that you made a mistake while I admit what you say.

就算你说得对，我仍认为你做错了。

有的译为无条件的条件从句：

例 30　No matter what misfortune befell him, he always squared his shoulders and said: Never mind, I'll work harder."

不管他遭遇什么不幸的事，他总是把胸一挺，说："没关系，我再加把劲儿。"

例 31　Plugged into the intercommunication system, the man can now communicate with the rest of the crew no matter what noise is going on about him.

不管周围是多么喧闹，插头一接上机内通话系统，他就能和同机其余的人通话。

（六）目的状语从句

有 so that, in order that, for fear that, lest, for the purpose that, to the end that, in case 等引导的句子，例如：

前置：

例 32 They stepped into a helicopter and flew high in the sky in order that they might have a bird's-eye view of the city.

为了对这个城市作鸟瞰，他们跨进直升机，凌空飞行。

例 33 He pushed open the door gently and stole out of the room for fear that he should awake her.

为了不惊醒她，他轻轻推开房门，悄悄地溜了出去。

后置：

例 34 The murderer ran away as fast as he could, so that he might not be caught red-handed.

凶手尽可能地跑开了，以免被人当场抓住。

例 35 Brackett groaned aloud, "You came from Kansas city in two weeks so that I could give you a job?"

布雷克特唉声叹气地说："你从堪萨斯城走了两个星期到这里，就是要我给你工作吗？"

课后练习

一、翻译下列句子，其中注意状语从句的翻译。

1. As we observe objects around us, one of the most noticeable properties is their motion.

2. When one form of energy disappears, other forms appear in equivalent amounts.

3. Our whole physical universe, when reduced to the simplest terms, is made up of two things, energy and matter.

4. Because two or more steps were involved, the processes came to be known as indirect processes.

5. The results of the investigation were not conclusive since the crucial experiment had been performed only once.

6. Since from now on frequent reference will be made to sample and population, it is necessary to distinguish between the mean of a sample and the mean of population.

7. He said that he felt like an alcoholic, in that moderate use of the Internet was just not possible for him.

8. Providing that solid is not soluble, the volume of an irregular solid can be found by the displacement of water.

9. If put together and heated to 25, at constant pressure, these substances will result in a new compound. There is no change in the motion of a body unless a resultant force is acting upon it.

10. The pressure of a gas is inversely proportional to its volume if its temperature is kept constant.

11. Lover of towns as I am, I realize that I owe a debt to my early country life.

12. Efficient as it is, the nuclear power station reactor is dangerous.

13. Even if someone is not a programmer, he can have a great impact on a piece of software by suggesting how to improve it to the development team.

14. The law of reflection holds good for all surfaces, whether rough or smooth, plane or curved.

15. I am going to start up the generator in case the power goes off.

16. Steel parts are usually covered with grease for fear that they should rust.

17. A much higher temperature is required so that we could change iron from a solid state into liquid.

18. I was about to speak when Mr. Smith cut in.

19. Until he had passed out of sight, she stood there.

20. Hardly had I got home when it began to rain.

21. Where there is sound, there must be sound waves.

22. The moment I heard the song, I felt cheerful.

23. As he finished the speech, the audience burst into applause.

24. You are free to go wherever you like.

25. Put on more clothes lest you should catch a cold.

26. I packed a swimsuit in case I should have time to go to the beach.

27. You can go out on condition that you promise to be back before 12 o'clock.

28. He never played with the children that a quarrel did not follow.

29. The travel plan was cancelled in order that the spread of SARS could be prevented.

30. You will have some money by then, if you last the week out.

二、翻译下面的段落，注意其中状语从句的翻译。

1. Though fond of many acquaintances, I desire an intimacy only with a few. The Man in Black, whom I have often mentioned, is one whose friendship I could wish to acquire, because he possesses my esteem. His manners, it is true, are tinctured with some strange inconsistencies, and he may be justly termed a humorist in a nation of humorists. Though he is generous even to profusion, he affects to be thought a prodigy of parsimony and prudence; though his conversation be replete with the most sordid and selfish maxims, his heart is dilated with the most unbounded love. I have known him profess himself a man-hater, while his cheek was glowing with compassion; and, while his looks were softened into pity, I have heard him use the language of the most unbounded ill-nature. Some affect humanity and tenderness, others boast of having such dispositions from Nature; but he is the only man I ever knew who seemed ashamed of his natural benevolence. He takes as much pains to hide his feelings, as any hypocrite would to conceal his indifference; but on every unguarded moment the mask drops off, and reveals him to the most superficial observer.

2. Possession for its own sake or in competition with the rest of the neighborhood would have been Thoreau's idea of the low levels. The active discipline of heightening one's perception of what is enduring in nature would have been his idea of the high. What he saved from the low was time and effort he could spend on the high. Thoreau certainly disapproved of starvation, but he would put into feeding himself only as much effort as would keep him functioning for more important efforts.

The effort is the gist of it. There is no happiness except as we take on life-engaging difficulties. Short of the impossible, as Yeats put it, the satisfaction we get from a lifetime depends on how high we choose our difficulties. Robert Frost was thinking in something like the same terms when he spoke of "The pleasure of taking pains". The mortal flaw in the advertised version of happiness is in the fact that it purports to be effortless.

We demand difficulty even in our games. We demand it because without difficulty there can be no game. A game is a way of making something hard for the fun of it. The rules of the game are an arbitrary imposition of difficulty. When someone ruins the fun, he always does so by refusing to play by the rules. It is easier to win at chess if you are free, at your pleasure, to change the wholly arbitrary rules, but the fun is in winning within the rules. No difficulty, no fun.

第五章
长句的翻译

英语习惯于用长的句子表达比较复杂的概念，而汉语则不同，常常使用若干短句，作层次分明的叙述。因此，在翻译长句时，要特别注意英语和汉语之间的差异，认真分析句子结构和逻辑关系，根据汉语的特点和表达习惯，正确地译出原文的意思。由于英汉思维习惯和表达方法的差异，在长句翻译中改变句序、重组结构便成了翻译中的一种常用手段。长句的译法主要有以下几种：顺译法、分译法、逆译法和综合法。

一、长句定义

长句指的是词数多、结构复杂、修饰成分较多、内容层次在两个或两个以上的复合句，亦可指含义较多的简单句。英语长句一般适用于精确、周密、细致地描述事理间的复杂关系，多用于书面语体，如政论、科技语体。据统计，现代英语各类文体的平均每个句子含有17.8个单词。一般把超过25个单词的句子称为长句。

二、英汉长句比较

英、汉两种语言在句法上存在差异，英语多为形合句，汉语多为意合句。汉语句子多属于紧缩型，英语的句子多属于扩展型。英语修辞语位置相对灵活，前置后置，比较自如，尤其倾向于后置，十分有利于句子的扩展。英语句子较长，且较多使用关联词和从句。多种从句（主语、状语、定语、表语从句）并存的长句比比皆是。因为英语结构复杂，层次变化多样，容易产生误解，所以英语长句翻译成为了难点。

三、英语长句的分析

在分析长句时可以采用下面的方法：

（一）找出全句的主语、谓语和宾语（主干/句），从整体上把握句子的结构。

（二）找出句中所有的谓语结构、非谓语动词、介词短语和从句的引导词。

（三）分析从句和短语的功能，例如，是否为主语从句，宾语从句，表语从句等，若是状语，它是表示时间、原因、结果、还是表示条件等等）。

（四）分析词、短语和从句之间的相互关系，例如，定语从句所修饰的先行词是哪一个等。

（五）注意插入语等其他成分。

四、英语长句翻译方法

英语长句之所以很长，一般是三个原因造成的：一是修饰语多，二是联合成分多，三是结构复杂、层次迭出。翻译英语长句所涉及的基本问题，一是汉英语序上的差异。语序上的差异主要表现为定语修饰语（或状语修饰语等）在语言转换中究竟取前置式、后置式还是插入式。而汉语的修饰语不采用后置式，因此遇到后置修饰语较多的英语长句就面临一个句子安排的问题。英语的修饰语很多，主要是名词后面的定语短语或从句（包括同位语），以及动词后面或句首的状语短语或从句。这些修饰成分可以一个套一个连用，形成迂回曲折，叠床架屋的长句结构。汉语多半是流水句，由多个短句铺排而成，读起来如行云流水。翻译长句时，首先要弄清楚原文的句法结构，找出整个句子的中心内容及其各层意思，然后分析几层意思之间的相互逻辑关系（因果、时间顺序等），再按照汉语特点和表达方式，正确地翻译出原文的意思，不拘泥于原文的形式。具体为：①紧缩主干（找出主句主语、谓语及宾语）。②区分主从（析出从句并找出从句的主语、谓语及宾语以及修饰关系）。③辨析词义（特别是主干中的词义）。④分清层次（推断句子思维逻辑发展形式，查明重心、时间或逻辑顺序）。⑤调整语序（按照中国人的思维方式和表达习惯安排语序）。⑥润饰译文（选词、炼句并考虑文体的风格）。例如：

1. ① A World Bank report ② released at the time of the conference, ③ which ended on 10 November, insists ④ that Vietnam's overall growth will depend more on its own policies than on the volume of external financing.

①一份世界银行的报告……坚持认为……②在这次会议上披露了世界银行的一份报告。③这次会议在 11 月 10 日结束。④越南经济的全面增长将更主要地取决于其本国的政策，而不是外来资金的数额。

③—②—①—④

英汉两种语言的语序差异是：英语时间顺序灵活（表示时间的从句可以在主句之前或之后）；汉语一般是从先到后。英语逻辑顺序也比较灵活（表示原因、条件的从句可以在主句之前或之后）；汉语一般是前因后果。英语中的句词性从句（主语从句、表语从句、宾语从句、同位语从句）与汉语句子主谓宾的语序基本一致，因此，一般都可按汉语的表达方式处理。由于英汉思维习惯和表达方法的差异，在长句翻译中改变句序、重组结构便成了翻译中的一种常用手段。长句的译法主要有以下几种：顺译法、分译法、逆译法和综合法。

第一节　顺译法

顺译法是指在英语的长句的叙述层次和逻辑关系与汉语基本相同时，可按照原文顺序，依次译出。这当然不是逐字翻译，也不排除个别词或词组的倒置。换句话，有些英语长句叙述的一连串动作按发生的时间先后安排，或按逻辑关系安排，与汉语的表达方式比较一致，可按原文顺序译出。例如：

例 1 As it was a fine day and I was in no hurry, I was taking my time, looking in shop windows, strolling in the park, and sometimes just stopping and looking around me.

由于天气晴朗，当时又无急事，我便慢悠悠看看橱窗，逛逛公园。有时干脆停下脚步，四处张望。

本句时间状语从句在前，用顺序法译。

例 2 "Neither believe nor reject anything," he wrote to his nephew, "because any other person has rejected or believed it..."

他在给侄子的信中写道："不要因为别的人相信或拒绝了什么东西，你也就去相信它或拒绝它……"

如果英语长句的时间顺序、逻辑顺序与汉语句子的语序相反，一般可逆原文顺序译。

例 3 Even when we turn off the beside lamp and are fast asleep, electricity is working for us, driving our refrigerators, heating our water, or keeping our rooms air-conditioned.

即使在我们关掉了床头灯深深地进入梦乡时，电仍在为我们工作：帮我们开动电冰箱，把水加热，或使室内空调机继续运转。

该句子由一个主句，三个作伴随状语的现在分词以及位于句首的时间状语从句组成，共有五层意思：A. 即使在我们关掉了床头灯深深地进入梦乡时；B. 电仍在为我们工作；C. 帮我们开动电冰箱；D. 加热水；E. 或是室内空调机继续运转。上述五层意思的逻辑关系以及表达的顺序与汉语完全一致，因此，我们可以通过顺序法。

例 4 But now it is realized that supplies of some of them are limited, and it is even possible to give a reasonable estimate of their "expectation of life", the time it will take to exhaust all known sources and reserves of these materials.

可是现在人们意识到，其中有些矿物质的蕴藏量是有限的，人们甚至还可以比较合理的估计出这些矿物质"可望存在多少年"，也就是说，经过若干年后，这些矿物的全部已知矿源和储量将消耗殆尽。

该句的骨干结构为"It is realized that..."，it 为形式主语，that 引导着主语从句以及并列的 it is even possible to ... 结构，其中，不定式作主语，the time ... 是"expectation of life"的同位语，进一步解释其含义，而 time 后面的句子是它的定语从句。五个谓语结构，表达了四个层次的意义：A. 可是现在人们意识到；B. 其中有些矿物质的蕴藏量是有限的；

C. 人们甚至还可以比较合理地估计出这些矿物质"可望存在多少年"；D. 将这些已知矿源和储量将消耗殆尽的时间。根据同位语从句的翻译方法，把第四层意义的表达作适当的调整。

下面我们再列举几个实例：

例 5　We sincerely hope / that your congratulations will be matched by your collective effort / to seek a just and practical solution to the problem / which has challenged the United Nations for so many years.

我们诚恳地希望，你们在表示祝贺之后，能采取与之呼应的共同行动，以寻求一个公正合理又切实可行的方案，来解决这个多年来一直困扰着联合国的难题。

例 6　Although, in the last century, / it was accepted / that the body has been programmed to last for 70 years, / until the 1960s it was all too obvious / that very few bodies ever did, / and for a man to enjoy good health in old age was exceptional.

虽然在上个世纪，人们普遍认为人能活到70岁，但是事实很清楚，20世纪60年代以前，很少有人能活到这个年龄。至于老年时享有一个健康的体魄，那更是极为罕见的。

例 7　In international buying and selling of goods, there are a number of risks, which, if they occur, will involve traders in financial losses.

（在）国际贸易货物的买卖(中)存在着各种各样的风险，这些风险的发生将会给（有关的）商人们带来经济损失。

例 8　In Africa I met a boy, who was crying as if his heart would break and said, when I spoke to him, that he was hungry, because he had had no food for two days.

在非洲，我遇到一个小孩，他哭得很伤心。我问他为什么哭，他说肚子饿，两天没有吃东西了。

例　The world is undergoing profound changes: the integration of economy with science and technology is increasing, the restructuring of the world economy is speeding up, and economic prosperity depends not only on the total volume of resources and capital, but also directly on the accumulation and application of technological knowledge and information.

世界正在发生深刻的变化：经济与科学技术的结合与日俱增；世界经济的重组加快步伐；经济繁荣不仅取决于资源和资本的总量，而且直接有赖于技术知识和信息的积累及其应用。

例 10　The problem is that in the last generation or so we're come to assume that women should be able, and should want, to do everything that by tradition men have done at the same time as pretty well everything that by tradition women have done.

问题是，大约在上一代里，我们已经认定，妇女们应该能够且应该想做男人们传统上所做的一切，而同时也能够做得跟妇女们传统上所做的一切同样好。

例 11 As an obedient son, I had to accept my parents' decision that I was to be a doctor, though the prospect interested in me not at all.

作为一个孝顺的儿子，我不得不接收父母的决定，去当医生，虽然我对这样的前途毫无兴趣。

例 12 I dream only that someday—perhaps as a senior—I will be able to win a race with a cheer as big as the one I got when I lost that race as a freshman.

我只是梦想将来某一天——也许在大四时——我能赢得比赛，得到与我在大一输掉比赛时得到的同样热烈的欢呼。

例 13 When our ship cleared the harbor, taking my family and me on the first leg of our journey home to the United States, I watched the receding coastline of Japan with mingled relief and regret: relief from the oppressive feeling that I was being watched; regret that the book I envisaged writing would not make me welcome again in the land of my birth.

当轮船离开港口，带着我们一家人驶向返回美国的第一段航程时，我怀着既宽慰又怅然的心情凝视着从视野中慢慢消失的日本海岸——因为从被人监视的气氛中解脱出来而感到宽慰；又因为我即将动笔的书稿将使我在我的出生地成为不受欢迎的人而惆怅。

例 14 In oxygen we have a different problem, for although both a research chemist and a chemical manufacturer know the element O means oxygen, in practice they have different ideas about it. Thus, if the researcher performed a delicate experiment, using the manufacturer's oxygen, it might easily be a failure since the so-called O, whether used us a solid, liquid or gas, would almost certainly contain other substances.

就氧气而言，我们遇到了一个不同的问题。因为尽管化学研究人员和化学成品制造商都知道元素 O 指的是氧，但在实际中他们关于氧的概念是不同的。因此，如果研究人员用制造商生产的氧来做精确度很高的实验，这实验很有可能会失败。因为这种所谓的氧不论是用作固态，液态还是气态，几乎肯定含有其他物质。

例 15 Prior to the twentieth century, women in novels were stereotypes of lacking any features that made them unique individuals and were also subject to numerous restrictions imposed by the male-dominated culture.

在 20 世纪以前，小说中的妇女都是一个模式。她们没有任何特点，因而无法成为具有个性的人；她们还要屈从于由男性主宰的文化传统强加给她们的种种束缚。

例 16　This method of using "controls" can be applied to a variety of situations, and can be used to find the answer to questions as widely different as "Must moisture be present if iron is to rust?" and "Which variety of beans gives the greatest yield in one season?"

这种使用参照物的方法可以应用于许多种情况，也能用来找到很不相同的各种问题的答案，从"铁生锈，是否必须有一定的湿度才行？"到"哪种豆类一季的产量最高？"

例 17　It begins as a childlike interest in the grand spectacle and exciting event; it grows as a mature interest in the variety and complexity of the drama, the splendid achievements and terrible failures; it ends as deep sense of the mystery of man`s life of all the dead, great and obscure, who once walked the earth, and of wonderful and awful possibilities of being a human being.

我们对历史的爱好起源于我们最初仅对一些历史上的宏伟场面和激动人心的事件感到孩童般的兴趣；其后，这种爱好变得成熟起来，我们开始对历史这出"戏剧"的多样性和复杂性，对历史上的辉煌成就和悲壮失败也感兴趣；对历史的爱好，最终以我们对人类生命的一种深沉的神秘感而告结束。对死去的，无论是伟大与平凡，所有在这个地球上走过而已逝的人，都有能取得伟大奇迹或制造可怕事件的潜力。

例 18　If parents were prepared for this adolescent reaction, and realized that it was a sign that the child was growing up and developing valuable powers of observation and independent judgment, they would not be so hurt, and therefore would not drive the child into opposition by resenting and resisting it.

如果做父母的对这种青少年的反应有所准备，而且认为这是一个显示出孩子正在成长，正在发展珍贵的观察力和独立的判断力的标志，他们就不会感到如此伤心，所以也就不会因对此有愤恨和反对的情绪而把孩子推到对立面去。

例 19　The very successes of physics and chemistry have ensured that biology should now present the key problems of the whole of natural science, offering a challenge to the understanding of the world in which we live, which will call for far more extensive and at the same time better coordinated efforts than all those which science has dealt with in the past.

正是物理学和化学的成功已确保生物学提出整个自然科学的关键问题，对我们所居住的世界提出新的看法。这些问题的解决需要付出的协作和努力比过去科学上所解决的一切问题所付出的协作和努力都要多得多。

例 20　Twenty-five years after the founding of the United Nations we can not fail to recognize the changes that have occurred in the world of today in all essential aspects and, most particularly, with respect to international life upon the emergence of new States, all of which makes it incumbent upon us to find new formulae to bring the constituent principles of the Organization up to date taking into account the experience gained over a quarter of a century and the ideals that justify its existence.

联合国已经成立25年了，我们不能不承认今天的世界在一切主要方面所发生的变化，特别是一些新兴国家出现后国际生活所发生的变化，所有这些变化都使得我们有义务找出新的方案，使本组织的基本原则适应当前的形势。同时要把本组织在1/4世纪中所取得的经验和本组织的存在所依据的理想考虑进去。

顺译法是翻译长句时最常用，也是最方便的方法。先按照英语句子的语序把英语长句"化整为零"，运用英语关联词的功能，把长句分割成几个分句，为了使前后语气衔接，可增加必要的词语，用汉语关联词体现各个分句的关系，这样翻译成汉语后意思就很清楚了。

课后练习

一、翻译下列句子，注意长句的翻译方法。

1. Prior to the twentieth century, women in novels were stereotypes of lacking any features that made them unique individuals and were also subject to numerous restrictions imposed by the male-dominated culture.

2. This method of using "controls" can be applied to a variety of situations, and can be used to find the answer to questions as widely different as "Must moisture be present if iron is to rust?" and "Which variety of beans gives the greatest yield in one season?"

3. It begins as a childlike interest in the grand spectacle and exciting event; it grows as a mature interest in the variety and complexity of the drama, the splendid achievements and terrible failures; it ends as deep sense of the mystery of man's life of all the dead, great and obscure, who once walked the earth, and of wonderful and awful possibilities of being a human being.

4. If parents were prepared for this adolescent reaction, and realized that it was a sign that the child was growing up and developing valuable powers of observation and independent judgment, they would not be so hurt, and therefore would not drive the child into opposition by resenting and resisting it.

5. The implied inclusion of books among the world's perishable goods is hardly made more agreeable by the reflection that increasing numbers of books these days do seem to be written with just such consumption in mind, and that most bookstores have become little more than news stands for hard cover publications of this sort which are merchandised for a few weeks sometimes only as long as they remain on the best-seller lists—and are then retired to discount store (those jumbled graveyards of books, so saddening to the hearts of authors) shortly before dropping out print altogether.

6. We hold these truths to be self-evident, that all men are created equal, that they are endowed by their Creator with certain unalienable Rights that among these are life, Liberty and the pursuit of Happiness.

7. Up to a point, flyovers and underpasses, being the first really decisive steps to speed up and divert traffic, have eased the situation, but a considerable contribution toward a satisfactory solution can be made by underground railway networks.

8. What is questioned is whether a country like Britain has a chance, assuming it has the will, to succeed where so many have failed and even assuming that it has, should make the tremendous effort and take substantial financial risk of trying to leapfrog into leadership in entirely new technology or whether it should take the softer option of merely catching up with the rest of the industrialized world.

9. If we consider what happens in conversation, in reveries, in remorse, in times of passion, in surprises, in the instructions of dreams, wherein often we see ourselves in masquerade-the droll disguises only magnifying and enhancing a real element, and forcing it on our distinct notice-we shall catch many hints that will broaden and lighten into knowledge of the secret of nature.

10. Andrea Pininfarina, the chief executive of the Italian car design firm founded by his grandfather that counts Ferraris and Alfa Romeos among its creations, died Thursday in a road accident near the northern Italian city of Turin.

11. In the months ahead, our patience will be one of our strengths-patience with the long waits that will result from tighter security, patience and understanding that it will take time to achieve our goals, patience in all the sacrifices that may come.

12. "The only people for me are the mad ones, the ones who are mad to live, mad to talk, mad to be saved, desirous of everything at the same time, the ones who never yawn or say a

commonplace thing, but burn, burn, burn like fabulous yellow roman candles exploding like spiders across the stars."

13. "What is that feeling when you're driving away from people and they recede on the plain till you see their specks dispersing? —it's the too-huge world vaulting us, and it's goodbye. But we lean forward to the next crazy venture beneath the skies."

14. "A pain stabbed my heart, as it did every time I saw a girl I loved who was going the opposite direction in this too-big world."

15. "Boys and girls in America have such a sad time together; sophistication demands that they submit to sex immediately without proper preliminary talk. Not courting talk — real straight talk about souls, for life is holy and every moment is precious."

16. "I realized these were all the snapshots which our children would look at someday with wonder, thinking their parents had lived smooth, well-ordered lives and got up in the morning to walk proudly on the sidewalks of life, never dreaming the raggedy madness and riot of our actual lives, our actual night, the hell of it, the senseless emptiness."

二、翻译下列段落，注意长句的翻译方法。

1. I woke up as the sun was reddening; and that was the one distinct time in my life, the strangest moment of all, when I didn't know who I was—I was far away from home, haunted and tired with travel, in a cheap hotel room I'd never seen, hearing the hiss of steam outside, and the creak of the old wood of the hotel, and footsteps upstairs, and all the sad sounds, and I looked at the cracked high ceiling and really didn't know who I was for about fifteen strange seconds. I wasn't scared; I was just somebody else, some stranger, and my whole life was a haunted life, the life of a ghost.

2. In some societies people want children for what might be called familial reasons: to extend the family line or the family name, to propitiate the ancestors; to enable the proper functioning of religious rituals involving the family. Such reasons may seem thin in the modern, secularized society but they have been and are powerful indeed in other places.

In addition, one class of family reasons shares a border with the following category, namely, having children in order to maintain or improve a marriage: to hold the husband or occupy the wife; to repair or rejuvenate the marriage; to increase the number of children on the assumption that family happiness lies that way. The point is underlined by its converse: in some societies the failure to bear children (or males) is a threat to the marriage and a ready cause for divorce.

Beyond all that is the profound significance of children to the very institution of the family itself. To many people, husband and wife alone do not seem a proper family—they need children to enrich the circle, to validate its family character, to gather the redemptive influence of offspring. Children need the family, but the family seems also to need children, as the social institution uniquely available, at least in principle, for security, comfort, assurance, and direction in a changing, often hostile, world. To most people, such a home base, in the literal sense, needs more than one person for sustenance and in generational extension.

第二节　分译法

有时，英语长句中的从句、分词短语或词组与其修饰部分的关系并不密切，而表达了相对完整的意思，具有一定的独立性。翻译时，可以把这些成分拆出来，翻译成独立的句子，这就是分译法。由于的英语可有各种后置修饰语，所以有些英语句子很长。为了符合汉语表达习惯，我们常将长句中的一连串后置修饰语与其修饰成分分开来译，即把短语或从句拆译为短句，有时还需将后置修饰语另作适当安排并适当增加词语。这一译法可以使译文层次分明，上下语义关联。分译法，是一种基本的句法变通手段。从被分译成分的结构而言，分译大致可以分为单词的分译、短语的分译和从句的分译三种。单词的分译即拆词，将难译的词从句子主干中拆离出来，另作处理，这种方法常常引起句式上的调整，英译汉中要拆译的词常常是形容词和副词。短语的分译即将英语的某个短语单独拿出来译成一个独立成分、从句或并列句。从句的分译则是根据译文需要打散句子，重新组织。英语的长句主要由主从复合句构成，结构严谨，只要明确其主从关系，就能正确分译。将英语句子中有些成分，比如词、短语或者从句，从句子的主干中拆分出来处理，或变成短句，或变成独立句。例如：

例 1　A physically mature female deer in good condition who has conceived in November and given birth to two fawns during the end of May or the first part of June, must search for food for the necessary energy not only to meet her body's needs but also to produce milk for her fawns.

一只成熟健壮的母鹿，在十一月份怀胎，五月底或六月初生下两只幼鹿，这时，它必须寻找食物以获得必要的能量，这不仅是为了满足自身的需要，而且也是为了给幼鹿生产乳汁。

本句的中心词 deer 后跟了一个长定语从句，用分译法译，化长为短。

例 2　It was equally clear that the Chinese agree on what is right or wrong in most situations; in casual encounters with Benjamin and other Western children, they were simply exhibiting their shared beliefs.

另外一点也很清楚，在多数情况下，什么是对的，什么是不对的，这些中国人都有一致的看法。在和本杰明及其他西方小孩的随意交往中，他们都展现了自己的共同看法。

把英语原句中用分号连接的两个并列从句，拆分成两个独立的句子，并将每个句子中的不同成分，也按照意思和逻辑关系分成一个个短句，这样使译文的句子不会太长，而且层次分明，意思清晰。

例3 Some people may worry that this is suggesting one sex is better than the other, but a moment's reflection should allay this fear.

一些人也许会担心：这意味着一种性别比另一种性别更优越。但稍稍思考一下，就清楚对此不必过分担忧。

英语原句是由转折连词but连接的并列句，在译成汉语时，将两个并列句译成了两个独立的句子。

例4 Then we begin to read novels, which are stories about people like ourselves, who have to meet either difficulties which are known to all of us or an exceptional set of circumstances calling for the exercise of great courage and skill.

然后我们开始阅读小说。这些小说的主人公都像我们一样，他们不得不遇到我们熟知的困难，或需要坚强勇气及熟练技巧才能度过的特殊环境。

英语原句中第一部分是主句，第二部分是关系代词which引导的定语从句，翻译时把主句和从句在关系代词处作了拆分。

例5 Even top corporate managers, who have mostly affected styles of leadership that can be characterized only as tough, cold and aloof, have begun to learn the lesson, and earn the benefits, of writing notes that lift people up.

那些通常比较做作的公司高层经理们，其领导作风可以被形容为强硬、冷漠、脱离群众。甚至这些人也开始学习写便笺去鼓舞人心，且获益匪浅。

从译文中可以看出，由who引导的定语从句被翻译成独立的句子，并放在由主句译成的另一个独立的句子前面。

例6 "She doesn't like boys, and just listens to the girls," said a boy in another class, where his sex got 63 per cent of the teacher's attention.

"她不喜欢男生，她只听女生发言，"另一个班上的一位男生说。而在他的班上，男生占据了老师63%的注意力。

英语原句中第一部分是主句,第二部分是关系副词 where 引导的定语从句,翻译时把主句和从句在关系副词处作了拆分。

例 7　It was the moment I ceased being a child, when I began to have an adult's awareness of the pain and tragedy in life.

在那一刻,我不再是个孩子了。那时,我开始用成人的眼光来看待生活中存在的痛苦与悲伤。

此句第一部分是主句,第二部分是关系副词 when 引导的定语从句,翻译时在此处切断,译成两个独立的句子。

例 8　Chinese "cross-talk" is a special type of slap-stick in which two Chinese comedians humorously discuss topics such as bureaucrats, family problems, or other personal topics.

中国的相声是一种特殊的滑稽剧。相声中两名中国喜剧演员幽默地谈论诸如官僚主义者、家庭问题或其他一些个人话题。

把英语原句中 in which 引导的定语从句拆开,译成一个独立的句子,使译文结构清晰,意思明确,句子又不会太长。

例 9　Then they went to the southern part of the island, but found it rocky and covered with bushes, growing so thickly that it was not easy to push one's way through.

接着他们到岛的南部,只见遍地岩石与灌木丛。灌木丛长得相当浓密,要穿过去实在不容易。

此句的非谓语动词短语 growing so thickly that it was not easy to push one's way through 作为定语修饰 bushes,在翻译时把此处与主句作了拆分,而且这一短语本身也分译成汉语的两个短句。

例 10　Another dimension of sex-biased education is the typical American teacher's assumption that boys will do better in the "hard" "masculine" subjects of math and science while girls are expected to have better verbal and reading skills.

美国教师中一个具有代表性的想法是,男孩擅长数学和自然科学,这些学科都是"难懂的""适合于男性的",而女孩则在语言和阅读技能上比男孩强。这是教育中性别偏见的另一种表现。

英语原句中,有一个由 that 引导的同位语从句,该从句中又有一个由 while 引导表示对比的并列句,将对女孩和男孩的不同看法进行对比。翻译时根据汉语表达的习惯将主句和从句,并列复合句之间进行了拆分。

例 11　Flying from Australia to Hong Kong, the tourist group then traveled thousands of interest-filled miles through China by train.

旅行团从澳大利亚乘飞机到香港，又乘火车在中国旅行了数千里，一路上兴趣盎然。又兴致勃勃地乘火车在中国旅行了数千里。

例 12 Chairman Mao might have spoken with understandable pride of the policy of "self-reliance".

毛主席在谈到"自力更生"的政策时，颇为自豪，这是可以理解的。

例 13 Having just left school or technical institute, where they had their place and a task to fulfill and where they were known and esteemed by their colleagues, those young people who do not land that first job they were so eagerly looking forward to have to face up for the first time to unemployment, a situation for which neither family nor school has prepared them.

青年人在学校或技术学院都各得其所，各有自己需要完成的任务，受到同学的了解和尊重。而现在，他们刚刚离校，却找不到自己孜孜以求的第一个职业，不得不面对有生以来的第一次失业。对于这种情况，无论是家庭还是学校都没有帮助他们做好准备。

例 14 At the same time, Cornelius Vanderbilt, Jr., a newspaper columnist who provided Roosevelt with accurate surveys in the past, sent him disturbing reports based on 2000 miles of travel through eight southern and Midwestern states.

与此同时，报纸专栏作家小科尼厄斯·范德比尔呈交罗斯福的报告令人不安。这位作者过去曾向罗斯福提供过一些准确的调查材料。这次报告是他跋涉两千英里，走遍南部和中西部八个州之后完成的。

例 15 After that two-and-a-half-year's trial, which was commended for its fairness even by the Japanese vernacular press, the Tribunal sentenced twenty-five Japanese leaders death or imprisonment for having conspired to wage aggressive war and for being responsible for the conventional war crimes—the atrocities—which had been committed by their subordinate.

经过两年半的审讯，法庭判决 25 名日本国家领导人死刑或监禁。这是因为他们阴谋发动侵略战争，并对常规的战争罪行——即他们部属的累累罪行——承担责任。法庭审判之公正，甚至连日本本国报界也予以赞扬。

例 16 Now it might be thought that Benjamin's appearance—he is Chinese, and we adopted him in Taiwan—encouraged this intervention; but similar intrusive interventions are reported by Westerners whose children do not look the least bit Chinese.

可能会有人认为本杰明的外貌容易让人这样做，因为他是中国人，是我们在台湾收养的。但是其他西方人也报道过类似的干预，他们的孩子可是一点儿都不像中国人。

例17　(1) After regular intervals (2) which depend partly upon the amount of traffic carried and (3) partly upon the local conditions, (4) the so-called "permanent way" requires replacement.

每隔一段时间之后，所谓"永久性道路"（即铁路轨道）就需要更换。这段时间的长短，部分取决于运输量，部分取决于当地的条件。(1)-(4)-(2)-(3)

例18　(1)While China welcomes the endorsement of its model, (2)which the previous administration of Barack Obama refused to do, (3) we need to observe the US's words and deeds going forward to see if it is credible, (4)said Shi Yinhong, (5)director of the Center for American Studies at the Renmin University of China.

人民大学美国研究中心主任时殷弘说，奥巴马执政期间美方拒绝接受这种关系模式，如今得到美方认可，中方表示欢迎。虽然如此，我们仍需观察美方的言行是否可靠。(5)-(4)-(2)-(1)-(3)

例19　(1)"Romeo and Juliet" is arguably Shakespeare's best-known and most-performed play, (2)and the story (3)of Shakespeare's "starcrossed" young lovers whose fate is sealed by their quarreling families, (4)the Montagues and the Capulets, (5)is the touchstone fable of romantic love.

《罗密欧与朱丽叶》可以说是莎士比亚最广为人知、上演次数最多的戏剧。蒙太古和凯普莱特家族间的仇怨注定这对年轻恋人命运多舛，他们的故事也被视为浪漫爱情的试金石。(1)-(4)-(3)-(2)-(5)

例20　A spirited discussion springs up between a young girl who insists that women have outgrown the jumping-on-the chair-at-the-sight-of-a-mouse era and a colonel who says that they haven't.

一位年轻的女士和一位上校激烈地争论起来了。女士认为，妇女进步了，不再是过去那种一看见老鼠就吓得跳起来的妇女了。而上校则认为妇女并没有多大的改变。

例21　Whatever the enthusiasm of the English, who seemed to believe that the Prime Minister was making the long journey to do what Mr. Asquith and Sir Edward had failed to do in 1914—warm Germany that any aggression against a small power would bring not only France but Britain into war against it—Hitler realized, as the confidential German papers and subsequent events make clear, Chamberlain's action was a godsend to him.

英国人似乎认为首相的长途跋涉是要完成阿斯奎先生和爱德华爵士在1914年所没有做到的事情，就是：警告德国对小国的任何侵略，不但会引起法国而且还有英国的参战，联合反抗德国。然而，不管英方如何热心，从德国的秘密文件和历来的事态演变过程看来，希特勒已意识到，张伯伦的行动对他来说是一个天赐良机。

由此可见，因为部分英语句子所包含的信息大大超过汉语单句的承受力，所以汉语句子往往要把它进行化解，各个击破。英语句子中有些成分，比如词、短语或者从句，从句子的主干中拆分出来处理，或变成短句，或变成独立句。当长句中的并列成分较多，或主句与从句、短语与其所修饰的词之间关系不很紧密，各具有相对的独立性时，可按汉语中多用短句的习惯，把分句分割成若干短句译出。为了使句子之间相互衔接，可以适当地增减词语。

● 课后练习

一、翻译下列句子，注意长句的翻译方法。

1. The ball's best review has come from England's star midfielder David Beckham who calls the ball's accuracy "exceptional". Incidentally, Beckham is sponsored by Adidas and helped design the ball.

2. There is a tide in the affairs not only of man, but also women too, which, taken at the flood, leads on to fortune.

3. The big problem of comprehension of the English text and the bigger problem of how to express it in rich, present-day Chinese which ranges from the classical to the colloquial both have to be solved in the course of translation.

4. The more we can enjoy what we have, the happier we are. It's easy to overlook the pleasure we get from loving and being loved, the company of friends, the freedom of living where we please, even good health.

5. The physical size of a diffused resistor will involve a compromise between a large pattern with an easily controllable value, and a small pattern which will occupy a smaller area and have a less predictable value.

6. The little girls loved the theater, that world of personages taller than human beings, who swept upon the scene and invested it with their presences, their more than human voices, their gestures of gods and goddesses ruling a universe.

7. The day before I was to leave I went walking across the river to the red mesa, where many times before I had gone to be alone with my thoughts.

8. Manufacturing processes may be classified as unit production with small quantities being made and mass production with large numbers of identical parts being produced.

9. The real challenge is how to create systems with many components that can work together and change, merging the physical world with the digital world.

10. This is, for instance, one of the main reasons why over the last ten centuries scientific progress has been mostly associated with universities, where scholars from many different disciplines were gathering together.

11. Sleep is influenced by the circadian timing system, a bundle of neurons, embedded deep in the brain, that regulates production of a sleep-inducing chemical called melatonin and sets natural bedtime and rise time.

12. American prisoners are permitted to receive Red Cross food parcels and write censored letters.

13. The total expenditure of the US government for the so-called Fiscal Year 1970 that is the period from July 1, 1969 to June 10, 1970, were about 195 billion dollars, of which about 80 billion was for national defense.

14. When you listen to people speak a foreign language that you understand, have you noticed that the native speakers of that language use words and phrases in a manner different from what you are used to?

15. At school the student needs to increase his knowledge in an organized way, to acquire sufficient vocabulary in science for effective communication, and to learn some facts because they are important in everyday living, such as knowledge that is useful for his health, for his safety and for an understanding of his surroundings.

二、翻译下列短文，注意长句的翻译方法。

1. (When one individual inflicts bodily injury upon another, such injury that death results, we call the deed man-slaughter; when the assailant knew in advance that the injury would be fatal, we call his deed murder.) But when society places hundreds of proletarians in such a position that they inevitably meet a too early and unnatural death, one which is quite as much a death by violence as that by the sword or bullet; when it deprives thousands of the necessaries of life, places them under conditions in which they cannot live—forces them, through the strong arm of the law, to remain in such conditions until that death ensues which is the inevitable consequence—knows that these thousands of victims must perish, and yet permits these conditions to remain, its deed is murder just as surely as the deed of the single individual; disguised, malicious murder, murder against which none can defend himself, which does not

seem what it is, because no man sees the murderer, because the death of the victim seems a natural one, since the offense is more one of omission than of commission. (But murder it remains.)

2. The Reagan administration's most serious foreign policy problem surfaced near the end of the president's second term. In 1987 Americans learned that the administration had secretly sold arms to Iran in an attempt to win freedom for American hostages held in Lebanon by radical organizations controlled by Iran's Khomeini government. Investigation also revealed that funds from the arms sales had been diverted to the Nicaraguan contras during a period when Congress had prohibited such military aid.

The ensuing Iran-contra hearings before a joint House-Senate committee examined issues of possible illegality as well as the broader question of defining American foreign policy interests in the Middle East and Central America. In a larger sense, the Iran-contra hearings, like the celebrated Senate Watergate hearings 14 years earlier, addressed fundamental questions about the government's accountability to the public, and the proper balance between the executive and legislative branches of government.

3. Although the American economy has transformed itself over the years, certain issues have persisted since the early days of the republic. One is the continuing debate over the proper role of government in what is basically a marketplace economy. An economy based on free enterprise is generally characterized by private ownership and initiative, with a relative absence of government involvement. However, government intervention has been found necessary from time to time to ensure that economic opportunities are fair and accessible to the people, to prevent flagrant abuses, to dampen inflation and to stimulate growth.

Ever since colonial times, the government has been involved, to some extent, in economic decision-making. The federal government, for example, has made huge investments in infrastructure, and it has provided social welfare programs that the private sector was unable or unwilling to provide. In a myriad of ways and over many decades, the government has supported and promoted the development of agriculture.

第三节 逆译法

逆着或基本逆着原文的词序或句序进行翻译，词序与思维方式和表达习惯有关。在翻译较长的英语句子时，将分句或一些从属成分倒置译是常见的翻译方法。汉语时空观上大体遵循逆序法，即由大至小，由远及近，由重而轻；而英语的时空观大体遵循顺序法在表达法上多有不同。英语长句的叙述层次、表达习惯不同于汉语，如果按原文次序翻译就会感到译文模糊，不通顺，这时就需要逆着原文的顺序去译，从后面的部分译起。从后往前译感到更自然，更能表达原文，符合汉语习惯。例如：

例 1 A student of mathematics must become familiar with all the signs and symbols commonly used in mathematics and bear them in mind and be well versed in the definitions, and formulas as well as the technical terms in the field of mathematics, *in order that* he may be able to build up the foundation of the mathematical subject and master it well for pursuing advanced study.

为了能打好数学基础，掌握好数学，以利于深造，学数学的学生必须熟悉和牢记数学中的所有常用的符号和代码，精通数学方面的定义、公式和术语。

这是个主从复合句。其中主句的主语 A student of mathematics 带三个平行结构的谓语 must become familiar with, bear them in mind and be well versed in…，然后由 in order that 引导一个目的状语从句，这个目的状语从句同时也带有两个平行结构的谓语 may be able to build up the foundation and master it well for pursuing advanced study。汉语表达习惯上总是目的在前，行动在后。所以，翻译时可按逆译法从后往前翻译，把目的先译置前，便是规范的汉语译文。

例 2 It was our view that the United States could be effective in both the tasks assigned by the President, i.e., of ending hostilities, and making a contribution to a permanent peace in the Middle East—if we conducted ourselves so that we could remain in permanent contact with all of these elements in the equation.

如果我们采取行动以便能继续与中东问题各方面保持接触，美国就能担当起总统布置的两项任务，即结束中东敌对行为，并对该地区的永久和平做出贡献，这就是我们的看法。

这是 it 作形式主语的主从复合句。主句是 it was our view，it 代替 that 引导的名词性从句，作形式主语。从句的主语是 the United States，谓语是 could be effective in…，过去分词短语 assigned by the President 修饰 tasks，另两个现在分词短语 ending hostilities, and making a contribution to 是介词 of 的宾语，一起补充说明 tasks 的实际内容。从句后又有一个 if 引导的条件状语从句，这个条件状语从句又带有 so that 引导的目的状语从句。翻译时把状语从句提前先译，其状语从句中的条件状语又先于目的状语去译。

例 3 Neither Goebbels nor Hitler nor anyone else, certainly not Bruening and most certainly Groener, to whom Schleicher owed his rapid rise in the army and in the councils of government, had as yet surmised the infinite capacity for treachery of the scheming, political general.

这个诡计多端、热衷政治的施莱彻尔将军是什么背信弃义的勾当都干得出来的，而且其寡廉鲜耻的程度，不论是戈培尔也好，希特勒也好，或者任何人也好，都一点底也没摸到。勃鲁宁肯定没有摸到，格罗纳就更不用说了，尽管他在军队和政府中的迅速升迁完全是靠格罗纳提拔的。

根据句子的逻辑关系判断 Schleicher 指的就是下面提到的 the scheming, political general, the infinite capacity for treachery 是 the general 的行为，这样采用逆译法翻译此句就容易多了。

例 4　Although her characters were portrayed in many settings and situations, they all reflected, by the often tragic outcome of their lives, her profound conviction that no human could be happy if that happiness was rooted in the wretchedness of another.

如果幸福是建立在另一个人的痛苦之上，那就没有人会有幸福。她的这种深切信念全都反映在一些人生结局通常都很悲惨的人物身上，虽然她笔下的人物出现在多种多样的背景和情节中。

主句是 they all reflected her profound conviction，that 引导的从句是 conviction 的同位语，Although her characters were portrayed in many settings and situations 是让步状语从句，if that happiness was rooted in the wretchedness of another 是条件状语从句。按照汉语的逻辑关系以及条件在前结果在后的习惯，采用逆译法翻译这句话比较合适。

例 5　Time goes fast for one who has a sense of beauty, when there are pretty children in a pool and a young Diana on the edge, to receive with wonder anything you can catch!

当可爱的孩子们站在池子里，又有个年轻的狄安娜在池边好奇地接受你所捉上来的东西的时候，如果你懂得什么叫美的话，时间是过得很快的！

主句 Time goes fast，两个定语从句 who has a sense of beauty 和 you can catch，一个时间状语从句 when there are pretty children in a pool and a young Diana on the edge 组成英语长句。

例 6　It was a keen disappointment when I had to postpone the visit which I had intended to pay to China in January.

我原打算一月份访问中国，后来不得不推迟，这使我深感失望。

例 7　Both plants and animals of many sorts show remarkable changes in form, structure, growth habits, and even mode of reproduction in becoming adapted to different climatic environments, types of food supply, or modes of living.

在逐渐适应不同气候环境、养料来源、或生活方式的过程中，许多种类的动植物在外形、构造、生活习性甚至繁殖方式方面都发生了显著的变化。

例 8　His business connections with the penurious great both in France and in England secured the foothold he has obtained on his arrival in Europe as a young man with letter of introduction to persons of consequences.

他初到欧洲时，还是个拿着介绍信去见名流的年轻人，后来和英法的大款们发生商务关系，这才站住了脚跟。

例 9　I put on my clothes by the light of a half-moon just setting, where rays streamed through the narrow window near my crib.

半轮月光渐渐坠下，月光透过小床旁边的一个窄窄的窗子射了过来，我趁着月光穿上衣服。

例 10　I feel that every book opens me a window through which I see an unthinkably new world when the book tells me about never-heard-of and never-seen characters, sentiments, ideas and attitudes.

我觉得，当书本给我讲到闻所未闻、见所未见的人物、感情、思想和态度时，似乎是每一本书都在我面前打开了一扇窗，让我看到一个不可思议的新世界。

例 11　The face she lifted to others was the same which, when she saw him, always looked like a window that has caught the sunset.

她的脸当她看见他的时候，总是像映着晚霞的窗子，现在她把它抬起来向别人。

例 12　Let me once more thank you for the constructive way you helped to settle all the problems that were in the way of signing the contract.

您本着建设性的求实的态度，协助解决了影响签订合同的若干问题，请允许我再次向您表示感谢。

例 13　In December 1980, two bronze carriages, each with a driver and four horses, were found near a big tomb.

1980 年 12 月，在一座大墓附近发现两辆青铜马车，每辆配有一名车手、四匹骏马。

例 14　Nobody with any sense expects to find the whole truth in advertisement any more than he expects a man applying for a job to describe his shortcomings and more serious faults.

凡是有头脑的人都不会指望申请工作的人说出自己的缺点和更为严重的过失。同样，他也不会指望广告里的话全都是真的。

例 15　The Conservative party was hard hit when War Minister John Profumo was involved in a moral scandal that furnished the British press with headlines for weeks.

国防大臣约翰·普罗夫莫卷入了一件有伤风化的丑闻,给英国报刊一连数周提供了头条新闻,这件事使保守党受到了沉重的打击。

例 16　And I take heart from the fact that the enemy, which boasts that it can occupy the strategic point in a couple of hours, has not yet been able to even the outlying regions, because of the stiff resistance that gets in the way.

由于受到顽强抵抗,吹嘘能在几个小时内就占领战略要地的敌人甚至还没有能占领外围地带,这一事实使我增强了信心。

例 17　Since natural water contains dissolved oxygen, fishes, which also need oxygen though they live in water, will die if hot days persist so long that the dissolved oxygen is evaporated.

鱼类虽然水栖,但也需要氧气,而天然水是含有溶解氧的,因此如天热得过久使水中的溶解氧蒸发掉了,鱼就要死亡。

例 18　Perhaps the factor that makes a positive outcome most likely is the clear recognition by the Japanese government and business community that there is an overriding need for innovation, and a wide agreement that the national interest requires that major effort be concentrated in this area.

日本政府和企业团体清楚地认识到革新是压倒一切的需要,而且人们普遍认识到民族利益要求对该领域共同努力。也许上述这些认识就是可能引起积极结果的因素。

例 19　Aristotle could have avoided the mistake of thinking that women have fewer teeth than men, by the simple device of asking Mrs. Aristotle to keep her mouth open while he counted.

亚里士多德认为女人的牙齿比男人的少,其实(很简单),他只需请他的夫人张一张口来让他数一数,就完全可以不犯这一错误的。

● 课后练习

一、翻译下列句子,注意长句的翻译方法。

1. Anthropologist Thomas Kochman gives the example of a white office worker who appeared with a bandaged arm and felt rejected because her black fellow workers didn't mention it.

2. The American confessed to feeling what I believe most Americans would feel if a next-door neighbor passed within a few feet without acknowledging their presence—snubbed.

3. Not surprisingly, it was an unwelcome change for senior citizens such as Sabine Wetzel, a 67-year-old retired bank teller, who was told that her state pension would be cut by $12.30 a month.

4. The most important fact in Washington's failure on Thursday to be re-elected for the first time since 1947 to the UN Human Rights Commission is that it was America's friends, not its enemies that engineered the defeat.

5. The progress to the statute book of the necessary legal infrastructure for electronic commerce has in many countries been delayed by a difficult and politically sensitive debate created by the concerns of law enforcement authorities that the widespread use of strong encryption may facilitate crime and terrorism to a degree that will destabilize civilized governments.

6. The story took place in a bitterly-fought 1929 textile strike at Gastonia N.C. in America.

7. Paradoxically, though they are the providers of food to the remaining mankind and constitute lifeline for the urban dwellers, yet the interests of inhabitants in many rural areas continue to be consigned to revolting neglect.

8. The Counselor for Commercial Affairs of China Embassy and the representative of import and export corporations, economic and technical corporations exercise their functions and power *abroad* under the leadership of the Ministry for Foreign Economic Relations and Trade of China.

9. They would have had to live the rest of their lives under the stigma that he had recklessly precipitated an action which wrecked the Summit Conference and conceivably could have launched a nuclear war.

10. If she had long lost the blue-eyed, flower-like charm, the cool slim purity of face and form, the apple-blossom colouring which had so swiftly and so oddly affected Ashurst twenty-six years ago, she was still at forty-three a comely and faithful companion, whose cheeks were faintly mottled, and whose grey-blue eyes had acquired a certain fullness.

11. Aluminum remained unknown until the nineteenth century, because nowhere in nature is it found free, owing to its always being combined with other elements, most commonly with oxygen, for which it has a strong affinity.

12. Great, therefore, was the rejoicing throughout Egypt when a traveler down the river Nile declared he was court physician to the king of a far country and would gladly, if he was allowed, examine the eyes of the blind man.

13. Accident may put a decisive blunderer in the right, but eternal defeat and miscarriage must attend the man of the best parts, if cursed with indecision.

14. So many of the super-computers we think of as costly many millions of dollars today will suddenly become things that we're carrying around in our pockets.

15. What has changed, many experts believe, is that Americans have grown more reluctant to cast stones at friends and neighbors who fail to meet the moral standards they set for themselves.

16. Towers, domes, balanced rocks, and arches have been formed over millions of years of weathering and erosion, and the process continues, constantly reshaping this fantastical rock garden.

二、翻译下列段落，注意长句的翻译方法。

1. I used my daily dose of hope like a drinker sipping a rationed ounce of Scotch: the day Ed said he longed for baking-powder biscuits and ate two of the home-made beauties Harris Russell produced overnight; the afternoon when around the hospital bed we played out the games in Peter Buckman's book Playground, the four of us relaxed and laughing as if we were spending a late Sunday morning at home; the first walk Ed took down the hallway, joking with the accompanying nurse about his shuffle; the morning I parked the car a block from the clinic and met Ed out buying a newspaper at the corner kiosk — we walked back to his room planning his trip to Peking before the official United States presidential visit there.

2. The Warwickshire Avon falls into the Severn here, and on the sides of both, for many miles back, there are the finest meadows that ever were seen. In looking over them, and beholding the endless flocks and herds, one wonders what can become of all the meat! By riding on about eight or nine miles farther, however, this wonder is a little diminished; for here we come to one of the devouring WENS, namely, CHELTENHAM, which is what they call a "watering place", that is to say, a place to which East India plunderers, West India floggers, English tax-gorgers, together with gluttons, drunkards, and debauchees of all descriptions, female as well as male, resort, at the suggestion of silently laughing quacks, in the hope of getting rid of the bodily consequences of their manifold sins and iniquities. When I enter a place like this, I always feel

disposed to squeeze up my nose with my fingers. It is nonsense, to be sure; but I conceit that every two-legged creature, that I see coming near me, is about to cover me with the poisonous proceeds of its impurities. To places like this come all that is knavish and all that is foolish and all that is base; gamesters, pick-pockets, and harlots; young wife-hunters in search of rich and ugly and old women, and young husband-hunters in search of rich and wrinkled or half-rotten men, the former resolutely bent, be the means what they may, to give the latter heirs to their lands and tenements.

These things are notorious; and, Sir William Scott, in his speech of 1802, in favor of the non-residence of the Clergy, expressly said, that they and their families ought to appear at watering places, and that this was amongst the means of making them respected by their flocks! Memorandum: he was a member of Oxford when he said this!

第四节 综合法

我们讲述了英语长句的顺译法、分译法和逆译法，事实上，在翻译一个英语长句时，并不只是单纯地使用一种翻译方法，而是要求我们把各种方法综合使用，这在我们上面所举的例子中也有所体现。尤其是在一些情况下，一些英语长句单纯采用上述任何一种方法都不方便，这就需要我们的仔细分析，或按照时间的先后，或按照逻辑顺序，顺逆结合，主次分明地对全文进行综合处理。对长句意义层次进行分析。弄清句中究竟讲了多少件事，将长句分解为语义相对完整的单句，分析各个单句之间的语义逻辑关系，然后用合乎汉语表达习惯的排列方式对各个单句进行重新组合。例如：

例1 People were afraid to leave their houses, for although the police had been ordered to stand by in case of emergency, they were just as confused and helpless as anybody else.

尽管警察已接到命令，要做好准备以应付紧急情况，但人们不敢出门，因为警察也和其他人一样不知所措和无能为力。

该句共有三层含义：A. 人们不敢出门；B. 尽管警察已接到命令，要做好准备以应付紧急情况；C. 警察也和其他人一样不知所措和无能为力。在这三层含义中，B表示让步，C表示原因，而A则表示结果，按照汉语习惯顺序，

例2 As regards health, I have nothing useful to say since I have little experience of illness. I eat and drink whatever I like, and sleep when I cannot keep awake. I never do anything whatever on the ground that it is good for health, though in actual fact the things I like doing are mostly wholesome.

谈到健康问题，我就没有什么可说的了，因为我没生过什么病。我想吃什么就吃什么，眼睛睁不开了就睡觉，从来不为身体有益而搞什么活动，然而实际上我喜欢做的事大都是有助于增进身体健康的。

原句有三个分句，但译文可并为两句来表明前后句是因果关系，第一句用顺译法，第三句用逆译法把原因说在前面。因此，本句可采用综合法翻译。

例 3 It should be realized that we are really expressing its velocity relative to something when we assign a magnitude and direction to the velocity of body, which is, for this particular purpose, imagined to be stationary.

应当认识到，当我们确定某一物体的速度大小和方向时，实际上我们表示的是相对于某一参考物的速度，对于这一特定场合来说，可以设想该参考物是静止不动的。

这是一个主从复合句。第一句为主句，第二句为主与从句，第三句为世间状语从句，说明第二句谓语行为发生的时间，第四句为定语从句，修饰第二句的 something。

例 4 But without Adolf Hitler, who was possessed of a demoniac personality, a granite will, uncanny instincts, a cold ruthlessness, a remarkable intellect, a soaring imagination and until towards the end, when drunk with power and success, he overreached himself—an amazing capacity to size up people and situations, there almost certainly would never have been a Third Reich.

然而，如果没有阿尔道夫·希特勒，那就几乎可以肯定不会有第三帝国。因为阿道夫·希特勒有着恶魔般的性格、花岗石般的意志、不可思议的本能、无情的冷酷、杰出的智力、深远的想象力以及对任何局势惊人的判断力。这种判断力最后由于权力和胜利冲昏了头脑而不自量力，终于弄巧成拙。

这个句子是由一个主句、一个非限定性定语从句和一个状语从句组成。插入主语中间的是一个由 who 引起的非限定性定语从句。这个从句较长，中间又插入了一个用破折号分开的、由 until 引起的时间状语从句。这个状语从句对非限定性定语从句的后面部分作了些补充说明，因而虽然具有相对独立的意义，仍可根据逻辑关系将该句译文置于句尾。全句有两层主要意思：A: 如果没有希特勒，那就几乎可以肯定不会有第三帝国；B: 希特勒在性格、智力、能力等方面有某些特点。原文各句的逻辑关系和表达顺序与汉语大致一致，但因从句是插入成分，和汉语表达习惯不同，所以翻译时顺中有逆，可以综合处理。

例 5 By the middle of the year, he warned, the Soviet Union would overtake the United

States in the number of land-based strategic missiles, the result of a massive Soviet effort beginning in the mid-1960, after the Cuban fiasco, to achieve at least parity and possibly superiority in nuclear weapons.

他警告说，到本年年中，苏联将在陆上发射战略导弹的数量超过美国，因为苏联在古巴事件中遭到失败后，从六十年代中期就大力发展导弹，目的是为了在核武器方面至少达到同美国均等，并力争超过美国。

这是一句简单句。有一个插入语 he warned 可以提前。另外有一个表示结果的名词短语，但这个短语中有两个表示时间的短语和一个表示目的的短语，需要按逻辑关系来安排。表示结果的名词短语可译为表示原因的句子。

例 6 Energy is the currency of the ecological system and life becomes possible only when food is converted into energy, which in turn is used to seek more food to grow, to reproduce and to survive.

能量是生态系统的货币，只有当食物转变为能量，能量再用来寻找更多的食物以供生长、繁殖和生存时，生命才成为可能。

这是一句并更复合句。第二个主要分句中有一个由 only when 引导的时间状语从句和一个非限制性定语从句。用逆序法将时间状语从句提前的，用分译法译非限制性定语从句。

例 7 Many man-made substances are replacing certain natural materials because either the quantity of the natural product can not meet our ever-increasing requirement, or, more often, because the physical property of the synthetic substance, which is the common name for man-made materials, has been chosen, and even emphasized, so that it would be of the greatest use in the fields in which it is to be applied.

人造材料统称为合成材料。许多人造材料正在代替某些天然材料，这或者是由于天然产品的数量不能满足日益增长的需要，或者往往是人们选择了合成材料的一些物理性质并加以突出而造成的。因此合成材料在应用的领域中具有极大的用途。

例 8 In that infinitesimal fraction of time, inconceivable and immeasurable, during which the first atomic bomb converted a small part of its matter into the greatest burst of energy released on earth up to that time, Prometheus had broken his bonds and brought a new fire down to earth, a fire three million times more powerful than the original fire he snatched from the gods for the benefit of man some five hundred years ago.

在这难以想象，无法计算的刹那之间，普罗米修斯挣脱了身上的锁链，又把新的火种送到了人间。这时第一颗原子弹把它的物质的一小部分化为地球上迄今为止所释放出来的最大的能量。这个新火种与大约五百年前普罗米修斯为了造福人类从天庭盗走的旧火种相比，其威力要大 300 万倍。

例 9 Just advanced by the Russians and later picked up and made much of by certain American writers, was the claim that U-2 pilots were worried that if the device had to be used the CIA had rigged it in such a way that it would explode prematurely, thus eliminating, in one great blast, all incriminating evidence, planes and pilot.

U-2 飞机驾驶员感到担心的是：中央情报局已在 U-2 飞机上安上了一种装置，这种装置在必要时能提前爆炸，把包括飞机和驾驶员在内的一切罪证一下子都消灭干净。这种说法原是俄国人提出来的，后来又被美国一些写文章的人接过来大肆宣扬。

例 10 The president said at a press conference dominated by questions on yesterday's election results that he could not explain why the Republicans had suffered such a widespread defeat, which in the end would deprive the Republican Party of long-held superiority in the House.

在一次记者招待会上，问题集中于昨天的选举结果，总统就此发了言。他说他不能够解释为什么共和党遭到了这样大的失败。这种情况最终使共和党失去众院中长期享有的优势。

例 11 By the middle of the year, he warned, the Soviet Union would overtake the United States in the number of land-based strategic missiles, the result of a massive Soviet effort beginning in the mid-1960.

他警告说，到本年中，苏联将在陆上发射战略导弹的数量超过美国，因为苏联在古巴事件中遭到失败后从六十年代中期就大力发展导弹。

例 12 Computer language may range from detailed low level close to that immediately understood by particular computer, to the sophisticated high level which can be rendered automatically acceptable to a wide range of computers.

计算机语言有低级也有高级的。前者比较繁琐，很接近于特定计算机直接能懂的语言；后者比较复杂，适应范围广，能自动为多种计算机所接受。

例 13 Up to the present time, throughout the eighteenth and nineteenth centuries, this new tendency placed the home in the immediate suburbs, but concentrated manufacturing activity, business relations, government, and pleasure in the centers of the cities.

到目前为止，经历了 18 和 19 两个世纪，这种新的倾向是把住宅安排在城市的近郊，而把生产活动、商业往来、政府部门以及娱乐场所都集中在城市的中心地区。

例 14　Modern scientific and technical books, especially textbooks, requires revision at short intervals if their authors wish to keep pace with new ideas, observations and discoveries.

对于现代书籍，特别是教科书来说，要是作者希望自己书中的内容能与新概念、新观察到的事实和新发现同步发展的话，那么就应该每隔较短的时间，将书中的内容重新修改。

例 15　Complaints of poverty of poets are as old as their art, but I never heard that they wrote the worse verses for it. It is enough, probably, to call forth their most vigorous efforts , that poetry is admired and honored by their countrymen.

自古以来，诗人即以贫困而怨诉不绝。但因贫而不功于艺者，于我则闻所未闻。盖天下爱诗而敬之，则诗人虽尽其才力仍因以自慰。这大概就是原因所在吧。

例 16　Digital computers are all similar in many ways such as having at least the five parts which all work together when solving a problem.

各种数字计算机在许多方面都相似，例如，至少具备五个部分，这五个部分在解题时都一起工作。

在尝试运用顺译法、分译法和逆译法等方法，译文未达到原文效果时，就可以考虑使用综合法。所以，在翻译时可顺中有序，化整为零，进行综合处理。

课后练习

一、翻译下列短文，注意长句的翻译方法。

1. The general public might be well-acquainted with the songs composed by Qiao Yu, but they might actually know very little about his two major hobbies-fishing and wine-drinking.

In his later years (Late in his life), Qiao Yu has become enamored of fishing (developed a penchant / special fondness for fishing). He asserts: "Mostly speaking, a place with water and fish must necessarily be blessed with a nice setting, which in return keeps people in good mood. I believe that the optimum fishing places are not those commercial fishing centers/resorts which provide the fishermen with all the conveniences and where fish are kept hungry for ready capture, but those naturally-formed places in the wilderness which exert a special appeal." According to him, fishing can constitute an activity conducive to the cultivation of one's temperament and to one's health, at once physical and psychological. Qiao Yu claims: "Fishing can be divided into three stages. The first stage consists of mere fish-eating; the second a combination of fish-eating and the pleasure (enjoyment) of fishing; the third primarily the pleasure of fishing when, confronted with a pond of clear water, one puts aside all his troubling vexations and annoyances and enjoys the total relaxation both mentally and physically."

2. The first generation of museums are what might be called natural museums which, by means of fossils, specimens and other objects, introduced to people the evolutionary history of the Earth and various kinds of organisms. The second generation is those of industrial technologies which presented the fruits achieved by industrial civilization at different stages of industrialization. Despite the fact that those two generations of museums helped to disseminate / propagate / spread scientific knowledge, they nevertheless treated visitors merely as passive viewers.

The third generation of museums in the world is those replete with / full of wholly novel concepts / notions / ideas. In those museums, visitors are allowed to operate the exhibits with their own hands, to observe and to experience carefully. By getting closer to the advanced science and technologies in this way, people can probe into their secret mysteries.

The China Museum of Science and Technology is precisely one of such museums. It has incorporated some of the most fascinating features of those museums with international reputation. Having designed and created exhibits in mechanics, optics, electrical science, thermology, acoustics, and biology. Those exhibits demonstrate scientific principles and present the most advanced scientific and technological achievements.

3. In 1986, Vancouver, Canada, just marked its centennial anniversary, but the achievements made by the city in its urban development have already captured worldwide attention. To build up a city and model its economy on the basis of a harbor is the usual practice that port cities resort to for their existence and development. After a century's construction and development, Vancouver, which boasts of a naturally-formed ice-free harbor, has become an internationally celebrated port city, operating regular ocean liners with Asia, Oceania, Europe and Latin America. Its annual cargo-handling capacity reaches 80 million tons, with one third of the city's employed population engaged in trade and transportation business.

The glorious achievements of Vancouver is the crystallization (fruition) of the wisdom (intelligence) and the industry of the Vancouver people as a whole, including the contributions made by a diversity of ethnic minorities. Canada is a large country with a small population. Although its territory is bigger than that of China, it only has a population of less than 30 million people. Consequently, to attract and to accept foreign immigrants have become a national policy long observed by Canada. It can be safely asserted that, except for Indians, all Canadian citizens are foreign immigrants, differing only in the length of time they have settled in Canada. Vancouver, in particular, is one of the few most celebrated multi-ethnic cities in the world. At present, among the 1.8 million Vancouver residents, half of them are not native-born and one out of every four residents is from Asia. The 250,000 Chinese there have played a decisive role in facilitating the transformation of the Vancouver economy. Half of them have come to settle in Vancouver only over the past five years, making Vancouver the largest area outside Asia where the Chinese concentrate.

第六章
常见文体的翻译

文体，即指文章的类别、体裁或风格。从根本上来讲，文体可以理解为说话或写作的方式。按照传统的划分，文体一般分为两大类，即文学文体与实用文体（有些学者也将其分为文学文体和非文学文体）。而每一类又可分为不同的子类。如文学包含诗歌、小说、散文、戏剧，而实用文体包含广告文体、新闻文体、经贸文体、旅游文体、科技文体等。文章与文章之所以会有文体上的不同，是因为文章的写作目的不同，反映的社会生活不同，使用的语言也不相同。

功利性与审美性，是区分实用文体和文学文体最主要的尺度。实用文体与文学文体都会对社会产生影响，但影响的方式、程度都有所不同。实用文体对社会产生直接的效应，因为其根本特征就是实用性，其写作目的是现实的，其目标是明确的，其效果也因此是直接的。实用文体都具有明确的写作目的，如广告诱导人们购买产品或服务，合同是为了明确缔约方的权利和责任，科技论文是为了传播科技信息、进行学术交流等，新闻文体是为了及时传播资讯等。而文学文体不求通过文学写作解决现实生活中的具体问题，主要是为了抒写个人对社会的感受、认识，体现个人的个性、情趣等，即文学创作没有明显的实用目的和功利性，其所追求的是情感的愉悦和精神的享受。文学文体借助艺术化的语言塑造形象，反映社会生活，表达思想情感，倾向于虚构。非文学作品反映客观事实，注重信息传达，倾向于写实。这两大文体的分野主要是基于创作手法的不同，前者力求表现世界，而后者则力求再现世界。诚然，这种区分只是相对的，在这两者之间还存在着若干层次。如广告文体、新闻文体等的部分内容表现性就较强。但是，这种表现性不是主流，改变不了其再现世界的本质。实用文体面向的是真实的世界，注重信息的真实性。即便某些文体如广告有夸大其词的成分，但仍然侧重的是对产品或服务的介绍，不以误导消费为底线，否则会承担相关的法律责任。

翻译的原则与策略要和特定的文本相对应。实用文体是人们传播信息、进行交往的重要手段。随着社会的发展和科技的进步，实用文体的翻译规模已经远远超过文学翻译，成为当今翻译活动的主流。实用文体主要有信息功能，人际功能，认知功能，呼唤功能，元语言功能等。在这些功能当中，又以信息功能为主。因此，实用文体的翻译侧重于信息的传达。基于此，我们认为，表现型的文本应采用翻译上的表现手法，而再现型的文本应采取翻译上的再现手法。尽管如此，每一种文体又有其独特的功能和语言特征，因此遵循的原则和采取的策略也会不尽相同。接下来，我们将按照文学性依次递减的顺序，就较为常见的文学文体，广告文体，新闻文体，商务文体和科技文体的翻译分别进行探讨。

第六章 常见文体的翻译

第一节 文学文体的翻译

一、文学文体概说

文学文体，是以语言的艺术反映人生和社会的一种文学综合体，主要包含诗歌、小说、戏剧、散文四大类。诗歌作为语言艺术的最高表现形式，又可以与其他体裁相对分开（在英语中，小说、戏剧和散文一般统称为 prose，与韵文 verse 相对应）。文学作品以经过提炼的艺术语言为媒介，以意象、形象和意境表现作者的思想情感，以作者的人格与作品的风格陶冶读者的心灵与情操。文学文体虽然在内容和体裁上各不相同，但作为一种艺术性文体仍然具有若干共同特征：一是现实性，文学创作源于生活又高于生活，集中而典型地反映了形形色色的社会现实，人生的悲欢离合。文学的现实不仅指文学以现实为基础，还指以现实为内容；二是虚构性，除了以现实为基础之外，文学还是作者构建的虚幻世界。它借助虚构的时空让人物在其中活动、思想，是现实事物的变形或精神世界的延伸；三是艺术性，这种艺术性表现在多个层面，如语言的艺术，结构的安排，形象的塑造以及意境的营造，等等。文学以语言来塑造典型形象，并通过具体的形象或意象来反映作者的思想情感、精神世界和艺术追求。简言之，文学追求的是艺术的真实性。

一般认为文学具有三大基本功用，即认识功用、教育功用和审美功用。文学的认识功能是指文学具有帮助人获得自然、社会和人生等方面的知识的作用，加深对社会、世界的认知与理解。文学的教育功能是指文学作品具有影响人的思想情感、是非判断、伦理道德等的功能。《诗经》上所说的"诗可以兴，可以观，可以群，可以怨""迩之事父，远之事君，多识于鸟兽草木之名"主要是从认识和教化两个层面对文学作品的功用进行概括的。其实，文学最根本的功能是审美功能。文学的审美功能是指文学具有沟通文学活动中主体与客体的美感和情感需求，使人获得精神对现实的超越、实现审美理想的功能，不像非文学文体那样具有明确的实用功用。要言之，审美是文学最基本的功能，即培养健全的人格，丰富人的情感世界，以及提高人的思想境界。

翻译不仅是一种跨语言的交流行为，更是一种跨文化的传播过程和交流活动。异语文化之间的传播属于跨语言和文化的传播，必须通过翻译才能够实现。没有翻译就没有异语文化之间的交流、融合与发展。文学翻译作为文化交流沟通中外文化的一种重要方式，更是起到了不可估量的作用。季羡林（2007：10）曾这样说道："中华文化这一条河之所以没有间断过，是因为有两次注水，一次是从印度来的水，一次是从西方来的水。

中华文化之所以能长葆青春,万应灵药就是翻译。翻译之为用大矣哉!"

二、文学文体的语言特征

文学文体与其他类型的文本在语言层面的差异,主要体现在文学性上。不可否认,任何类型的文本都具有文学性,但就文学作品而言,其文学性占据主导地位。这主要是由文学语言的符号属性决定的。文学符号学把符号分为两大类,一类是所指优势符号,大部分科学的、理性的日常符号都属于所指优势符号,这种文类注重的是文本的信息性,如法律文书、学术论文、科普文章等,它们以达意为旨归,属于所指优势符号,这种符号属于规约性符号。另一类属于能指优势符号,如文学、艺术作品等,其强调的是语言符号的可感性和自指性。这并不是说,其他文体不具备文学性,如广告、新闻等都具有文学的特质,但是这种文学特征不占主流,而是为各自的文体功能服务的。文学作品借助各种诗学手段,延长了人们的认知过程。文学语言在本质上是反常规的。常规语言只能作为一种背景,用来衬托文学语言的艺术化扭曲,而这种扭曲的语言就在这个背景上被前推出来。换言之,文学语言在传达一般信息之外,还要传达审美信息。具体表现在以下几个方面。

音乐性 文学语言的音乐性主要是指文学语言语音手段所形成的节奏与韵律。文学语言反映社会生活,创造艺术形象,表达思想感情,不只具有形象上的意义,也有音乐性上的意义。文学的节奏和韵律相互作用,相互影响,这就是文学语言音乐性特征的体现。文学语言的音乐美,主要由两个审美层面构成:首先是文学语言本身的音乐审美追求,这里主要指充分利用文学语言语音手段所产生的各种音乐美,如节奏的整体美,旋律的抑扬美等,从而使文学作品产生独特的音乐氛围。其次是文学语言本事的音乐审美特性与文学语言形象性、情意性的音乐审美特性的完美结合,形成对文学语言音乐性的高层次的审美追求。美国散文家 E.M. White 在《风格指南》(The Elements of Style)中曾以英国作家托马斯·佩恩的一句名言 These are the times that try men's souls,以说明文字节奏的重要性。这句话之所以被广为传诵,经久不衰,除了其本身的寓意之外,还与句子本身的节奏、结构以及轻重音有关。这种音乐性也经常用在演讲里面,以营造强烈的感染力,如肯尼迪就职演讲中的一句名言 Ask not what your country can do for you-ask what can do for your country。该句前后对称,而且 ask not 的倒装形成了两个重音,读起来铿锵有力。"凡文学作品,不论是小说、散文或诗歌,写在纸上是文字,读出来就是声音。"(刘士聪,2019:20)这种声音就是文学语言的音乐性。

丰富性 文学语言的丰富性体现在多个层次上。从文学语言的运用来看,它既包含常规语言，又包含变异语言；从文学语言的来源来看，它既有来自古语的成分，又有来自现代汉语的成分，既有方言成分，又有外来语成分。这些都是语言修辞构成的基本材料。其次，文学句式、句型的丰富多彩也是文学语言丰富性的具体表现。诸如长句和短句、整句和散句，书面语句式和口语句式，常式句和变式句等综合运用，既要服从表达主题刻画形象的需要，又要适应不同文体的风格特点。再次，文学语言的丰富性还表现在多种修辞格上，如比喻、拟人、夸张、对象、排比、反复等。由此构成了一个语言丰富的文学世界。下面几个例句分别使用了不同的文学手段，由此可管窥文学语言的丰富性。

例1　But the Vichy men are a loathsome form of life—crawling, sycophantic, pretentious, lying, self-righteous, anti-Semitic, reactionary, feebly militaristic and altogether base and unworthy of French culture.

例2　I'm a very humble person... I am well aware that I am the humblest person going... My mother is likewise a very humble person. We live in a humble abode.

例3　I hear her hair has turned quite gold from grief.

例4　When the evening is spread out against the sky like a patient etherized upon table...

例5　You should get married. A misanthrope I can understand—a womanthrope, never.

例6　A poor relation—is the most irrelevant thing in nature, —a piece of impertinent correspondency, —an odious approximation, —a haunting conscience, —a preposterous shadow, lengthening in the noon-tide of our prosperity, —an unwelcome remembrance, —a perpetually recurring mortification, —a drain on your purse...

个性化　前面所谓的音乐性、丰富性，属于文学语言的共性，而个性化的话语则属于作者本人。但凡有一定成就的作家都会以独特的方式表现其所营造的文学世界，因此形成了自己个性化的话语方式。散文翻译家高健（1990：20）曾在《浅谈风格的可译性及其他——翻译英美散文的一点体会》一文中对不同作家的风格进行了界说：

培根的简古，布朗的委婉，密尔顿的雄浑，戴登的俊逸，笛福的矫健，斯威夫特的犀利，艾狄生的温文，蒲柏的警策，约翰逊的典重，兰姆的天真，海士列特的晓畅，欧文的华美，霍桑的沉丽，爱默生的恣肆……

这里我们分别选取培根的《论财富》（*Of Riches*）和爱默生的《论超灵》（*The Over-Soul*）中的一段文字来感受一下前者的简古和后者的恣肆。

例7　Riches gotten by service, though it be of the best rise, yet when they are gotten by flattery, feeding humors, and other servile conditions, they may be placed amongst the worst. (*Of Riches*)

例8　If we consider what happens in conversation, in reveries, in remorse, in times of passion, in surprises, in the instructions of dreams, wherein often we see ourselves in masquerade-the droll disguises only magnifying and enhancing a real element, and forcing it on our distinct notice-we shall catch many hints that will broaden and lighten into knowledge of the secret of nature. (*The Over-Soul*)

诚然，文学的语言特征还不限于这些，但上述这些特点基本能涵盖文学语言的基本特征。而且，这些特征并不是孤立的，而是彼此融合的。要言之，文学的语言是一种艺术性的语言，借助艺术性语言来表现一种意境和氛围，进而陶冶人的情操，提升人的精神世界。

三、文学文体翻译的原则与策略

任何文体的翻译，都涉及两个过程，即理解与表达。如何表达涉及翻译的策略或方法问题。但是由于文学文体的特殊性，其翻译原则与策略不同于其他文体翻译。文学翻译的原则与策略，可以说是仁者见仁，很难有较为统一的看法。但毋庸置疑的是，文学的翻译不仅要考虑到英汉两种语言在遣词造句之间的差异，还要体现文学翻译的审美境界。"文学只有保持和再现原文的这种意境和氛围，才能使译文具有和原文类似的审美韵味。"（刘士聪，2019：22）。为论述方便，这里我们以陈大亮教授提出的文学翻译的三重境界为分析框架，来探讨文学文体的翻译。陈教授在《文学翻译的境界：译意·译味·译境》一书中把文学作品划分为意义、意味与意境三个层次，以对应文学翻译的译意、译味和译境三个境界。"译意主要涉及概念、命题等信息文本的翻译，具有抽象性、普遍性、表意性等特征；译味主要涉及意象、节奏、修辞等情感文本的翻译，具有具体性、特殊性、表情性等特征；译境主要涉及象外之象、味外之旨、韵外之致等虚性氛围的翻译，具有空灵性、淡远性、整体性。"（陈大亮，2019：126）这三重境界并非截然分开，而是一个有机的连续体。"从境界的高低而言，译意最低、译境最高、译味居中；从文学性的强弱而论，译意文学性最弱，译味较强，译境最强；从可译性的大小而言，译境最小，译味较大，译意最大。"（同上：114-115）下面就以文学翻译的三重境界分析文学翻译的具体操作过程。

（一）译意

所谓译意，是指"把字句的意念上的意义，用不同种的语言表示出来。"（同上：116）译意又分为两种情况，一是按照字面意义即指称意义进行翻译，二是根据译入语的语言规范进行重写，使译文尽量符合译入语的表达习惯，从而读起来仿佛是用译入语直接写出来的文本。如：

例 9　I cannot call riches better than the baggage of virtue.

译文 1：对于财富我叫不出更好的名字来，只能把它叫作德行的行李。

译文 2：我认为财富不过是德行的包袱。

例 10　The Bench was nothing to me but an insensible blunder.

译文 1：我看这些法官只是些不动感情的错误的制造者。

译文 2：我看这些法官无非是不动感情的人，只会把事弄错。

例 11　He is not an originator, but merely a calculator.

译文 1：他不是一个创始者，只是一个计算者。

译文 2：他没有创见，只会计算而已。

例 12　Those privileged to be present at a family festival of the Forsytes have seen that charming and instructive sight-an upper-middle-class family in full plumage.

译文 1：那些有幸出席福尔赛家庭节日的人们已经看到了那迷人而有教育意义的景象——一个全身盛装的上层中产阶级家庭。

译文 2：碰到福尔赛家有喜庆的事情，那些有资格去参加的人都曾看见那派中上层人家的兴盛气象，不但看了开心，也增长见识。

例 13　It is a curious fact, of which I can think of no satisfactory explanation, that enthusiasm for country life and love of natural scenery are strongest and most widely diffused precisely in those European countries which have the worst climate and where the search for the picturesque involves the greatest discomfort.

译文 1：这是一个奇怪的事实，我想不出任何令人满意的解释，对乡村生活的热情和对自然风光的热爱，在那些气候最恶劣，寻找风景最令人不适的欧洲国家，是最强烈和最广泛传播的。

译文 2：欧洲有些国家天气极为糟糕，那里的人们要辛苦一番才能找到景色如画之地。奇怪的是，他们最喜欢过那里的乡村生活，也最爱欣赏自然美景，这个情形极为普遍。此种实情令人费解。

以上例句的译文 1 均按照字面意义或句式结构进行翻译，译文 2 则不受原文拘束采取了较为大胆的改写。相比之下，译文 2 更符合中文读者的阅读习惯。不过，有时为了丰富汉语的表达方式而按照原文结构直译也是可以的。如：

例 14　Hearing that they had won the match, the children rejoiced.

听到他们比赛胜利的消息，孩子们欢腾起来。

例 15　He was one of the greatest writers in modern times.

他是近代最伟大的作家之一。

由于汉语没有现在分词，只能把主语移到句首。按照汉语传统语法，例 6 应该译为："孩子们听到比赛胜利的消息，全都沸腾起来了。"但是译文 1 按照原文结构译出，将主语"孩子们"置后，丰富了汉语的表达方式。"之一"结构，也是从欧洲语言尤其是英译引进而来的。按照传统的中文习惯，上面的英文可以直接翻译为"他是近代一位伟大的作家。"而原文语意并没有受到任何影响。这涉及文学语言欧化的问题。关于这个问题，我们在下面的"欧化的语言"小节中再讲。

至于文化负载词的翻译，两种方法均可使用。可以按指称意义翻译，如：crocodile's tears（鳄鱼的眼泪），stick and carrot（大棒与胡萝卜），sour grapes（酸葡萄），the heel of Achilles（阿喀琉斯的脚踵），armed to the teeth（武装到了牙齿），等等。也可按照内涵义翻译，如：carry the can（代人受过），by the seat of one's pants（根据经验或直觉做事），smell a rat（起疑心），cut to the chase（做正经事），cut someone some slack（放某人一马），等等。有些时候似乎两种策略均适用，如 crocodile's tears 既可以翻译为"鳄鱼的眼泪"，又可以翻译为"假慈悲"，stick and carrot 既可译为"胡萝卜加大棒政策"，又可译为"软硬兼施"。采取哪种策略，主要取决于表现的需要以及读者的接受程度。

文学作品虽然属于能指优势符号，但是所指优势符号同样大量存在，这些所指符号大多表达的是语义信息，尤其是散文、小说、戏剧记叙与叙事成分。对于这些所指优势符号，采取不受原文拘束的译意是必要的。文化负载词的翻译另当别论。当然，为了丰富汉语的表达方式而采取的直译也是可以的。总之，"译意是文学翻译的基础，没有译意作为依托，一切翻译都是不可能的。"（陈大亮，2019：137）

（二）译味

"译味是把句子所有的各种情感上的意味，用不同的语言文字表示出来。译味注重的是意象、情感或想象，侧重于具体的特殊的'象'。"（同上 2019：116）根据陈教授的观点，译味包含四个层面，即：音乐效果，情真意切，文采优美，风格相似。这里我们不单独谈文采问题，但在分析其他三个方面时会涉及到。

音乐效果　"文学作品里语言的声响与节奏，特别是语言的节奏感，要在翻译里体现出来，这是保持和再现文学作品语言审美价值的一个不可忽视的方面。"（刘士聪，2019：21）这里所谓的声响与节奏，其实就是文学语言的音乐效果。如下面几个句子的翻译。

例 16　Tiny sounds from the city drift through the room. A milk bottle clinks on a stone. An awning is cranked in a shop on Marktgasse. A vegetable cart moves slowly through a street.

A man and woman talk in hushed tones in an apartment nearby.

细碎的市里隐隐地进屋里来：是牛奶瓶放到石板上的铿锵声，是马可巷里一家店铺撑起遮阳篷时的嘎嘎声；是运菜车缓缓地碾轧作响，是一男一女在附近的公寓里小声说话。（童元芳，2015：125）

英文原文是独立的五句话。但从逻辑上来看，首句为统领句，后四句呈现为平行句式，结构对称。译文将后四句处理为以"是"开头的排比、对称结构，同时把原文中的拟声词全部译为拟声词，以保留回荡在空气中的各种声响。

例 17 The waiting-room appears to me like an aquarium and the arriving and departing travelers swim to and fro at all levels between the floor and the ceiling. This is very disconcerting and induces in me a kind of soporific reverie in which past and future combine and inextricably overlap, so that it is impossible for me to tell what I am looking back upon with nostalgic regret and what I am looking forward to with anticipatory delight. It is as though I am lying at the bottom of a river swayed by contradictory currents. The travelers-fish keep moving this way and that in endless shoals above my head.

候车室看来是个大水族箱，来来往往的游客在地板与屋顶之间各处穿梭往返，情况相当混乱，只引得我昏昏沉沉，一时里但觉过去与未来交融相叠，难分难解，所以无法说出自己究竟在缅怀什么而满腔惆怅，展望什么而衷心喜悦。我好似躺在河床的底部，受到互相对冲的水流摆弄，而旅客鱼群继续不断在我的头顶处无止无休地进进出出。（金圣华，2011：96）

原文选自《黑娃的故事》（*The Story of Noire*），共有 4 句构成，其中前 2 句为长句，一连用了 8 个 and，是为了表现"我"等待的焦灼与期盼。为了表现了这种心情，译文采取了"来来往往""昏昏沉沉""穿梭往返"，以营造连绵不绝的感受。同时，对于第二句的排比句，译文也采取了对仗较为工整的句式，以还原原文的节奏感。

有时候，原文的音乐性并不明显，但是经过译者的创造性翻译，同样使译文悦耳动听。如：

例 18 There aren't more than two hundred people in Loma. The Methodist church has the highest place on the hill; its spire is visible for miles. Two groceries, a hardware store, an ancient Masonic Hall and the Buffalo Bar comprise the public buildings. (*Johnny Bear*)

洛曼镇上顶多只有二百人。卫理公会教堂坐落在小山顶上，从好几英里外就能望见教堂的塔尖。两家杂货铺、一爿五金店、一座古老的共济会大厅和那个布法罗酒馆便构成了全镇的公共建筑。（曹明伦，2019：5）

这段文字节选自美国作家 John Steinbeck 的 *Johnny Bear*，译文由翻译名家曹明伦提供。这段文字看似简单，但若要译出文采却并非易事，尤其是数量词的翻译。原文中的 two, a, an, the 并未译成"两个，一个，一个，那个"，而是采取了变换手法，分别将其译为"两家、一爿、一座和那个"，措辞不仅富于变化，而且呈现为"平平仄仄"的韵律，读来朗朗上口。

情真意切 所谓情真意切，其实指的就是文本的情感意义。即"依附在字词句上边的情感寄托、感情色彩、情趣意味以及态度语气等审美要素。"（陈大亮，2019：247）情感意义是文学文体的重要特色。无论是体现在字里行间，还是蕴含在历史文化意象之中。情感意义属于译味的重要组成部分，译者应尽可能减少意味的损失或变形。如：

例 19 With only 3% of Americans in agriculture today, brain has supplanted brawn. Yet cultural preferences, like bad habits, are easier to make than break. But history warns repeatedly of the tragic cost of dismissing too casually the gifts of the so-called weaker sex.

今天在美国，脑力已经取代体力，只有3%的美国人在从事农业。但文化上的习俗正如陋规，形成容易冲破难。面对所谓"阴柔"性别，历史再三告诫我们，若对她们的禀赋过于轻率地否认，其代价将会何等惨重。（乔萍等：2010：346）

原文标题为《为育庸才损英才》（*Genius Sacrificed for Failure*），作者为福建省外国专家。该散文主要指出了一个问题：尽管文化不同，但是重男轻女的现象是普遍存在的。这段文字尤其是最后的长句明确地表明了作者对这种现象极为反感、痛心的态度。译文借助"轻率地否认""何等惨重"等语气沉重的修饰词，很好地将原作者对重男轻女的语气和态度表现出来。

例 20 Everything is the same, but you are not here, and I still am. In separation the one who goes away suffers less than the one who stays behind.

此间百凡如故，我仍留而君已去耳。行行生别离，去者不如留者神伤之甚也。

这是拜伦写给情妇的一封书信中的一段。译文由钱钟书提供。钱钟书采取了浅近的文言来翻译，契合了拜伦作为诗人的身份。译文情真意切，表达了留者的神伤之甚，而且文采斐然，符合诗人的身份品味。

例 21 How many loved your moments of glad grace,

And loved your beauty with love false or true,

But one man loved the pilgrim soul in you

And loved the sorrows of your changing face;

多少人爱你青春欢畅的时辰，

爱慕你的美丽，假意或真心，

只有一个人爱你那朝圣者的灵魂，

爱你衰老了的脸上痛苦的皱纹。（袁可嘉译）

这是叶芝的名诗 When you are old（《当你老了》）中的一段文字，译者是九叶派诗人之一的袁可嘉。原文表达了诗人对爱恋之人的真挚情意。译者在文字的雕刻上着实下了一番功夫，如"青春欢畅""朝圣者的灵魂""痛苦的皱纹"，从而生动地表现了原诗"与子偕老"的强烈情感。

风格意义 风格是译味的构成要素之一。这种风格可以是人物语言的风格，可以是场景描写的风格，甚至可以是整篇文章或作品表现出来的风格。客观来讲，风格很难翻译。但这并不是说，风格不可译。只要能做到情词相称，不失原文意旨，风格的翻译还是具有可操作性的。

例22　Well, well; what's done cannot be undone! I'm sure I don't know why children o'my bringing up forth should all be bigger simpletons than other people's-not to know better to blab such a thing as that, when he couldn't find it out till too late!

得得；已经泼出去的水还有什么法儿收回？俺不明白，怎么俺养的女儿，比别人的都傻——连这样的事该不该说都不知道！你要是不说，他自己会知道吗？等他发现，那就生米做成熟饭了。（张谷若，1984：272）

原文选择《德伯家的苔丝》，译文由张谷若翻译。苔丝的母亲听说女儿婚变之后的反应。张谷若采取了方言土语，以对应苔丝母亲的乡下人身份以及其无奈的心情。只不过个别译文稍显过分，如"生米做成熟饭了"。

例23　朴公摆了摆手止住雷委员道，"他倒真是做过了一番事业的。不过你老师发迹得早，少年得志，自然有他许多骄纵的地方，不合时宜。这个不能怨天尤人……"（《梁父吟》）（白先勇，2017：107-108）

初稿：In fact, he had a magnificent career, all right. But your teacher made his mark early; he distinguished himself at such a young age, naturally he did things with a somewhat cocky air that simply didn't suit the times. You can't blame Heaven or man…

定稿："In fact, he had a magnificent career. The thing is, your teacher made his mark early—as a result, he was sometimes guilty of overweening pride, which simply wasn't the way to get along. For this you can't lay the blame on Heaven or man…（Pai Hsien-yung, 1982: 95）

朴公是一位退役的儒将，其学养和身份决定了其语言的文雅与含蓄，如"一番事业""发迹得早""骄纵""怨天尤人"等。译者白先勇和叶佩霞在初稿中，竭力在译文中寻求符合人物身份的表达方式，如 magnificent career，made his mark early。但有些地方的处理不甚妥当，如"骄纵"译为 cocky 失之于粗俗。编辑高克毅将其改为 guilty of overweening pride 这一稍微复杂但却文雅的说法。Guilty of 可以表示"有……过失"之意，属于较为正式的表达。Overweening 在英文中有"自负"之意，较 cocky 显得含蓄而文雅，也更符合人物的身份。此外，高克毅还将"怨天尤人"从原译 blame Heaven or man 改为 lay blame on Heaven or on man，也是出于同样的考虑。修改之后的译文整体上保持了人物语言风格的一致性。

有时，原文各种风味兼具，如将这些味道悉数译出，自然是难上加难。但也有许多成功的例子。如下面这段文字的翻译。

例 24　On one of those sober and rather melancholy days in the latter part of the autumn, when the shadows of morning and evening almost mingle together, and throw a gloom over the decline of the year, I passed several hours in rambling about Westminster Abbey. There was something congenial to the season in the mournful magnificence of the old pile; and as I passed its threshold, it seemed like stepping back into the regions of antiquity, and losing myself among the shades of former ages.

时方晚秋，气象肃穆，略带忧郁，早晨的阴影和黄昏的阴影，几乎连接在一起，不可分别。岁云将暮，终日昏暗，我就在这么一天，到西敏大寺散步了几个钟头。古寺巍巍，森森然似有鬼气，和阴沉沉的季候正好调和；我跨进大门，觉得自己好像已经置身远古世界，忘形于昔日的憧憧鬼影之中了。（夏济安，2000：90-91）

原文选自华盛顿·欧文的散文《西敏大寺》（Westminster Abbey），描写了审美移情的心境融合。译文较好地体现了此种情景交融的艺术效果。而且，译文不仅文采斐然，富于节奏感，而且"气象肃穆""古寺巍巍""置身远古""憧憧鬼影"还营造出一种时空交织的意境氛围。

（三）译境

译味与译境有交叉重叠的部分，但是译境具备更深一层次的意义，体现为一种人生感、历史感和宇宙感等。陈大亮（2019：275）认为，"译境表现为三个层面，即：言外之意，象外之意，以及形而上的意义。"

言外之意　这里的言外之意，指的是含蓄意义，"它表达的是不在场的意义。是由读者的想象而获得的言外之意。"（同上：276）具体到翻译，则是译者经由想象得到的言外之意。如：

例 25　Le grondement du fleuve monte derriere la maison.

From behind the house rises the murmuring of the river.

江声浩荡，自屋后上升。（傅雷译）

这是罗曼·罗兰《约翰·克里斯多夫》开篇的第一句，原文为法语。中文译文出自著名翻译家傅雷。法语单词 grondement 意指"沉闷的声音"，英译本的 murmuring 似乎是正确的译法。然而，傅雷的"江声浩荡"却最为大家称道。其实，这四个字是对小说主题的概括，为全书奠定了基调。也体现了约翰·克里斯朵夫生命不息、奔腾不止的"浩荡"人生。此外，许渊冲将《红与黑》中的最后一句 Elle mourut 译为"魂归离恨天"而不是"她死了"，也是基于人物的命运而做出的适当选择，表达了不在场的"言外之意"。

象外之意 文学中的象可以指隐喻、象征，文化意象或其他。这些象外之意往往蕴含着作品的深层寓意。意境的生成关键在于从象内到象外的转化。具体到文学翻译，译文是否有意境，关键在于译者要创造一种景外之景或象外之象，让读者感悟到景外之意或象外之意。如：

例 26 Let life be beautiful like summer flowers and death like autumn leaves.

生如夏花之绚烂，死如秋叶之静美。（郑振铎译）

原文源自印度诗人泰戈尔的《飞鸟集》第 82 首。这首哲理小诗借助"夏花"和"秋叶"表现了作者对生死的看法，即生命要像夏花那样去盛开，即使是面临死亡，也要淡然的看待，就像秋叶般静美地接受所有的结局。郑振铎的译文不仅对称，节奏和谐，而且尤为重要的是，借助"绚烂，静美"两个象外之意，将人生的两极表现出来，较为完美地诠释了原文蕴含的人生哲理。

例 27　　　　　　　　《枫桥夜泊》

月落乌啼霜满天，江枫渔火对愁眠。

姑苏城外寒山寺，夜半钟声到客船。

译文 1

The moon goes down and crows caw in the frosty sky,

Dimly-lit fishing boats' neath maples sadly lie.

Beyond the Suzhou walls the Temple of Cold

Rings bells which reach my boat, breaking the midnight still.

译文 2：

At moonset cry the crows, streaking the frosty sky,

Dimly lit fishing boats neath maples sadly lie

Beyond the city wall, from Temple of Cold Hill

Bells break the ship-borne roamer's dream and midnight still.（转自童元芳，2015：16-19）

《枫桥夜泊》是传颂千古的名诗。上面这两个译文均出自许渊冲。译文 2 是在译文 1 的基础上修改而成。最大的修改体现在第一句和第二句上。这里我们重点分析最后一句，因其最能体现意境的凸显。译文 2 最明显的改动有：删掉代词 my，将客船改为 ship-borne roamer，以保留原诗的模糊性；把 reach 去掉，使 break 同时修饰 roamer's dream 和 midnight still。由此，修改后的译文更能凸显原诗蕴含的羁旅之思以及身处乱世尚无归宿的漂泊感。

形而上的意义　"意境除了有意象的一般规定性（情景交融）之外，还有自己的特殊的规定性，即象外之象所蕴含的人生感、历史感、宇宙感的意蕴。"（陈大亮，2019：254）这种人生感、历史感和宇宙感便是文学中的形而上意，也是译者竭力捕捉进而在译文中再现的主要内容。如：

例 28　To see a world in a grain of sand / And a heaven in a wild flower / old infinity in the palm of your hand / And eternity in an hour.

一花一世界，一沙一天国，君掌盛无边，刹那含永劫。（宗白华译）

原文是英国诗人威廉·布莱克（William Blake）《天真的预言》（*Auguries of Innocence*）的第一小节，充满哲理。这首在欧美不为人知的小诗，却能在中国广为流传，翻译功不可没，尤其是宗白华的译文最受欢迎。宗白华不受四行诗的语法结构所缚，而以中国诗歌的传统手法——意象并置再现原作。宗的译文不仅典雅，还赋予其禅意，体现了原文所蕴含的玄学色彩以及宇宙观。

例 29　"To be, or not to be, that is the question."

译文 1：生存还是毁灭，这是一个值得考虑的问题。（朱生豪译）

译文 2：死后是存在，还是不存在——这是问题。（梁实秋）

译文 3：活着好，还是死了好，这是个难题啊！（方平）

译文 4：死还是不死，这是个问题。（许渊冲）

译文 5："活人呢，还是不活？这就是问题哪！"（王宏印）

原文是莎剧《哈姆雷特》中哈姆雷特的一句独白。该句独白的翻译至今已有十余种不同的版本。译者王宏印认为原文包含三层含义：一是宇宙观层次，指人乃至万物的终极存在或不存在；二是个人形体存在层次，指具体的个人的存在方式，即生存还是毁灭的生死问题；三是人的存在的精神层次，指个人是否能够按照自己的存在方式生活下去，能否保持自我与尊严或心灵是否高贵的问题（王宏印，2015：267）。前人对此句的翻译只译出了三个层次中的一个或两个。王宏印译文中使用了动词"活人"，涵盖"活得像一个人""活得要挺直腰板""活得要活到你的自然的寿命",基本涵盖了上述三个层次的含义。

四、文学语言的欧化现象

20世纪初,出于对中国文化发展的反思,以鲁迅为代表的一些中国文人希望直译欧文句法以改造中文,进而改造国人的思维方式。鲁迅(2006:113)认为:"欧化文法渗透中国白话的一大原因,并非因为好奇,乃是为了必要。"郑振铎在1921年发表的《语体文欧化之我观》一文中,也赞成适度的欧化并认为:"中国的旧文体太陈旧而且成了滥调了。有许多很好的意思与情绪都为旧文体的成式所拘,不能尽量的精微的达出。"可见,欧化的动因与救亡图存有着莫大的关联。五四以来,英语对汉语的影响越来越大,众多欧化词汇、句法出现在文学译作之中。这些词汇和句法丰富了汉语的表达方式,同时使汉语的表达更加精密,但在一定程度上危害了汉语的规范性和纯洁性。在现代汉语日趋成熟的今天,我们应该竭力避免过度的欧化。

学界对欧化的定义不尽相同,但基本所指大体相同。这里我们采取较为中性的一种定义:中国人学习直接或间接传来的欧洲语言,在汉语中除旧布新,并留下痕迹,而由此形成的语言形式(主要是书面语)即为欧化汉语(刁晏斌,2019:28)。中国著名语言学家王力(2019)将欧化归为以下几类:"复音词的创造,主语和系词的增加,句子的延长;可能式、被动式、记号的欧化;联结成分的欧化;新替代法和新称数法。"诚然,如再细分的话,可能还不止这些。这里我们无意于面面俱到,只撷取主要的欧化现象来分析其对文学翻译的影响。具体包括:主语(包括代词)的增加;描述句改为判断句;句子的延长;"的"字的泛滥;联结词的增加。

(一)描述句改为判断句

汉语欧化的一个表现,就是采用判断句的形式替换原文的描述句。简单来讲,即把To be+adj结构译为"是……的"。汉语中"是什么的"是一种判断句:你来是对的;他不去是不应该的;这个人是难缠的,等等。如:

例30 We come nearest to the great when we are great in humility.

当我们大为谦卑的时候,便是我们最近于伟大的时候。

郑振铎(1898—1958)的译本《飞鸟集》是在1922年出版发行的,时值新文化和新文学运动高潮,有关文言翻译和白话翻译的论战正酣。郑振铎坚定地站在后者一边,并赞成译文的适度欧化。如译文"当我们是大为谦卑的时候"就是将描写句改为判断句。郑振铎的这种译法是时代使然,带有试验性质。而这种句式结构充斥着现代翻译之中。如:

例 31　The explanation is pretty thin.

原译：这个解释是相当不充实的。

改译：这个解释相当薄弱（牵强）。

例 32　His refusal is not final.

原译：他的拒绝不是不可改变的。

改译：他的拒绝并非不可改变。

例 33　Now his health is poor, his mind vacant, his heart sorrowful, and his old age short of comforts.

原译：如今他的健康是糟糕的，他的头脑是空虚的，他的心灵是悲哀的。

改译：如今他的健康失去了，他的头脑虚空了，他的心里充满了悲哀。

这些译文均将原文译为了"是什么的"结构，不仅显得啰嗦，而且缺乏力量。改后的译文更自然、流畅一些，也更富于文采。

（二）人称代词的增加

在英文中，代词是构成语篇衔接与连贯的重要手段。而在汉语中，代词使用相对较少。然而，由于受到欧化的影响，如今的很多译文出现了大量的代词，致使译文冗长、啰嗦。如：

例 34　My maternal grandmother, after having nine children who survived, one who died in infancy, and many miscarriages, as soon as she became a widow, devoted herself to woman's higher education. She was one of the founders of Girton College, and worked hard at opening the medical profession to women. She used to relate how she met in Italy an elderly gentleman who was looking very sad. She inquired the cause of his melancholy and he said that he had just parted from his two grandchildren. (*How to Grow Old* by Bertrand Russell)

她一守寡，便投身于妇女的高等教育事业了。她是格顿学院的创始人之一，她为了让医学专业向妇女开放而历尽了辛劳。她常常说自己怎样在意大利遇见过一位神情十分悲伤的老绅士。她问起他为什么闷闷不乐，他说他刚刚和他的两个孙女分手。（《谈人之将老》）

译文将原文中的人称代词 she 和 he 悉数保留，显得有些啰嗦。其实，这里可以适当地删减几处，而丝毫不影响逻辑关系，语义也更为清晰。

改译：她一守寡，便投身于妇女的高等教育事业了。她是格顿学院的创始人之一，为了让医学专业向妇女开放而历尽了辛劳。她常常说自己怎样在意大利遇见过一位神情十分悲伤的老绅士。问起这位绅士为什么闷闷不乐时，对方回答说刚刚和两个孙女分手。

(三) 句子的延长

"西洋的句子就比中国的句子长。中国人如果像西洋人那样运用思想，自然得用长句子；翻译西洋的文章，更不知不觉地用了许多长句子。因此，句子的延长也是欧化文章的一种现象。"（王力，2019：377）必要的欧化长句可以使表述更为严谨，逻辑性更强。我们这里反对的是冗长、不忍卒读的长句。其表现之一就是长定语的前置。

例 35　On the morning of August 8, 1965, Robert Kincaid locked the door to his small two-room department on the third floor of a rambling house in Bellingham, Washington.

原译：一九六五年那八月八日早晨，罗伯特·金凯德锁上了他在华盛顿州贝灵汉一栋杂乱无章的房子里三层楼上的两居室公寓的门。

例 36　This is the cat that killed the rat that ate the cake that was put in the house that Jack built.

原译：这就是那只捕杀了偷吃放在杰克所建房间里的蛋糕的老鼠的猫。

这两个译文从逻辑上讲，词语排列没有问题，意思也清楚，只是限定语太长，削弱了中心语。改进的方法是在尊重原文基本结构的前提下，进行适当的拆分。

改译：罗伯特·金凯德锁上了他的两居室公寓的门，即告别了位于华盛顿州贝灵汉市一栋杂乱的三层小楼。

改译：就是这只猫，捕杀了偷吃放在杰克所建房屋里的蛋糕的老鼠。

这并非说传统汉语中没有长句，如"我却是蒸不烂煮不熟捶不扁炒不爆响当当一粒铜豌豆。""天打雷劈五鬼分尸的没良心的东西！"王力认为，"只有那些极度形容词，才放在首品的前面，使文气更生动些。"可见，长句并非西文的专利。下面的译文体现这一点。

例 37　But without Adolf Hitler, who was possessed of a demoniac personality, a granite will, uncanny instincts, a cold ruthlessness, a remarkable intellect, a soaring imagination and—until toward the end, when drunk with power and success, he overreached himself-an amazing capacity to size up people and situation, there almost certainly would never have been a Third Reich.

但要是没有那个盛行残暴、意志坚韧、心肠冷酷、直觉超人、才智出众且想象丰富的阿道夫·希特勒，没有那个在因被权力和成功冲昏头脑而招致失败之前对人和局势都具有惊人判断力的阿道夫·希特勒，那历史上几乎不可能有一个第三帝国。（曹明伦译）

(四)"的"字的增加

余光中（2020：238）在《论的的不休》一文中曾指出："无论在中国大陆或是台湾，

一位作家或学者若要使用目前的白话文来写作或是翻译，却又不明简洁之道，就很容易陷入'的的不休'。"根据余的看法，这种现象源自西文形容词与副词的滥用与混淆，以至积习难改。香港著名翻译家金圣华（2011：27）对此深有同感。她举了两个"的"字充斥的译文，并进行了改正。例证如下：

例 38　She was forced to face up to a few unwelcome truths about her family.

原译：她不得不正视有关她的家族的几个尴尬的事实。

改译：她不得不正视有关她家庭的几桩尴尬事。

例 39　There are plenty of restaurants for those who tire of shopping.

译文：有很多的餐馆可以成为厌烦购物的人的去处。

改译：厌烦购物的人有很多餐馆可去。

例 40　An old, mad, blind, despised, and dying king…

译文 1：一位衰老的、疯狂的、瞎眼的、被人蔑视的、垂死的君王。

译文 2：一位衰老、疯狂、瞎眼、遭人蔑视、垂死的君王。

译文 1 与译文 2 最大的区别在于后者省略掉了不必要的"的"字，有时译文去掉不必要的"的"字，译文不仅显得干净，而且更有力量。

诚然，也不是说"的"字不能使用，使用恰当的话还可以表现出一定的节奏感甚至诗意，如徐志摩的诗《偶然》中有这样的诗句："你我相逢在黑夜的海上，你有你的，我有我的，方向"，这里的"的"字虽然重复，却不能省略，因为它不仅体现了一种节奏感，还表现了诗人的一种无奈而又坚定的情绪。

（五）连接词的增加

现代汉语中很多连接词的使用，是受欧化的影响，如"和""在""当"字，"对于""关于""就说""作为""一……就"，等等。这些连接词一方面丰富了汉语的句法，同时使句意表达更为严谨。如：

例 41　To abolish as soon as possible Hong Kong's status as a port of first asylum.

译文 1：要尽快取消香港作为第一收容港的地位。

译文 2：要尽快取消香港第一收容所的地位。

这里的"作为"是从英语 as 翻译而来，属于连词欧化之一种，体现了严谨性。"香港作为第一收容港"强调的是，"香港"这个范畴大于"第一收容港"，"第一收容港"只是香港的一个方面而已，去掉"作为"则将香港与收容港等同起来。

但在一些译文中，有些连接词的使用未必恰当。这里以表示时间状语的 when 与 as soon as 的翻译为例。大多数中国的英语语言学习者看到 when、as soon as 这些表示时间状语的连接词时，第一反应就是"当……的时候""一……就……"。这种受英语语言影响所形成的思维方式，使得当代汉语在句法上不断出现时间状语从句的"欧化"现象。如：

例42 "I will give her a ring as soon as I get home."

原译："我一到家就给她打电话"。

改译："我到家就给她打电话。"

例43 As soon as its branch becomes tender and puts out its leaves, you know that summer is near.

原译：当树枝发嫩长叶的时候，你们就知道夏天近了。

改译：树枝发嫩长叶的时候，你们就知道夏天近了。

例44 When you are in doubt, don't hesitate to let me know.

译文：当你有疑问时，要立刻告诉我。

改译：如有疑问，可以随时告诉我。

例45 Noah was six hundred years old when the flood of waters came upon the earth.

原译：当洪水泛滥在地上的时候，挪亚整六百岁。

改译：洪水泛滥在地上的时候，挪亚整六百岁。

一般情况下，汉语的时间成分比较短，用"……时/的时候"这种形式来表达时间成分即可，这是传统汉语的表达习惯。但英语等印欧语言的时间状语从句往往比较长，当译者此种句式去翻译这些时间状语从句时，就会感到为难，因为读者要读到末尾才知道这是一个时间成分，这对读者理解整个句子都会有一定的影响。这时在时间成分的开头加上标记性的"当"字，就显得非常有必要。如叶芝的名诗 When you are old (《当你老了》)中的第一句英文的翻译。

例46 When you are old and grey and full of sleep, and nodding by the fire, take down this book, and slowly read, and dream of the soft look.

当你老了，头发花白，睡意沉沉，倦坐在炉边，取下这本书来，慢慢读着，追梦当年的眼神。

欧化是不同语言在文化交流过程中不可避免的现象。正如王力所说，"咱们对于欧化的语法，用不着赞成，也用不着反对。欧化是大势所趋，不是人力所能阻隔的；但是，西洋语法和中国语法相离太远的地方，也不是中国勉强迁就的。"（2019：363）曹明伦（2019：294）结合多年的翻译经验总结道："在现代汉语已近完善的今天，我们应该有足够的语言手段尽可能保存原文的形态（在神似的基础上追求最大限度的形似），或根据原文形态构建与之相似的译文形态（以原文语篇为模本构建译文语篇），从而做到形具而神圣，使译文尽可能神形兼备。"

结语

本节主要从译意、译味、译境三个层次解读了文学文体的翻译。这三个层次是由低到高且互相关联的。说到底，文学作品的翻译从根本上讲是一种情感移植。这种情感的移植，需要译者的灵感和顿悟，以及丰富的社会经历与人生阅历。如果译者的此种能力得不到充分的锻炼，译文必将生硬晦涩，没有美感可言。文学语言本身的模糊性、陌生化、多义性赋予了译者一定的创作自由。这种自由需要译者深厚的文化素养和语言功底才能把控好。要提高这两方面的能力，常读文学作品尤为重要。"宏观上，读书的过程是接受审美的熏陶和陶冶的过程；对于译者，通过读书学习语言，这是增强语言修养的主要途径，不论是以英语为母语的人，还是以汉语为母语的人，都是如此，不读书，谁也写不出好文章。"（刘士聪，2019）

课后练习

一、翻译下列句子。

1. The cold weather frosted up the track last night.

2. A gulf had opened between them over which they looked at each other with eyes that were on either side a declaration of the deception.

3. The beauty of our country is as hard to define as it is easy to enjoy.

4. That morning I met Mrs. Effingham, a woman as flat as a pancake.

5. He was thirty-six, his youth pad passed like a screaming eagle, leaving him old and disillusioned.

6. Harvy was among the guests at the wedding; and he sought Miss Nathalie out in a rare moment when she stood alone.

7. He didn't have a bath every day as he had done when he was well because Mum had to help him with it and it was really quite a business.

8. It happened in one of those picturesque Danish taverns that cater to tourists where English is spoken. I was with my father on a business-and-pleasure trip, and in our leisure hours we were having a wonderful time.

9. Today, being driven by the necessity of doing something for himself, he entered the drug store which occupied the principal corner, facing 14th street at Baltimore, and finding a girl

cashier in a small glass cage near the door, asked of her who was in charge of the soda fountain.

10. To find genius and happiness united is nearly a scandal. Ordinarily those to whom the gods give their largesse are envied, even hated, by their peers and contemporaries. Yehudi Menuhin is probably the most widely loved personality in the history of the performing arts. It was so after his triumphant debut in 1927; it is so today.

二、翻译下面一则短文。

Music

When music affects us to tears, seemingly causeless, we weep not, as Gravina supposes, from "excess of pleasure"; but through excess of an impatient, petulant sorrow that, as mere mortals, we are as yet in no condition to banquet upon those supernal ecstasies of which the music affords us merely a suggestive and indefinite glimpse.

三、翻译下面一段诗文。

Far from the heart of culture he was used:

Abandoned by his general and his lice,

Under a padded quilt he closed his eyes

And vanished, He will not be introduced

When this campaign is tidied into books:

No vital knowledge perished in his skull;

His jokes were stale; like wartime, he was dull;

His name is lost forever like his looks.

He neither knew nor chose the Good, but taught us,

And added meaning like a comma, when

He turned to dust in China that our daughters

Be fit to love the earth, and not again

Disgraced before the dogs; that, where are waters,

Mountains and houses, may be also men.

第二节 广告文体的翻译

一、广告文体概论

广告，即广泛的告知公众某种事物的宣传活动。广告的兴起、繁荣与市场经济密切相关。市场离不开广告的宣传，而广告宣传又可助推市场的能见度，从而更好地服务于人们大众。《中华人民共和国广告法》对广告的定义为：广告是指商品经营者或服务提供者承担费用，通过一定媒介和形式直接或间接地介绍自己所推销的商品或者所提供的服务的商业广告。陈培爱（2003：5）在《广告学原理》一书中把广告定义如下：广告是由广告主付出某种代价的信息，经过艺术加工，通过不同的媒介向大众传播，达到改变或强化人们观念和行为的目的。在英文中，较为流行的定义为：Advertising is paid non-personal communication from an identified sponsor using mass media to persuade or influence an audience.（William ells & John Burnet, 1999：13）（即广告是一种由某个特定出资人发起的，通过大众传媒进行的非个人化的有偿沟通方式，其目的是说服或影响某类受众。）

结合不同的广告定义，可以发现广告具备的五个基本要素，即公众性（non-personal），说服性（persuasive），有偿性（paid），广告信息（advertising information），以及特定的广告主（identified sponsor/advertiser）。要言之，广告是大众传播的一种形式，由赞助商或广告客户支付费用，其本质特征都是通过一定的媒介手段，向大众传播特定的信息，具有明确的劝导功能。

广告属于应用型文体，是以传达信息为主的呼唤型文本。按照不同的划分标准，广告的分类自然也会不尽相同。从广告覆盖地区来看，广告分为国际性广告、全国性广告、区域性广告；按照传播形式，广告可分为印刷广告、户外广告、电子广告、移动广告等。按照是否盈利，广告又可划分为商业广告和非商业广告。前者又称为狭义的广告，仅指市场学体系中的经济、商业广告。后者属于广义广告。广义上的广告不仅包括经济广告、文化广告、社会广告，举凡通知、声明、启事、招标、求职、招生、倡议等，都可以纳入广告之范畴。本书如不做说明，主要是从商业广告和非商业广告两个方面进行探讨。

尽管广告类型繁多，侧重点也不尽相同，但作为一种应用型文本，它们在很大程度上有着共同的功能。广告的主要功能主要体现在如下几个方面：一是与同类产品相区分（differentiate products from others，此功能侧重于商标）；二是信息的交流（communicate information）；三是吸引新的消费者（induce new customers）；四是赢得回头客（gain repeated customers）；五是促进销售（stimulate the distribution）；六是树立产品偏好和忠实性（build preference and loyalty）（夏政，2003：6）。

上面的论述虽然倾向于商业性广告，但从中仍可看出，真实而有效的信息传递是广告功能的主要任务，并进而影响人们的行为。而非商业性的功能则在于：告知、说服或提醒人们广告中的特定思想、原因或理念。（The general objective of noncommercial advertising is to inform, persuade, or remind people about the particular idea, cause, or philosophy being advertised.）（赵静，1997：243）

可见，无论是商业性还是非商业性广告，其本质在于通过传播不同种类的广告信息促成一定的影响力。广告文体虽然属于应用文体，但特别讲究词句优美、注重韵律和谐，因而兼具文学与非文学的特征。因此，为了使英文广告翻译更加有效、更加广泛的传播，有必要对广告语言的构成及其特点进行全面的了解。

二、广告语言的构成与特征

广告语言有广义和狭义之分。广义的广告语言是指广告中所使用的一切手段与方法，包括声音、图案、图像、色彩、人物，自然也包括文字语言。狭义的广告语言专指广告作品中的文字语言，具体包括商标词、广告标题、广告正文等。其中，广告标题和正文又统称为广告文案。这里我们只涉及广告的语言文字部分。

（一）商标词

商标（trademark），作为一种标识符号，是区别其他产品或企业的标志。而商标词是商标重要的组成部分，即可视觉分辨的文字。商标词是由个人或个别企业精心挑选或创造出来的用于区别其他企业商品的一种专有符号。商标与广告文案同样具有宣传作用。它作为一种标志符号，可以体现商品的品质和企业的形象，自然就成了一种广告手段。与广告文案相比，商标更具有经济性、灵活性、广泛性和持久性等特点。受众在选购商品或寻求服务时，多数人记住的往往是商标词。一个精心设计的商标词，可以在宣传产品或企业形象的同时，还能给人以丰富而美好的联想。如 Kleenex（洁净纸巾），其中 kleen 与 clean 谐音，ex(excellent) 又代表精美、完美之意。所以该商标词不但暗含了产品的性质，还使受众领略到其语言魅力。概括来说，商标词应具备的一般特点是：发音响亮，简短易记，措辞讲究，标新立异，国际性强，为读者所接受。（顾维勇，2005：66）商标词可以大致分为以下四种情况：专有名词，普通词汇，杜撰词汇以及缩略词等。

专有名词 为了防止产品被假冒等行为的出现，产品一般都具有专利权。商标注册权，其中专有名词颇受青睐。因此，在英语广告中专有名词的出现率比较高。这类商标词又可分为以下三种情况。（1）以人名姓氏为商标，如 Ford（福特），Honda（本田），McDonald's（麦当劳），Heinz（美国亨氏食品），Harley-Davidson（哈利·戴维森），Louis Vuitton（路斯威登）；（2）以地名为品牌名，如 Pizza Hut（必胜客），Amazon（亚马逊），Sandwich（三明治），Marlboro（万宝路），Santana（桑塔纳）；（3）以神话中的人物或神灵名称为品牌名，如 Nike（耐克），Apollo（太阳神），等等。

普通词汇 即日常生活中较为常见的语词，如 Dove（德芙），Jaguar（捷豹），Coca Cola（可乐），Cosmos（宇宙），Rejoice（飘柔），Paramount（派拉蒙电影公司），Subway（赛百味），Polo（三角马），Apple（苹果），等等。

杜撰词汇 该类商标词主要采用合成的方法，杜撰出新的词汇，也不乏字母的随意组合。这类词汇往往比较新颖，通过语言的变异，赋予品牌名一种变异美，迎合了人们追求时尚的口味。如 Lexus(凌志)，Rolex（劳力士手表），Timex（天美时），Kleenex（克里内可斯纸巾），Xvision（扫描仪），Ikea（宜家家具）等。

缩略词 顾名思义，即通过简单的字母（或数字）组合而成。虽然表面看来没有特定意义，但因其简洁醒目而能较好地维护商标的形象统一性。如：IBM（美国国际商用机器公司），KFC（肯德基），AOL（美国在线服务公司），BMW（宝马车），HP（惠普），XO（人头马），M&M（巧克力），H&M（瑞典服饰零售商），MAC（魅可）等。

此外，还有一些商标词是由两个单词合并而成的，如 Starbuck（星巴克），Polar bear（白熊脂），Burger King（汉堡王），New Balance（新百伦），Kinglion（金利来），Land Rover（路虎），等等。

（二）广告标题

标题由于其特殊的位置和功能，最能引起人们的注意。标题在整个文案中往往起到画龙点睛的作用。广告标题有四大职能：首先，它能迅速引起读者的注意，第二，能够抓住主要的目标对象，第三，能够吸引读者阅读广告正文；第四，说明其所宣传事物能给受众带来的好处。著名广告学大师大卫·奥格尔威总结多年的广告创作经验指出：平均来说，读标题的人数是读正文人数的五倍（赵静，1997：13）由此看出，广告标题在整个文案中的重要地位。它是对正文的概括，并通过艺术性的语言引导读者探知正文内容。概括来讲，广告标语及标题由于其特殊的位置及功能，非常注重语言的艺术性，而广告正文则侧重整体效果，其主要目的是传达广告文案的具体信息。但不论是广告标语、标题还是广告正文，都以凝练的语言突出尽可能多的新信息。正所谓"广告不言，言必中的；言简意赅，言近旨远。"（马永堂、华英，2005：276）这也是广告行文的基本要求。具体来讲，广告标题或标语的语言具有如下基本特征。

韵律　好的广告语要动听，读起来有韵律感，能激发读者的兴趣，进而增强受众的记忆。如下面这些广告标题：

例 1　Safety, security and simplicity (Mobile Phone)

例 2　Wonder where the yellow went (Pepsodent)

例 3　Talk global, pay local (Telecommunication)

例 4　My goodness! My Guinness! (Guinness Beer)

例 5　Workout without wearout (Sneakers)

对比　对比也是广告标题修辞之一种，通过词义的反差，突出某一理念或商品的特性或建议忠告的方式，这种方式往往能给读者留下深刻的印象。如：

例 6　Cancer is often curable. The fear of cancer is often fatal. (American Cancer Society ACS)

例 7　No business too small, no problem too big. (IBM)

例 8　The driver is safer when the road is dry; the road is safer when the driver is dry. (Traffic slogan)

例 9　A business in millions, a profit in pennies. (Retailer Ad)

例 10　All new Mitsubishi has more power and economy, less weight and noise. (Mitsubishi)

仿拟　所谓仿拟就是借用人们所熟知的谚语或典故，将其恰当地镶嵌在广告行文中的一种做法，这种策略能唤起受众的亲切感，起到一种意想不到的宣传效果。如：

例 11　We take no pride in prejudice. (*The Times*)

例 12　To Teach or Not to Teach—That is the Question? (Patient Education in Radiation Therapy)

例 13　The pros without the con (*Times Magazine*)

例 14　Just a reminder. This why save money. Easy as UCB (United Commercial Bank)

例 15　A Mars a day keeps you work, rest and play (Mars chocolate)

这种仿拟其实体现了一种互文性。广告语中的互文性除了巧妙的暗示所宣传事物的某些特征之外，更重要的是让读者去思考，去体会其中之妙处，无形之中会大大地增强广告语的魅力。

变异在英语广告创作中，撰写人往往将人们熟悉的词语故意拼错或杜撰词汇以达到吸引受众的目的。变异表现了人们求异的探究心理。人们看多了常规语言，就会对其听而不闻、视而不见。而当人们听到或看到变异的语言时，就会产生新的刺激，在大脑中形成新的兴奋点，改变原有的精神和心理状态，而美感就会油然而生。如：

例 16 We know eggsactly how to sell eggs. (Egg Ad)

例 17 P-P-P-Pick up a Penguin (Penguin biscuits)

例 18 Every motor**stree-ee-eets** ahead. (Motor vehicle)

例 19 Orangemostest Drink in the world (Orange juice)

例 20 Not just digital, Samsung digit ALL (Samsung)

双关语 双关又分为语音双关和语义双关两种情况，广告标题标语中使用双关语，其主要目的同样是为了吸引读者的注意力。如：

例 21 Trust us. Over 5000　ears of experience. (Hearing aid)

例 22 Try our sweet corn. You will smile from ear to ear. (Sweet corn)

例 23 Have a nice trip. Buy-Buy. (Heathrow)

例 24 When you see Dirt, see Red. (Dirt Devil Vacuum)

例 25 From Sharp minds, come Sharp products. (Sharp)

简洁性 有些广告标题只有寥寥数语，虽然没有使用特定的修辞手段，但因为简洁而醒目，便于受众记忆。如：

例 26 The taste is great. (Nestle)

例 27 Love is a treasure. (Lancome)

例 28 Your future is our future. (Hong Kong Bank)

例 29 It's all within your reach. (AT&T)

例 30 UPS. On time, every time. (United Parcel Service)

此外，还有其他形式的广告标题，如拟人、比喻、重复、排比等，这里不再赘言。

（三）广告正文

广告正文是指广告文案中处于主体地位的语言文字部分。其功能在于详细地介绍所宣传产品或服务的信息，对潜在的目标受众展开诉求。广告正文可以使受众了解到各种希望了解的信息，在阅读过程中建立起对产品的了解、兴趣，进而产生购买欲望。在行文措辞方面，英文广告正文倾向于简洁凝练，注重细节的刻画。如下面这则广告：

例 31 The older your feet get, the more you have to baby them.

Everyone is born with fat feet; and extra padding of fatty tissue that cushions footstep. But as we grow older, we lose that tissue. Until there's little left to absorb the bumps and jolts.

That's why your feet get tired and sore.

Dr. Scholl's Air Insoles help take the place of that fatty tissue. They're soft, so you'll feel the comfortable difference with every step. They're thin, so slip into your shoes without bunching and binding. And they help keep feet cooler and drier.

Because the older your feet get, the more you have to baby them.

Dr. Scholl's

Air Insoles

Baby your feet.

这是英国知名品牌"爽健"（Dr. Scholl）对新推出的"气垫鞋垫"的宣传广告。较为详细地介绍了新产品的功用，其优势所在。语言质朴，简洁，无华丽辞藻。当然这并不是说，英文广告正文不用华丽词语，而是相对较少。如下面这则广告。

例 32　Sometimes nothing but pure indulgence will do. The nights are longer, the evening is your own …, and the perfect accompaniment to make you feel special is the delicious Terry's Chocolate Orange Bar.

And we really do mean indulgence. It's the unique blend of rich chocolate and deliciously orangey flavours, together with that melt-in-the-mouth quality, that gives the Terry's Chocolate Orange Bar its delectably decadent feel. And its convenient size makes it just right for you to eat alone…

So, picture the scene. It's your first evening in for weeks. You've kicked off your shoes, turned the lights down low and put on some slow music, perhaps a little soft soul or gentle jazz. The whole evening is a "me-time", a special time just for you to relax. Make it complete with a Terry's Chocolate Orange Bar …it's sumptuous, luxurious and delectable. Go on … indulge. You deserve it.

这是"特里巧克力橙"（Terry's Chocolate Orange Bar）的广告文案，相比第一则广告要稍显华丽，这种华丽既体现在词语层面如"perfect accompaniment""delectably decadent feel"，也体现在句式层面，如"it's sumptuous, luxurious and delectable. Go on … indulge."但总体来讲，英文广告文案在语言上尚简，注重产品信息、功用的介绍。

三、英语广告语言的翻译

前面已经介绍，广告语言由商标词，广告标题以及广告正文三部分构成。虽同属于广告语言，但各有各的特点，因此翻译的原则与策略并不相同。下面分别予以讨论。

（一）商标词的翻译

我们知道，商标词具备"发音响亮，简短易记，措辞讲究，标新立异，国际性强，为读者所接受"等特点。因此，商标词的翻译也应具备这些特点。具体来讲，商标词的翻译主要有以下几种实现方法，即音译、意译、移译、再创造等。

音译 音译是指用发音近似的汉字将商标词翻译过来，这种用于译音的汉字不再有其自身的意义，只是保留其语音与书写形式。音译又分为两种情况，即绝对音译和相对音译。前者表现为："所选汉字为中性词，汉字的组合无特定的语义，也无所为褒贬，符合商标排他性的需求。"（彭朝忠，2019：198）这种音译的好处在于能保持商标发音的统一性，便于受众识别与记忆。如：Siemens（西门子），Philips（飞利浦），FIAT（菲亚特），CONBA（康恩贝），Rolls Royce（劳斯莱斯），Paramount（派拉蒙），Jeanswest（真维斯），SASSOON（沙宣），YAMAHA（雅马哈），Volvo（沃而沃），Wal-mart（沃尔玛），McDonald's（麦当劳），等等。

还有一种音译属于相对音译，它一方面照顾到原词的发音，另一方面兼顾产品的性质或表达企业的理念。如 Good Year 为美国著名的轮胎，以公司的创始人也是硫化橡胶发明人 Charles Good Year 的姓命名，其译文"固特异"在保留发音的同时，还凸现了产品的性能。美国波音飞机 Boeing 也是为了纪念该航空公司创始人 William Edward Boeing 而以其姓氏命名的。译名"波音"贴切而形象。BMW 在原文中没有太大的意义，只是几个字母的组合而已，而译者仅利用字母 BM 与汉语中的宝马首字母相同这一特点而将其译为"宝马"，较之原文更为生动形象。采用这种译法的例子很多，如 Johnson（强生），Sprite（雪碧），Parliament（百乐门），Marlboro（万宝路），Hewlett Packard（惠普），Uni-lever（联合力华），Ford（福特），Gillette（吉列），Fanta（芬达），Fun（奋牌服装），Puma（彪马），Reebok（锐步），Dove（德芙），Oil of Ulan（玉兰油），Pantene（潘婷），Whisper（护舒宝），SLEK（舒蕾），Mazda（马自达），Palid（拍立得），Decis（敌杀死），Legalon（利肝灵），等等。

相对音译往往改变了商标词的形象，而在目的语中赋予其另外一种形象。此方法既考虑到了原品牌名发音类似的一面，又体现了商品的性质或凸显了企业的理念，同时兼顾目的语读者的审美意向。是较为理想的商标词翻译方法。

值得一提的是，有些商标词的译名采取了一半译音一半译意的策略，如 Starbuck（星巴克），New Balance（新百伦），Maan Coffee（漫咖啡），或者是一半译意，一半创造，如 Land Rover（路虎），Jaguar（捷豹），等等。

需要注意的是，采用拼音的时候切记音节不要太长。冗长的话，不但不易理解，更不利于记忆，达不到商标词对外宣传的功能效果。

意译 顾名思义，就是将商标词的意义译出来。采用这种策略能客观地反映原品牌的信息与内涵，体现撰写人的初衷和希冀。在无法音译兼顾的情况下，可以采用意译的方式。如：Lion（狮牌文具），Skinice（肤美灵），Elegance（雅致羊毛衫），Transformer（变形金刚），Crown（皇冠），Blue bird（蓝鸟），Microsoft（微软），Crocodile（鳄鱼），Apple（苹果电脑），Nestle（雀巢），Playboy（花花公子），UvWhite（优白），Shell（壳牌石油），等等。

有些商标词难以完全意译，即部分意译，另外一部分进行适当的改动，因此具有一定的创意，如 AQUAIR 的译文"水之密语"将原文的 air 即空气改为"密语"，Land Rover 的译文"路虎"是将原文的 Rover 即"漫游者"改为了"虎"字，La Mer 的译文"海蓝之谜"增加了"之谜"。（La mer 在法语里是"大海"之意）

移译 所谓移译就是原封不动的将商标词移植到目的语中去的一种做法，有时也称为零翻译，即不需要任何翻译。移译是为了更好地维护企业品牌的统一形象，同时也便于人们记忆。IBM 已成为美国国际商用机器公司的形象标志，该商标词简洁、响亮，便于人们记忆。类似的还有 AT & T/ 美国电话电报公司，MTV（音乐电视），AOL（美国在线服务公司），BP（英国石油公司），iPad（平板电脑），XO（洋酒人头马），SUV（越野车），M&M（巧克力），LV（箱包），等等。

再创造 有些商标词的"译名"与原品牌名无论在发音上还是在意义上都没有什么关系，属于再创造的范畴。如 Mild-seven（万事发），Rejoice（飘柔），Carefree（娇爽），Cortina（跑天下），夏新（Amoi），Fortune spa（喜洋洋娱乐中心）等，这些名字已与原品牌名无论在发音上还是意义上都不存在一定的关系。这种做法是出于对目的语读者的考虑，可以避免传统翻译过程中容易出现的困难和尴尬。这类通过目的语而另外创造品牌名的做法虽然已不属于翻译的范畴，但由于其特殊的目的及原因是可行的，有时也是必要的。

商标词的翻译灵活性很强，未必限于一种翻译方法。而应根据其要达到的目的或要表现某种特定的情感而采取灵活的对应策略，如 Dove 就根据产品的不同性质而分别采用了德芙（巧克力）和多芳（肥皂）两个译名。Volvo 也有两个名字，大富豪和沃尔沃。从形象的统一性角度出发，商标词的翻译往往不得不改变原来的形象，在译名中又赋予了其另外一种形象，译文也因此与原品牌名的内涵有很大的出入。此外，商标词的翻译还需要考虑民族禁忌的问题，如日本汽车品牌 Prado，就曾译为"霸道"而触犯了中国人民的民族情感，后来不得不改为"普拉多"。

（二）广告标题的翻译

由于标题和标语的特定位置和特殊职能，侧重语言表达的艺术性，它首先要能够引起读者的注意，进而阅读广告正文，或倡导某一理念思想等，最终达到宣传的目的。广告标题一般具备"易读、易懂、易记、易传播"等特点。因此，标题和标语的翻译在尊重原信息的基础上，要充分利用目的语言的优势展现标题及标语的艺术美。实现手法有直译、增译、创译、仿译等策略。

直译 有些广告标题、标语表达形式浅显易懂，语言平实，采用直译策略即可。如：

例 33　DHL worldwide Express: the Pulse of the Business. (Deutsche Post DHL)

敦豪快递，感受企业的脉动。（DHL 物流公司）

例 34　We lead. Others copy. (Ricoh)

我们领先，他人效仿。（理光复印机）

例 35　Take time to indulge. (Nestle)

尽情享受吧！（雀巢冰淇淋）

例 36　Life is a journey. Enjoy the ride. (NISSAN)

生活就是一次旅行，祝您旅途愉快。（尼桑）

例 37　Future for my future. (Chevrolet)

未来，为我而来。（雪佛兰）

例 38　Take TOSHIBA, take the world. (TOSHIBA)

拥有东芝，拥有世界。（东芝）

例 39　The biggest thing to happen to iPhone since iPhone. (iPhone)

迄今为止改变最大的 iPhone。（iPhone）

增译 增译分两种情况，一是为了美感的需要而采取必要的解释或适当增加语言措辞的一种技巧。上面这些译文，无论是意义还是语言结构都与原文基本相同，采取直译即可。但绝大部分的广告标语标题注重语言的艺术性，很难做到单纯的语义翻译，往往要按照目的语的规范重新组合。因此，翻译过程中往往要进行语言上的增润。如雀巢咖啡的广告语 Good to the last drop 的译文"滴滴香浓，意犹未尽"，即是一例。还一种情况就是解释性的增译，因为有些信息在原文化中可能是已知信息，而在目的语国家中则未必，因此应进行适当的解释。如 Any shape and size to Europe (Federal Express) 的译文"不同大小各种形状，火速直飞欧洲。"就增加了部分内容，如不增加，语义不清。减译情况较少，主要是对部分重复的内容进行压缩或提炼。

例 40　Trust for us. (American international insurance)

<u>财务稳健</u>，信守一生。（美国国际保险公司）

例 41　Anytime (Global Logistics)

随时随地，<u>准时无误</u>。（全球物流）

例 42　Live with focus. (Ford focus)

生活有焦点，<u>才是真享受</u>。（福特福克斯）

例 43　Elegance is an attitude. (Longines)

优雅态度，<u>真我性格</u>。（浪琴表）

例 44　Be good to yourself. (Fly emirates)

纵爱自己，<u>纵横万里</u>。（阿联酋航空）

例 45　Wherever you are, whatever you do, the Allianz Group is always on your side. (Allianz Group)

安联集团，永远站在你身边。（安联集团）

前面五个译文（即例 8 至例 12）都增加了原文不具备的形式内容。增译之后的文本取得了一种平衡美，读起来朗朗上口，便于记忆。广告标语及标题一般来讲以凝练简洁为主，故减译的情况很少，但也有非常经典的例子，如最后一例。全部译出会显得啰嗦。但是减词不能减意，其目的是为了使译文更加符合目的受众的审美习惯。

创译　广告标语标题艺术性的语言决定了创译的必要性。广告语言要雅俗共赏，生动有趣，要具有特殊的感染力，能在瞬间引起读者的注意力，尤其是双关语、诗词的运用。这些在语言结构和表达上存在着难以逾越的障碍，即可译性的问题。然而广告语言的翻译是不会不得已而求其次的。前面讲过，广告标语标题具有很强的艺术性，如诗词，双关语的大量使用等，有时很难做到形式甚至内容上的统一，而广告的翻译是不讲求退而求其次的。因此，在这种情况下，就应该对原文进行大胆的调整，从形式或内容上。但须以将广告标语或标题潜在的信息传达出来为前提。而这正是变通翻译之精髓。它将不可译变为可译，在某种程度上解决了广告翻译中的一些难点问题。

例 46　Connecting people. (Nokia)

科技以人为本。（诺基亚）

例 47　A great way to fly. (Singapore Airlines)

新加坡航空，飞跃万里，超越一切。（新加坡航空）

例 48　It happens at the Hilton. (Hilton)

希尔顿酒店有求必应。（希尔顿酒店）

例 49　Easier dusting by a stre-e-etch. (Stretch)

拉拉拉长，除尘力强。（Stretch 牌除尘布）

上面几个译文虽然在形式与内容上都与原文有较大的出入，但却反映了广告标语标题的潜在意义和内涵,可读性并不比原文差,部分译文甚至比原文表现力更强。本部分主要论述了广告标题标语的翻译。广告标语标题的特殊作用及其语言的艺术性是决定翻译策略的重要因素。

仿拟 所谓仿拟,就是借用译入语中某些惯用结构进行翻译的一种方法。被借用的结构可以是成语、谚语、诗词等等。总之,被借用的结构必须是译入语广告读者喜闻乐见、家喻户晓的表达。下面广告标题均采取了这种翻译策略。

例 50 Vander mint isn't good because it's imported, it's imported because it's good. (Vandermint)

好酒不在进口,进口必是酒好。

例 51 Only your time is more precious than this watch. (Rolex watch)

手表诚可贵,时间价更高。

例 52 Think before you act. Read before you think. (Canadian Airlines)

加航信舒适,北美若比邻。

例 53 Slim Express (A modern beauty salon)

大家归瘦。

例 54 Taking you forward. (Erissson)

以爱立信,以信致远。

例 55 Sense and Simplicity. (Philips)

精于心,简于形。

从信息交际理论来看,人们能否理解某个话语取决于交际负荷的大小。所谓交际负荷,通俗地说,就是在交际系统中话语未知信息的量。未知信息的大小与交际负荷成正比。而仿拟是拉近与读者距离的一种有效手段。因为成语、诗词等,要么预定俗成,要么为民众所熟悉。但仿拟也不是万能的,须注意以下两点。一是内容要能够准确有效地反映原文的信息,否则无论多动听悦耳都是失败的。二是套译切忌滥用。套译固然能起到很好的宣传效果,但用得多了,也就失去了新鲜感。如 where there is a South, there is a way; where there is a man, there is a Marlboro; where there is a way, there is a Toyota,等等。多次的仿拟就成陈词滥调了。

(三)广告正文的翻译

由前面的分析可知,英文广告正文以详细介绍产品信息为根本任务,对目标受众展开细部诉求,使受众进一步了解各种希望得到的信息。在行文措辞方面,英文广告正文倾向于简洁凝练。因此,面对此类广告文本,译者可以采取简洁明了的译意方式,如下面这则介绍劳斯莱斯的广告文案。

例 56 **Rolls-Royce**

At 60 miles an hour the loudest noise in this new Rolls-Royce comes from the electric clock.

What makes Rolls-Royce the best car in the world? "There is really no magic about it—it is merely patient attention to detail," says an eminent Rolls-Royce engineer.

1. "At 60 miles an hour the loudest noise comes from the electric clock," reports the technical Editor of *THE MOTER*. Three mufflers tune out sound frequencies—acoustically.

2. Every Rolls-Royce engine is run for seven hours at full throttle before installation, and each car is test-driven for hundreds of miles over varying road surfaces.

3. The Rolls-Royce is designed as an owner-driven car. It is eighteen inches shorter than the largest domestic cars.

4. The car has power steering, power brakes and automatic gearshift. It is very easy to drive and to park. No chauffeur required.

5. The finished car spends a week in the final test shop, being fine-tuned. Here it is subjected to 98 separate ordeals. For example, the engineers use a stethoscope to listen for axle whine.

6. The Rolls-Royce is guaranteed for three years. With a new network of dealers and parts-depots from coast to coast, service is no problem.

7. The Rolls-Royce radiator has never changed, except that when Sir Henry Royce died in 1933 the monogram RR was changed from red to black.

8. The coachwork is given five coats of primer paint, and hand rubbed between each coat, before nine coats of finishing paint go on.

9. By moving a switch on the steering column, you can adjust the shock-absorbers to suit road conditions.

10. There are three separate systems of power brakes – two hydraulic and one mechanical. Damage to one will not affect the others.

The Rolls-Royce is a very safe car, and also a very lively car. It cruises serenely at eighty-five. Top speed is in excess of 100 m.p.h.

参考译文：

劳斯莱斯

60 英里的时速下，这辆最新劳斯莱斯车内最大的噪音来自于电子钟。

劳斯莱斯为什么是世界上最好的车？"其实真的没有什么秘密——就是对细节不厌烦

的关注。"劳斯莱斯的一位著名工程师介绍道。

1."60英里的时速下,这辆最新的劳斯莱斯车内最大的噪音来自于电子钟。"《机动车》杂志的技术编辑如是报道。声频由3个消声器调节,消除噪音。

2. 劳斯莱斯每一部引擎在安装前都经过7小时的全油运转,每一辆车都在不同路面上经过几百英里的试驾。

3. 劳斯莱斯为车主而设计,比最大的家用轿车短18英寸。

4. 机动方向盘,机动刹车,自动排档,驾驶和停止都十分便捷,不需要专业的司机。

5. 组装完毕的每一辆车送往终极检查站,接受为时一周,98个项目的细微检测,包括工程师使用听诊器听轮轴声响。

6. 劳斯莱斯承诺3年保修,随着全国经销商和零配件站网络的完善,服务会越来越好。

7. 劳斯莱斯散热器从未改变,唯一例外是1933年,亨利·莱斯先生去世,上面的字母标志R由红色刷成黑色。

8. 车身涂刷5层底漆,每一层都经过手工打磨,再以同样方式刷9层面漆。

9. 方向盘上有一个减震器调节按钮,以应付不同路况。

10. 3个独立机动刹车系统:两个液压,一个机械,3个系统互不影响……

劳斯莱斯安全性能高,灵活自如。轻松运行时最高时速85英里,极限时速100英里。

该广告主要是对高级品牌车劳斯莱斯性能的全方位介绍,语言风格简洁明快。译文完整地再现了原文的所有信息,准确、规范、流畅,基本体现了原文的风格。但是,在多数情况下,中文广告行文讲求文笔优美。

鉴于审美方面的差异,对于英文广告文案的翻译宜适当增加一些修饰性内容,使之更富吸引力,尤其是旅游广告正文及其他描述性的广告正文。如下面这则旅游广告的翻译。

例57 I saw a city with its head in the future and its soul in the past;

I saw ancient operas performed on the modern streets;

I saw a dozen races co-exist as one;

I didn't see an unsafe street;

Was it a dream I saw?

—Singapore! So easy to enjoy, so hard to forget.

译文1:

我看到一个城市，她有过去与未来的结合；

我看到古老的歌剧在摩登的街头上演；

我看到不同的种族融洽共存为一；

我看不到一条不安全的街道；

只疑身在梦中？

——新加坡！逍遥其中，流连忘返。

译文 2：

有一座城市，工业立足高科技，民间传统不能忘；

有一座城市，海边花园建高楼，摩登街头演古戏；

有一座城市，十余民族一方土，情同手足睦相处；

有一座城市，大街小巷无盗贼，夜不闭户心不惧；

是天方夜谭，痴人说梦？

啊，新加坡——如此享受，铭心刻骨。

译文 3：

未来与历史相连

古雅与摩登并肩

各族居安多融洽

繁华若梦君所见

——新加坡，触手可及，永世难忘。（转自彭超中，2019：105-106）

原文是一则旅游广告，语言风格整体来讲偏于简洁、凝练。我们现在看到的三个译文各有特色。译文 1 偏于直译，语言质朴，但感染力不强；译文 2 偏于华美，创造成分较多，浮夸较重；译文 3 不仅简练，而且体现了汉语广告文雅、华丽的一面。整体来看，译文 3 效果最佳。但最后一句话的翻译"触手可及，永世难忘"似乎不如译文 1 中的"逍遥其中，流连忘返"更贴切。

相反，如果将中文广告文案翻译为英文广告的话，则要对华丽甚至浮夸的成分予以酌情压缩或删除。如下面这则介绍苔干的宣传文案。

例 58 涡阳苔干，名优特产，驰名中外，声震古今，翠绿、清脆、可口，有天然海蜇之称；清乾隆年间奉献皇宫，故又名"贡菜"。

译文：Taigan is a celebrated product of Woyang, Anhui Province, which is also sought after all over the world. Green, tender, crisp and pleasant to the taste, it has been styled as jellyfish-on-land. And it was deemed suitable as an article of tribute during the Qing Emperor Qian Long's reign (1736—1796).

译文在保留原文基本信息的同时，同样对华丽的部分如"名优特产，驰名中外，声震古今"进行了适当的弱化，使译文更加符合英文广告的表达需求。

四、广告翻译需要注意的问题

广告翻译除了需要注意语言文字上的问题，还需要特别注意法律、宗教、政治制度等敏感话题。Athieu Guidere（2003）在 *the Translation of Advertisement: from Adaptation to Localization* 一文中曾指出：

Localization of international advertising campaigns consists of adapting the company's communication to the specificities of the local environment of the hosting countries targeted by the campaign. This local environment could be divided in several components. The socio-cultural component which includes the local particularities stemming from religion, mores, social and commercial habits, rules of conduct and ethical norms. In short, this component is related to the main features of the hosting culture and society. The politico-legal component which includes the local particularities stemming from the nature of the political system, the stage of opening onto the world, the restrictions imposed on advertisements and the regulations related to information and to certain products (such as spirits and tobacco).

大意是说：国际广告活动的本地化，包括使公司的传播适应所针对主办国当地环境的特殊性。这种当地环境又可以分为几个部分。其中社会文化包括宗教、风俗习惯、社会和商业习惯、行为准则和道德规范。简言之，这一部分与主办文化和社会的主要特征有关。政治法律方面包括：由于政治制度的性质、对外开放的阶段、对广告的限制以及与信息和某些产品（如白酒和烟草）有关的规定而产生的地方特殊性。

这段文字指出了语言文字翻译之外的问题，涉及宗教、法律和意识形态等诸多方面。例如，我国《广告法》第九条第三款就明确禁止"使用国家级、最高级、最佳等用语"。而在西方国家的广告法中则没有相应的规定。如 Finest food, most attractive surroundings and a friendly disposition. 其中的 finest, most attractive 译为中文时就不宜再用最高级。另外，第 18 条禁止利用广播、电影、电视、报纸、期刊发布烟草广告。西方对此则相对宽松一些。如摩尔牌广告语：Ask for more；万宝路香烟的广告标题：Come to where the flavor is—Marlboro Country 等。有些西方国家广告中含有一定的情色内容，而在中国，这种情况是不允许出现在广告语言中的。翻译时应酌情处理或删除不译。

此外，有些种类的广告排斥华丽的词藻，或者忌讳过多的软信息或夸大的功效，如招聘、招标、医药、食品等诸如此类的宣传。因此，这些广告正文的翻译宜采取"平实的语言"。否则误导受众，引发不必要的纠纷。如：

例59 Avon perfect Day Moisture Cream Nourishes skin with the moisture it needs for a softer, more healthy appearance.

雅芳保湿营养霜<u>蕴涵丰富维生素和天然保湿成分</u>，具有滋养和保湿功效，为肌肤提供营养分和水分，令肌肤全日滋润亮泽、平滑柔软，保持健康的动人光彩。（郑玉琪、郭艳红，2005：72）

这是一则化妆品广告，画线部分为添加成分，其实原文中没有，有夸大之嫌，应该删除。而下面另外一则医药广告则避免了类似的问题。

例60 How to relieve Arthritis pain and Inflammation

Take Bufferin to relieve minor arthritis pain fast. Bufferin goes to the heart of the pain and works where you hurt to quickly relieve minor arthritis pain. So you feel better for hours.

Take Bufferin to relieve inflammation that Tylenol cannot effectively reach. Many people with arthritis pain, swelling and stiffness don't realize that inflammation is the primary cause. And many don't know that while Tylenol works on pain, it doesn't effectively reduce inflammation, but Bufferin does. Taken regularly, Bufferin reduces inflammation, so after several days you begin to feel relief from the swelling and persistent pressure around joints.

Arthritis can be serious. If pain persists more than 10 days or redness is present, consult your doctor immediately.

Bufferin for the pain and inflammation of arthritis.

Used only as directed.

Bristol-myersco.

译文：服用布啡啉，很快就能解除轻微关节疼痛。布啡啉直接作用于疼痛部位，并迅速解除关节疼痛。用后几小时内，您能恢复自如。

服用布啡啉可消除炎症。泰诺（Tylenol）无此效果。尽管许多患者关节疼痛，肿胀或麻木僵硬，但他们没有认识到这些痛苦的根源是炎症。泰诺止痛却不消炎，布啡啉既止痛又消炎。按时服用布啡啉，您会从关节疼痛，肿胀或麻木僵硬的病痛解脱出来。

关节炎危害很大。如果疼痛持续10天，或出现红肿，请务必去求医。

布啡啉止痛又消炎。

服用时请遵医嘱。（杨荣琦、陈玉红，1995：78）

这是一则医药广告，其语言准确，通俗，易懂。译文本着"诚实守信"的原则，语言平实质朴，未见随意增删内容。这样做是为了避免误导消费者。

结语

广告语言注重措辞的精炼，结构的精美，广告翻译虽然属于非文学翻译，但兼具文学特性。因此，广告语言的翻译具有较大的灵活性，不苛求表层结构和字面意义的忠实。而是应该在考虑到中英两种语言在审美和文化差异的基础上，充分发挥译者的创造性，在最大程度上再现原文的呼唤功能与感染性。商标词作为一种标识符号，具有一定的永久性。它的翻译在很大程度上是一种形象的转化而非单纯的意义对等。这主要是由于商标要保持其对外的统一性以及实现原品牌名意义、内涵等。广告标题由于其特定的位置及特殊职能而格外受人注目。广告标题往往是对整个文案的概括或浓缩，表现了某一宗旨、服务理念或某一倡议等等。其首要任务就是首先引起人们的注意，通过艺术性的语言来传达特定的信息。因此它的翻译也必须兼顾艺术性。广告正文应是整个广告文案最重要、最有价值的组成部分。正文的翻译应从整体考虑，既要考虑到信息的准确传达，又要兼顾语言的感染力。此外，广告语言的翻译还须注意民族文化禁忌，法律法规等非常规情况问题。

课后练习

一、翻译下列商标词。

1. Nivea 2. Lux 3. Prada 4. Starbucks 5. ARROW
6. Gucc 7. Pizza Hut 8. Loreal 9. Pamper 10. Longines

二、翻译下列广告标题。

1. Finest food, most attractive surroundings and a friendly disposition.(Hotel Ad)

2. Spend a dime, save your time. (Home appliance)

3. Mercedes Benz is the car by which other cars are judged. (Mercedes Benz)

4. Less is more. (Lilanz)

5. A business in millions, a profit in pennies. (Wholesale business)

6. The relentless pursuit of perfection. (Lexus)

7. Fine in quality, fare in price, novel in design, prompt in delivery. (Mansha)

8. No business too small, no problem too big. (IBM)

9. M&Ms melt in your mouth, not in your hand. (M&Ms)

10. A diamond lasts forever. (De beers)

三、翻译下面一则广告文案。

Relaxed Riders

Your body is beautiful.

It's your jeans that are out of proportion.

Even the most beautiful body can get lost under the wrong pair of jeans.

That's why it's important to wear jeans that let you look your best. Jeans that make the most of what you've got. Like our Relaxed Riders. When we make Relaxed Riders, we cut our material on a curve to conform to the natural contours of your body. So where your proportions change, Relaxed Rider jeans change too.

If you've been thinking that something is wrong with you just because your jeans don't fit. Try Relaxed Riders. You'll see it's not a better body you need. It's better jeans.

第三节 新闻文体的翻译

一、新闻文体概论

新闻是对正在发生、新近已经发生或过去发生但新近发现的有价值的事实的及时报道。新闻种类繁多，按照不同的分类标准，可实现多种不同的分类方法。根据报道内容，可将新闻划分成政治新闻、科技新闻、体育新闻、娱乐新闻等；根据新闻事实发生的地域范围，可将新闻划分成国际新闻、国内新闻、地方新闻等；根据新闻传播媒介，可将新闻划分成报纸新闻、广播新闻、电视新闻、网络新闻等。如果按照事件性质划分的话，新闻又可分为硬新闻（hard news）和软新闻（soft news）两大类。所谓"硬新闻"，是指题材严肃，具有一定时效性的客观事实报道。有时也称"现场短新闻"或"纯新闻消息报道"，强调时间性和重要性，重在迅速传递消息。而"软新闻"是指情感味浓，写作方法诙谐，轻松幽默的社会新闻。这种"软新闻"时效性相对较弱。但是不论哪种类型的新闻，大都具备新闻的基本特点，即真实性、准确性以及简明性。

新闻英语中常见的体裁主要有三大类：消息（news）、特写（features）和新闻评论（commentaries and columns）（张健，1994）。所谓消息就是狭义的新闻，属于硬新闻范畴，文字干净利落，报道及时，注重事实。构成消息的基本要素有五个 W 和一个 H，即 Who（何人）、What（何事）、When（何时）、Where（何地）、Why（何因），以及 How（如何)。借助这六个要素,读者可以迅速地把握其主要内容。特写属于软新闻,是对某一事件、人物进行形象化报道的一种新闻。这类新闻往往选取精彩的生活片段进行生动的刻画,语言生动活泼,具有较强的感染力。而新闻评论则常常是对社会上重大事件或热点问题的评论,语言犀利,观点鲜明。

新闻文体主要由标题、导语、正文三部分组成。标题(headline)是新闻的"眼睛",是对新闻中心问题的浓缩。导语(Lead or Introduction)是对新闻内容的浓缩与概括,引导读者判断是否读下去,通常位于新闻的第一段,提供主要话题与主要事实。正文(body)是新闻的主干部分,是在导语的基础上,较为详细地引入更多与主题相关的事实,使之更加详实,并展开评论,或得出结论。在结构安排上,正文主要有三种形式:时间序列(chronological order),即按照事件发展的先后顺序进行安排;金字塔式序列(pyramid form),即按照事件的重要性递增的顺序进行安排(in the order of descending importance);"倒金字塔形式"(the Inverted Pyramid Form),即以事实的重要性递减的顺序来安排(in the order of descending importance)。但从整体来看,英语新闻内容的结构安排以"倒金字塔式"为主流。

英语日益成为一种国际语言已是不争的事实。据统计,在当今世界,80%以上的新闻信息是用英文写成和传播的。(刘其中,2018)新闻不仅是人们获取全球信息的重要手段,还是语言学习者了解语言发展趋势的一大途径。在全球一体化加速发展的背景下,国际交流越来越频繁,英语学习者、新闻从业人员掌握英语新闻的特点及其翻译方法,一方面可了解全球先进的方法理念,一方面可发挥其纽带作用,将全球发展的最新动态及方向及时展现给大众。鉴于直接读英语新闻的国人人数有限,因此新闻的翻译可以让更多国人了解国际资讯,这也是信息化时代的必然趋势。因此,英汉新闻的翻译意义可以概括为:帮助中文读者扩大视听范围,及时了解国际信息,增长见闻见识,进而提高分析和判断问题的能力。

英语新闻涉及的层面十分广泛,作为英语语言的一种延伸,形成了独特的措辞及句法特点。

二、新闻英语的语言特点

新闻的基本属性决定了其语言风格。新闻是对事实的反映,这就要求新闻语言必须客观、准确,慎用主观色彩较强的词汇。同时,新闻面向的对象是大众群体,其语言宜通俗易懂。此外,为吸引眼球、争取读者,也要考虑到措辞的时尚型与趣味性。这就要求新闻语言尽可能生动、形象。概言之,新闻英语的整体风格表现为:客观性、简洁性和趣味性。下面从词汇和句式两个层面进行分析。

（一）词汇特点

概括来讲，新闻英语的词汇具有以下几个主要特征：使用小词，创造新词，跨专业借词以及外来词。

使用小词 英语新闻力求用有限的字数来表达尽可能多的新闻内容，为此偏爱选用那些短小精悍的动词，以单音节词居多，即所谓的小词（midget words）。由于报纸篇幅有限，使用小词可以免于移行。此外，小词的词义范畴较宽，生动灵活，可以增强新闻的简洁性和可读性，如表示"破坏"或"损坏"时，标题一般不用 damage，而用 hit, harm, 或 wreck 等。类似的小词还有：aid=assist（帮助），alter=change or modify（改变），axe=dismiss/reduce（解雇，减少），ban=prohibit（禁止），bar=prevent（防止，阻止），bare=expose or reveal（揭露），boost=increase（增加，提高），check=examine（检查），curb=control or restrict（控制），dip=decline or decrease（下降），ease=lessen（减轻，缓和），flay=criticize（批评），foil=prevent from（阻止，防止），grill = investigate（调查），map=work out（制订），mark=celebrate（庆祝），moot=discuss（讨论），mull=consider（考虑），nab=arrest（逮捕），nip=defeat（击败），foil=prevent from（阻止），trim=reduce（削减），vie=compete（竞争），等等。

创造新词 创造新词是新闻文体写作的一个重要特点。新闻反映了人们日新月异的现实生活、科学技术的迅速发展与人类文明的不断提高。所有这一切促使人们寻求新的表达方式以适应新的需要。新事物层出不穷，原有的词汇已经很难满足需求，无法准确反映出其特征与含义。因此创造新词势在必行。新词的出现反映了时代的特点，记录了时代的发展。各大报刊媒体的记者也在想尽办法以便从语言上制造轰动效果。因此，使用新词便成为新闻报道不可避免的现象。如 sexting（Sex+Texting 发送色情短信），vaping（电子烟），twitterati（twitter+glitterati 社交网络红人），photobomb（成功抢镜），chillax（chill+relax 淡定），trendsetter（trend+setter 潮人），cyberbullying（cyber+bullying 网络暴力），phishing（网络钓鱼），Webcast（网络播放），infotainment（information+entertainment 资讯娱乐），cross-dresser（伪娘），holiday getaway（假日出行，尤指短期假日），等等。

跨专业借词及外来词 英语新闻文体还大量地借用体育、军事、商业、科技、文学、娱乐业等方面的专业词汇或其他外来词，以便增强大众读者的亲切感或新鲜感，如：package deal（经济用语：一揽子协议），throw somebody a curve ball（棒球用语：虚晃一招，行骗），throw the sponge（拳击用语：认输或投降），schmuck（意大利语：蠢货），macho（墨西哥语：男子汉气概），nadir（天文术语：形容两方关系的最低点），downer（医学用语：镇定剂，意指令人沮丧的人），long-arm jurisdiction（法律用语：长臂管辖），banana-republic（文学修辞：香蕉共和国），high-water marks（经贸用语：高水位条款），等等。

（二）句法特点

新闻句法有多种表现形式，这里我们根据新闻语言的特点总结为三点，即简单句、省略句和被动句。

简单句 新闻英语倾向于使用简单句或拓展的简单句，即遵从 "the simpler, the better" 的原则，一般来讲，英文句式较中文句式偏长。但是新闻主要是面对大众的，讲究言简意赅，注重句式的简洁。因此，简单句或拓展的简单句较多。如下面这段文字。

例 1 Getting caught up in fishing ropes or nets is one of the biggest threats to whales. The animals can suffocate or starve after becoming trapped. Reports of very large whales getting entangled in fishing gear are rare compared with smaller species, leading to the assumption that the biggest whales might largely avoid such threats. A new study, led by experts at the University of St Andrews in Scotland, cast doubt on this idea. The researchers analysed images taken by drones of blue and fin whales in Canada's Gulf of St Lawrence—an important summer feeding ground for whales.

在这段由 5 个句子构成的文字中，有 4 句为简单句，只有 1 句为复合句，而且相对来讲该复合句并不算长。要言之，新闻英语里简单句较多，长句句式不占主流。这既与新闻注重时效性有关，又与传播的大众对象有关。

省略句 省略句的使用主要体现在新闻标题上。为了达到信息浓缩的效果，标题常常使用分词短语、介词短语等扩展简单句。在新闻标题中，很多成分都被省略，如冠词、介词、系动词、代词、连词等。如：

例 2 Buried lakes of liquid water discovered on Mars

例 3 Two-fifths of plants at risk of extinction, says report

例 4 Longer overlap for modern humans and Neanderthals

例 5 Climate change: Top tips to reduce carbon footprint revealed

例 6 Climate anxiety: children losing sleep over the environment

例 7 Plug pulled on 5,000 post-GCSE qualifications

被动句 英语新闻语言的另外一个特点是被动句使用较多。原因主要有如下几种：一是在报道不好的新闻时如天灾人祸、事故死伤等；二是特意强调动作的受事者；三是有意回避动作的施事者，避免不必要的麻烦；四是信息源不确定，或是已经掌握却不便透漏。如下面 4 个例文。

例 8　The blue and fin whales are the two largest species in the oceans. Both are endangered, though the blue whale's starting to make a comeback in Antarctic waters.

例 9　In footage of the alarming incident, he can be seen attempting to hurriedly walk away from the throng.

例 10　"Details of the visit are being discussed and will be officially announced as soon as a decision is made," the spokesman said.

例 11　There are an estimated 145,000 people living with Parkinson's in the UK, but there is no cure and no definitive test for the disease.

诚然，新闻英语的语言特点不限于这些，但也基本体现了其主要特征。限于篇幅，其他方面不再赘言。

三、新闻英语的翻译

基于英语新闻的语言特点和功用，新闻翻译应遵循以下几种翻译原则。一是确保译文准确，避免错误。不同于其他文体的翻译，新闻出版周期非常短，需要在极短的时间内翻译完毕。出错的几率相对较大。这对译者和编辑都提出了较大的挑战；二是在尊重新闻表述规范的前提下，译文要通俗易懂，简单明了，避免晦涩难懂；三是根据二次传播的需要，允许适当的文字编译，对部分文字进行删减或结构上的调整。

（一）新闻标题的翻译

标题是新闻报道的"眼睛"，是其灵魂所系。为了尽量吸引读者，新闻编辑往往运用各种修辞手段，以凝练的文字告知读者新闻的核心内容。大众读者一般先看标题，再决定是否阅读正文。因此，译好新闻标题尤为重要。标题翻译与标题写作一样，贵在创意、醒目。其次译文要本着简洁的原则。在不违背原意的情况下，可以允许适当的增补或运用汉语习语。概括来讲，新闻英语的标题翻译，主要直译、套用、增补等几种策略。

直译　英语新闻写作历来奉行"越简洁越好"的原则。绝大多数英语新闻有着句式简短的标题，在对这些标题进行翻译时，通常可采用简洁明了的直译法即可。如：

例 12　Extinction: Freshwater fish in "catastrophic" decline

淡水鱼物种数量将"灾难性"减少

例 13　Indonesia coral reef partially restored

印度尼西亚部分珊瑚礁重现生机

例 14　Future-proofing coffee in a warming world

经得住气候变暖考验的咖啡品种

例15　Self-driving cars to be allowed on UK roads this year

英国或将在年底前允许自动驾驶汽车上路

例16　Deaf sheepdog learns how to herd using "sign language"

失聪牧羊犬通过识别手势指令放羊

例17　Early cherry blossom in Japan likely to be result of climate change

日本樱花盛花期提前或因气候变化所致

这几则新闻标题简洁明了，直接表明主题。而译文也本着简洁的原则，采取了不增不删的直译法。

套用　新闻标题通过运用各种修辞技巧，既有效地传递一些隐含信息，又使读者在义、音、形等方面得到美的享受。中文受众对新闻标题具有较高的期望，这种期望除了言简意赅，提供尽可能多的信息，还表现在行文修辞上，注重文字的对仗、工整，讲求文采。因此，译文可以适当借助中文的典故或成语，或四字结构，拉近与读者的心理距离和审美期待。如：

例18　UK woodlands "at crisis point" amid wildlife decline

英国林地野生动物数量下降树木状况"危在旦夕"

例19　Extinction: "Time is running out" to save sharks and rays

拯救濒危物种鲨鱼和鳐鱼"时不我待"

例20　Will anyone ever find Shackleton's lost ship?

英国探险家沙克尔顿的南极沉船能否"失而复得"？

例21　Squirrels are "climate culprit"

松鼠是"气候变化的罪魁祸首"

例22　US astronaut arrested for trying to kidnap love rival

美宇航员三角恋千里追情敌遭拘

例23　After the Booms Everything Is Gloom

繁荣不再，萧条即来

增补　新闻标题中如果出现国人不太熟悉的背景信息，则要进行必要的变通，如添加有关人物的国籍、事件发生的地点等，便于中国读者的理解，消除误会。如下面几个新闻标题的翻译：

例24　For Beslans children, a legacy of nightmares

（俄罗斯）劫后相逢，别城孩童仍似噩梦中

例25　Blue whale numbers increase

南乔治亚岛蓝鲸数量有所增长

例26　Covid jail opens in Germany

德国"关押"拒绝隔离人员

例27　Skin cancer

皮肤癌发病率增长与廉价全包假期有关

例28　Ants in space

蚂蚁在太空的表现

例29　Record TV football deal

英超直播权拍卖再创历史新高

例30　A fourth dimension to film

4D影院引领看片新潮流

例31　Wildlife crime prints "breakthrough"

科学家找到从猛禽羽毛上提取偷猎者指纹方法

例32　Ebola airport checks

英国将对机场旅客进行埃博拉病毒检测

例33　Deadly substances found

美国实验室发现被遗忘致命病毒

这几则新闻标题的翻译均出现了不同程度的增补内容。增补的原因，不外乎以下几种。一是标题过于简单，如 Skin cancer, Ants in space，不添加必要的信息，读者不清楚标题内容，因此需要适当的扩充。二是背景信息缺少，如 Ebola airport checks, Deadly substances found，直译的话，读者不清楚新闻发生于何地，因此需要交代。三是修辞效果的需要。有些新闻标题直译的话，不够生动。如 A fourth dimension to film 译为 4D 电影，显然不如"4D影院引领看片新潮流"更能打动中文读者。因此翻译标题时，可以结合汉语新闻标题的特点，适当增加一些词语，使标题的意义更趋完整，修辞效果更好。

（二）新闻导语的翻译

　　导语是新闻消息的起始部分，通常位于第一段，是帮助读者了解新闻内容的核心部件。导语是新闻内容的浓缩，因此它的翻译至关重要。导语翻译的精彩，才能吸引读者，使之产生继续读下去的强烈欲望。因此，译者应该花费精力研读中英文新闻导语的异同，然后采取适切的翻译策略与手段，以保证译文准确、地道、精彩。

　　中英文导语在行文结构上有同有异。这里我们重点强调两者之间的差异及其对翻译的影响。"英文导语常常采取先虚后实的写法（即先写出一个 general statement，后提供

specific information），将新闻要素一点一点地批露出来。就是说，他们喜欢在第一段里只提供宏观的或概念性的信息，而中文导语更强调开门见山，着笔伊始就把何人、何事、何时、何地和盘托出。"（刘其中，2018：27）

鉴于这种差异，一般有两种应对翻译策略。一是按照原文结构进行翻译，二是按照中文新闻的行文结构进行处理。如：

例 34　The chief of the International Monetary Fund (IMF) said he believed China would pursue economic policies that benefit both the country and the world.

Completed in a one-day meeting with top Chinese officials, IMF Managing Director Rodrigo Rato said he shared the view with Chinese policy makers about the need to rebalance the growth pattern of the Chinese economy.

译文 1：国际货币基金组织的负责人说，他相信中国奉行的是一种既惠及中国也惠及世界的经济政策。

国际货币组织执行主席罗德里戈·拉托与中国官员举行了一整天会谈。他在会谈后表示，他同意中国政策决策者关于需要重新平衡中国经济增长模式的看法。

托拉是在他与中国总理温家宝昨天会谈后举行的记者会上发表这些意见的。

译文 2：国际货币基金组织执行主席罗德里戈·拉托昨天说，他相信中国奉献的是一种既惠及中国，也惠及世界的经济政策。

托拉昨天与中国总理温家宝举行了一整天会谈。他在会谈后举行的记者会上表示，他同意中国决策者关于需要重新平衡中国经济增长模式的看法。

译文 1 是根据原文结构进行翻译的，译文 2 是根据中文导语的行文习惯进行改译的。从阅读效果来看，译文 2 要好一些。

此外，新闻导语的翻译还需要注意行文逻辑的问题。虽然新闻语言从整体上来讲，以简单句为主，但有时也会存在不同程度的长句。如果这种长句出现在导语中，就需要理清其中的逻辑关系。其关键在于分清已知信息和未知信息。未知信息是导语传达的核心内容，而已知信息则提供相关的背景知识。这两者之间有主次轻重之分。在翻译时要注意它们之间的逻辑顺序，以免颠倒。如：

例 35　A bomb explosion caused the crash of an Air India jumbo jet off Ireland last year in which all 329 people aboard were killed, investigation for the Boeing Company and the Indian government have testified.

译文 1：去年一枚炸弹爆炸使印度航空公司的一架大型客机在爱尔兰离岸坠毁；造成机上 329 人遇难；这是波音公司和印度政府调查人员证实的。

译文 2：据波音公司和印度政府的调查人员证实，印航的一架大型客机去年在爱尔兰离岸坠毁，造成机上 329 人死亡；原因是机上炸弹爆炸。

译文 3：据波音公司和印度政府的调查人员证实，去年印航大型客机在爱尔兰离岸坠毁的事件是由于炸弹爆炸造成的；该次空难使得机上 329 人全部丧生。

分析不难发现，原文的已知信息为空难，因为是去年的消息。经过调查，发现空难的原因为炸弹爆炸造成的。因此，从这个意义上来讲，译文 3 更符合原文的语义信息结构。

（三）新闻消息的翻译

新闻消息属于硬新闻，要求报道快捷，开门见山，以便能立即吸引读者。一条新闻一个中心或主题，要求抓住一件事物的一个侧面下笔，使得主题明确，思路清晰。把最新最重要的信息写在新闻开头。硬新闻的文字简短精炼，表现手法以叙述为主，多用动词，少用形容词。结构多采用"倒金字塔"式。把新闻高潮结论放在最前面，然后根据事实的重要性依次递减的顺序进行安排，由高到低地突出最重要最新鲜的事实。因此，在翻译新闻消息时，可以遵循原文的结构。同时要以事实为准绳，以准确为基本原则，在行文方面，要做到文从字顺，符合汉语新闻的语言规范。从策略上来讲，新闻消息的翻译，主要有全译、编译两种。

全译 英语新闻的全译，是将原文所包含的全部信息在译文中悉数呈现。这种新闻一般都比较重要，具有较高的二次传播价值，且篇幅相对较短。在尊重译入语表达规范的基本前提下，译者需要逐段甚至逐句进行翻译（出于译入语语言表达规范的考虑，可以适当调整句式结构），同时在最大程度上体现原文的风格特征。如下面这则新闻的翻译。

例 36　　　　　　　　Bezos steps down as CEO

Jeff Bezos is stepping down as the CEO of Amazon, 27 years after founding it with his ex-wife and building it into one of the most successful companies of all time now worth \$1.7 trillion. He will be replaced by 53-year-old Andy Jassy, the current CEO of the Amazon empire cloud business Amazon Web Services.

Bezos, 57, announced the move in an email to his 1.3 million Amazon employees Tuesday where he insisted he isn't retiring but wants to focus on his "passions", including his space and climate change ventures.

Bezos will move to the role of Executive Chair, where he says he wants to focus on "new products and initiatives".

The move will not happen until the third quarter of this year.

译文：贝索斯将卸任亚马逊 CEO

杰夫·贝索斯将卸任亚马逊首席执行官一职，亚马逊云计算业务亚马逊网络服务首席执行官、53 岁的安迪·贾西将接任他的职位。27 年前，贝索斯和前妻共同创建了亚马逊，并将其打造成美国历史上最成功的公司之一，目前亚马逊市值 1.7 万亿美元。

现年 57 岁的贝索斯 2 月 2 日在一封致亚马逊 130 万员工的电子邮件中宣布了这一变动，他在邮件中坚称自己并非要退休，而是要专注于自己"热爱的事业"，包括太空和气候变化事业等。

贝索斯将转为担任亚马逊董事会执行主席，他表示希望专注于"新产品和新方案"。

这一变动要到今年第三季度才会实施。

英文原文由四个自然段组成，层次分明，主题突出，语言较为严谨，是一则典型的消息类新闻。从内容来看，新闻正文首先以导语开头，对事件进行概括，之后按照时间顺序进行具体报道。译文整体来看，非常完整，没有删节，用词专业，语义清晰。尤其是第一段导语的翻译，译者抓住了原文的未知信息，即贝索斯卸任亚马逊 CEO 一职，取而代之的是 53 岁的安迪·贾西。而将其他已知信息如亚马逊的创立时间，市值等置于其后。可见，所谓的全译也允许部分内容结构的调整，主要是已知信息与位置信息的调换。

编译 新闻编译是通过翻译和编辑的手段，将以源语语言写成的新闻进行翻译、综合、加工，使之成为用译语语言表达出来的新闻的翻译方法。（刘其中，2018：9）新闻编辑集翻译与编辑为一身，对原文信息进行加工处理，便于更好的二次传播。其原因一是外电的新闻稿件一般都比较长，内容丰富，背景资料较多。而中文新闻相对较短，不习惯长篇报道。因此，删繁就简就成了新闻翻译常规性任务。二是涉及敏感内容，不适合二次传播。但需要声明的是，不论是全译，还是编译，译文的中心思想和深层含义都应该与原文保持一致，不能随意歪曲。前面我们已经提及，英语新闻一般采取"倒金字塔"式结构，即重要信息大都安排在新闻的前面，次要信息或背景资料则往往后置。因此，在编译的过程中一般删减的是后面不甚重要的信息，或予以整合，尤其是对国人来讲无关紧要的内容。如：

例 37　　Akbar Charged in Grenade Attack on 101st Airborne Division

Fort Campbell, Ky-A soldier from the 101st Airborne Division has been charged with murder in a grenade attack on officers' tents in Kuwait that killed two.

The charges against Sgt. Hasan K. Akbar, 32, were announced Friday afternoon. Fort Campbell officials said Akbar was charged March 25 with two counts of premeditated murder and 17 counts of attempted murder, under military law.

If convicted, Akbar could face the death penalty, according to Dennis Olgin, a retired military judge.

Akbar was also charged with one count each of aggravated arson of an inhabited dwelling and misbehavior as a sentinel while receiving special pay.

Akbar was returned to the United States last Friday and was being held at an undisclosed military facility.

Akbar is the only person charged in the grenade attack that killed two U.S. officers and wounded 14 other soldiers on March 23. He was transferred from Kuwait to the military detention center in Mannheim, Germany, after the attack, then to the United States.

Officials are still investigating the attack, which killed Army Capt. Christopher Scott Seifert, 27, of Easton, Pa., and Air Force Maj. Gregory Stone, 40, of Boise, Idaho.

The attack happened in the early morning hours in the command center of the 101st Division's 1st Brigade at Camp Pennsylvania. Days later, the 1st Brigade began moving into Irap.

Fort Campbell said military defense counsel had been assigned to Akbar and that he could hire a civilian lawyer on his own. Military lawyers representing Akbar said they had no comment.

Akbar, a black Muslim, has been described as resentful about alleged religious and racial discrimination in the Army.

编译译文：

炸死己方军人的美国兵被控谋杀罪

美联社肯塔基州坎贝尔要塞3月25日电 那个用手榴弹炸死两名军官、炸伤14名士兵的美国兵今天被控犯有谋杀罪。

对哈桑阿克巴尔的制控是今天宣布的。这名32岁的中士被控犯有两宗预谋杀人罪和17宗故意杀人罪。

一位军法法官说，如判定有罪，他可能会被处以死刑。

阿克巴尔已于上星期五被遣送回国。

上述事件于3月23日发生在美军第101空降师驻科威特的兵营里，一名少校、一名上尉被当场炸死。

阿克巴尔是黑人穆斯林，有人说他对美军内部存在的"宗教歧视和种族歧视"有不满情绪。

这则编译新闻简化并突出了最重要的新闻事实,在保留主要信息的同时,删去了对中文读者并不是特别重要的资讯。如被杀死的两名军官的身份背景,以及阿克巴尔申请律师事宜等。至于如何删减,主要取决于不同媒体二次传播的需要。

四、新闻特写的翻译

新闻特写(news feature)是以文学性手段报道新闻人物或趣闻的特殊新闻文体。兼具新闻性和文学性。特写娱乐性较强,人情味较浓,写作风格轻松活泼,易于引起读者的兴趣,或愉悦,或同情等。主题可能会不应时或不甚重大,常使读者欢笑或悲泣,喜爱或憎恨,嫉妒或遗憾。特写属于软新闻的范畴,主要是从感情上吸引读者,而非以理性赢得读者。向受众提供娱乐,使其开阔眼界,增长见识,或供人们茶余饭后的谈资。软新闻写作常用"散文笔法",文笔生动活泼。因此,新闻特写的翻译除了保证信息的准确无误,可以允许译者一定程度的发挥,使之具备文学色彩。如下面这段新闻特写(片段)的翻译。

例 38 "The two warring images will be linked forever, each denying—and completing—the other: Christopher Reeve, built and beautiful in his superman suit, roaring invincibly into the stratosphere. And Christopher Reeve, strained and drawn, hooked to a ventilator and living another motionless day in his wheelchair. The cartoon hero had suffered a horrible fall and emerged as a real-life hero." (Washington Post, October 12)

两个互相抵触的形象将永远地联系在一起:互相否定又互相补充。一个克里斯多夫·里夫,在《超人》电影里英俊、健美,总是以胜利者的姿态冲入云霄;另一个克里斯多夫·里夫,身体僵硬、面部走形,带着呼吸器,日复一日地坐在轮椅上一动不动。太多的不幸降临在这位卡通般的英雄身上,但最终使他历练成一位真正的英雄。

这段文字描写的是《超人》中的英雄形象克里斯多夫·里夫。文字采用对比递进的手法,让人物形象跃然纸上。译文同样再现了人物特写生动、细腻的笔法,让读者看到了英雄"豪迈、虚弱、磨难"的生动过程。但是在运用散文笔法翻译的同时,也要注意文字的适切性,即要与所描写的人物或场景相符合。

例 39 The most eye-catching ornament in Ke Xiuhua's home is a white cotton cloth embroidered with striking colors. It is carefully arranged atop three folded comforters on the family's clay bed, which fills up one-third of the living room. The traditional Chinese love motif in the stitching shows a pair of birds singing in a tree, a family of mandarin ducks swimming together, and a lion playing with two balls on the ground.

译文1：柯秀花家最引人注意的装饰，是一张色彩绚丽的绣花布。这张装饰布被小心地摆放在三床折叠好的被子上。堆放着被盖的土坑，占据了客厅1/3的面积。装饰布上表现的是中国传统关于爱的主题：小鸟唱歌，鸳鸯戏水，狮子滚绣球。

译文2：在柯秀花家里，最抢眼的摆设就是那块绣着花的白布。这块布整整齐齐地摆放在三床叠好的被子上。堆放着铺盖的土坑占了屋子的将近1/3。绣花布上绣的是中国传统关于爱的主题：小鸟唱歌，鸳鸯戏水，狮子滚绣球。（转自刘其中，2018：202）

译文1出自原文作者之手，属于自译。整体来讲，译文较为流畅、生动。但也有个别地方显得过分如"色彩绚丽"或者显得不够自然如"这张装饰布被小心地摆放在三床折叠好的被子上。"译文2在原译的基础上进行了改进，收到了较好的效果。

五、新闻英语翻译需要注意的几个问题

新闻翻译需要注意的问题很多，如行文体例，人名地名机构名，意识形态，甚至包括标题符号。限于篇幅，这里主要讲两个问题：人名的翻译与统一，意识形态内容的处理。

（一）人名的翻译与统一

在英语新闻中会涉及大量的新闻人物，以及与这些人物紧密相连的人名称谓问题。人名在第一次出现时，一般要全部译出（中间名字可以不译），如在 The charges against Hasan K. Akbar, 32, were announced Friday afternoon 句中，应全部译出，即"哈桑·阿克巴尔"，后面再出现时可以直接保留人物的姓"阿克巴尔"即可。不过对于目的语较为熟悉的人名则可直接从简，如"奥巴马""克林顿""小布什""特朗普"等等。而中国人名却需要全部保留。如：

例40 The Chinese government has always attached great importance to the health of Taiwan compatriots and will do whatever is beneficial to safeguard their interests, Chinese Health Minister Gao Qiang said here Monday.

"We will do our utmost to safeguard the health rights and interests of the Taiwan people. This is not only what we have promised, but also what we have done," Gao told the 60th World Health Assembly (WHA)."

在这段文字中，中国文化部长"高强"是以完整的形式出现的，但再次出现时报道按照英文的习惯只保留了姓"高"字，在回译时还是要完整保留的"高强"二字。

此外，人名的翻译还涉及统一的问题。大陆与台湾在人名（也包括地名）的翻译上存

在较大差异。如美国前总统 Obama 台译为"欧巴马",前国务卿 Kissinger 为"季辛吉",这两位人物在大陆的译名分别为"奥巴马""基辛格"。诸如此类的例子还有很多,需要译者格外留意,以免造成不必要的混乱。对于人名的翻译,如果没有把握的话,可以参考一些权威的工具书,如《英语姓名译名手册》《外国地名译名手册》,确保译文准确与统一。

(二)意识形态内容的处理

新闻传播是世界各国文化交流传播的一种重要途径,而英语新闻媒体"主导着世界舆论,每天都在影响甚至操纵着人们的思想意识。许多英语新闻语篇看似客观公正,实则含而不露地表达各种意识形态意义,对读者产生潜移默化的影响"。(辛斌,2005:83)这种不平衡的国际新闻传播现状有利于西方国家强化西方文化在全球的影响力,打压其他国家的国际话语权,进而传播自身的意识形态。在严重失衡的国际新闻话语格局中,中国无论是对外建构还是对内维护自己正面的国家形象,发展文化软实力,都需要对各种来源的媒体信息养成审慎的意识态度,发挥新闻翻译在国家形象建立和传播中的积极作用。如何正确处理原文中的意识形态在新闻翻译中已经成为一个重要的前沿关注点。因此,在翻译意识形态意义丰富的新闻文本时,译者应该以显性或隐性的方式来强化或弱化其介入叙事的某些方面。如:

例 41 The two playwrights would not have heard of each other: Contacts between China and Europe were rare at the time. But that has not deterred China's cultural commissars from trying to weave a common narrative.

这两位剧作家应该从未听说过彼此,因为当时中国和欧洲的接触非常少。但这并没有阻止中国文化官员为两者牵线搭桥的尝试。(邓静锶、王祥兵,2020:52)

Commissar 一词本指 1946 年以前苏联的政治教育委员(或政委),原文使用该词来指代中国的文化官员,意图营造出一种中国仍然停留在几十年前的落后印象,讽刺中国政府的文化活动都是刻意谋划强力推进的,引起英语读者不好的联想。Weave a common narrative 是说中国这些活动是在故意编造子虚乌有的联系,目的在于宣传自己的文化。为了弱化这种贬损的意识形态,译者需要将带贬义的词语以中性意义的词语来替代。此处译者用中性词语"文化官员"和"牵线搭桥"在翻译中分别改写了原文中带有贬义的 cultural commissars 和 weave a common narrative,以此消除译文对中文读者可能造成的不良影响。再如:

例 42 Taiwan's "premier" Su Tseng-chang, the top figure in the pro-independence administration of Chen Shui-bian, announced yesterday he would seek his party's nomination for the 2008 "presidential" election.

台湾行政部门负责人、倾向于台独的陈水扁行政当局的头号人物苏贞昌昨天宣布，他将寻求民进党提名，参加2008年台湾地区领导人的竞选。

这则消息涉及台湾问题，译文进行了必要的改动。但凡涉及与国家主权、领土完整的问题，译者必须按照国家有关规定进行执行。《关于正确使用涉台宣传用语的意见》中有这样的规定：

> 对1949年10月1日之后的台湾地区政权，应称之为"台湾当局"或"台湾方面"，不使用"中华民国"，也不使用"中华民国"纪年。
>
> 不直接使用台湾当局以所谓"国家""中央""全国"名义设立的官方机构中官员的职务名称，可称其为"台湾知名人士""台湾政界人士"或"××先生（女士）"。台湾市级以下的机构及人员职务，在相关新闻报道中，原则上可以直接称呼。

由此可见，新闻翻译不是死板地将两种语言进行单纯的语码转换，而要在传达原文积极意义的基础上凸显译者的主体性和家国立场，通过对源语新闻话语的改写与重构，对抗西方媒体不公正的新闻叙事。作为译者，应该充分运用批评话语分析方法，在解码过程中对原文进行细致的语言分析和社会历史分析，识别带有意识形态偏见的叙事，在国外新闻的对内翻译传播中采取正确翻译策略，重构新闻叙事，向国内读者消解外媒蓄意对中国国家形象造成的负面影响。

结语

本节在分析新闻英语文体与语言特征的基础上，探讨了新闻标题、新闻导语、新闻消息和新闻特写的翻译，尝试性地指出了新闻翻译的基本原则和策略。如准确性、通俗性、简洁性以及必要的编译等。但不论是新闻消息，新闻评论，还是新闻特写，其目的都是客观而准确地传递消息。因此，新闻英语的翻译宜避免浮夸和粗俗两种倾向。同时还要避免过激语言的使用。译者要慎用带有个人感情色彩的语词，做一个平静的事实陈述人。同时，从事新闻翻译的人士要不断提高自己的新闻素养语言文化修养，唯有如此才能在时间紧迫的情况下，交出质量上乘的新闻译作。

课后练习

一、翻译下列新闻中经常出现的语词。

1. China hand   2. head in the sand policy   3. coupling effect

4. Brain trust   5. draw the line   6. tax haven

7. hush money   8. rotating presidency   9. affirmative action

10. deep fakes

二、翻译下列新闻标题。

1. If America's economy runs hot, what happens to the rest of the world?

2. How to Design Language Tests for Citizenship—and How Not to

3. Inoculating non-whites is the first step to reducing vaccine hesitation

4. Loneliness is a widespread problem with complex roots

5. Topsy turvy: Have banks now got too much cash?

6. As Northern China struggles, the South surges ahead

7. Once endangered, the MBA is emerging stronger from the pandemic

8. Joe Biden sets out to restore American leadership with an old team in a new world

9. The returns on housing investment are not what they are cracked up to be

10. Treating forgotten killers, Herbal remedies can help ameliorate neglected diseases

三、翻译下面一则新闻导语。

Supported by a group of British business leaders, Eurostar reiterated its request to the British government for a bail-out. Operating trains through the tunnel linking Britain and France, Eurostar's passenger numbers have plummeted by 95% since March. The British government sold its stake in 2015. Eurostar is majority owned by SNCF, the French state-owned railway company.

四、翻译下面一则新闻消息。

The Biden administration has pledged to deliver 150m covid-19 vaccinations within the president's first 100 days in office, but who should get those shots? Most states are prioritising frontline health-care workers and long-term care-home residents, followed by people aged 75 or older and essential workers. Few states are making sure African-Americans or Hispanics get vaccinated, even though they are three times more likely to die from the virus than whites. In fact minorities may be at the back of the queue for something that is of great value to all Americans.

五、翻译下面一篇新闻特写。

Margaret Zhang Named Vogue China Editor-in-chief

As a 27-year-old Chinese Australian fashion influencer, Margaret Zhang is the youngest person to land an editor-in-chief role at the magazine and replaces Vogue China founding editor-in-chief Angelica Cheung, who had led the title for 16 years.

Margaret Zhang is an Australian-born Chinese filmmaker, photographer, consultant and writer.

At the age of 16, she launched a successful fashion blog and has worked as a consultant. For now, she has 1.2 million Instagram followers. In 2016, she was named in Forbes' 30 Under 30 Asia list and shot fashion week in Sydney for the publication she will now lead.

Anna Wintour, Vogue's global editorial director says: "I am so delighted that Margaret is our new editor in chief of Vogue China. Her international experience, exceptional multiplatform digital expertise, and wide-ranging interests are the perfect combination to lead Vogue China into the future."

In announcing her appointment, Vogue described Zhang as "an unmistakable presence on the front row" of fashion shows around the world.

Zhang sees her new responsibilities as both outward and inward facing. Outlining her vision for Vogue China, she believes her international experience positions her well to achieve them: "there's a lot of context about China that is lost; often it's looked at as this one monolithic entity, as opposed to a country of individuals and innovations."

Zhang was born in Sydney and grew up in the suburb of West Ryde in Australia after her parents moved from Taizhou, in Zhejiang province. She studied commerce and law at the University of Sydney. She scored 99.85 in her HSC and graduated from the University with a degree in commerce/law.

Her father was a professor of mechanical engineering at the University of Sydney. She came to fashion through her passion for ballet.

第四节　商务文体的翻译

一、商务英语文体概论

商务英语是在商业实践中规范使用并形成的一种具有专业交流方式特征的功能性英语。它以英语为载体，由商务背景知识和商务交际技能构成。商务英语以适应职场生活的语言要求为目的，内容涉及商务活动的各个层面。这些商业活动包括技术引进、对外贸易、招商引资、国际金融、涉外保险、商务谈判、电子商务等，涉及的文本类型有商务信函、商品说明书、商务合同、公司介绍、商务公告等。

科学技术的发展促进了全球范围内国际化、社会化大生产的发展，增强了世界经济贸易一体化的进程。新时代下，我国经济朝向纵深发展，对外贸易合作更趋频率，与世界各国的联系也越来越密切。在这种背景下，商务英语就成为国际间贸易合作和交流的必然选择，成为企事业合作各方不可或缺的沟通桥梁和纽带。商务英语的内容范畴从专业化的英语读写逐步包含了如何与对方进行交流，如何合作、合作方式，生活习惯、文化差异等。可以说商务英语的内容已经涉及商务活动的方方面面。与此同时，国内人才市场由于大批外资公司的登陆，对商务英语的人才的需求也愈来愈大。商务英语的翻译任务也更加繁重。可以说，商务英语翻译的前景比较广阔。初涉商务英语的译者，首先需要掌握扎实的国际商务知识，深入了解商务英语的内涵、特征、功用，其次要掌握一定的商务翻译技巧和基本的翻译理论。

二、商务英语的语言特点

在长期的国际贸易实践中，逐渐形成了独具特色的贸易术语。通过这些贸易术语，可以更好地解决货物的检验、包装、运输、保险等方面的问题，进而促进交易的达成。在国际商务实践中，商务英语就成为各方在交易磋商和合同订立过程中不可缺少的专门用语，因而被称为"对外贸易语言"。商务英语是程式化较为突出的一种文体。商务英语源于普通英语，具有普通英语的语言学特征。同时，商务英语又是商务知识和普通英语的综合体，属于英语的一个功能性变种，因而又具有自身的特点。接下来我们分别从词汇和句法两个层面分析商务英语的语言特点。

（一）词汇层面

概括来讲，商务英语词汇主要有三方面的特征，即缩略词、古语以及专业词汇的使用。

缩略词 商务英语缩略词汇根据单词的组成可以分为两大类。第一类是指在合成词中利用两个以上的词汇前部或者多于两个字母进行缩略，如净重 weight 缩略成为 Wt，股份有限公司 incorporated，缩略成为 Inc，应用程序 application 缩略为 app。类似的还有：min prem（minimum premium 最低保险），chpd（charges paid 费用已付），Co（company 公司），Gal（Gallon 加仑），Sq.ft（平方英尺），等等。第二种类型是由多个单词的首字母组合而成的缩略词，如 for your information 缩略成为 FYI（供你参考），关于 in respect of 缩略成为 I. R.O，离岸价 Free on Board 缩略成为 FOB。这样的例子还有很多，如 FAS（Free Alongside ship 船边交货），FOB（free on board 离岸价格）离岸价格，L/C（letter of credit 信用证），B/L(bill of lading 提单），CIF(cost insurance and freight 成本保险和运费），VAT（value added tax 增值税），S/O No (shipping order 装货单号），LLC(Limited Liability Company 有限责任公司），IMF（International Monetary Fund 国际货币组织），等等。

古语 古语的使用也是商务英语语言的一大特色。对于商务英语来说，古语的适用范围是相对固定的。而且这些古语词大都是以 here，there, where 等为词根再加介词形成的。如：hereinafter（以下，下文中），hereby（特此，由此，兹），hereunder（在此之下，在下文中），thereupon（于是，因此）；thereunder（据此，在其下）；hereto（至此，于此）；wherein（那里，其中，在那种情况下）；whereby（凭此），等等。具体例证如下：

例 1　Please find the check enclosed herewith.

请查收随函所附的支票。

例 2　This Contract shall come into force from the date of execution hereof by the Buyer and the Seller.

本合同自买卖双方签署之日起生效。

例 3　In Witness Whereof, the parties hereto have caused the Agreement to be executed on the day and year first before written in accordance with their respective laws.

本协议书于上面所签订的日期由双方根据各自的法律签订，开始执行，特立此据。

这些古英语词汇，在一些公司合约条款、法律文书等方面出现的频率较高，给人一种庄严、郑重之感。

专业术语 商务文体涉及的体裁类型较多，因此形成的专业术语也较为繁杂。尽管繁杂，但是这些专业词汇的意义是相对固定的，不随译者的主观意愿而改变。例如，"procurement of goods" 中的 procurement 只能解读为"采购"，因此该词语就是"货物采购"之意。类似的专业词汇有：real estate（不动产房地产），available capital（可用资产），reserve（准备金或储备金），buffer fund（缓冲基金、平准基金），endorsement（背书），exchange rate（汇率），foreign exchange（外汇），hard currency（硬通货），devaluation（货币贬值），deflation（通货紧缩），capital flight（资本外逃），dividend（红利），stock-jobber（股票经纪人），preference stock（优先股），par value（股面价格或票面价格），creditor（债权人），debtor（债务人，借方），discount（贴现，折扣），annuity（年金），maturity（到期日或偿还日），amortization（摊销，摊还，分期偿付），overhead expenses（间接费用或管理费用），social charges（社会负担费用），graduated tax（累进税），等等。

由此可见，商务英语中的专业术语词汇意义相对固定。此外，还有一些专业词汇具有一词多义的现象。因此，需要根据具体的语境来判断该词语的含义，比如 acceptance, acquire, average, collection, tender 在商务英语中词义分别为"承兑、收购、海损、托收、投标",而在普通语境中却依次是"接受、获得、平均(数)、收集、提交"的意思。

我们主要从三个方面分析了商务英语的词汇特征。其实,这三个特点都不同程度地体现了商务英语的专业性。这种专业性要求每位从事商贸的人员,须对商务英语的构成及其特点有充分的了解,以便在实际业务中能够正确、规范地运用。

(二)句式层面

商务英语的句法特点,主要呈现为两种趋势。一方面,随着时代的发展,生活节奏的加快,商务英语有简化的趋势,表现在语言结构上,就是简单句、并列句的使用增加。另一方面,一些商务文本的法律属性如商务合同,又决定了商务英语语言的严谨性和专业性。表现在语言结构上就是同义词/近义词的重复、并列,条件句、情态动词、长句的使用较为普遍。同时,商务英语的交际性又决定了其礼貌和委婉的一面。

同义词/近义词的重复、并列 同义词或近义词重复、并列的现象在商务英语中较为普遍。在商务合同或法律文书中,经常用成双成对的同义词或近义词,用 and 或 or 连接。这种做法是为了避免诉讼时双方律师利用词义之间的细微差别大做文章而引起的混乱。如下面例句中的划线部分:

例 4 Party A agrees to purchase from Party B the following commodity under the terms and conditions set out below:

例 5 This agreement is made and entered into by and between Party A and Party B.

例 6 The decision by such arbitration shall be accepted as final and binding upon both parties.

这种近义词并列的结构还有:secret and confidential(保密)、null and void(无效)、rights and interests(权益)、ships and vessels(船只)、modification and alternation(修改和变更)、obligation and liability(义务和责任)、interpretation and construction(理解和解释)、sign and issue(签发)、force and effect(效力)、fulfill or perform(履行)、furnish and provide(提供),make and enter into(达成),transferable or assignable(可转让),等等。

条件句的使用 国际商务谈判参与的双方,为了协调、改善彼此的贸易关系或满足各自的贸易需求,都会提出一些符合自己利益的条件。因此如何提出和接受这些条件就显得至关重要。这里的条件句又可分为两种情况,一是虚拟条件句,二是真实条件句。这里主要谈第二种情况。虚拟条件句在后面的礼貌性和委婉性部分再提及。真实条件句是为了表达真实准确的信息。商务谈判双方既可能存在冲突的利益,还可能存在共同点或许彼此可以兼容的利益。一项商务合同谈判的背后会涉及诸多利益因素。商务谈判者必须分析交易双方的利益所在，认清哪些利益对于己方是重要的，是不能让步的；哪些利益是可以让步的，是可以谈判的。特别是在正式签约文书上要做到准确无误。下面这些例句都是合同中的真实条件句。

例 7　Should the carrying vessel be advanced or delayed, the Buyer or their chartering agent shall advise the sellers immediately and make necessary arrangements.

若装运轮提前或推迟抵达，买方或其运输代理人须立即通知卖方并做出必要安排。

例 8　In case that no written objection is raised by either party one month before its expiry, this Agreement will be automatically extended for another year.

在期满前一个月，如果双方未书面提出任何异议，本协议将自动延长一年。

例 9　Either side can replace the representatives it has appointed provided that it submits a written notice to the other side.

任何一方都可更换自己指派的代表，但须书面通知对方。

例 10　Providing that one of the parties fails to abide by the terms and conditions of this Agreement, the other party is entitled to terminate this Agreement.

如果一方未按本协议条款执行，另一方有权终止协议。

例 11　In the event that the Contract Price or any other terms of the Contract changes after the issuance of the Letter of Credit, the Owner shall arrange for such Letter to be amended accordingly as soon as possible after any such changes.

如果在信用证开立后，合同总价或合同其他条款发生变化，业主应尽快安排对信用证进行相应的修改。

情态动词的使用　商务英语中使用的情态主要有 shall，should，will，may 等。这些情态动词与日常意义不尽相同，甚至悬殊较大。如 shall 在合同中，并非指单纯的将来时，而是常用来表示法律上强制执行的义务，表示当事人需要承担的义务，如未履行，即视为违约，并构成某种赔偿责任。有"应该""必须"之意。这是英语合同用词与基础英语用词的不同之处。Should 通常只用来表示语气较强的假设"万一"，极少用来表示"应该"。may 表示合同上的权利（right），权限（power）或特权（privilege）的场合中使用。May not 用于禁止性义务，即"不得做什么"，但不可用 cannot 或 must not 来替代。will 一般使用在没有法律强制的情况下，也用来表示承担义务的声明，但语气和强制力比 shall 要弱。如：

例 12　The parties hereto **shall**, first of all, settle any dispute arising from or in connection with the contract by friendly negotiations. **Should** such negotiations fail, such dispute **may** be referred to the People's Court having jurisdiction on such dispute for settlement.

双方<u>应</u>首先通过友好协商解决因合同而发生的或与合同有关的争议。<u>如协商未果，可</u>将争议提交有管辖权的人民法院解决。

例 13　The parties **will** attempt in good faith to resolve any controversy or claim arising out of or relating to this contract promptly by negotiations between executives of the parties.

所有与合同有关的争端和索赔双方项目执行人<u>要</u>努力地通过迅速友好地协商解决。

长句的使用　在商务合同中，经常会使用大量结构复杂、语义严谨的句式。这些长句修饰成分较多，其定语或是状语环环相扣，形成了错综复杂的树状结构。如：

例 14　Both party A and party B agree that a technology transfer agreement shall be signed between the Joint Company and Party B (or a third party) so as to obtain the advanced production technology needed for realizing the production scale stipulated in Chapter 4 to the contract, including product design, manufacturing technology, means of testing, material prescription, standard of quality, and the training of personnel.

例 15　In consideration of your granting and/or continuing to make available advances, credit facilities or other financial accommodation for so long as you may think fit, to the "Customer", the undersigned "Covenanter" as primary obligator and not merely as surety, hereby irrevocably and unconditionally guarantees and will procure, punctual payment to you, on the respective due dates, of all moneys which are now or may at any time hereafter be or become from time to time due or...

这两个长句都超过了 50 个单词，而且例 15 还只是节选了其中的一部分。合同中之所以会使用大量的长句，主要是为了能够准确、清晰、严谨地传递内容信息，以免出现漏洞，防止法律纠纷的出现。

礼貌性与委婉性　商务英语作为一种谈判语言，还具有礼貌性和委婉性的特点。礼貌原则要求尽量从对方利益出发，站在对方的立场上表达我方的意愿，站在对方立场上看问题，进而推动贸易的达成。礼貌不仅仅是简单使用一些礼貌用语诸如 your kind inquiry, we appreciate, your esteemed order, looking forward to 等就可以了。毋宁说，它是从"您为重"（You-attitude）的角度考虑问题，尊重、赞誉、体谅对方，使对方受益。在此基础上，尽可能在平等的基础上恰当地使用 you、we，避免过激、冒犯和轻视的措辞。体谅原则强调对方的情况而非我方，要体现一种为他人考虑、体谅对方心情和处境的态度。尤其当对方发生了不幸或不愉快的事情时往往会向对方表达慰问或同情之意，以便体现一种"人情味"策略。下面这些句式以及措辞便体现了商务英语的礼貌性和委婉性。

例 16　Your complaint is being looked into.

例 17　I was wondering if you could possibly send us your latest sample machine.

例 18　We are sorry for the trouble caused you by the error and wish to assure you that care will be taken in the execution of your further orders.

例 19　You could rest assured that we would make every effort to affect the shipment as soon as possible so as to meet your demand.

例 20　We sincerely recommend you to accept our proposal as our stocks are getting lower and lower day and day, and we are afraid we shall be unable to meet your requirements if you fail to let us have your confirmation by return.

三、商务英语文体的翻译

前面提到，商务英语涵盖面较为广泛，涉及的次文体较为繁多，因此商务英语的翻译有其特殊性。但是，无论哪种文体，商务英语文体均以传递信息为其根本。因此，商务英译的翻译应遵循信息对等的基本原则。而奈达的功能对等比较契合这一原则。功能对等理论（functional equivalence theory）由美国语言学家尤金·A·奈达在这一理论中，他指出："翻译是用最恰当、自然和对等的语言从语义到文体再现源语的信息。"（Translating consists in reproducing in the receptor language the closest natural equivalent of the source—language message, first in terms of meaning and second in terms of style. Nida&Taber, 1969:12）奈达有关翻译的定义指明翻译不仅是词汇意义上的对等，还包括语义、风格和文体的对等。就商务英语的翻译而言，这种对等又分为语义信息的对等，文体风格的对等，以及文化信息的对等。语义信息是商务信息的关键所在。没有语义信息，就谈不上文体信息和文化信息。一般来讲，语义信息又分为表层语义信息和深层语义信息。而商务英语侧重于表层语义信息，一般不允许有多种意义的解读。下面我们以商务信函、商务合同、产品介绍为例来说明商务英语的翻译，并分析这些体裁是如何实现各个层面的对等的。

（一）商务信函的翻译

商务信函是商务交流中重要的组成部分，涉及商贸活动的各个方面，如建立贸易联系，发出邀请，提出投诉，解决问题等。随着世界贸易的一体化融合，中国与外商之间的合作与交流日益频繁。因此，商务信函的英汉互译成为一种基本技能。具体来讲，商务信函又可分为请求函、商洽函、投诉函、感谢函、邀请函、推销函等。要进行规范、得体的商务信函翻译，首先要对其语言特点进行分析。相对于普通信函，商务信函格式固定、用语礼貌、内容简明等。一封完整的商务信函一般包括信头（letter head），日期

(date)，地址（address），经办人（attention），称呼（salutation），事由（subject），正文（body），结尾套语（complimentary close），签名（signature）等。

商务函电体现了发出方和接收方之间的合作伙伴关系，比较正式，因此在翻译商务信函时，首先要注意信函的格式要求，其次要措辞礼貌正式，用语规范。如英语商务信函钟情态动词使用居多，以示礼貌，如 we should be grateful if you would help us with your suggestion, we shall be very pleased if… 等等。而中文信函则常用"盼""烦请""希望"等句型。其实，无论是英文信函，还是中文信函，都有大量的套语，熟悉这些套语可以提升信函翻译的规范性。如：We are in receipt of your letter./we acknowledge receipt of your letter（来函获悉，或来函收悉），In reply to your letter of…/regarding your letter of…/Referring to your letter of…（兹回复贵方来函），Please do not hesitate to contact…（请随时……与联系）；We would like to apologize for…（对……谨表谢意）；We would appreciate it/should be obliged/ for an early reply（如蒙早日。不胜感谢），Enclosed we hand you…/Enclosed please find…/We are enclosing…（随函附上……），Please find…（请查收……），等等。

下面是一则英文商务信函及其译文。

例 21

Eastern Corp

15 Dundas Street

Toronto, Canada

Jan. 15, 1988.

Jingxing Corp

32 Heping Street

Beijing 100013

China

Dear Sirs,

We write to introduce ourselves as one of the leading exporters of a wide range of Electric Goods from Canada

We attach a list of products we are regularly exporting and trust some of these items will be of interest to you. We would be interested in receiving your inquiries for all types of electric goods, against which we will send you our quotations.

We look forward to hearing from you soon.

Yours faithfully

James Parrinto

Vice President

参考译文

敬启者：

现具函自我介绍。本公司是加拿大主要电器用品出口商之一，经营多种电器产品。

随函附寄我公司常年出口的产品目录一份，相信其中有些产品贵公司会感兴趣。我们欢迎贵公司来函询购各种类型的电器用品，并将按贵方的询价单寄去我方报价。

盼即复。谨此

詹姆斯·帕林托

1988.1.15

这是一封完整的商务信函，信函的主要内容是向对方发出邀请，表现出洽谈业务的热心。整体来看，语体较为正规，多用礼貌语如 trust（表相信），we would be interested in...（表欢迎）。因此，翻译时候，需要注意格式和措辞这两个方面，即所谓的文体对等。译文同样采取了书信体各式，在措辞上也注意到了规范性和礼貌性，如"敬启者"（也可译为各位先生），"具函""盼即复""谨此"，同时把时间从信头调到了信尾，做到了格式和文体上的对等。

例 22

Dr. Simon Smith

1221 Tennessee Blvd

Murfreesboro, TN 37130

Dear Dr. Smith:

Thank you for your letter of 20 March. I have given much thought to the equipment we need in the Art Education. We need to purchase several new computers and programs to learn about graphic designing. Attached is a list of needed computer-related equipment and a floor plan sketch after the installation of the new equipment.

Sincerely,

Jane Doe,

Art teacher

Enclosures:

Equipment Proposal

Floor Plan

参考译文：

尊敬的西蒙·史密斯博士：

3月20日来信收悉。谨致衷心谢意。现已对我校艺术教育部设备更新事宜重新进行了考量。现需要购置几台新的计算机及程序用于图形设计学习。随函附上计算机相关设备清单及新设备安装后的楼层布局草图。

此致

简·多伊

艺术教师

Janeannedoe@email.com

附：设备购置计划及楼层布局方案

这封信函的翻译同样遵守了体例格式、措辞方面的规范原则。只不过相较于第一封信函，有些措辞出现了细微的变化，如结尾改为"此致"而非"谨此"。其实，表示尊敬的信函用语也是多种多样，应根据具体的写作内容和对象而有所区别。这是译者需要熟练掌握的。

（二）商务合同的翻译

商务合同是买卖双方达成交易的协议书，是商务英语重要的组成部分。合同明确了交易双方的权利和义务，对两者均具有法律约束力，在日常的贸易活动中起着非常重要的作用。合同一般包括合同名称、合同编号、合同的基本条款、特别条款、通用条款、其他条款、结尾条款等几部分。合同是非常正式而严谨的一种文体，一般具有以下几个特点：语言规范，符合国际惯例；表达清楚、明确有条理；多专业术语，多长句。商务合同其行文特定在于简练、严谨、顺畅、专业。因此，合同的翻译也应再现原文的这种行文规范，体现严谨性、逻辑性和专业性。

严谨性 商务合同涉及权利、义务、利害等问题，经双方签署之后便会自动产生法律效力。因此，合同的翻译务必忠实、准确、严谨。不能出现任何的错误，或表述不清。如：

例23 You are entitled to a refund of all the money you paid EXCEPT for $200 or 0.2% of the purchase price(whichever is more) if you end the contract in this way.

whichever is more 是合同中较为常见的表达方式，意指"以较……者"为准。这里根据语境可以翻译为"以较高者为准"(类似的还有 whichever is greater)。因此,整句可以翻译为:如果你以这种方式终止合同,你有权获得扣去 200 美元或购买价格的 0.2%(以较高者为准)以外的全额退款。

例 24 If either of the contracting parties be prevented from executing the contract by such events of Force Majeure as war, serious flood, fire, typhoon and earthquake, or other events agreed upon between both parties, the term for the execution of the contract shall be extended for a period equivalent to the effect of such events.

译文 1:若双方中的任何一方,由于战争、严重水灾、火灾、台风、地震以及双方同意的其他原因而无法按期履行合同时,则延长履行合同的期限,延长的期限相当于事故影响所及的时间。

译文 2:若缔约双方中之任何一方因战争、严重水灾、火灾、台风、地震以及经双方认可的其他此等不可抗力事件阻碍而无法按期履行合同,应当延长合同的履行期限,延长的期限相当于事故所影响的时间。

译文 1 的主要问题有两点,一是未将 contracting parties 译为"缔约方",不够严谨。二是 other events agreed upon between both parties 的译文"双方同意的其他原因"不完整,甚至可以说不准确。因为这里面有一个限定词即"不可抗力事件"。译文 2 则改正了这两处不严谨的地方。

例 25 Notwithstanding any other provision of this agreement or contract, the University of Central Arkansas shall not be responsible or liable for any type of special or consequential damage to the other party, specifically including, but not limited to, lost profits or commissions, loss of goodwill, or any other damages of such nature.

无论本协议或合同中涉及任何其他相关条款,中阿肯色大学对于协议或合同另一方所遭受的直接损失或间接损失概不负责,具体包括但不限于利润损失或佣金损失、商誉损失或其他任何类似性质的损失。(转自赵刚、杜振东,2019:215)

这是中阿肯色大学自拟自译的中英文合同。因为翻译的不够严谨几近造成了孔子学院与中阿肯色大学合作破产的危机。问题主要出在 special or consequential damage 的汉译上,原译为"直接损失或间接损失"。Consequential damage 可以译为"后续损害"或"间接损害"。但是 special damage 是否可以翻译为"直接损失"呢?查证于各种权威词典,我们不难发现,special damage 并非直接损害。如在线韦伯斯特 Online Merriban Webster 词典的一种解释为:damage not ordinarily expected to be caused by defendant's wrong or breach of duty but in fact caused thereby under circumstances making defendant responsible(即:

通常不认为是由于被告的错误或失职造成的损害，但实际上是在使被告负有责任的情况下造成的）。可见，special damage 是一种附带损害，并非直接损害。其实，这两个术语虽然有细微的差别，但在合同中是可以互换的。孔子学院中方负责人赵刚发现了这一问题，并告知了中阿肯色大学，才避免了一场不必要的危机。

逻辑性 前面提到，商务英语中长句较为常见，尤其是合同条款。长句的使用可以行文表述严谨，但同时也给译者带来了不小的麻烦。译者首先要理清句式之间的逻辑关系，在此基础上再按照中文合同的行文逻辑进行安排，否则就可能出错。如：

例 26 Both party A and party B agree that a technology transfer agreement shall be signed between the Joint Venture Company and Party B (or a third party) so as to obtain the advanced production technology needed for realizing the production scale stipulated in Chapter 4 to the contract, including product design, manufacturing technology, means of testing, material prescription, standard of quality, and the training of personnel.

原译：甲、乙双方同意由合资公司与乙方（或第三方）签订技术转让协议，以取得为达到第四章规定的生产经营目的、规模所需要的先进生产技术，这些技术包括：产品设计、制造工艺、测试方法、材料的配方、质量标准、人员培训。

改译：甲、乙双方同意由合资公司与乙方（或第三方）签订技术转让协议，以取得为达到第四章规定的生产经营目的、规模所需要的先进生产技术及人员培训，这些技术包括：产品设计、制造工艺、测试方法、材料的配方、质量标准。（王相国，2008：19）

原译的问题出在"人员培训"（the training of personnel）的位置安排上。细读原文不难发现，这里的"人员培训"与前面的"先进生产技术"是并列关系而非从属关系，因为"先进生产技术"无法包括"人员培训"。改后的译文纠正了这一问题。

例 27 This insurance shall take effect from the time the insured goods leave and Consignor's warehouse at the place of shipment named in the policy and shall continue in force in the ordinary course of transit including sea and land transit until the insured goods are delivered to the Consignee's warehouse at the destination named in the Policy. The Cover shall, however, be limited to sixty days upon discharge of the insured goods from the seagoing vessel at the final port of discharge, before the insured goods reach the Consignee's warehouse.

本保险自被保险货物运离保险单所载明的起运地仓库或储存处所开始运输时生效，包括正常运输过程当中的海上、陆上、内河和驳船运输在内，直至该项货物到达保险单所载明目的地收货人的最后仓库或储存处所或被保险人用作分配、分派或非正常运输的其他储存处所为止。

专业性　要保证译文的专业性，译者首先要深入地理解、掌握并使用正确地使用商务专业术语。有些专业术语其含义较为固定。而有些专业术语因为源自其他行业，或者具有一词多义现象，这时候就需要根据上下文仔细甄别。合同语言表述中会涉及各类不同的专业。同一词汇的词义根据专业不同也会发生变化。因此，根据不同的专业来确定词义也是重要的选词翻译手段。如：

例 28　We need to get a written quotation before they start work.

我们需要在他们开始工作前得到一份书面报价。

例 29　These are the latest quotations from the Stock Exchange.

这些就是证券交易所的最新行情。

例 30　Subsequent to the execution of this agreement, ABC Cor. changed its name to XYZ US Investment Company.

本协议签署并交付后，ABC 公司更名为 XYZ 美国投资有限公司。

例 31　Party B shall lodge a 60-day note in China Construction Bank Zhengzhou Branch for discount.

乙方须把一张 60 天的期票提交中国建设银行郑州分行贴现。

例 32　The Seller shall present the following documents required for negotiation /collection to the banks.

卖方必须将下列单据提交银行议付或托收。

例 28 中的 quotation 根据语境应为"报盘"之意，而例 29 中的 quotation 则应解读为"行情"。例 30 中的 execution 在本句中应为"签署"之意，而不是"执行"。在银行业中，discount 意为"贴现"而非"折扣"。negotiation 和 collection 的一般含义是"谈判"和"收取"，但在例 32 中是国际金融的专业术语，分别指"议付"和"托收"。

此外，还要辨别专业术语意义相近的语词或表面相似的表达方式。如在商务英语中，change A to B 表示的是把 A 改为 B，而 change A into B 则表示为"把 A 折合成或兑换成 B"。二者语义差别之大不可混淆。再如 shipping advice 与 shipping instructions。shipping advice 是由出口商发给进口商的，可以翻译为"装运通知"。而 shipping instructions，是进口商发给出口商的，通常翻译为"装运须知"，其意义正好与前者相反。

下面我们看一则中英对照版的合同文书，以更为全面的体会合同翻译的专业性、严谨性。

例 33

1. Scope of Cover

This insurance is classified into three forms-Total Loss Only (T.L.O), With Average (W.A.) and all risks. Where the insured goods sustain loss or damage, this Company shall undertake to indemnify therefore according to the risks insured and the Provisions of these Clauses.

(1) Total Loss Only (T.L.O)

This company shall be liable for

(a) Total loss of the insured goods caused in the course of transit by natural calamities-heavy weather, lightning, floating ice, seaquake, earthquake, flood, etc. or by accidents-grounding, stranding, sinking, collision or derailment of the carrying conveyance, fire, explosion, etc. And falling of entire package or packages of the insured goods into sea during loading or discharge;

(b) Sacrifice in and contribution to General Average and Salvage Expenses.

(2) With Average (W.A.)

This Company shall be liable for

Aside from the risks covered under Total Loss Only Condition as above, this insurance also covers partial losses of the insured goods caused by heavy weather, lightning, tsunami, earthquake and/or flood.

(3) All Risks

In addition to the liability covered under the aforesaid Total Loss Only and With Average insurance, this Company shall also be liable for total or partial loss of the insured goods caused by shortage, shortage in weight, theft & or pilferage, leakage, contact with other substance, breakage, hook, rainwater, rust, wetting, heating, mould, tainting by odor, contamination, etc, arising from external causes in the course of transit.

Goods may be insured on Total Loss Only or With Average Risks conditions and may also be insured against additional risks upon consultation.

2. Exclusions

This Company shall not be liable for

Loss or damage caused by the international act or fault of the Insured;

Loss or damage falling under the liability of the Consignor or arising from inherent vice or normal losses of the insured goods;

Loss or damage caused by strikes of workers or delay in transit;

Risks covered and excluded in the Ocean Marine Cargo War Risk Clauses of this Company.

3. Commencement and Termination of Cover

This insurance shall take effect from the time the insured goods leave and Consignor's warehouse at the place of shipment named in the policy and shall continue in force in the ordinary course of transit including sea and land transit until the insured goods are delivered to the Consignee's warehouse at the destination named in the Policy. The Cover shall, however, be limited to sixty days upon discharge of the insured goods from the seagoing vessel at the final port of discharge, before the insured goods reach the Consignee's warehouse.

译文：

一、责任范围

本保险分为全损险、水渍险及一切险三种。被保险货物遭受损失时，本保险按照保险单上的条款规定，负赔偿责任。

（一）全损险

本公司负责赔偿

（1）被保险货物在运输途中由于恶劣气候、雷电、海啸、地震、洪水自然灾害造成整批货物的全部损失或推定全损。由于运输工具遭受搁浅、触礁、沉没、互撞、与流冰或其他物体碰撞以及失火、爆炸意外事故造成货物的全部或部分损失。

（2）共同海损的牺牲、分摊和救助费用

除包括上列平安险的各项责任外，本保险还负责被保险货物由于恶劣气候、雷电、海啸、地震、洪水自然灾害所造成的部分损失。

（3）一切险

除包括上列平安险和水渍险的各项责任外，本保险还负责被保险货物在运输途中由于外来原因所致的全部或部分损失。

货物可以只投保全损险，也可以投保普通险，也可以协商投保附加险。

二、除外责任

本保险对下列损失不负赔偿责任：

1. 因被保险人的国际行为或过失所造成的损失。

2. 属于托运人责任的损失或者因被保险货物的固有缺陷造成的损失或者正常损失；

3. 因工人罢工或运输延误造成的损失或损害；

4. 本公司海洋运输货物战争险条款规定的责任范围和除外责任。

三、责任起讫

本保险自被保险货物运离保险单所载明的起运地仓库或储存处所开始运输时生效，包括正常运输过程当中的海上、陆上、内河和驳船运输在内，直至该项货物到达保险单所载明目的地收货人的最后仓库或储存处所或被保险人用作分配、分派或非正常运输的其他储存处所为止。

如未抵达上述仓库或储存处所，则以被保险货物在最后卸载港全部卸离海轮后满六十天为止。如在上述六十天内被保险货物需转运到非保险单所载明的目的地时，则以该项货物开始转运时终止。

这是一则有关海运方面的保险合同文书（节选），涉及责任范围，除外责任，责任起讫等核心部分，而每一部分又分为诸多条款。对照原文，我们发现译文无论在准确性、专业性上都十分的规范和到位。商务英语合同属于庄严体英语，要求用词规范，符合约定俗成的涵义，一般不能随意改动，除非双方经协商才能变动措辞。因此，翻译商务合同必须十分熟悉本行业务，要具有高度的责任感，并在实践中培养自己严谨的翻译作风。

（五）商品说明书的翻译

商品说明书，也称为产品说明书、使用说明书、使用手册，是生产商提供商品信息和如何使用商品的说明性文件，是商品销售过程中不可或缺的组成部分。其对应的英文名称有 Instruction Manual，Operation Manual，Instructions，Directions，Description 等。说明书的主要功能是向消费者详细介绍产品的成分、结构、性状、功用等各方面的特征，以便指导消费者正确使用该产品。总体来讲，商品说明书的语言和文体具有以下三点。1. 用词专业、体例固定。产品说明书会涉及很多专业术语，以突出产品的性质、功用等。而且每种产品的说明书其体例格式相对固定。2. 句式结构简单，行文通俗易懂。产品说明书通常要面对不同阶层、不同文化程度的用户，其表达风格应当遵循"就低不就高"的原则，那些面对大众的产品说明书尤其如此。3. 常用祈使句。祈使句有强调、警告等功能，提醒消费者注意事项，应该做什么，不应该做什么。结合产品说明书的语言特点和实际功用，我们认为商品说明书的翻译，要力求做到译文与原文在语言和文体上的对等。译文既要简洁易懂，又不能随意增删。说明书不刻意去鼓动消费者购买，只是客观地将产品的特点和用法呈现给消费者。因此，选词不能过于华丽，句型、语气风格应该与原文一致。在翻译专业术语时，要严谨规范，否则会误导消费者。如下面这则产品说明书的翻译，便很好地体现了语言风格和体例格式的对等。

例 34　Aspirin description (excerpt)

Name: Aspirin Tablets

Why it is prescribed

1. Aspirin relieves mild to moderate pain.

2. It reduces fever, redness, and swelling.

3. It prevents blood from clotting.

4. It is used to relieve discomfort caused by numerous medical problems including headaches, infections, and arthritis.

Specification type: 0.5g*100s

How it should be taken

1. Aspirin comes in the form of suppositories, capsules, and regular, coated extended-release, chewable, and effervescent tablets.

2. If aspirin tablets cause a bad taste or burning sensation in the throat, try taking coated tablets to avoid these problems.

3. Regular, coated, and extended-release aspirin tablets and capsules should be swallowed with a full glass of water or milk or after meals, to avoid stomach upset.

4. Chewable aspirin tablets may be chewed, crushed, dissolved in a liquid, or swallowed whole; a full glass of water, milk, or fruit juice should be drunk immediately after taking these tablets.

5. An oral liquid form of aspirin can be prepared by dissolving effervescent tablets according to the directions on the package.

Special instructions

1. Children should not take aspirin for fevers associated with flu or chickenpox because such use has been linked with a serious illness known as Reye's Syndrome.

2. Adults should not take aspirin for pain for more than 10 days (five days for children) without consulting a doctor.

3. Aspirin should not be taken by adults or children for high fever, fever lasting longer than three days, or recurrent fever without a doctor's supervision.

4. Do not give more than five doses to a child in a 24-hour period unless directed to do so by a doctor.

5. If you miss a dose, take the missed dose as soon as you remember it and resume the prescribed schedule.

Side effects:

1. Although side effects from aspirin are not common, they can occur.

2. Nausea, vomiting, stomach pain, indigestion and heartburn are common, aspirin after meals, with a full glass of water or milk. If these effects continue, contact your doctor.

3. Ringing in the ears, bloody or black stools, wheezing, difficulty breathing, dizziness, mental confusion and drowsiness are rare. Stop taking the drug and contact your doctor.

Storage conditions:

1. Store aspirin suppositories in a cool place or in a refrigerator.

2. Keep aspirin tablets and capsules in a tightly closed bottle in a cool and dry place.

3. Do not store aspirin in the bathroom because the dampness there can cause it to lose its effectiveness.

4. Throw away aspirin that smells strongly of vinegar.

5. Keep this medication out of the reach of children.

EXP: 01/10/202124

译文：阿司匹林药品说明书

【药品名称】阿司匹林片

【适应证/主治功能】1. 本品可以缓解轻度和中度疼痛。2. 解热，消除红肿。3. 防止血液凝结。4. 缓解由于头痛、感染和关节炎等多种疾病引起的不适。

【规格型号】0.5g*100s

【用法】

1. 阿司匹林有栓剂、胶囊、包衣缓释片、咀嚼片和泡腾片几种类型。

2. 如果服用阿斯匹林片引起口臭或喉咙烧灼感，尝试服用包衣片，以避免这些问题。

3. 普通药片、包衣片、缓释片和胶囊应用水或牛奶冲服，或饭后吞服，以避免胃部不适。

4. 咀嚼阿司匹林片可咀嚼、粉碎、溶解于液体中或吞服；服用后，应立即饮用一杯水、牛奶或果汁。

5. 可根据包装上的说明溶解泡腾片制备口服阿司匹林。

【注意事项】

1. 儿童不宜服用阿司匹林治疗流感或水痘引起的发烧，因为服用阿司匹林会导致一种称为雷氏综合征的严重疾病。

2. 成年人在没有咨询医生的情况下服用阿司匹林治疗疼痛不能超过10天（儿童为5天）。

3. 对于发高烧、发烧超过三天或经常发烧而没有医生监督的情况下，成人或儿童不应服用阿司匹林。

4. 除非医生指示，否则24小时内儿童服用的剂量不能超过5次。

5. 如果错过用药时间，记起后请立即服用，并恢复规定的用药时间表。

【副作用】：尽管阿司匹林的副作用并不常见，但也可能发生。1. 常见的副作用有：恶心、呕吐、胃痛、消化不良和胃灼热，饭后服用阿斯匹林，喝一杯水或牛奶。如影响持续，请联系医生。2. 罕见的副作用有：耳鸣、血便或黑便、喘息、呼吸困难、头晕、精神错乱或嗜睡。如出现上述症状，请停止服药，并联系医生。

【储存条件】：1. 将阿司匹林栓剂储存在阴凉处或冰箱里。

2. 将阿司匹林片剂和胶囊放在密封的瓶子里，置于阴凉干燥处。

3. 切勿将本品放在浴室里，以免湿气使其失去效用。

4. 扔掉有强烈醋味的阿司匹林。

5. 将此药物放在儿童接触不到的地方。

【有效期限】2022年10月1日

这则关于阿司匹林的产品说明书在具备自身的特殊性时，也有与其他说明书共同的特征：专业术语较多（如 arthritis, suppositories, capsules, extended-release, effervescent tablets 等）。祈使句较多，简单句较多。此外，格式和某些表达方式也属于程式化的内容，如 description, specification, side effect, storage conditions。这些表达都有相对较为固定的中文表达方式。（有的可能有两种译法，如 side effect 可以译为"副作用"或"不良反应"）。译者本着准确性、专业性、规范性和简洁性的原则进行了转化处理，基本实现了体例格式和文字表达上的功用对等。

结语

本节主要从功能对等的角度分析了商务英语的翻译，具体涉及商务信函、商务合同、产品说明书的翻译。诚然，商务英语的体裁远不止这几种类型，但也能管窥商务英语翻译的一般特征，即功能对等，包括语言、风格、体例格式等层面。随着国际贸易的加速发展，商务英语及其翻译发挥了越来越重要的作用。从事商务翻译的译者需要不断地学习国际商务知识，深入了解商务英语的文体与语言特点及其功用，并勤于翻译实践，唯此才能更好地胜任商务翻译这一艰巨任务。

课后练习

一、翻译下列句子。

1. The parcel you post must be well packed. Inadequate packing can mean delay, damage or loss at your expense.

2. After 10 months of the financial roller coaster, there were few signs of changing attitudes.

3. Everyone knows that John lost his shirt when the business he had invested failed.

4. Unless one is aware of the local culture he may end up insulting the people with whom he hopes to establish trade relations.

5. This credit is available by draft at 90 days from the Bill of Lading date. You may draw in excess of the L/C amount via your draft on ourselves, interest at 1.3% for 30 days (the first 60 days being interest rate).

6. The Seller shall be entitled to terminate this Contract in the event of failure by the Buyer to comply with any terms or conditions stated in this Article.

7. The establishment, remuneration and the expenses of the staff of the preparation and construction office, when agreed by both parties, shall be covered in the project budget.

8. Both party A and party B agree that a technology transfer agreement shall be signed between the Joint Venture Company and Party B (or a third party) so as to obtain the advanced production technology needed for realizing the production scale stipulated in Chapter 4 to the contract, including product design, manufacturing technology, means of testing, material prescription, standard of quality, and the training of personnel.

二、将下面有关仲裁的合同条款翻译为中文。

Arbitration

All disputes, controversies, claims or differences arising between the parties hereto in connection with or relating to the execution of this Contract shall be settled through amicable negotiations. In case no settlement can be reached, the case in dispute shall then be submitted for arbitration Commission of the China Council for the Promotion of International Trade in accordance with the Provisional Rules of Procedure promulgated by the said Arbitration Commission. The arbitration shall take place in Beijing and the decision made by the Commission shall be final and binding upon both parties. The arbitration fee shall be borne by the losing parties, unless otherwise awarded.

三、将下面的商务信函翻译为中文。

Dear Sirs,

Having had your name and address from the Commercial Counselor's office of the Embassy of the People's Republic of China in Tokyo, we now avail ourselves of this opportunity to write to you in the hope of establishing business relations with you.

We have been both importers and exporters of Arts and Crafts for many years. In order to acquire you with our business lines, we enclose a copy of our Export List in regard to the main items available at present.

If any of the items be of interest to you, please let us know. We shall be very pleased to give you our lowest quotation upon receipt of your detailed requirements.

We expect to receive your inquiries soon.

Yours faithfully

Encl. As stated

第五节　科技文体的翻译

一、科技文体概论

科技文体，专指以科学技术为主要内容的各种文章与论著，是人们在从事科学技术活动的过程中所形成的一种文体形式，涵盖科技专著、实验报告、技术说明等。此外，也可包括科技大会的发言记录或是声像资料的解说词等。科技文体虽然类型繁多，但是具有共同的基本特征，这些特征可以概括三种。一是客观性。科技文体以客观事物及其规律为研究对象，多用于描述事物的性质、特征、形成过程，一般采用时间顺序和逻辑顺序，不带有个人感情色彩地进行客观描述、推理、论证。二是专业性。就内容而言，科技文体所包含的各种专业主要是根据技术手段的发展和科学研究的对象性知识的积累，因此专业性较强，有时一种文体还会涉及不同的学科专业。三是规范性。科技文体一般采用规范的专业语言，配以有关公式、图像、列表等非语言表达形式。有些文体还遵循特定的写作程序和体例格式。作为科技文本的载体，科技英语同样具备上述特征，不追求语言的艺术性，而把适切性、准确性、客观性、逻辑性、简明性和规范性作为其基本特征。

科技英语 (EST—English for Science and Technology)，作为科学技术的载体，已经发展成为一种重要的英语语体。随着经济的融合和社会的进步，世界上各个国家的联系日益密切。在全球化趋势的影响下，科技的发展和经济全球一体化正在逐步加剧，科技英语作为相互交流的一种特色语言，彰显出其重要性。目前世界上许多国家已经建立了科技英语研究机构，旨在帮助国家之间更好地进行学术交流。中国仅仅依靠国内的科学技术还远远不够，还要使用别国的科学技术。特别是现今中国的改革开放走向纵深之时，中国科技事业的蓬勃发展更是离不开科技英语的翻译。因此,科技英语翻译显得特别重要,其在中国科技的发展过程中起到不可或缺的作用。因此,为了更好地做好科技英语的翻译,我们需要对其语言特征进行较为全面深入的系统了解。

二、科技英语的语言特征

科技英语是随着科学技术的发展逐渐形成的一种英语文体,专业性较强。本小节主要从词汇和句法两个层面分析科技英语的语言特点。

(一)词汇特征

随着 21 世纪经济全球化向纵深推进,科技英语也得以迅猛发展,专业词汇也越来越丰富。人们在阅读和翻译科技文献时,经常会碰到许多新的术语。虽然科技词汇数量大、来源广泛,但它们的构成是有一定规律的。大致来讲,主要有以下几种来源。

常用词 科技英语中的专业术语,有相当一部分源自日常用语。许多科技词汇都是由一般生活词语转换而成,与原义有着直接或间接的联系。如单词 pit 在日常语境中有"坑、槽"之意,而在采矿行业中则指的是"煤矿",在纺织业则为"麻点"之意。carrier 的日常意义为"搬运者"或"运输工",但是在医学领域,却是"带菌者"或"携带者"。burst 其基本含义为"爆炸、迸发",在光电学中则为"脉冲"之意。lunch-box 本指午餐盒,科技英语中可以指"便携式计算机",等等。

专有词 有时借用外来词、人名、地名、商标等直接用作科技英语词汇。这种方法在科技英语中用得十分普遍。科技英语里专有名词较多,如:kuru(库鲁癫痫症,源自几内亚的 kuru Highlands,库鲁高地),Xerox 复印(源自美国商标词"施乐"),Gaussian function(高斯函数,源自法国数学家 Gaussian),Hill reaction(希尔反应,源自英国植物学家 Robert Hill),Roussarcoma virus(劳氏肉瘤病毒,源自美国病理学家 Francis Peyton Rous),Down syndrome(唐氏综合征,源自英国医生约翰·朗顿·唐 John Langdon Down),Wernicke's area(韦尼克区,源自德国医生和神经学家卡尔·韦尼克 Carl Wernicke),等等。

缩略词 缩略词按照结构又可分为截短词和字母缩略词。截短词(clippings)如 chute=parachute(降落伞),aerodrome=drome(飞机场),eq=equation(方程式)fig=figure 图等。字母缩略词(Acronyms)则更为常见,如:QR=quick response(二维码),AC=alternate current(交流电),ADM=adaptive delta modulation(自适应增量调制),AI=artificial intelligence(人工智能),DC=direct current(直流电),MSE=mean-square error(均方误差),RMS=root-mean-square(均方根),DNA=deoxyribonucleic acid(脱氧核糖核酸),

TB=tuberculosis（肺结核），Ic=integrate circuit（集成电路），RPM=revolutions per minute（转数/分），等等。

派生词 科学技术的不断发展为英语增加大量的新词汇。派生法是科技英文中常见的构词手段，一般是通过词缀加上词根构成，词缀的意义相对来讲较为固定，译者可以根据已有的构词知识推断词义。如词根 photo 在希腊文中为"光"（lumin）之意，由此派生出的新词有 photometer（光度计），photocurrent（光电流），photodiode（光电二极管）等。cyber 源自希腊语 Kubernetes 意为"操舵员"或者"飞行员"。诺伯特·维纳在《控制论》中使用 Cybernetics 一词，后来作为前缀代表与 Internet 相关或电脑相关的事物，由此派生的新词有：cybersquat（网上盗名登记），cybersecurity（网络安全），cyberworld（虚拟世界），等等。nano 也是较为流行的科技术语前缀，nano 来源于希腊，有"微小"之意，现在 nanos 表示"十亿分之一"，一般翻译为"纳（诺）"或"毫微"，如 nanowatt（毫微瓦），nanosecond（毫微秒），nanometer techonology（纳米技术），等等。

诚然，科技英语中的词汇构成还有其他方法，限于篇幅这里只涉及主要的四种。

（二）句法特征

科技英语的句式结构紧凑，逻辑性强，表述严谨。具体表现为如下主要特征：名词化结构；常用被动句式与非人称句式；复杂句式较多；多用一般现在时。

名词化结构 科技英语常用名词化结构分为两种情况，一是动词的名词化以及名词的连用或叠加。第一种情况如：

例 1 Graves' ophthalmopathy usually occurs in association with hyperthyroidism.

例 2 Lower shear stress shows the greatest increase in permeability in combination with TNF-α..

第二种情况是名词的叠加，即多个名词连在一起使用。如：Computer programming teaching device manual（计算机程序编制教学装置手册）上面几个例子都是名词的叠加，如果换成普通的表达方式，则为：manual of teaching device for computer programming，这样显得稍微繁琐。下面的例子同样体现了名词叠加的特征。the Trend Micro QR Scanner（趋势科技二维码扫描仪），human immune deficiency virus（人类免疫缺陷病毒），illumination intensity determination（照明强度测定），Transfer Adaptation Learning（迁移自适应学习），sample selection bias（采样选择偏差），等等。

科技论文的目的在于叙述事实和论证推断，要求简洁明了。而动词的名词化以及名词的连用有效地简化了叙事层次和语言结构，减少了使用从句的频率，使行文更加紧凑。

被动句与非人称句式 科技文本主要描述科技活动的过程、结果，进而探究其自然规律。因此，在科技英语中，大量使用被动句式、非人称句式，以便读者把注意力集中在所叙述事物的本身，从而突出科技文本侧重叙事和推理论证的特征。如：

例 3　The behavior of a fluid flowing through a pipe is affected by a number of factors including the viscosity of the fluid and the speed at which it is pumped.

例 4　It is now known that food protein is not absorbed as much, but must first be broken down into constituent amino-acids.

例 5　Since this iBTA technology cannot be applied in medical treatment in Japan, it is necessary to develop a new process for obtaining regulatory approval in this case.

使用被动语态不仅客观，而且还可以使读者的注意力集中在叙述事物的本身。不过，被动语态只是一种主流趋势。事实上，近年来科技论文中泛主语 we 的使用也在逐渐普遍。如：

例 6　It is worth noting that, with JDA, we can usually obtain a more accurate labeling for the target data. Thus, if we use this labeling as the pseudo target labels and run JDA iteratively, then we can alternatingly improve the labeling quality until convergence.

例 7　To tackle the non-convexity, we decouple the optimization problem into two stages (subproblems) where we minimize the distributional discrepancy and maximize the structural similarities alternatively. Specifically, we have the following two stage optimization algorithm.

在上面这两段文字中，每段都出现了三次 we，这并非偶然现象。在描述实验操作过程时，这种情况较为常见。所以科技英语的被动语态不能一概而论。这是值得注意的一种现象。

复杂句式　科技英语是随着科学技术的发展逐渐形成的一种英语文体，具有高度的专业化。科学的根本任务在于认识事物和现象的本质，揭示其运动规律。科研人员要对这些事物和现象进行分析、归纳、推理、论证。因此，科技文体的语言自然具有专业性、抽象性、精确性、逻辑性等特点。科技文体不讲究修辞效果，但注重用词的准确和句子的平衡，句子所含信息量较大，因而复杂句较多。句式虽长，但是层次清晰，逻辑性强。如：

例 8　Unless otherwise noted, oxide folds and suckbacks are acceptable if the thickness in the area is not less than the minimum sheet or plate thickness allowed in the material specification and/or the drawing tolerance for machined or formed sheets or parts, whichever is applicable.

例 9　We developed an endothelialized microfluidic device where the two-layer microfluidic channels are compartmentalized, which enables independent flow modulation in each channel and supply of controlled shear stress and stimuli to the cells

一般现在时 科技英语一般倾向于多用一般现在时，来表示无时间性的一般叙述。即通常发生或并无时间限制的自然现象、过程、常规，等等。一般现在时在科技英语中用于表述科学定义、定理或公式的解说以及图表说明，或者表述观点与结论时。目的在于排除任何与时间相关的误解。

例 10　Our results indicate molecular targeting of atherosclerotic plaques.

例 11　Application of nano-DDS is a unique and promising approach to prevent life-threatening cardiovascular events including acute myocardial infarction by regulating inflammation in the cardiovascular system.

例 12　To our knowledge, the 50 cm long Biotubes are the world's longest tissue-engineered vascular grafts. The Biotubes successfully functioned as arterial grafts and AV shunt grafts within a limited acute phase of implantation in beagle dogs and goats, indicating the potential use of the iBTA technology to develop long Biotubes that are biocompatible and can be used in clinical practice.

需要指出的是，过去时、完成时态也会使用，尤其是在描述实验过程时，过去时的使用较为普遍，如下面这段文字。

例 13　For accurate diagnosis of this inflammatory disease, molecular imaging is required. Toward this goal, we sought to develop a nanoparticle-based, high aspect ratio, molecularly targeted magnetic resonance(MR) imaging contrast agent. Specifically, we engineered the plant viral nanoparticle platform tobacco mosaic virus (TMV) to target vascular cell adhesion molecule (VCAM)-1, which is highly expressed on activated endothelial cells at atherosclerotic plaques.

三、科技英语的翻译原则与策略

科技英语是实用文体中最为严谨的一种，因此它的翻译要求也较高。下面我们就科技文体的翻译应该遵从的原则与策略进行讨论。

（一）翻译原则

基于上述科技文体与科技英语特定及其功用的分析，我们认为科技文体的翻译应遵循三点，即：准确规范、通俗易懂、简洁明晰。（赵萱、郑仰成，2018：2）准确是科技文体翻译的第一要务，准确是指完整无误地传达原文的所有信息，而规范则指译文要符合科技术语或某一专业领域内专业语言的表达规范。要搞清楚所涉专业内容和有关的科学原理。深入理解句子含义并灵活进行切换。通顺易懂，是指译文的语言符合译入语语言的表达习惯及句法结构，易为读者所理解和接受。换言之，译文要明白晓畅、逻辑清晰，无佶屈聱牙、晦涩难懂的现象。简洁明晰是科技文体的特征之一，因此科技英语的翻译自然也要体现这一特点。要避免繁琐冗长的句式表达。要分清句子的主次和搭配性质，长句的断句和顺序安排。在校对时要特别注意数字、单位、图形的准确无误，要保证译文在语言、逻辑和专业知识三方面都经得起推敲。

（二）策略与方法

关于科技英语具体的翻译策略与方法，我们不求面面俱到，而是选取重要的几种进行分析与讨论。

科技术语翻译的准确性与表达的规范性　首先区分一般用语和专业术语，然后再确定其专业范围。要注意旧词新义和新词的创造以及外来词的使用。尤其要注意较长的名词词组内部的修饰和限定关系。如：

例 14　Velocity changes if either the speed or the direction changes.

译文 1：假如速度的大小或方向改变了，速度要跟着变化。

译文 2：如果速率和方向有一个发生变化，则运动速度也随之发生变化。

例 15　Oil and gas will continue to be our chief source of fuel.

译文 1：油和气体将继续是燃料的主要来源。

译文 2：石油和天然气将继续作为燃料的主要来源。

例 16　To prepare a nano fluorescent probe (Anti-CD47 NP) linked with Anti-CD47 antibody, 1.5 mg TPETPAFN probe, 2.0 mg MPEG-DSPE2000 and 2.5 mg PEG-DSPE-COOH$_{2000}$ were respectively weighed and dissolved in 1 ml THF. 1 ml of the above mixed solution in a cell breaker was added dropwise into 9ml deionized water, and ultrasonic treatment was performed for 60s.

为**制备**成连接 Anti-CD47 抗体的纳米荧光**探针**（Anti-CD47　NP），依次称取 1.5 mg TPETPAFN 探针、2.0 mg MPEG-DSPE$_{2000}$、2.5 mg PEG-DSPE-COOH$_{2000}$，溶解于 1 ml 的 THF。在细胞破碎仪中将溶解好的 1 ml 的上述混合溶液逐滴缓慢滴入到 9 ml 的去离子水中，超声处理 60s。

例 14、例 15 的译文 1 都是不准确的。在科技术语中，velocity 与 speed 是有区别的，不能混为一谈。在科技英语中，在没有特殊说明的情况下，oil 与 gas 分别指石油和天然气。例 16 则体现了术语的准确性和表达的规范性。如 prepare 应译为"制备"而不是"准备"，probe 译为"探针"而不是"刺针"。但在某些情况下，科技英语中常用词汇的词义较为灵活，必须根据上下文进行推断。如：

例 17　The test confirms again that smokers are most prone to develop lung cancer...

这个测试再次确定了吸烟者最容易患（或感染）肺癌。

例 18　Shorts frequently develop when insulation is worn.

绝缘受到磨损时往往会发生短路（现象）。

例 19　First, there are the industrial historians. Second, the analysis and chronicles. Third and finally, the "hands-on" industrial engineers. In some cases, the foregoing divisions are separated by flexible curtains, rather than brick walls.

首先是工业历史学家，第二是分析与编年史，第三，也是最后一个，"动手"的工业工程师，有些情况下，上述分类是柔性的，而不是刚性的。

Develop 在不同的语境下其语义也不尽一致，有"研发""研究""提出""恶化"等。而例 17 和例 18 中的 develop，根据语境，却只能被分别理解为"患""得"或"感染"，以及"发生""产生"。而例 19 中的 "flexible curtains""brick walls" 则更不能直译，而只能根据上下文分别译为"柔性的"（或弹性的）和"刚性的"。

科技词语和术语在某一专业范围内其词义较为稳定，只要勤于查找各种资料，一般即可正确使用。随着科技的日新月异，新生的科技术语也往往大量涌现。如何翻译这些新生术语呢？这里有一些约定俗称的译法。大致来说，主要分为两种情况，一种是译意，二是译音，三是音译+注释词。第一种情况较为简单，即如果原名有词义，译意即可，如果无词义，则取音译。音译时，一般要遵从"名从主人"的原则，即源自哪国术语，即采用哪国的发音。如奎宁（quinine），法兰（flange），凡士林（vaseline）。第三种方法是，在音译之后再加上注释性语词，凸显术语的属性，如来复枪（rifle），普米族（Pumi），这里的"枪"和"族"便表示事物的属性。此外，还有一些术语其译名尚未统一，如 ergonomics 就有"工效学""人体工学""人类工效学"等数种译文，myocardial infarction 也存在"心肌梗塞""心肌梗死"两种译法。面对此种情况，可以采用译名+原文的方式。如工效学（ergonomics），心肌梗死（myocardial infarction）。至于科技译名的统一性问题，自然由专门机构负责。但是从事科技英语翻译的人员，应本着负责任的态度，遵循基本的科技译词原则，将译名混乱的现象控制在最小范围内。

被动语态的适当转化　科技文体注重事理的客观叙述，竭力避开作者的主观判断，因而常用被动语态，以及其他表示客观陈述的句式，如含有 it 的评价结构。但在翻译成中文时，这些被动语态要适当地转化为汉语的主动语态。

例 20   In each pig, one of two grafts was cannulated with a 16G dialysis needle. After removal of the needle, the cannulation site was digitally compressed for at least 3 min or until hemostasis was reached. Time to hemostasis was recorded.

在每只猪身上，每头猪的两个移植物中的一个用 16G 透析针插管。拔出针头后，将针管部位数字压缩至少 3 分钟或直至止血，并记录止血时间。

例 21   As oil is found deep in the ground, its presence cannot be determined by a study of the surface. Consequently, a geological survey of the underground rock structure must be carried out. If it is thought that the rocks in a certain area contain oil, a drilling rig is assembled.

由于石油是在地下深处发现的，不能通过研究地表来确定石油的存在。因此，必须对地下岩石结构进行地质调查。如果认为某一区域的岩石中含有石油，就装配钻机。

在这两个原文中，被动语态较多。尤其是第二个例文中，被动语态一共出现了 5 次。而译文中并没有出现一次"被"动结构。而语义同样清晰，结构严谨。原文短短的一段文字，共有 4 处被动语态，但在译文中却都变为了主动语态。这并不是说，译文不能用被动语态。如果特别强调动作的承受者，也可以采取被动结构。如：

例 22   The substance which gives up hydrogen is said to be oxidized and the one which accepts the hydrogen is said to be reduced.

放出氢的物质被称为氧化了的物质，而接受氢的物质被称为还原了的物质。

再现非人称句式的客观性　此外，含有 It 的评价性结构在科技英语中也较为常见。在传统语法中，it 作为形式主语的结构，它使真正的主语后置避免了结构的头重脚轻。另外，it 还可用于投射句，将命题当成事实陈述，发话者无需介入而显得客观，因而被称为评价性 it。这种结构在学术、科技英语中应用较多。它能使作者的观点客观中立。符蓉、李延林（2020：11）总结了五种类型的评价型主位：似然性、重要性、难易度、确定性与可行性。如果 it 作为形式主语，翻译时，般将真正主语前移，还原主语 + 谓语结构。在翻译 it 主位评价句时，要尽量保持原文的主位结构，如果不能保留，也要通过其他手段。因此，应将 it 小句前置，如必须后置，也要补充适当的语词，以弥补评价因后置而消失的主位凸显性。如：

例 23   In any FSO network, it is possible that multiple users might try to access the same optical link at the same time.

在任何访问网络中，都有可能出现多个用户同时访问同一光链路的情况。（似然性）

例 24   Therefore, it is important to consider the neighboring tiles together to make sure the errors are properly compensated.

因此，**请务必将相邻切片一起考虑，以确保错误得到修正**。

例 25　Besides, it is desirable to be able to accommodate non-trivial CFO values in the system.

此外，**一个理想的办法**就是调试该系统中的非平凡的 CFO 值。（可行性）

这些译文都保留了原文的主位结构，避免了观点表述的主观性。但是，在表示否定或然性 unlikely/impossible 时，却不能放在句首，译为"不可能的是"。必须后置时，可用这等话题标记，将评价内容变为话题，用"是"突出 it 小句作为评价的焦点。如：

例 26　Due to the restricted size of a femtocell light cone, **it is unlikely** that any given user will have to share their FSO connection with many other users

由于蜂窝基站光锥的大小有限，要一个用户必须与许多其他用户共享其 FSO 连接，**这是不太可能的**。

时态的保留或适当切换　前面分析可知，科技英语多用一般现在时，来表示无时间性的一般叙述。需要注意的是，科技英语中的一般现在时可以表示过去，进行甚至将来。刘宓庆（2015：210）认为应该根据具体的情况进行适当的时态转移。如：

例 27　Enzyme *plays* an important role in the complex changes in tooth growth.

酶在牙齿生长的复杂变化中起着重要的作用。（转变为现在进行时）

例 28　As the disease progresses, the large muscles also *grow* steadily weaker. Without treatment, the patient becomes paralyzed, *has* great difficulty breathing and eventually *dies*.

译文：随着病情发展，大肌肉会逐渐衰竭。不经治疗，病人就会瘫痪，呼吸会发生困难，最终将导致死亡。（转变为将来时）

例 29　Tifflin must be saying something right when he *points out* that the focus is man's adaptation to the environment.

梯夫林曾经指出，关键在于人对环境的适应能力。他一定说对了。（转变为过去式）

在上面的三个例子当中，原文均为一般现在时，但在翻译成为中文时，却相应的转化为了将来时、现在进行时和过去式。例1描述了在病情发展过程中，会出现的一些现象，因此用将来时较为恰当。例2用进行时更能凸显突出了 ensyme 在牙齿生长的过程中的重要作用。例3指出的是人物的观点，采用过去时能够与前面的 must be saying 形成一种时间上的照应。

虽然一般时态占据主流，但其他时态同时并存。时态的不同体现了的语义诉求，以及科技论文的严谨。这些时态也应该在译文中准确地体现，以确保语义的准确。如：

例 30　This, too, was something which was completely at variance with the known laws of nature.

这同样完全不符合当时已知的自然法则。

例 31 Such plants have evolved to depend on hummingbirds rather than insects as pollinators.

这类植物**已经**进化到依靠蜂鸟而不是依靠昆虫来传授花粉（的程度）。

例 32 The cyclones will make the removal efficiency increase.

旋风分离器**会**使分离效率得以提高。

由于英汉动词的形态变化属于不同的类型，因此在转化过程中就不应机械的进行对应。译者应对中英科技文体的时态要非常敏感，唯有如此才能准确地在两种语态之间切换自如。

连接词的适当删减或保留 科技英语十分注重连接词、虚词、介词等的使用，这一点与科技英语重视叙事的逻辑性、层次感、推理过程等有关。因此衔接手段在科技英语中的应用较为广泛，尤其是体现在复杂的长句、复合句里。因为中英语言在形合和意合方面的差异，在翻译为汉语时，却只能部分地保留这些连接词，否则容易造成译文啰嗦。如：

例 33 When the ship is moving close to a wall or bank, because of reduced cross section, accelerated flow between the ship and bank, so the fluid pressure is reduced in this space, and the suction force draws the ship closer to the bank.

船舶靠近槽壁或岸壁时，横向距离减小，船体和壁岸之间的流速加快，导致该区间流体压力减小，吸力将船体吸向岸边。

例 34 To detect the distribution of Free NP and Anti-CD47 NP in ApoE-/-mice, 8-week-old male ApoE-/-mice were equally divided into three groups: Saline group (n = 5), Free NP group (n = 5) and Anti-CD47 NP group (n = 5). After fed on a high-fat diet for 12 weeks, 150μl saline, 150μl free NP solution and 150μl anti-CD47 NP solution were absorbed respectively with a disposable insulin syringe and then injected intravenously into the mice through the tail vein. The mice were euthanized at 6h, 12h, and 24h after the nanoparticle injection. And then the heart, liver, spleen, lung, kidney and aortic organs were isolated. Cambridge Research & Instrumentation (CRI) fluorescence imaging system was applied to collect the fluorescence signals of nanoparticles in atherosclerotic plaques .

为检测 Free NP 和 Anti-CD47 NP 在 ApoE-/- 小鼠体内的分布，将 8 周雄性 ApoE-/- 小鼠平均分为三组：生理盐水组（n=5）、Free NP 组（n=5）、Anti-CD47

NP 组（n=5）。喂养高脂饲料 12 周后，用一次性胰岛素注射器分别抽取 150μl Saline、Free NP 溶液和 Anti-CD47 NP 溶液通过尾静脉注射入小鼠体内。在纳米粒注射 6h、12h、24h 后迅速处死小鼠取心、肝、脾、肺、肾和主动脉器官。使用 CRI 荧光成像系统采集纳米粒在动脉粥样斑块中的荧光信号。

在上面的原文中，我们发现有诸多连词、介词如 when, because of, so, and, then, and then, 等等，这些连接词将整句连接了起来，句子内部结构紧凑，体现了科技英语的严谨性。为了使译文符合汉语行文习惯，译文对句法结构进行了转换，采用意合手段，去形存意，省略了这大部分连接词。相形之下，译文则体现了意合的特性，以及对语境的高度依赖性。

但有些时候，为了体现科技文体的严谨性，译文中必要连接词的保留还是必要的。如：

例 35　Underwater currents and several other factors swing the sled about, making it impossible to tow the device over exact, predetermined routes *unless* we know precisely where it is all times.

深海洋流及其他因素使撬状装置摇摆不定，**因此**我们无法将它在确定、预定的路线上拖曳，**除非**我们每时每刻都能准确地知道它的位置。

例 36　The production function is responsible for the selection of a production system, made up of facilities and equipment, that will provide a product or service, and thus will carry out the organization's strategic policy.

生产部门负责选择由设施设备组成的生产系统。此生产系统将生产产品或提供服务，**进而**执行企业的战略方针。

例 37　A computer is a device that takes in a series of electrical impulses representing information, combines them, sorts them, analyses and compares the information with that stored in the computer.

计算机是一种装置，该装置接受一系列含有信息的电脉冲，对这些脉冲进行合并、整理、分析，并将它们与储存在机内的信息进行比较。

这三个译文都部分地保留了原文的连接词（见粗体部分）。这里的"因此""除非""进而"很难省略。如果省略的话，语义则不甚明朗。由此可见，科技英语的汉译过程中，去形留意只是一种整体倾向。如果去掉原文中的连接词，而原文的语义、逻辑不受任何影响，则可采取这种措施，反之则要保留。

四、科技论文摘要的翻译

摘要(abstract),是对论文主体内容的浓缩。作为学术论文的重要组成部分,论文摘要一般包括研究过程、研究视角、研究方法、研究发现以及主要结论等。论文摘要一般有相对固定的表达,体现在词汇和句式层面。常用的词汇有:introduce, to analyze, to focus on, apply to/to use, indicate, suggest, show, to summarize/sum up to put forward/to propose;句式结构有:this paper gives a brief introduction of(本文简要地介绍了),this research sets out to analyze and compare(本研究拟就对比分析),it indicates(研究表明),it finds that(研究发现),it concludes that(研究得出结论),this study suggests that(研究提出/建议),等等。在时态方面,一般过去时或完成时主要用于对实验和研究过程的具体描述,一般现在时主要介绍研究的目的或是结论。

论文摘要的翻译,一是要保证内容的完整性和信息的准确性,不能有任何的遗漏或是歪曲;二是要注意语言表达的规范性。三是注意时态的转化;四是要注意行文的逻辑性和层次感。要区别哪些是已知信息,哪些是未知信息,哪些是主要信息,哪些是次要信息。总之,要理清不同信息的轻重缓急。如:

例 38　Tissue engineered blood vessels are considered a promising alternative for prosthetic vascular grafts as arteriovenous vascular access for hemodialysis. In a goat model of arteriovenous grafting, we have demonstrated sufficient mechanical characteristics of *in situ* engineered vascular grafts to allow safe vascular grafting with similar patency rates compared to ePTFE AV-grafts. This indicates that *in situ* TEBVs are a robust vascular graft, with the potential to be used in as arteriovenous vascular access for hemodialysis.

译文1:组织工程血管作为血液透析的动静脉通路,被认为是人工血管移植的一种有前途的选择。在山羊动静脉移植模型中,我们已经证明了原位组织工程血管移植的足够的力学特性,使得安全的血管移植具有与ePTFE AV血管移植相似的通畅率。这表明原位TEBVs是一种强大的血管移植物,有可能用作血液透析的动静脉通路。

译文2:组织工程血管作为血液透析的动静脉血管通路,被认为是人工血管移植很有前途的一种替代方法。在山羊动静脉移植模型中,我们已经证明了原位组织工程血管移植物具有足够的力学特性,能够以与ePTFE AV移植物相似的通畅率进行安全的血管移植。这表明,原位TEBVs是一种强有力的血管移植物,具有用作血液透析动静脉血管通路的潜力。

译文1与译文2都再现了原文的全部信息。但在精确度和规范性上,译文1不如译文

2. 如对原文 we have demonstrated sufficient mechanical characteristics of *in situ* engineered vascular grafts to allow safe vascular grafting with similar patency rates compared to ePTFE AV-grafts 的处理上，译文 1 出现了偏差。这里的 safe vascular grafting 其实是一种结果，因为前面交代原位组织工程血管移植物具有足够的力学特性。因此，翻译为"安全的血管移植"这种偏正关系欠妥，译文 2 则避免了这个问题。此外，在措辞方面，译文 1 也存在一些瑕疵，如最后一句的翻译，译文 1 "这表明原位 TEBVs 是一种强大的血管移植物，有可能用作血液透析的动静脉通路"中的"强大"和"可能"有些随意。译文 2 使用了"强有力""潜力"，显得更规范一些。

五、科普文章的翻译

科技英语中还有一类体裁较为特殊，即科普文章。科普文章担负着向大众普及科学知识、启蒙思想的功用。科学性是所有科技作品的生命，科普作品也不例外。科普是科学技术与社会生活之间的一座桥梁，它在向读者传授知识、宣传科学的世界观和方法论，以提高人们的科学素质的同时，也使其受到科学思想、科学精神的熏陶。因此，科普文章的主要特点就是通俗性，即用明白晓畅的文字介绍科技知识。因此，科普文章的翻译，要在尊重原文基本事实的基础上，采用平实的语言再现原文的思想性，有时允许个人一定程度的语言艺术性发挥，如下面一则科普文章的翻译。

例 39　QR codes are everywhere now. Here's how to use them.

The pandemic and our desire to minimize contact with objects and surfaces as much as possible has spread the use of Quick Response (QR) codes.

How QR codes work

While you might have only heard about them recently, this technology has been around since the 1990s. They're essentially a type of code that holds information in a form that other hardware and software can understand. In the same way that a store checks barcodes to identify the prices of various goods, you can scan a QR code to launch a website, register at a doctor's office, sign into a service, get a Wi-Fi password, or install an app.

Scanners can only read standard barcodes in one direction, top to bottom. But your phone can read QR codes in two directions: top to bottom, and left to right. This means these patterns can contain significantly more information—just about any type of data, and up to about 4,000 characters of text.

You might be surprised at how easily your phone can read QR codes. The three black squares in the corners of the graphic tell your phone where the code is, before the actual scanning takes place. This means angles aren't usually a problem, and you won't need to get the framing exactly right or have a perfectly steady hand.

This technology can be really useful, but don't go down the street scanning every QR code you find. There is potential for abuse from shady operators, mainly through attempts to send you to websites designed to capture login details or install malware on your phone. As long as your device is running up-to-date software, it should be able to spot and block these malicious techniques. But it's still worth being cautious when scanning QR codes in public places, especially when you're not sure who's behind them.

While it's unlikely that fraudsters will have replaced all the QR codes on the menus at your local restaurant, a code randomly stuck to a wall in a public space is more likely to be risky. Exercise common sense and caution and you shouldn't run into any security or safety problems.

In terms of privacy, QR codes can't actually store data—they just display it. How much information about yourself you're giving away depends on the app you're using to scan. If it asks you to sign in before or after reading a code, the app could be storing that data as a sort of browsing history. As always, check app privacy policies if you're unsure.

How to use QR codes

Using QR codes is easy: just point your phone's camera at the graphic, and your device processes the data the moment it recognizes it.

Some apps use this technology as a means for authentication, where all you need to do is follow instructions. One example of this is WhatsApp, which asks you to scan a QR code on their web client to load up your account with all your contacts and conversations in a browser.

If you've come across a QR code in the wild, you can use your phone's camera app. On Android, open the Camera app and get the QR code in focus within the frame. Once your device recognizes the pattern, you'll see a link appear on screen. Tap the link to open it.

The process is very similar on iOS. Launch the Camera app, point your phone's camera at a QR code, and when you've got the framing and the focus right, you'll see a notification asking you if you want to open the link embedded in the code.

Most of the time, your phone's built-in camera app will do just fine, but there are plenty of QR code reader apps available, too. They offer extras such as the ability to keep a log of all the codes you've scanned, and to process many more types of barcode.

If you want to be ultra-cautious, you can install a reader app from a trusted security company. One example is the free Kaspersky QR Scanner app for Android and iOS. When it scans QR codes, the platform puts up a warning if you're about to visit a URL that's known to be harboring malware or associated with phishing attempts.

Another option is the Trend Micro QR Scanner for Android, or the QR scanner built into Trend Micro Mobile Security for iOS. Again, the platform will flag potentially problematic links in the QR code so you can stay away from harmful sites. Android and iOS have their own similar security features built in, but a third-party app gives you an extra level of protection if you feel like you need it.

参考译文：二维码如今无处不在，小贴士助你应对自如

全球新冠疫情的影响，以及我们尽可能减少与物体和物体表面接触的意愿，使二维码（QR）的使用迅速流行起来。

二维码的工作原理

虽然最近你才可能听说，但这项技术早在20世纪90年代就出现了。二维码其实是一种代码，它以其他硬件和软件都能解读的形式保存信息。就像商店检查条形码来识别各种商品的价格一样，你可以通过扫描二维码来打开一个网站，预约医生，登陆某项服务（平台），也可获得wi-fi密码或者安装应用程序。

扫描仪只能在一个方向上即从上到下读取标准条形码。但是手机可以从两个方向读取二维码：从上到下，从左到右。这意味着这些模式可以包含更多的信息——几乎任何类型的数据，最多可以包含4000个字符的文本。

或许你会感到惊讶，手机居然如此容易地读取二维码。其实，在扫描之前，二维码图案中三个黑色的方框就告诉手机代码在哪里了。就是说，角度一般不是问题，你无需对准图案或是用手拿稳手机。

这项技术的确有用，但切勿在街上扫描你发现的每一个二维码，以防可疑运营商的欺诈。他们会尝试不同方法诱导你登录网站，以获取登录详细信息或在手机上安装恶意软件。只要你的手机运行的是最新的软件，就应该能够发现并阻止这些恶意技术。但是在公共场所扫描二维码时，还是谨慎为好，尤其是当你不确定幕后操纵者是谁时。

虽然诈骗者不太可能把你们当地餐厅菜单上的二维码全部替换掉，但在公共场所随机贴在墙上的二维码更有风险。运用常识并保持谨慎，应该不会遇到任何风险和安全问题。

就隐私而言，二维码实际上不能存储数据，只能显示数据。提供多少信息取决于你使用的扫描应用程序。如果应用程序要求在阅读代码之前或之后登录，应用程序可能会将该数据存储为一种浏览记录。如往常一样，如果存有疑问，可事先查阅应用程序隐私政策。

如何使用 QR 码

使用二维码很容易：只要将手机的摄像头指向图形，设备识别图案之后就会即刻处理数据。

有些应用程序使用该技术作为认证手段，你所需要做的就是按照说明操作就行了。Whatsapp 软件便是一例，它要求你在其网络客户端上扫描二维码，然后在浏览器中加载你所有的联系人和对话内容。

如果你在户外发现了一个二维码，可以使用手机的相机应用程序。在安卓系统上，打开摄像头应用程序，对准二维码团。一旦设备识别到该模式，你会看到屏幕上出现链接。点击链接打开它。

这个过程在 iOS 程序上也非常相似。启动摄像头应用程序，将手机的摄像头指向二维码，对准框架时，你会看到一个提示，询问是否要打开嵌入在代码中的链接。

多数情况下，手机内置的摄像头应用程序同样有效，不过也有很多二维码码阅读器应用程序可供选择，还提供额外的功能，例如记录你扫描的所有代码，并处理更多类型的条形码。

如果需要格外小心，你可以从信誉良好的安全公司安装阅读应用程序。如免费版的卡巴斯基二维码扫描仪应用程序，用于 Android 和 iOS 系统。在扫描二维码时，如果访问一个已知包含恶意软件或与"网络钓鱼"企图相关联的统一资源定位器，在扫描二维码时，平台将会发出警告。

另一个选择是 Android 上安装的趋势科技二维码扫描仪，或者内置在 iOS 上内置的网络趋势科技移动安防二维码扫描仪。同样，平台将在二维码中标记出潜在的问题链接，这样你就可以远离有害网点。Android 和 iOS 内置了自己类似的安全功能，但是如果你觉得必要的话，第三方应用程序会为你提供更多的保护措施。

这是一则介绍二维码工作原理和使用指南的科普文章，文字简单明了，通俗易懂。译文同样采取了简洁明快的语言，不局限于字面意义和句式结构的局限，体现了一定的主体发挥，尤其是标题的翻译"二维码如今无处不在，小贴士助你应对自如"，采用了平衡结构和四字格，可顿时引起读者的关注，进一步引起阅读正文的兴趣。

结语

本节主要探讨分析了科技英语的翻译，包括科技文章、科技论文摘要的翻译，以及科普文章的翻译。可以看出，科技文体的翻译较为严谨。科技英语表达严谨的科学事实或进行预测，不允许有任何的差错。即便是科普文章，也要尊重原文的基本事实。为此，专业的科技翻译人员应当通晓本专业各个方面的基础知识，掌握本专业的发展动态。只有勤于学习，勤于翻译实践，科技翻译的主观能动性才能得到很好的发挥。事实证明，译者的科技背景在科技英语翻译中起着重要的作用。只有当译者有着厚实的科技背景时，才能在科技英语翻译中表现出色。

课后练习

一、翻译下列句子。

1. Hence, in addition to geometric shapes, it is possible to use different material compositions to optimize the mechanical properties of a component for given design requirements.

2. The lifejacket can be stowed in the life-boat or taken from the ship and placed under the seat or on the knees during the launch. It is not allowed to take any other loose objects in the boat.

3. First, there are the industrial historians. Second, the analysis and chronicles. Third and finally, the hands-on industrial engineers. In some cases, the foregoing divisions are separated by flexible curtains, rather than brick walls.

4. The current increases faster than resistance decreases, leading to more heating and less heat radiation and resistance.

5. Using this reasoning, we can estimate the number of detectable civilizations in our galaxy.

6. The transfer of information from one part of the computer to another depends on the electrical current being conducted over wires.

7. Agricultural technique spreading centers have been set up everywhere in that province, helping farmers to do their work in a more scientific way.

8. Captured underwater noise was transmitted directly from the hydro-phone to operator's ear-phones.

9. Odd though it sounds, cosmic inflation is a scientifically plausible consequence of some respected ideas in elementary-particle physics, and many astrophysicists have been convinced for the better part of a decade that it is true.

10. Aluminum remained unknown until the nineteenth century, because nowhere in nature is it found free, owing to its always being combined with other elements, most commonly with oxygen, for which it has a strong affinity.

二、翻译下列一则科技短文（节选）。

Diabetes is a common metabolic disease worldwide. 463 million people were estimated to have diabetes in the world in 2019, and this number is expected to increase to 700 million in 2045. For people living with diabetes, cardiovascular disease (CVD) is the main problem they face, which remains the most prevalent cause of death in patients with diabetes. Specifically, the relative risk of CVD morbidity and mortality in people with diabetes ranges from 1 to 3 in men and 2 to 5 in women compared with those without diabetes.

三、翻译下面一则科技摘要。

Aims: To provide global estimates of diabetes prevalence for 2019 and projections for 2030 and 2045.

Methods: A total of 255 high-quality data sources, published between 1990 and 2018 and representing 138 countries were identified. For countries without high quality in-country data, estimates were extrapolated from similar countries matched by economy, ethnicity, geography and language. Logistic regression was used to generate smoothed age-specific diabetes prevalence estimates (including previously undiagnosed diabetes) in adults aged 20–79 years.

Results: The global diabetes prevalence in 2019 is estimated to be 9.3% (463 million people), rising to 10.2% (578 million) by 2030 and 10.9% (700 million) by 2045. The prevalence is higher in urban (10.8%) than rural (7.2%) areas, and in high-income (10.4%) than low-income countries (4.0%). One in two (50.1%) people living with diabetes do not know that they have diabetes. The global prevalence of impaired glucose tolerance is estimated to be 7.5% (374 million) in 2019 and projected to reach 8.0% (454 million) by 2030 and 8.6% (548 million) by 2045.

Conclusions: Just under half a billion people are living with diabetes worldwide and the number is projected to increase by 25% in 2030 and 51% in 2045.

四、翻译下面一则科普文章

Oil

What was the origin of the oil which now drives our motor-cars and aircraft? Scientists are confident about the formation of coal, but they do not seem so sure when asked about oil. They think that the oil under the surface of the earth originated in the distant past, and was formed from living things in the sea. Countless billions of minute sea creatures and plants lived and sank to the sea bed. They were covered with huge deposits of mud, and by processes of chemistry, pressure and temperature were changed through long ages into what we know as oil. For these creatures to become oil, it was necessary that they should be imprisoned between layers of rock for an enormous length of time. The statement that oil originated in the sea is confirmed by a glance at a map showing the chief oilfields of the world; very few of them are far distant from the oceans of today. In some places gas and oil are of marine origin too. They are sedimentary rocks, rocks which were laid down by the action of water on the bed of the ocean. Almost always the remains of shells, and other proofs of sea life, are found close to the soft rock and was obviously formed by being deposited on the sea bed. And where there is shale there is likely to be oil.

Geologists, scientists who study rocks, indicate the likely places to the oil drillers. In some cases oil comes out of the ground without any drilling at all and has been used for hundreds of years. In the island of Trinidad the oil is in the form of asphalt, a substance used for making roads. Sir Water Raleigh visited the famous pitch lake of Trinidad in 1595; it is said to contain nine thousand million tons of asphalt. There are probably huge quantities of crude oil beneath the surface.

There is a lot of luck in drilling for oil. The drill may just miss the oil although it is near; on the other hand, it may strike oil at a fairly high level. When the drill goes down, it brings up oil. The samples of soil from various depths are examined for traces of oil. If they are disappointed at one place, the drillers go to another. Great sums of money have been spent, for example in the deserts of Egypt, in prospecting for oil. Sometimes little is found. When we buy a few gallons of petrol for our cars, we pay not only the cost of the petrol, but also part of the cost of the search that is always going on.

When the crude oil is obtained from the field, it is taken to the refineries to be treated. The commonest form of treatment is heating. When the oil is heated, the first vapors to rise are cooled and become the finest petrol. Petrol has a low boiling point; if a little is poured into the hand, it soon vaporizes. Gas that comes off the oil later is condensed into paraffin. Last of all the lubricating oils of various grades are produced. What remains is heavy oil that is used as fuel.

参考答案

第一章

第五节

一、翻译下列句子，注意"忠实"和"通顺"的原则。

1. 我认为那篇讲话口气强硬，大可不必。

2. 职业和工作对于获得幸福和满足起了很大的作用，我们大多数人却对此认识不足。

3. 气候变化，他仅稍稍作了一头变通，赴宴时穿了件白色的短礼服。

4. 但下个世纪我们将能从根本上改变DNA，能在构建新的生命时把我们的种种想象、种种出于虚荣的要求，都编入遗传密码。

5. 他有一种习惯让人无法忍受，意见反复不定，一会儿一个变化。

二、翻译下列句子，注意直译法和意译法的运用。

1. 见风使舵

2. 厨子太多煮坏汤。

3. 满堂喝彩

4. 人皆有短处

5. 徒劳无功/枉费心机

三、翻译下列句子，注意归化法或异化法的运用。

1. 过着牛马一样的生活

2. 缘木求鱼

3. 旧瓶装新酒

4. 王牌

5. 象牙塔

第二章

第一节

翻译实践

一、英汉语言结构

（一）翻译下列句子，注意思考英汉语言结构的差异。

1. 这所大学造就了他。

2. 他的一番话表明他决心完成这件棘手的工作。

3. 园艺还为许多娱乐活动提供环境，包括户外家庭生活区的野炊地以及足球场上的耐寒草皮。

4. ……每当它敏捷而机械的迈出一步，或者果断地驻足观察时，总是流露出一副自命不凡，不求他人，十分自信的神情，俨然认为世界就是为苍蝇而创造的。

（二）翻译下列句子，注意思考英汉语言结构的差异。

1. 我们必须加强国防建设。

2. 我们和中国人双方都是怀着谨慎、不安甚至是惶恐的心情来互相探讨这初次的接触的。

3. 这个主题突出了三个方面的特点：时代性，独创性和普遍性。

4. 长江后浪推前浪，世上新人换旧人。

（三）翻译下列句子，注意思考英汉语言结构的差异。

1. 他开始变得惊恐万分。

2. 近来发现，馆藏图书量惊人地减少。

3. 我们认为，他今天上午发言的内容和口气都无助于在中东建立持久的和平。

4. 深化改革开放，激发经济社会发展活力。

5. 继续把简政放权、放管结合作为改革的重头戏。

二、英汉文化差异

（一）翻译下列词组，注意思考词汇背后的文化内涵。

1. 先发制人

2. 健康极佳

3. 春风得意

4. 满面春风

5. 雨后春笋

6. 很会喝酒

（二）翻译下列句子。

1. 他在家中地位显赫。

2. 会计科那个女科长是个十足的母夜叉。

3. 是别人放的火，让我背了黑锅。

4. 你给我们讲的那个笑话简直老掉牙了，但是我认为还是很有趣的。

（三）翻译下列词组或句子。

1. 美钞

2. 无用而累赘的东西

3. 人才济济

4. 被打得青一块，紫一块

5. 临阵换将

（四）翻译下列词组或句子。

1. 害群之马

2. 对牛弹琴

3. 缘木求鱼

4. 音痴、五音不全

5. 亡羊补牢，为时未晚

6. 别高兴得太早。

课后练习

一、词语翻译

1. 一贫如洗 as poor as a church mouse

2. 付诸东流 go down the drain

3. 皇天不负有心人 heavens helps those who help themselves

4. 说曹操，曹操到 talk of the devil and he will appear

5. 心有余而立不足 the spirit is willing but the flesh is weak.

二、句子翻译

1. 由于接触包括原子武器实验产生的放射性散落物在内的辐射，人类基因可能遭到损伤，这一问题近年来已经理所当然地引起了人们的广泛重视。

2. 可是现在人们意识到，其中有些矿物质的蕴含量是有限的，人们甚至还可以比较合理地估计出这矿物质有望存在多少年，也就是说，经过若干年后，这些矿物的来源和储备将消耗殆尽。

3. 土地龟裂，泉水干涸，牛群也无精打采地啃着干树枝。

4. 而特许经营真正的春天则始于20世纪50年代后期，此时假日酒店之类的旅馆和宾馆迅速扩散开来，巴斯金—宾斯和唐金甜面包圈之类的快餐企业更是遍地开花。

5. 你必须要有锦囊妙计，否则你不会成功。

三、段落翻译

1. 恐怖主义是人类社会的公敌，是国际社会共同打击的对象。恐怖势力通过暴力、破坏、恐吓等手段，肆意践踏人权、戕害无辜生命、危害公共安全、制造社会恐慌，严重威胁世界和平与安宁。极端主义思想的渗透与蔓延极易催生暴力恐怖行为，对人们享有各项人权直接构成威胁。中国政府反对一切形式的恐怖主义、极端主义，对任何宣扬恐怖主义、极端主义，组织策划实施恐怖活动，侵犯公民人权的行为，依法严厉打击。

2. At the southern terminus of the Grand Canal and amid a region known as the "land of fish and rice" is Hangzhou, the imperial capital during the Southern Song period. The centrepiece of the city's seductive landscape is West Lake, a shallow man-made reservoir, the creation and alternation of which owes much to the efforts of some of China's great poets. As officials, both Bai Juyi in the ninth century and SuDongpo in the eleventh century built sea walls, dykes, causeways, and bridges as well as restored temples and pagodas.

四、篇章翻译

1. 沿河上下都可以听见那歌声。它响亮而有力，那是船夫，他们划着木船顺流向下，船尾翘得很高，桅杆系在船边。它也可能是比较急促的号子，那是纤夫，他们拉纤逆流而上，如果拉的是小木船，也许就只五六个人；如果拉的是扬着横帆的大船过急滩，那就要200来人。船中央站着一个汉子不停地击鼓助威，引导他们加劲。于是他们使出全部力量，像着了魔似的，腰弯成两折，有时力量用到极限就全身趴在地上匍匐前进，像田里的牲口。他们使劲，拼命使劲，对抗着水流无情的威力。领头的在纤绳前后跑来跑去，见到有人没有全力以赴，竹板就打在他光着的背上。每个人都必须竭尽全力，否则就要前功尽弃。就这样他们还是唱着激昂而热切的号子，那汹涌澎湃的河水号子。我不知道词语怎样能描写出其中所包括的拼搏，它表现的是绷紧的心弦，几乎要断裂的筋肉，同时也表现了人类克服无情的自然力的顽强精神。虽然绳子可能扯断，大船可能倒退，但最终险滩必将通过，在筋疲力尽的一天结束时可以痛快地吃上一顿饱饭……

2. 经过多年不懈奋斗，中国农村贫困人口显著减少，贫困发生率持续下降，解决区域性整体贫困迈出坚实步伐，贫困地区农民生产生活条件显著改善，贫困群众获得感显著增强，脱贫攻坚取得决定性进展。据世界银行测算，按照人均每天支出1.9美元的国际贫困标准，过去40年中国共减少贫困人口8.5亿多人，对全球减贫贡献率超过70%。按中国现行贫困标准，1978年至2017年，中国农村贫困人口由7.7亿人减少到3046万人，贫困发生率由97.5%下降到3.1%。2012年至2017年，中国每年有1000多万人稳定脱贫。中国是世界上减贫人口最多的国家，也是率先完成联合国千年发展目标减贫目标的发展中国家。中国的减贫成就是中国人权事业发展的最显著标志。

第二节

翻译实践

一、英汉词汇对比

（一）翻译下列词汇。

1. 盆栽，盆景

2. 旗袍

3. 苦力

4. 易经

5. 小费，赏钱

（二）翻译下列词组。

1. 虔诚的教徒

2. 慈爱的父母

3. 孝顺的儿女

4. 贤良的妻子

5. 尽职的丈夫

（三）翻译下列词汇。

1. 新约

2. 不公正地划分选区，弄虚作假

3. braised pork ball in brown sauce

4. fotiaoqiang (steamed abalone with shark's fin and fish maw in broth)

5. double-flavored hot pot

二、英汉句法对比

（一）翻译下列句子，注意句中语态的转换。

1. 由首都渥太华和各省资助成立的加拿大健康技术合作办公室，就是朝创立一个全国性的医药机构这一方向迈进所踏出的一小步。

2. 8440个空白乡镇邮政局所完成了补建，全国总体实现"乡乡设所，村村通邮"。

3. 人们发现，当人们经常接触某种气味时，一开始时会突然变得对它很敏感。

4. 认为自己的思想太深奥，以至于不可能表达清楚使任何人都能理解，这是一种自我安慰。这样的作家当然不会想到，问题出在自己的头脑缺乏精确思考能力。

5. 同时，六月十七日曝光的盗取美国4,000万信用卡账号信息的事件也给一天前美国联邦商业委员会做出的重要决定蒙上了阴影，该决定向美国商界发出公告，如果企业不能充分保障数据安全，执法者将采取行动。

（二）翻译下列句子，注意中英文句式结构的转换。

1. 尽管它听起来很奇怪，宇宙膨胀说是在基础粒子物理学中一些公认的观点在科学上貌似可信的推论，并且在近十年中，很多天体物理学家已经相信这种理论是真实的。

2. 美国人不再期望公众人物在演讲或写作时可以娴熟地运用技巧和文采来掌握英语，而人们本身也不再这样去要求自己。

3. 上周，这家新英格兰的主要能源供应商宣布将停止履行"遵守该州严格的核能管理法规"这一长期承诺，这激起了佛蒙特州合情合理的公愤。

4. 鉴于本年度选择出来的高质量的公司，以及我们在这次多元文化活动的组织中从中国和欧洲的赞助商、合作伙伴中收到的积极回应，我相信这次会议将会获得圆满成功，为中国和欧洲之间的ICT创新合作建立一个良好的平台！

（三）翻译下列句子，注意中英文句式结构的转换。

1. 这是一次精心组织的会议，由斯特朗先生主持，市政厅济济一堂，热情洋溢。

2. 氧化膜表面具有轻微的渗透性，因此可以用有机或无机燃料着色。

3. 她说："有一个哥哥该多好啊。"这话说得十分有道理。她没爹没娘，又没有亲戚朋友，孤苦伶仃的。软心肠的阿米莉亚立刻同情起她来。

4. 最令女主人失望的是，她花了许多心思或费用来招待客人，可是，这位客人只顾津津有味地与她的丈夫谈政治或生意，却没注意到香气扑鼻的咖啡、松软的蛋糕或者房间内别具一格的陈设。

（四）翻译下列句子，注意中英文句式结构的转换。

1. 人们认为美国队将赢得这场足球赛，皮特也是这样想的，但是我认为结果并非如此。

2. 阅读训练人的眼睛，说话训练人的口齿，写作训练人的思维。

3. 近朱者赤，近墨者黑。

4. 狡猾之人轻视学问，愚昧之人羡慕学问，聪明之人利用学问。

5. 历史使人明智；诗歌使人灵秀；数学使人周密；自然科学使人深刻；伦理使人庄重；逻辑修辞使人善辩。

课后练习

一、句子翻译

1. 她入睡了。

2. 这座城市沦陷了。

3. 别在墙顶上走，你会摔下来的。

4. 当我告诉她这个消息的时候，她突然沉下脸来。

5. 上周利率下跌得很厉害。

6. 举行祷告是为了纪念战争中的阵亡将士。

7. 各国应以民主、包容、合作、共赢的精神实现共同安全，做到一国内部的事情一国自主办，大家共同的事情大家商量办。

8. 当复杂性超过极限时，这种现象就会发生，而我们现有的许多系统包括编纂和计算机操作系统已经超出了极限。

9. 读史使人明智，读诗使人灵秀，数学使人周密，科学使人深刻，伦理学使人庄重，逻辑修辞之学使人善辩。

10. 我们过了江，进了车站。我买了票，他忙着照看行李。这时我看见他的背影，我的泪很快地流下来了。我赶紧拭干了泪，怕他看见，也怕别人看见。

二、段落翻译

1. 卫星导航系统是人类发展的共同财富，是提供全天候精确时空信息的空间基础设施，推动了知识技术密集、成长潜力大、综合效益好的新兴产业集群发展，成为国家安全和经济社会发展的重要支撑，日益改变着人类生产生活方式。

2. Navigation satellite systems are public resources shared by the whole globe, and multi-system compatibility and interoperability has become a trend. China applies the principle that "The BDS is developed by China, and dedicated to the world" to serve the development of Belt and Road Initiative, and actively pushes forward international cooperation related to the BDS. As the BDS joins hands with other navigation satellite systems, China will work with all other countries, regions and international organizations to promote global satellite navigation development and make the BDS better serve the world and benefit mankind.

三、篇章翻译

1. 一年来，外交工作成果丰硕。习近平主席等国家领导人出访多国，出席二十国集团领导人峰会、金砖国家领导人会晤、上海合作组织峰会、东亚合作领导人系列会议、亚欧首脑会议、达沃斯论坛等重大活动。成功举办亚太经合组织第二十二次领导人非正式会议、亚信会议第四次峰会、博鳌亚洲论坛。积极参与多边机制建立和国际规则制定。大国外交稳中有进，周边外交呈现新局面，同发展中国家合作取得新进展，经济外交成果显著。推进丝绸之路经济带和21世纪海上丝绸之路建设，筹建亚洲基础设施投资银行，设立丝路基金。我们与各国的交往合作越来越紧密，中国在国际舞台上负责任大国形象日益彰显。

2. 中国是一个地域辽阔，有着数千年悠久历史的多民族国家，有着秀丽的自然风光、众多的名胜古迹和丰富多彩的灿烂文化，旅游资源十分丰富。改革开放以来，中国经济以年平均近10%的速度持续增长，各项事业蓬勃发展，人民生活水平显著提高，为旅游业的兴旺奠定了坚实的基础。中国政治稳定，经济发展，市场繁荣，中国政府坚持对外开放积极发展与世界各国的关系，也为旅游业的发展创造了极为有利的条件。中国政府十分重视旅游业的发展，将旅游业作为第三产业的重点，不断开发旅游资源，改善旅游设施，提高服务质量，促进了国际国内旅游业的快速发展。随着中国人民生活水平的提高，我国到国外旅行的人数也逐年增多，为国际旅游业的发展增添了新的活力。

第三章

课后练习

第一节

翻译下列句子，注意划线单词的词义。

1. 他个子很高，身材挺直，两眼明亮，皮肤黝黑。

2. 账目清楚。

3. 把你的房间整理好。

4. 她品行端正。

5. 有很多事情我们需要搞清楚。

6. 这可是个十分正经的地方。

7. 我和他的关系忽冷忽热。

8. 这首歌的音乐和歌词都给人留下非常深刻的印象。

9. 因为贫穷，我必须精打细算每一分钱。

10. 他这个人最会干伤天害理的事情。

11. 他一直生活在沙漠里，每杯水都是生死攸关之大事，必须精打细算地用。

12. 女孩们很容易沉浸在自我批评的谈话中，一旦开了个头，别人就很难掺和进去。

13. "你这个胆小鬼！"他轻蔑地看着威廉道。

14. 曾经是不登大雅之堂的言语，如今充斥于电影、戏剧、书籍之中，甚至充斥在电视上。

15. 他们向那个亿万富翁点头哈腰的行为看起来非常令人作呕。

16. 请不要惹是生非。

17. 他以为像这样花言巧语加上奉承就可以蒙蔽她，但她没有受骗。

18. 他是整个学校都仰慕的人。

19. 情人眼里出西施。

20. 这是个使所有老师都束手无策的孩子。

21. 不久，他就成为了全国的风潮级人物。

第二节

一、翻译下列句子，注意划线部分的词类转换。

1. 她工作十分努力。

2. 做完手术后，他还在恢复当中。

3. 她热衷于阅读爱情故事。

4. 我不会教你法语，我觉得我弟弟会教得更好。

5. 火箭已经用来探索宇宙。

6. 如果你每天不上网，你就会忽视国内外的发展。

7. 她非常担忧她妈妈的健康。

8. 盐可溶于水。

9. 我们不应该满足于当前的成绩。

10. 他的腿摔断了，在床上躺了一个月。

11. 向十八岁以下的未成年人出售香烟违反当地的规定。

12. 等了很久之后，我上了一辆出租车，但车子移动得和蜗牛一样慢。

13. 人们的说话声变低了，成了耳语。

14. 这台电脑性能很好。

15. 一个穿着讲究，外表和谈吐都像美国人的人上了车。

16. 设计的目的在于操作自如，调节方便，维护简易，生存率高。

17. X 在数学上用于表示方程中的未知数。

18. 他们对我们的问题表示同情和理解。

19. 伤员们已经被送往医院。

20. 我们要有全球观念。

21. 这就是你错误的地方。

22. 每天一个苹果能让你身体健康。

23. 上周五的路演非常成功。

24. 我们有各种各样的女士围巾。

25. 交流思想非常有必要。

26. 这个爱情故事使我印象非常深刻。

27. 下个月初很有希望能完成。

28. 交通事故和他的粗心驾驶脱不开干系。

29. 这完全是无稽之谈。

30. 一个成功的科学家必然擅长观察。

31. 贸易量增长迅猛，对两国都有利。

32. 很幸运我能见到他。

33. 我们必须全心全意服务于客户。

34. 我成功地说服了他。

二、翻译下列段落，注意使用词类转换法。

金婚纪念日

一对夫妇正在庆祝他们的金婚纪念日，他们多年平静的生活，成为小镇上流传的佳话，一个小报记者要求采访他们这段长久而幸福的婚姻的秘密。"这要从我们的蜜月说起，"男的说，"我们去旅行了大峡谷，而且用骡子驮着行李走到了谷底，我们没有走多远，我妻子的骡子就跌倒了，妻子平静地说：'这是第一次。'"

第三节

一、翻译下列句子，注意使用增词法。

1. 我狂热地爱上了她，她也狂热地爱上了我。

2. 这份报纸可以指导群众，教育群众，鼓舞群众。

3. 无知是畏惧之源，羡慕之根。

4. 他伸出双腿，露出腿上的道道疤痕。

5. 是不是有轻微的噪音？是什么噪音呢？

6. 肺癌如果能够早期确诊，也能进行满意的手术治疗。

7. 通货膨胀过去是，现在仍然是国家的首要问题。

8. 英语目前的情况良好，并正以不易为人发现的方式变化着。

9. 该病毒可能存活数周甚至数月。

10. 机器再响也不会妨碍你休息，对吧，杰克？

11. 你爱怎么办就怎么办吧!

二、翻译下列段落，注意使用增词法。

如果你饿了，你会怎么做？抓起你最喜爱的美食饱餐一顿，然后静静地待在那里？而你的大脑也像你的胃，是会感到饥饿的，但它却从不让你知道，因为你让它一直想着你的梦中情人，你最喜爱的明星和许多诸如此类的荒唐事。因此它只是默默地留意着你的需要却从不让自己成长。当思维恣意成长时，创造力就戛然而止。

第四节

一、翻译下列句子，注意使用减词法。

1. 不到长城非好汉。

2. 寒冷阴沉，乌云密布。

3. 这个城市工业人口稠密。

4. 如果你施恩于别人，不要耿耿于怀；如果你受人恩惠，请铭记于心。

5. 他们把他踩在脚下，压得粉碎，他们榨干了他的精髓，害死了他的父亲，摧残了他的妻子，毁了他全家。

6. 与人同乐才是真乐。

7. 不要自找麻烦。

8. 他被捕判刑，监禁在狱。

9. 无雪，叶落，草枯。

10. 应聘兼职女招待，有工作经验者优先。

11. 她踌躇了一会儿，静静地站着，有一两滴泪水溅落在破旧的红地毯上。

12. 我看到乘客们涌向站台，知道火车就要进站了。

13. 盼复。

14. 政府已经发行了新的硬币，但只有少数人见到过。

15. 狐狸会变老，但绝不会变好。

二、翻译下列段落，注意使用减词法。

词语"赢家"和"输家"有很多种意思。当我们说起赢家时，并非意味着他使别人一败涂地。所谓的赢家是能真实地表现出守信、可信、敏锐、诚恳的个体及社会的一员。

第五节

一、翻译下列句子，注意使用重译法。

1. 大家庭有大家庭的难处。

2. 人们往往更爱把脾气发在陌生人身上，尤其是电话里只闻其声而不见其人的人身上。

3. 虽然你被录取了，但你仍然有缺陷，而且缺陷很大。

4. 你决心成为什么样的人，你就可以成为什么样的人。只要决心做出个名堂，你就会做出名堂。

5. 先生们尽管可以高喊和平，和平！但是依然没有和平。

6. 一个人死后，人们忘记了他的脸，然后忘记了他的名字。

7. 大城市里的医生和医生是不一样的。

8. 这一直是我们的立场－而不是他们的立场。

9. 这一下不仅震痛了他的手，也震痛了他的肩膀。

10. 他既精于飞行，又善于导航。

11. 他粗心大意，马马虎虎的行为激怒了他的顶头上司。

12. 一群吵吵嚷嚷，喋喋不休的孩子一窝蜂地下了公共汽车。

13. 据说那位集邮者有一张独一无二的邮票。

14. 他给我们讲了他在非洲的一个栩栩如生，惟妙惟肖的故事。

15. 她想向那对收养她的老夫妇表达她真真切切的感谢。

16. 一整个下午，他都是一副心不在焉，迷迷糊糊的样子。

二、翻译下列段落，注意使用重译法。

我们的生命无非就是我们的时间，因此浪费时间也就是一种自杀。我们想到死便惊恐不已，因而不惜一切努力，麻烦和费用来保全我们的生命。可是我们对于损失一个小时或一天的时间无动于衷，忘记了我们的生命原本就是我们生活的每一天，每一小时的总和。因此浪费一天或一个小时就是丧失一天或一个小时的生命。人生短暂，总共不过七八十年。可是将近三分之一的时间必须用睡眠；吃饭也得花去好几年；陆路海上旅游又是几年；再加上娱乐活动的几年，在病床边照看至亲至爱的几年。现在如果从我们的寿命中扣除所有这些岁月，我们将会发现，能受我们支配的有效的工作时间大约仅二三十年而已。谁能记住这一点，谁就不会心甘情愿地浪费他生命的分分秒秒。

第六节

一、正反译法

（一）翻译下列句子，注意运用正反、反正译法。

1. 我没有得到这样一个机会。

2. 不久之前他金盆洗手，戒了赌博。

3. 你知道他为什么总是不愿意见你吗？

4. 交警不让骑车人上人行道。

5. 报社不愿意对公众隐瞒事实。

（二）翻译下列句子，注意划线部分名词的反译。

1. 不注意文化差异或当地习俗可能会产生问题。

2. 黑暗是因为没有光。

3. 这里没有水供应。

4. 她满脑子全是对过去的回忆，其他事情都不想了。

5. 所有的国际争端都应该通过协商解决，尽量不要使用武力。

（三）翻译下列句子，注意划线部分形容词或形容词短语的反译。

1. 这小孩写作业非常不细心。

2. 他不慌不忙地掏出工具开始制作书桌。

3. 她漫不经心地说："哼，这有什么关系呢？"

4. 不出所料，今年夏天更热。

5. 他已经变得焦躁不安了，这不难理解。

（四）翻译下列句子，注意划线部分介词的反译。

1. 我爸爸是最不可能责骂我的人了。

2. 父母经常对孩子的优点视而不见。

3. 他们正密切注视着动荡不安的局势。

4. 对老年人来说，现代流行音乐比不上传统音乐。

5. 公司的倒闭是因为经营不善。

6. 他的钥匙不见了。

7. 她胃里不舒服。

（五）翻译下列句子，注意划线部分介词的反译。

1. 不满十八岁的人禁止结婚。

2. 我的成绩不值一提。

3. 发言人讲的内容我理解不了。

4. 他成功地在不到两年的时间完成了晋升。

5. 如果没有其他的事情，我们可以结束会议了。

6. 他还来不及阻止我，我已经脱口而出了。

（六）翻译下列句子，注意划线部分连接词的反译。

1. 他不开口讲话，我都没意识到他是一个外国人。

2. 他的行为不是我能理解的。

3. 她宁愿尝试第十次也不愿放弃。

4. 她男朋友不仅帮不上忙，反而在这碍事。

5. 他家说不上好客，倒是很大方。

（七）翻译下列句子，注意固定短语（或者俚语）的反译。

1. 油漆未干！

2. 他的文章不缺优美的短语。

3. 还有很多未开发的能源。

4. 未经邀请不得入内。

5. 地平线与天空泾渭分明；在一个特定地点，一片银色磷辉逐渐升高，扩大，衬得地平线格外黝黑。最后，在恭候已久的大地的边缘，月亮堂皇地徐徐升起，她摆脱了地平线，无羁无绊地悬在空中。这时，他们又看清了地面的一切——广阔的草地，幽静的花园，还有夹在两岸之间的整条河，全都柔和地展现在眼前，一扫神秘恐怖的色调，亮堂堂如同白昼，但又大大不同于白昼。他们常去的老地方，又在向他们打招呼，只是穿上了另一套衣裳，仿佛它们曾经偷偷溜走，换上一身皎洁的新装，又悄悄溜回来，含着微笑，羞怯地等着，看他们还认不认得出来。

二、反正译法

（一）翻译下列句子，注意划线部分否定动词的正译。

1. 这个问题亟待解决。

2. 他违背了他的母亲，同一群家伙出去厮混。

3. 她一直反对收养那个可怜的婴儿。

4. "系上鞋带，凯文，"她说。

5. 这个话题的中心是揭开当今社会的价值问题。

（二）翻译下列句子，注意划线部分否定名词的正译。

1. 市政府官员们的欺诈行为被报纸披露。

2. 他出生在1946年战后的动荡年代，这使他具有强烈的使命感。

3. 基因工程是对生命的漠视。

4. 她的声音中流露出一丝迟疑。

5. 政府已宣布要扫除文盲。

6. 斯皮尔伯格被称为"忧虑大师"。

（三）翻译下列句子，注意划线部分否定形容词的正译。

1. 博物馆内的一切展品禁止触摸。

2. 那是一次极其痛苦的返回伦敦的旅行。

3. 我感觉到难以置信的轻松。

4. 这个老人的牙齿全掉光了。

5. 琳达这么讲是有点欠考虑。

6. 但他始终担心自己再次一贫如洗。

（四）翻译下列句子，注意否定副词的正译。

1. 我们要永远对生活抱有乐观的态度。

2. 他呆若木鸡地站在那里，一时不知该说什么。

3. 他焦躁地用手指敲打着桌子。

4. 她饥一顿饱一顿的，慢慢消瘦了下去。

5. 他电话刚一放下，门铃就响了。

6. 一雨即倾盆。

第七节

一、将下列英文被动句直接译为"被"字句。

1. 他被所有朋友看不起。

2. 公司被禁止使用虚假广告。

3. 可怜的孩子被打得青一块紫一块的。

4. 他被送到前线去了。

5. 这家著名的酒店已经被大火烧了。

6. 过度加热，维生素 C 会被破坏。

7. 我被困在倾盆大雨中。

二、将下列英文被动句译为变体"被"字句。

1. 电视机使我们能了解当今的国内外大事。

2. 那些做好事的人将会得到奖赏。

3. 翻译技巧应该得以充分重视。

4. 他遭到两个蒙面人的袭击。

5. 错误不应当加以掩饰，而必须加以揭露，才能得到改正。

6. 赵大妈为家境所迫，十二岁就到上海一家针织厂做童工。

三、将下列英文被动句译为中文主动句。

1. 这块地方满是纸屑，烟头，空瓶子和生锈的空罐头。

2. 这个老人住在一个十分古老的小镇上，这个小镇的四周有一片秀丽的树林。

3. 全世界都踢足球。

4. 当这位老师走进实验室时，有一群沉静的列队行进的学生跟随着他。

5. 大家估计这个项目会汲取国外经验。

6. 众所周知人口一直在增长。

7. 我们的前嫌已经冰释。

8. 必须警告烟民的是，医生们已经得出结论，吸烟会增加肺癌的概率。

9. 必须注意放射性物质的安全。

10. 让人不愉快的噪音必须立即停下来。

11. 于是，国会和盟友们驳斥了里根的提议。

四、将下列英文被动句译为中文的判断句。

1. 水是进化生命所必需的。

2. 这些书是我的朋友借给我的。

3. 自由女神像是十九世纪法国人民赠予美国的。

4. 彩虹是当太阳穿过雨滴照射下来形成的。

5. 他们是得到命令这样做的。

6. 包办婚姻给我们提供了一个很好的例子，告诉我们未来的爱人是如何相识的，文化价值观和习俗又是如何限制了伴侣的选择。

翻译下列段落，注意被动语态。

由于石油深埋地下，靠研究地面，不能确定石油的有无。因此，对地下岩层结构必须进行地质勘探。如果认为某地区的岩层含石油，则在该处安装钻机。钻机中最显眼的部件叫井架。井架用来吊升分节油管，把油管放入由钻头打出的孔中。当空钻成时，放入钢管防止孔壁坍塌。如果发现石油，则在油管顶部紧固地加盖，使石油通过一系列阀门流出。

第八节

一、分译法

（一）翻译下列句子，注意划线词语的分译。

1. 我总是克制自己，不去想那件事。

2. 这个小村庄有个美丽的湖，人人以此为自豪。

3. 因为他很富有，他可以做任何事。

4. 她以自己高超的厨艺为荣，这是可以理解的。

5. 人们已经认识到，无线电波是一种辐射能。

6. 天寒地冻，人人都躲进了室内。

7. 电脑可以让杰克上到合适的课程，不会太快，也不会太慢。

（二）翻译下列句子，注意划线部分的分译。

1. 他们之间十分坦率，直言不讳，气氛很轻松。

2. 她来到伦敦，就国际形势而言，时机正合适。

3. 本杰明富兰克林一生都在学习，他不仅从书本中学习，也从与人的交往中学习。

4. 演讲已经开始，他离开座位时那么轻，因此谁也不怪他干扰演讲。

5. 他疲惫不堪，天气也越来越热，于是他下了决心，一碰到舒适的阴凉处，就坐下来休息。

6. 外宾观看了这场在北京举行的锦标赛，看得十分入迷。

（三）翻译下列句子，注意使用分译法。

1. 音响效果不好，演出大为逊色。

2. 我们漫步街头，在中央大道附近发现了一个很大的棚户区，有很多迹象表明茅棚里还住了人。

3. 在数学教学中，一般采用传统方法：教师正规讲课，学生记笔记。

4. 现在此处已经成为冬夏两季的度假胜地，风光景物，蔚为奇观；而从前，筋疲力尽的旅游者到此只得止步。

5. 她经常提到她在意大利碰到一位老先生的事，她见他愁容满面，就问起他闷闷不乐的原因。

翻译下列段落，注意使用分译法。

世界经济正在发生着根本性转变。我们正迅速向一个世界告别，在此世界中，各国经济曾为相对自成体系的实体，因为跨境贸易和投资的壁垒重重，各国地理位置各异、时区不同、语言不通，以及各国政府管控制度不一、文化有别、经济体制相异，这些实体彼此独立。与此同时，我们正迈向一个新世界，在这个世界中，跨境贸易和投资的壁垒正在坍塌，随着运输手段和电信技术的进步，可感距离日益缩短，世界各地物质文化日渐趋同，各国经济日趋相互依存，逐渐融为全球经济体系。正在发生这一变化的过程通常称为全球化。

二、合译法

翻译下列段落，注意综合使用本章的翻译技巧。

人们对智力所指的有那些不同表现看法比较一致，而对这些表现如何进行解释和分类，意见就不那么一致了。但人们一般认为智力高的人在处理问题时能抓住要点，善于区分，能进行逻辑推理，和利用语言和数学符号。智力测试只能很粗地衡量孩子的学习能力，尤其是学习学校要求的东西的能力。智力测试并不能衡量一个人的个性，社会适应力，耐力性，劳动技能，或艺术才能。人们不认为能做到这些，当初也不是为这些目的设计的。批评智力测试不能做到这一些，就如同批评温度计不能测风速一样。既然对智力的评估是相对而言的，那么我们必须确保，在比较对象时，我们所使用的尺度能提供"有效的"或"公正的"比较。

第四章

课后练习

第一节

一、翻译下列句子，其中注意名词性从句的翻译。

1. 淋巴结肿大是对艾滋病或任何一种病毒的免疫反应。

2. 得出的结论是，我们不确定现在作弊是否比过去更糟。

3. 鲁尔小姐是一个全面发展的学生，品学兼优，堪称前程无量的 WOW 候选人；所谓 WOW，乃是为世界各国杰出妇女而设的一个国际性的奖学金项目。

4. 可以毫不夸张地说，镇上的大街小巷感人至深的事迹何止千百：邻里互相帮助，青年帮老年，富人帮穷人。

5. 濒临死亡的病人——特别是最容易受误导、也经常被蒙在鼓里的病人——因此不能做出对有关临终的种种选择：是否要住进医院，或进行手术；在何处与何人度过所剩余的时间；以及如何处理完自己的事务而后与世长辞。

6. 这些个人和组织通过贿赂来决定赛事的电视转播权和主办国，以及这个管理着全世界有组织足球运动的组织该由谁领导。

7. 我们不知道今天在体育运动中作弊是否比过去更普遍，但是机构腐败似乎在体育组织中正在成为一个日益严重的问题，其中大多数组织都缺乏正式的强制性命令保证其透明度或明晰责任。

8. 身体在水中比在空气中轻，这是一个普遍的经验。

9. 人们常说，广泛阅读是最佳的替代行动方案，但即使这样，也有必要做出一些选择。

10. 很明显，他不仅仅需要善意、墨水和纸张来回信。

11. 法律规定，父母必须确保其子女在学校或其他地方接受全日制教育，在英格兰、苏格兰和威尔士，孩子年龄在5岁至16岁，在北爱尔兰，孩子年龄在4岁至16岁。

12. 他说，部分问题在于制定目标时，欧盟却在拼命解决交通排放量不断上升的问题。

13. 几乎无法想象，如果没有城市的支持，大学、医院、大型企业甚至科学技术都不会诞生。

14. 营养实验表明，维生素对一个人的生长和健康是必不可少的。

15. 任何治疗最重要的部分不是你理解什么或谈论什么，而是你做了什么。

16. 关键的是你有没有尽力去完成这个任务。

17. 他曾经来过中国使所有在场的人都激动不已。

18. 他没有准时出席会议的原因是他遇到了交通堵塞。

19. 这就是他如何处理这件事的，这让我很担心。

20. 医生慢慢意识到了医院的环境对病情恢复是很重要的。

21. 困难在于这个事实，国与国对人口增长的态度不同。

22. 毫无疑问政府会采取措施来阻止新冠疾病的蔓延。

23. 据报道，到目前为止，已经有100多个孩子在洪水中失去了生命。

24. 现在我们要做的最重要的事是保护那些正受到灭绝威胁的野生动物。

二、翻译下面的段落，注意其中的名词性从句的翻译。

1. 我们经常听到人们说，电脑处理问题是因为电脑设有能让其处理问题的程序，它们只能按人的指令行事。我们应该知道，人类也设有程序。我们的基因给我们编写了程序，我们的所作所为无不受制于这个"程序"。我们大脑的程序极其复杂，我们或许可以从人类的文学、艺术、科学和技术上的创造力这个角度给"思维"下定义。从这个意义上说，电脑肯定无法思维。

2. 真正的幸福在于怎样开始而不是如何结束，在于我们的希冀而并非拥有。渴望是永远的乐趣，一笔如地产般真实稳固的财富，用之不尽，取之不竭。每年我们都会因为拥有渴望而充满活力。一个人如有许多希望，精神便会富足。人生只不过是一场单调乏味且编导拙劣的戏，除非我们对这戏有些兴趣；对于既没有艺术细胞也没有科学细胞的人来说，这个世界只不过是各种颜色的堆积，或者是一条崎岖小路，一不小心就会摔伤小腿。正是因为希望与好奇，我们才会以加倍的耐心继续生存，才会着迷于纷繁复杂、多姿多彩的人或事，早晨醒来才会以崭新的热情投入新一天的工作和娱乐。希望和好奇是人观看这绚丽迷人的世界的一双眼睛：正是这双眼睛使得女人美丽妩媚，又使顽石妙趣横生。一个人可以倾家荡产，沦为乞丐，可是只要他还有这两个"护身符"，他就仍然可能拥有无限的欢乐。

第二节

一、翻译下列句子，其中注意定语从句的翻译。

1. 刚刚向英国医学研究委员会报告的结果显示，一些表面健康的潜水员大脑损伤区域与中风患者相似。

2. 美国的许多州都在设定减少排放量的具体标准并为实现这些目标采取意义深远的行动。尤其是加利福尼亚州，去年我曾与其州长签署了关于这一问题的双边协议。

3. 我们相信，贵国政府负有重大责任来保证你们提供给古巴的武器不会用于干扰这种监督，因为这种监督对于我们双方获取改善局势所需要的可靠信息都是非常重要的。

4. 于是我们就面临这样一种选择：要么利用技术来提供并满足迄今为止一直被视为并无必要的各种需求，要么利用技术来缩短人们为了维持一定的生活水准而必须工作的时数。

5. 虽说在43岁的今天，她早已失去了她那双蓝眼睛和花儿一般的妩媚，失去了她身段的苗条和脸上那种恬静与纯真，失去了她犹如苹果花一样红润的肤色，失去了她26年前曾使阿舍斯特一见倾心的神奇魅力，而且她脸上已隐隐约约出现了斑纹，灰蓝色的眼睛也悄悄有点浮肿，但她依然是他相宜而忠实的伴侣。

6. 他走的路，是那些进入大学4年却未取得学位的人走的一条典型的路。

7. 苹果很可能是这个星球上唯一一家敢于与毕加索相比的技术公司。

8. 唐纳德·特朗普总统的第一任妻子伊万娜·特朗普正在写一本回忆录，重点讲述这对夫妇的三个孩子。

9. 悲观主义者是指利用机会制造困难的人；乐观主义者利用困难创造机会。

10. 决定在一个地区种植什么的条件包括气候、供水和地形。

11. 这是亚马逊河支流上农民渔民梦寐以求的一天。

12. 他在足球方面取得了巨大的成功，这使他成为每个足球运动员眼中的偶像。

13. 维修人员将把洗衣机送到维修车间，在那里进行检查和维修。

14. 一位当时在伦敦旅行的上海学者在20世纪30年代的一次姓名搜索比赛中为可口可乐（Coca-Cola）想出了一个完美的翻译"可口可乐"。汉字的意思是"美味和快乐"，很快就大受欢迎，从此它就成为中文中最受欢迎的品牌之一。

15. 有一次暴风骤雨，猛烈的程度实在是我平生所鲜见的，这场暴雨遮住了我的目标。

16. 获得A学位的学校制度是该国文化的基础，强调追求财富和地位必须具备的经济卓越。

17. 关于辐射，一个奇怪的事实是它可以在不引起疼痛的情况下造成伤害，这是我们期望从伤害中得到的警告信号。

18. 但我们很少意识到，工作在多大程度上提供了文化生活，而这种文化生活可以区分充实的生活和空虚的生活。

19. 这将是中国社会生产力的划时代革命，为社会主义和共产主义生产方式奠定物质基础。

20. 他经营着一家工匠公司，从固定窗帘杆到堵住滴水的水龙头，无所不包。他的员工主要来自50多岁的一代，他们一生都有为朋友和家人做事的经历。

21. 曾经只生长在中国的许多花卉如今能在世界各地看到。

22. 他们在一起的美好时光一去不复返了。

23. 在许多城市肆意传播的可怕病毒现在得到了控制。

24. 任何违反规定的人都要受到惩罚。

25. 她住在一幢屋顶上有一个美丽花园的大楼里。

26. 在所有影响农业生产的因素中，天气是对农民影响最大的一个。

27. 昨天在购物中心，我遇到了那位我在一次聚会上认识的教授。

28. 人们会永远记住香港和澳门回归祖国的那一时刻。

29. 没有吃过苦的人不知道什么是甜。

30. 他那富有感染力的笑声打破了沉寂。

二、翻译下面的段落，注意其中定语从句的翻译。

1. 中国有句谚语说：不到长城非好汉；如果你错过了北京烤鸭，那你的北京之旅是不完整的。北京烤鸭历史悠久，如果你想了解更多的中国美食、文化和习俗，北京烤鸭是一个很好的选择。吃北京烤鸭的最好季节是春天、秋天和冬天。厨师会把热烤鸭放在餐桌上，然后把它切成100多片薄片，每片薄片上都覆盖着酥皮。那种美妙的味道会让你终生难忘！

2. 我住在城里高价的公寓里。每天步行去上班，一路上，垃圾包臭不可闻。我还要向我一向厌恶的地方政府缴纳高额的税金。但相比之下，在别人眼里，我算是中产阶级了。使我感到不解的是，这些衡量标准是否有道理？我们是否只是按照那些容易计量的东西进行评估，比如只看财产价目表上的数字，而忽略了那些衡量富足生活的更为重要的价值标准？对于我的儿子们来说，当然，他们可以尽情享受田园的恩赐，像各种新鲜蔬菜、钓来的鱼等，还可以分享邻居们果园和菜园中的各种瓜果。家中有临时保姆帮助看小孩，她从不收报酬。作为回报，我的儿媳也为她看小孩。邻居们经常用自己的技艺和劳力进行换工交易。事情还远不止这些，你如何来估量乡村宁静悠闲的生活？如何来估量自我感觉？我并不想美化小乡村的生活。外部世界常常无情地侵扰这里的宁静。有时汽油价格上涨，有时土地开发商把目光瞄向尚未利用的农田。在小乡村暴力事件时有发生，偏执的观念盛行。大城市出现的许多恶习和丑行同样也在这里发生。而且，我们很难做到对其视而不见，因为我们无法从心理上将他们从身边赶走，也不能无端地把它们说成是外来团体的怪念头，而必须把它们看作"我们生活中的一部分"。

第三节

一、翻译下列句子，其中注意状语从句的翻译。

1. 当我们观察周围的物体时，最显著的特征之一就是它们的运动。

2. 当一种形式的能量消失时，其他形式的能量以等量出现。

3. 我们的整个物理宇宙，当简化为最简单的术语时，是由两种东西组成的，能量和物质。

4. 由于涉及两个或多个步骤，这些过程被称为间接过程。

5. 调查的结果不是决定性的，因为关键的实验只进行了一次。

6. 由于从现在起将经常参考样本和总体，因此有必要区分样本的平均值和总体的平均值。

7. 他说他感觉自己像上瘾了，有节制地使用因特网对他来说简直就不可能。

8. 如果固体不可溶，则不规则固体的体积可通过水的置换来确定。

9. 如果将这些物质放在一起并在恒压下加热到25，则会生成一种新化合物。

物体的运动没有变化，除非有合力作用在物体上。

10. 如果温度保持不变，气体的压力与其体积成反比。

11. 虽然我热爱城镇，但我意识到早年的乡村生活欠我一笔债。

12. 核电站的反应堆虽然效率很高，但却是危险的。

13. 即使有人不是程序员，他也可以通过向开发团队建议如何改进软件对软件产生巨大影响。

14. 反射定律适用于所有表面，无论粗糙或光滑，平面或曲面。

15. 我要启动发电机，以防断电。

16. 钢制零件通常涂上润滑脂，以免生锈。

17. 需要更高的温度，这样我们才能把铁从固态变成液态。

18. 我正想讲话，史密斯先生就插嘴了。

19. 她站在那里看着，直到看不到他的身影。

20. 我刚一到家，就下雨了。

21. 哪里有声音，哪里就有声波。

22. 我一听到这首歌，就感到很愉快。

23. 他结束讲话的时候，听众掌声雷动。

24. 你可以随意到你喜欢的任何地方去。

25. 多穿点衣服，以免感冒。

26. 我带上了游泳衣以防我万一有时间去海边。

27. 只要你保证12点之前能回来，你就可以出去。

28. 他跟孩子们玩耍，结果总是吵架。

29. 为了防止非典的传染，这次旅行计划取消了。

30. 到那时你该有点钱了，如果你能度过这星期的话。

二、翻译下面的段落，注意其中状语从句的翻译。

1. 尽管我喜欢广交朋友，但我只愿与为数不多的几人成为至交。我所提及的那位黑衣男士，就是那样一个我希冀与其成为莫逆之交的人，因为他深得我的景仰。诚然，其行为举止不乏某些怪异的出尔反尔，他全然可被称为幽默家王国中的幽默大师。虽然他慷慨大方，乃至奢靡无度，但他仍假惺惺地希望人们将其视作节俭与审慎之奇才。尽管其言谈之中满是污秽和自私的格言，其内心却充盈着最博大无际的爱心。据我所知，他常宣称自己是人类憎恶者；然而，他的脸庞上却总洋溢着怜悯之情。虽然其神情会柔化为一片慈悲，我却听到过他使用最为恶劣的言辞，其恶劣程度可谓无以复加。有些人佯装人道与柔情，也有一些人则夸耀说这样的秉性乃天性使然。但在我所有认识的人当中，唯有他似乎羞耻于其与生俱有的慈悲之心。他会竭力掩饰其真情，一如任何一个伪君子会掩饰其冷漠那样。然则，在每一个毫无防范的瞬间，那戴着的假面具便会脱落下来，使其毕露于哪怕是最为肤浅的观察者。

2. 梭罗所理解的"低层次",即为了拥有而去拥有,或与所有的邻居明争暗斗而致拥有。他心目中的"高层次",则是这样一种积极的人生戒律,即要使自己对自然界永恒之物的感悟臻于完美。对于他从低层次上节省下来的时间和精力,他可将其致力于对高层次的追求。毋庸置疑,梭罗不赞成忍饥挨饿,但他在膳食方面所投入的精力仅果腹而已,只要可确保他能去从事更为重要的事务,他便别无所求。

殚精竭虑,全力以赴,便是其精髓所在。除非我们愿意直面那些需要我们全身心投入的艰难困苦,否则便不会有幸福可言。正如叶芝所言,除却某些不可能的情形,我们于人生中所获取的满足皆取决于我们在多高的境界中选择我们所愿意面对的艰难困苦。当罗伯特·弗罗斯特言及"以苦为乐"时,他内心所思,大体如此。商业广告中所宣扬的那种幸福观,其致命的缺陷就在于这样一个事实,即它宣称,一切幸福皆唾手可得,不费吹灰之力。

即便于游戏之中,我们也需要有艰难困苦。我们之所以需要它,因为设若没有困难,便断无游戏可言。游戏即是这样一种方式,为了享受其中的情趣而人为地使事情变得不那么轻而易举。游戏中的种种规则,便是将困难武断地强加于人。当有人将情趣摧毁殆尽时,他总是因为拒不按游戏规则行事而使然。这犹如下棋;如果你随心所欲、心血来潮地去更改那些全然武断的游戏规则,这样去赢棋当然会更加容易。但下棋的情趣则在于,应在规则的限定范围内赢取胜利。一言以蔽之,没有艰难,断无情趣。

第五章

课后练习

第一节

一、翻译下列句子,注意长句的翻译。

1. 在20世纪以前,小说中的妇女像都是一个模式。她们没有任何特点,因而无法成为具有个性的人;他们还要屈从于由男性主宰的文化传统强加给他们的种种束缚。

2. 这种使用参照物的方法可以应用于许多种情况,也能用来找到很不相同的各种问题的答案,从"铁生锈,是否必须有一定的湿度才行?"到"哪种豆类一季的产量最高?"

3. 我们对历史的爱好起源于我们最初仅对一些历史上的宏伟场面和激动人心的事件感到孩童般的兴趣;其后,这种爱好变得成熟起来,我们开始对历史这出"戏剧"的多样性和复杂性,对历史上的辉煌成就和悲壮失败也感兴趣;对历史的爱好,最终以我们对人类生命的一种深沉的神秘感而告结束。对死去的,无论是伟大与平凡,所有在这个地球上走过而已逝的人，都有能取得伟大奇迹或制造可怕事件的潜力。

4. 如果做父母的对这种青少年的反应有所准备，而且认为这是一个显示出孩子正在成长，正在发展珍贵的观察力和独立的判断力的标志，他们就不会感到如此伤心，所以也就不会因对此有愤恨和反对的情绪而把孩子推到对立面去。

5. 无意中把图书归类于世界上易损的商品之行列，几乎不会因想到日前越来越多的图书的的确确是为了如此消费目的就会令人感到欣慰。也不会是因为想到多数书店已变得徒有虚名，成了只是销售这类精装书的民刊亭而令人欣慰。这类精装书出售没有几周，有时只要一旦不为畅销书，就会成为折扣书店的商品（这些乱七八糟的书堆也令作家们深感痛心），紧接着就不再再版了。

6. 我们认为这些真理是不言而喻的：人人生而平等，他们都从他们的"造物主"那里被赋予某些不可转让的权利，其中包括生命权，自由权，追求幸福的权利。

7. 在某种程度上，立交桥和地下通道的建设，在加速和分流交通方面迈出了决定性的第一步，从而缓解了交通不畅的局面。但要从根本上解决交通问题，仍须依赖地铁系统。

8. 现在提出的问题是，像英国这样的国家，假如愿意的话，是否有可能在很多国家已经失败的方面获得成功。假如有这种可能，英国是否应尽最大的努力，冒最大的财政风险，一步进入全新技术的前列，或者应该采取比较稳妥地选择，只是赶上其他工业国的步伐。

9. 若想想我们平时那些交谈、幻想、懊悔、激动、惊异和梦的谕示——那些我们常在其中发现自己披着仅凭美化真相而招人瞩目的奇幻伪装的生活场景——想想在这些场景中会发生什么，我们就会获得诸多暗示，而这些暗示将拓展并明晰为对人类本性奥秘的认识。

10. 意大利轿车设计公司总裁安德鲁·皮宁法瑞纳昨天在意大利北部城市都灵的一次交通事故中不幸身亡。意大利轿车设计公司是由他祖父创建的，法拉利和阿尔法·罗米欧等名牌轿车都是该公司设计的。

11. 在今后几个月里，我们的耐心就是我们的一种力量——那种为获得更安全的环境而需要进行长时间等待的耐心，那种对耗费时间才能达到我们的目的的理解和耐心，那种为可能会有牺牲而做好心理准备的耐心。

12. 对于我来说，最重要的就是那些疯狂的人，他们疯狂地活着，疯狂地谈论着万事万物，疯狂地等待着被人救赎，而同时也渴望着所有。他们从不枯燥无聊地说些普通平凡的事情，而是像那罗马美丽的蜡烛燃烧，又在空中爆散开来。

13. 当你开车离开大家,看着他们离你渐行渐远直到人影散乱、模糊不清,那会是一种怎样的感觉?偌大世界与我们错过,那就是再见,而我们却跳进了一个疯狂的冒险之中。

14. 每次我看见我心爱的女孩在这个大千世界中与我擦肩而过,这种伤痛都会刺戳我的内心。

15. 在美国,所有的男孩和女孩都有一段难过的时间,错误观念使他们没有进行过适当的谈话接触、没有真正的谈论过灵魂深处就发生了性关系。因为生活是神圣的,每时每刻都是弥足珍贵的。

16. 我意识到我们的孩子将会好奇地看到这些照片,他们会认为他们的父母生活地一帆风顺,生活井然有序,每天早上起床后都骄傲地走在人生之路上。他们不会想到那令人抓狂的、混乱不堪的窘困生活,痛苦的夜晚和毫无疑义的空虚。

二、翻译下列段落,注意长句的翻译。

1. 我醒来时,太阳红红的,那是我生命中完全不同最陌生的时刻,因为我不知道我是谁。我离开家时,整天疲倦于旅行,我住在一个从未见过的廉价旅馆里,听着窗外斯斯的汽笛声、旅馆破旧木板的嘎吱声、楼上的脚步声还有一切悲伤的声音。我望着屋顶开裂的天花板,大概15秒的样子,我不知道我是谁。我并不害怕,我是另外一个人,一个陌生人,我的生活中充满了鬼和灵魂。

2. 在某些社会中,人们希望拥有孩子是出于所谓的家庭原因:传宗接代,光宗耀祖,博取祖辈的欢心,使那些涉及整个家族的宗教仪式得以发挥其应有的作用。此类原因在现代世俗化的社会中似显苍白,但它们在其他地方曾一度构成并确实仍在构成强有力的理由。此外,有一类家庭原因与下列类别不无共通之处,这便是:生儿育女是为了维系或改善婚姻:能拴住丈夫或者使妻子不致无所事事;修复婚姻或为婚姻注入新的活力;多子多孙,以为家庭幸福,维系于此。这一点更可因其相反情形而得以凸现:在某些社会中,无法生儿育女(或无法生育男孩)于婚姻而言可构成一种威胁,并可作为离婚的一个顺理成章的(或现成的)缘由。

除了所有这一切以外,还有一个原因,那就是后代对于家庭这一体制本身所具有的深远意义。对许多人来说,夫妇两人尚不足以构成一个真正意义上的家庭 -- 夫妻需要孩子来丰富其两人小天地,赋予该小天地以真正意义上的家庭性质,并从子孙后代身上获取某种回报。

孩子需要家庭,但家庭似乎也需要孩子。作为一种社会体制,家庭以其特有的方式,至少从原则上说,可在一个变幻莫测、常常是充满敌意的世界中让人从中获取某种安全、慰藉、保障，以及价值取向。于大多数人而言，这样的一个家庭基础，即使从其表层意义上来讲，也需要不止一个人来维持其存在，并使其世代相传，生生不息。

第二节

一、翻译下列句子，注意长句的翻译方法。

1. 对此球的最好评价来自于英格兰队的中场球星贝克汉姆。他说，此球的准确性十分"杰出"。贝克汉姆受到阿迪达斯赞助，还参与了设计此球。当然，这是题外话。

2. 人生在世，有时会走运，只要抓住时机，就能飞黄腾达，非但男人如此，女人也一样。

3. 了解原文是一个大问题，现代汉语文言与口语兼收并蓄，如何用这样一个丰富多彩的文字来表达英语原文是一个更大的问题，这两个问题在翻译中都得解决。

4. 我们越能知足常乐，就越感到幸福。施人以爱，被人所爱，友人相伴，居之其所，乐之自由，身体健康，这一切所带来的快乐都易为人们所忽略。

5. 扩散电阻器的物理尺寸要作两方面的折衷考虑：图形大，电阻值就容易控制；图形小，占用面积就小，但电阻值却较难控制。

6. 两个小姑娘爱看戏，喜爱戏剧的世界。那个世界的人物比凡人高大。他们堂堂地穿行于舞台，各有风采；他们的声音洪亮，非凡人可比；他们的举止宛如统治一个宇宙的男神和女神。

7. 临行前一天，我淌过河来到红石山下。我以前曾多次来过这里，独自遐想一番。

8. 制造过程可分为单件生产和大量生产。单件生产就是生产少量的零件，大量生产就是生产大量相同的零件。

9. 我们所面临的真正挑战是如何建立这样一些系统，它们虽然由很多成分组成，但可互相兼容，交换使用，从而把物质世界与数字世界溶为一体。

10. 比如说，在过去一百多年中，绝大多数科学进步一直与大学联系在一起，其主要原因之一就在于：大学是许多不同专业学者的群英汇集之地。

11. 睡眠受体内生理节奏定时系统的影响。这种系统是镶嵌在大脑深处的一束神经元，能对诱发睡眠的一种叫作褪黑素的化学物质进行调节，并控制自然的入睡和起床时间。

12. 美国战俘可以领用红十字会派发的食品，也可以写信，不过信要受到检查。 13. 美国政府 1970 年财政年度总支出为 1,950 亿美元，其中 800 亿左右为国防开支；所谓 1970 年财政年度是指 1969 年 7 月 1 日至 1970 年 6 月 10 日这一时段。

14. 当你听别人讲你所懂的外语时，那些以这种外语为母语的人，他们使用词语的方式和你所习惯使用词语的方式是不同的，对此你注意到了吗？

15. 在学校里，学生需要有系统地扩大知识，掌握足够的科学词汇，以便有效地进行交际；还要懂得一些诸如对增进健康、保障安全以及了解周围环境等有用的常识，因为这些常识在日常生活中是十分重要的。

二、翻译下列短文，注意长句的翻译方法。

1.（如果一个人伤害了另一个人的身体，而且这种伤害置被害人于死，我们把这叫做杀人；如果杀人者事先知道这种伤害会致死，那么我们就把他的行动叫作谋杀。）但是，如果社会把千百个无产者置于这样一种境地，使他们不可避免地遭到过早的非自然的死亡，这如同被刀剑或枪弹所惨杀一样；如果社会剥夺了成千上万人的生活必需品把他们置于不能生存的境地，利用法律的铁腕强迫他们处于这种境地，知道不可避免的结局 — 死亡的来临，而且社会也知道这成千上万的人一定会死去，但又听任这种情况存在下去；那么这也是一种谋杀，和个人进行的谋杀完全一样，只不过这是一种隐蔽的，恶毒的谋杀，没有人能够防御，而且看起来又不像谋杀，因为这种罪行是一种不作为，谁也看不到谋杀者，被杀的人看起来好像是自然地死去的。（但这仍然是谋杀。）

2. 里根政府最严重的对外政策问题在总统第二任期行将结束之际浮出水面。1987年，美国人得知里根政府曾秘密向伊朗出售武器，试图为那些美国人质换取人身自由，这些人质被伊朗霍梅尼政府所控制的激进组织囚禁于黎巴嫩。此外，调查也披露，这些武器交易中所得的款项被转移到尼加拉瓜反政府武装组织的手里，但在这一时期，美国国会早已禁止此类性质的军事援助。

随后所举行的参众两院联合委员会的有关"伊朗 - 反政府武装组织事件"听证会审议了有可能存在的非法问题，以及对美国在中东和中美洲对外政策利益进行界定这一更为广泛的问题。从某种较为宽泛的意义上说，有关"伊朗—反政府武装组织事件"的听证会，犹如14年前著名的参议员水门事件听证会那样，所涉及的都是某些根本性问题，即政府应如何向公众负责，以及政府行政与立法部门之间如何才能达成某种恰如其分的平衡。

3. 虽然美国经济在过去几年中已实现了转型，但某些问题自美国建国之初以来一直持续至今，依然悬而未决。其中之一便是围绕着政府在一个基本上属于市场性质的经济中的恰当角色所展开的持久争论。以自由企业为基础的经济体制，其普遍特征便是私有制和个人创新精神，政府介入应相对微弱。然而，人们发现，政府的干预时不时地也是必要的，以确保经济机会人人均等，能为全部民众所获得，并防范肆无忌惮的权力滥用，平抑通货膨胀,刺激经济增长。自殖民地时期以来,美国政府或多或少地参与到经济决策中来。例如,联邦政府曾在基础设施方面进行过巨额投资,它也提供了私营业主们没有能力或不愿意提供的社会福利项目。在过去数十年中,政府也以无数的方式支持并促进农业发展。

第三节

一、翻译下列句子,注意长句的翻译方法。

1. 人类学家托马斯·科赫曼举出一个白人办事员的例子。她上班时一只手臂上绑着绷带,因为她的黑人同事看见她手臂上的绷带却只字不提,对此她感到不快。

2. 这个美国人坦承他感到自己受到了冷落,我相信如果隔壁邻居隔着自己几步之遥径自走过去连招呼也不打一声,大多数美国人也会有同样的感受。

3. 有一点不足为奇,即对于像 67 岁退休银行出纳员莎碧·维特尔这样的老人来说,这一变化是不得人心的,因为她被告知,她的养老金每个月要减少 12.30 美元。

4. 星期四,华盛顿未再次当选联合国人权委员会委员,这是自 1947 年以来的头一遭。这件事中最重要的事实是,导致美国失利的是美国的朋友,而不是美国的敌人。

5. 在许多国家,执法机关担心严格加密的广泛使用,会给犯罪分子和恐怖活动提供方便,从而破坏文明政府的稳定。这种担心引起了一场难以解决的、政治上敏感的辩论。而这场辩论则延误了必要的电子商务法律归入法典的进程。

6. 1929 年,美国北卡莱罗纳州加斯托尼地区爆发了一场激烈的纺织工人大罢工,故事就发生在这场大罢工中。

7. 尽管他们生产粮食养活了世界的另一部分人,维系着城镇居民的生命线,然而,许多农业人口的利益至今仍继续遭受令人厌恶的冷漠忽视。说起来荒谬,但这却是事实。

8. 在国外,中国使馆商务参赞及进出口公司经济和技术公司的代表在中国对外经济贸易部的领导下行使职权。

9. 他们可能已不得不蒙着一种臭名而终其余生,这个臭名就是:他曾贸然采取了一项行动,这项行动破坏了最高级会谈,并且可以设想,还可能已触发一场核战争。

10. 如果说她早已失掉了那蔚蓝色眼睛的、花儿般的魅力,也失掉了她脸儿和身段的那种玉洁冰清、苗条多姿的气质和那苹果花似的颜色 —— 二十六年前这种花容月貌曾那样迅速而奇妙地影响过艾舍斯特 —— 那么在四十三岁的今天,她依旧是个好看而忠实的伴侣,不过脸颊淡淡地有点儿斑驳,而灰蓝的眼睛也已经有点儿饱满了。

11. 铝总是跟其他元素结合在一起,最普遍的是跟氧结合;因为铝跟氧有很强的亲和力,由于这个原因,在自然界找不到游离状态的铝。所以,铝直到19世纪才被人发现。

12. 这时,有个从尼罗河下游来的游客,声称他是一个远方国家的御医,并且说,如果允许的话,他将非常乐意给国王诊治眼睛,因此埃及举国上下一片欢腾。

13. 容易出错的人,若遇事果断,仍可取得意外的成功;哪怕是最有才干的人,若优柔寡断,一定是屡遭失误。

14. 今天,我们认为那么多价值几百万美元的超级计算机,突然间竟变成了可以放在我们衣兜里能随身携带的小玩意儿,真有点不可思议。

15. 许多专家认为,与以前有所不同的是,美国人虽然为自己规定了道德准则,但是对于言行不符合这些准则的朋友或邻居,他们往往不愿进行谴责。

16. 历经数百万年的岁月沧桑,风化雨蚀,形成了山体奇特的地貌:高耸的巨塔、浑圆的穹丘、摇摇欲坠的不倒翁、凌空而立的大拱门。大自然造物不尽,还在不断重塑着这奇岩妙石公园。

二、翻译下列段落,注意长句的翻译方法。

1. 我像一个啜饮每天配给的一两苏格兰威士忌酒的酒鬼一样,每天喝着一杯希望之酒:例如有一天,埃德说他很想吃焙粉饼干,并且真吃了两块哈里斯·罗素连夜赶制出来的家做美味;有一天下午,我们围着他的病床,玩了彼得·巴克曼所著的《游戏场》一书中的游戏,我们一家四个人轻松地欢笑着,就像是星期日在家里度过一个傍午一样;有一天,埃德第一次在走廊上散步,他和随行护士开自己蹒跚而行的玩笑;有一个早上,我将车停在离医院有一街区远的地方,看见埃德出来在一街角上的商亭买了一份报纸——我们一起走回病房,谋划着在美国总统正式访问中国之前赶到北京。

2. 华立克夏的埃文河在此处流入塞纹河,两河沿岸若干英里水草丰美,前所未见。草地上牛羊成群,沿途不断。看着这景色、这牛羊,心想这些好肉可作多少用途,不禁感到神奇。但是再向前骑八九英里,这神奇之感就破灭了;原来我们已到达一个毒瘤似的害人地方,名叫却尔特能,所谓温泉胜地是也。这地方充满了东印度的劫掠者,西印度的奴隶主,英国的税吏、吃客、酒鬼、淫棍,各色各样,男女俱全。他们听了一些窃窃暗笑的江湖郎中的鬼话,以为在做了多少丑事之后,一身孽障,可以到此一洗而净!我每次进入这等地方,总想用手指捏住自己鼻子。当然这话没有道理,但我一看见这儿任何一个两腿畜生向我走来,实在觉得他们肮脏不堪,像是一有机会就要将他们的毒疮传染给我似的!来这地方的都是最恶劣、最愚蠢、最下流的人:赌鬼、小偷、娼妓,一心想娶有钱的丑老婆子的年轻男子,一心想嫁有钱的满脸皱纹、半身入土的老头子的年轻女人,这些少夫幼妻为了便于承继产业,不惜一切手段,坚决要为这些老妇衰翁生男育女!

　　这等丑事,尽人皆知。然而威廉·司各特爵士在1802年演讲时明确表示牧师不必定居教区,而应携眷到温泉游览,据说这样反而能得到他们教区子民的尊敬云云。查此人作此语时,官任代表牛津城的国会议员!

第四节

一、翻译下列短文,注意长句的翻译方法。

1. 乔羽的歌大家都熟悉。但他另外两大爱好却鲜为人知,那就是钓鱼和喝酒。

　　晚年的乔羽喜爱垂钓,他说,"有水有鱼的地方大都是有好环境的,好环境便会给人好心情。我认为最好的钓鱼场所不是舒适的、给你准备好饿鱼的垂钓园,而是那极其有吸引力的大自然野外天成的场所。"钓鱼是一项能够陶冶性情的运动,有益于身心健康。乔羽说:"钓鱼可分三个阶段:第一阶段是吃鱼;第二阶段是吃鱼和情趣兼而有之;第三阶段主要是钓趣,面对一池碧水,将忧心烦恼全都抛在一边,使自己的身心得到充分休息。"

2. 中国科技馆的诞生来之不易。与国际著名科技馆和其他博物馆相比,它先天有些不足,后天也常缺乏营养,但是它成长的步伐却是坚实而有力的。它在国际上已被公认为后起之秀。

　　世界上第一代博物馆属于自然博物馆,它是通过化石、标本等向人们介绍地球和各种生物的演化历史。第二代属于工业技术博物馆,它所展示的是工业文明带来的各种阶段性结果。这两代博物馆虽然起到了传播科学知识的作用,但是,它们把参观者当成了被动的旁观者。

　　世界上第三代博物馆是充满全新理念的博物馆。在这里,观众可以自己去动手操作,自己细心体察。这样,他们可以更贴近先进的科学技术,去探索科学技术的奥妙。

　　中国科技馆正是这样的博物馆!它汲取了国际上一些著名博物馆的长处,设计制作了力学、光学、电学、热学、声学、生物学等展品,展示了科学的原理和先进的科技成果。

3. 加拿大的温哥华1986年刚刚度过百岁生日,但城市的发展令世界瞩目。以港立市,以港兴市,是许多港口城市生存发展的道路。经过百年开发建设,有着天然不冻良港的温哥华,成为举世闻名的港口城市,同亚洲、大洋洲、欧洲、拉丁美洲均有定期班轮,年货物吞吐量达到8,000万吨,全市就业人口中有三分之一从事贸易与运输行业。

　　温哥华(Vancouver)的辉煌是温哥华人智慧和勤奋的结晶,其中包括多民族的贡献。

加拿大地广人稀，国土面积比中国还大，人口却不足 3000 万。吸收外来移民，是加拿大长期奉行的国策。可以说，加拿大除了印第安人外，无一不是外来移民，不同的只是时间长短而已。温哥华则更是世界上屈指可数的多民族城市。现今 180 万温哥华居民中，有一半不是在本地出生的，每 4 个居民中就有一个是亚洲人。而 25 万华人对温哥华的经济转型起着决定性的作用。他们其中有一半是近 5 年才来到温哥华地区的，使温哥华成为亚洲以外最大的中国人聚居地。

第六章

课后练习

第一节

一、翻译下列句子。

1. 昨晚天气寒冷，跑道上结了霜。

2. 在他们之间产生了一条鸿沟。双方隔沟相对而视，彼此的目光都在宣告受尽了对方的欺骗。

3. 我国的山川之美虽然难以描绘，却是众口皆碑。

4. 那天早上我遇见了艾芬汉太太，那个像博饼一样没有曲线的女人。

5. 他已经三十六岁，青春像一路鸣叫的鹰，早已一闪而逝，留给他的是衰老和幻灭。

6. 哈维参加了他们的婚礼。他好不容易找到一个娜塔莉小姐单独站在那儿的机会，约她出来。

7. 他不能像过去身体好的时候那样每天洗澡了，因为现在要有妈妈来帮他做这件事，这真是一件相当费劲的事情。

8. 故事发生在丹麦的一家美丽如画的小旅社里。这种旅社备有酒食招待客人，通用英语。我和父亲这次旅行，既为了公事，也为了游乐，有空的时候玩得挺开心。

9. 今天他因为急于要给自己像个办法，迫不得已，便走进了那家杂货铺。这家杂货铺坐落在巴尔的摩街口，正面是十四号街，地位正当要冲。他看见靠近门口的一座小玻璃柜房里有一个女出纳员，就去向她打听卖汽水的柜台归谁负责。

10. 天才与幸福竟能兼耳得之，简直匪夷所思。一般来说，得天独厚者往往招嫉惹怨，不为同侪友辈所喜。梅纽因可说是演奏史上最广受爱戴的人物，从 1927 年崭露头角开始，即备受欢迎，迄今仍历久不衰。

二、翻译下面一则短文。

音乐

当音乐使我们流下看似无端的泪水时，我们并非像格拉维纳认为的那样是"喜极而泣"，而是一种骤然而至且难以忍受的悲哀，因为作为凡尘的芸芸众生，我们尚不能尽享那种超凡的极乐，音乐赐予我们的只是朦胧飘渺的浮光掠影。

三、翻译下面一段诗文。

他被使用在远离文化中心的地方，
又被他的将军和他的虱子所抛弃，
于是在一件棉袄里他闭上眼睛，
而离开人世。人家不会把他提起。

当这场战役被整理成书的时候，
没有重要的知识在他的头壳里丧失。
他的玩笑是陈腐的，他沉闷如战时，
他的名字和模样都将永远消逝。

他不知善，不择善，却教育了我们，
并且像逗点一样加添上意义；
他在中国变为尘土，以便在他日
我们的女儿得以热爱这人间，
不再为狗所凌辱；也为了使有山、
有水、有房屋的地方，也能有人烟。

第二节

一、翻译下列商标词。
1. 妮维雅 2. 力士 3. 普拉达 4. 星巴克 5. 箭牌卫浴
6. 古驰 7. 必胜客 8. 欧莱雅 9. 帮宝适 10. 浪琴

二、翻译下列广告标题。
1. 饭菜上乘，环境迷人，服务可心。（酒店广告）
2. 花点小钱，省点时间。（某电器广告）
3. 奔驰轿车，行业标杆。（奔驰）

4. 简约不简单。(利郎)

5. 百万买卖,毫厘利润。(零售商广告)

6. 不懈追求完美。(凌志轿车)

7. 品质优良,价格合理,设计新颖,交货迅捷。(蔓莎服装)

8. 没有不做的小生意,没有解决不了的问题。(IBM 公司)

9. M&Ms 只溶在口,不溶在手。(M&M 巧克力)

10. 钻石恒久远,一颗永流传。(戴·比尔斯)

三、翻译下面一则广告文案。

修身骑士牛仔裤

您的身材是靓丽的!

是您的牛仔裤跟您的身材不协调。

穿着不合身的牛仔裤就算再好的身材也秀不出来。

这就是为什么穿着一条能秀出您靓丽身材的牛仔裤会这么重要。牛仔裤最能体现出您的身材。就像我们的修身骑士。当我们在设计轻松骑士的时候,我们于其上面裁出曲线以适合您本来的身材轮廓。所以如果您的身材比例变了,修身骑士也会跟着变。

如果您仅仅因为您的牛仔裤不合身而觉得不舒服不自信的话,就来试试我们的修身骑士吧。试了您就会明白,您需要的不是一副更靓丽的身材,而是一条更好的牛仔裤。

第三节

一、翻译下列新闻中经常出现的语词。

1. 中国通 2. 鸵鸟政策 3. 耦合效应 4. 智囊团 5. 划出界限

6. 避税港 7. 封口费 8. 轮值主席(国)9. 平权行动 10. 换脸(伪真)

二、翻译下列新闻标题。

1. 如果美国经济过热,世界其他地区会发生什么?

2. 如何设计入籍语言测试?要规避哪些方面?

3. 为非白人接种疫苗是减少疫苗犹豫的第一步

4. 孤独是一个普遍存在的问题,其根源很复杂

5. 七颠八倒,银行现在有很多钱?

6. 在中国北方挣扎之际,南方却奋起直追

7. 疫情使曾经濒危的 MBA 重新变成热门

8. 乔·拜登着手利用旧的团队恢复美国在新世界的领导地位

9. 住房投资的回报并不是他们所吹嘘的那样

10. 治疗被遗忘的杀手，草药可以改善被忽视的疾病

三、翻译下面一则新闻导语。

在一群英国商界领袖的支持下，欧洲之星再次向英国政府提出了紧急援助的请求。欧洲之星运营着连接英国和法国的隧道列车，自3月以来，乘客数量已经暴跌了95%。2015年，英国政府出售了其所持股份。欧洲之星的多数股权由法国国营铁路公司（SNCF）持有。

四、翻译下面一则新闻消息。

拜登政府承诺在担任总统的前100天内提供1.5亿剂新冠疫苗，但哪些人应该接种疫苗呢？大多数州优先考虑一线医护人员和常住疗养院的居民，其次是75岁及以上的老人和必要工作人员。很少有州会确保非裔美国人或西班牙裔人接种疫苗，尽管他们死于新冠的可能性是白人的三倍。事实上，少数族裔可能排在对所有美国人来说都很有价值的事情的后面。

五、翻译下面一篇新闻特写。

史上最年轻"女魔头"！90后华裔女孩成Vogue中国版新主编

27岁的澳大利亚华裔时尚博主章凝成为时《美国尚杂志》（Vogue）中国版新主编，接替任此岗位长达16年的前主编张宇，成为Vogue史上最年轻的编辑总监。

章凝（Margaret Zhang）是澳大利亚华裔，时尚圈的斜杠少女。她曾经做过倩碧全球代言人，掌镜拍摄过施华洛世奇广告大片，摄影师/设计师/作家/时尚顾问/制片人/创意总监都是她的标签。

章凝是澳大利亚出生的华裔电影人、摄影师、时尚顾问和作家。

16岁起，章凝就开启了她的时尚事业，如今，她的社交媒体粉丝已经超过120万。

16岁时，章凝就开始运营她的时尚博客，并且成为一名时尚顾问。如今，她在社交媒体上有超过120万的粉丝。2016年，她名列福布斯亚洲30位30岁以下精英榜，2016年，她还为Vogue中国版进行悉尼时装周的拍摄。

她常在社交媒体上分享自己的工作和日常，穿搭风格时尚多变。

也分享过一些具有中国元素的照片，比如"福"字和拔罐什么的……

Vogue全球编辑总监安娜·温图尔表示，"我很高兴章凝成为了Vogue的新任编辑总监，她国际化的成长背景、对数字媒体的精通，以及广泛的兴趣爱好，势必能为Vogue带来更好的发展。"

在宣布其任命时，Vogue形容章凝无疑是世界各大秀场前排的座上客。

提起她对新岗位的理解，章凝说自己是这样理解的。

章凝认为，她的岗位职责既要专注国内，也要面向世界。提起她对 Vogue 中国版的展望，她相信她的国际经验能够帮助她完成使命："有关中国的很多语境是不完整的，中国很多时候被看成是一个整体，而不是作为个体和创新的集合。"

章凝祖籍浙江台州，成长于澳大利亚悉尼，拥有悉尼大学商业与法律学士双学位。父亲是悉尼大学机械工程教授。她最早接触时尚起源自对芭蕾的热爱。

章凝出生在悉尼，在澳大利亚西莱德郊区长大，章凝父母来自浙江台州。她在悉尼大学学习商业和法律。她的 HSC 成绩为 99.85 分，大学毕业后获得商业/法学双学位。

章的父亲是悉尼大学机械工程教授。她最早接触时尚起源自对芭蕾的热爱。

第四节

一、翻译下列句子。

1. 你邮寄的包裹必须妥善包装。包装不妥会造成耽搁、损坏或丢失。由此造成的费用由你承担。

2. 在金融连续 10 个月发生剧烈震动之后，这种态度并没有明显改变。

3. 大家都知道，约翰投资的生意破产了，损失惨重。

4. 如果不了解当地文化，其结果可能会冒犯想与之建立贸易关系的人。

5. 本信用证在提单日期后 90 评汇票付款，其中 60 天免息，后 30 天利息在信用证金额按利率 1.3% 凭我行开出的即期汇票向我行提取。

6. 如果买方违反本条所规定的条件，卖方有权终止此合同。

7. 经甲乙双方同意后，工程预算应包括筹建工作人员的编制、报酬及费用。

8. 甲、乙双方同意由合资公司与乙方（或第三方）签订技术转让协议，以取得为达到合同第四章规定的生产经营目的、规模所需要的先进生产技术及人员培训，这些技术包括：产品设计、制造工艺、测试方法、材料配方和质量标准。

二、将下面有关仲裁的合同条款翻译为中文

凡与本合同有关的，或在执行本合同过程中发生的一切争议、争论、索赔或分歧，双方应友好协商解决。如协商不能解决，则将分歧提交中国国际贸易促进委员会对外贸易仲裁委员会，按该会仲裁程序暂行规定进行仲裁。仲裁应在北京进行。该委员会的决定是终局性的，对双方均具有约束力。除另有规定外，仲裁费用由败诉方负担。

三、将下面的商务信函翻译为中文。

尊敬的先生：

我们从中华人民共和国驻东京大使馆商务参赞处获悉贵公司名称和地址，现借此机会致函，希望与你们建立业务联系。

我公司从事工艺品进出口业务已多年。为方便你们熟悉我们的经验范围，随函附上我公司目前主要出口产品一览表一份。

倘若你们对我方产品感兴趣，请来函告知。俟得知你方的详细需求量，我们即提供低报价。

盼早日回复

诚挚问候

附件：如文

第五节

一、翻译下列句子。

1. 因此，除几何形状外，还可以使用不同材料的组合来优化组件机械性能，满足给定的设计要求。

2. 救生衣应存放于救生艇中，或从大船带入救生艇中，在救生艇下方时，将其置于座位下火膝盖上。救生艇中不允许携带任何松散物体。

3. 首先是工业历史学家。第二，分析和编年史。第三，也是最后一个，"动手"的工业工程师，有些情况下，上述分类是柔性的，而不是刚性的。

4. 电流的增长比电阻的下降要快，这就导致进一步加热，进一步减小热辐射和电阻。

5. 我们根据这种推理，就可以估计出银河中的可探测到的文明世界的数目。

6. 信息从计算机的一个部分传送到另一个部分，靠的是电线中传导的电流。

7. 该省已普遍成立农技推广中心，帮助农民以更加科学的方法种田。

8. 水中听音器将捕捉到的水下噪声直接传递到操作员的耳机中。

9. 宇宙膨胀说虽然听似奇特，但它是基本粒子物理学中一些公认理论的科学合理的推论。许多天体物理学家过去十年来都认为这是论说是正确的。

10. 铝总是和其他元素结合在一起，最常见的是和氧结合在一起，因为铝对氧有很强的亲和力，因此，在自然界任何地方都找不到处于游离状态的铝，所以铝直到十九世纪才为人所知。

二、翻译下列一则科技短文（节选）。

糖尿病是世界范围内一种常见的代谢性疾病。据估算，2019年全球有4.63亿糖尿病患者，到2045年将上升到7亿[1]。对糖尿病患者来说，心血管疾病（CVD）是他们面对的主要问题，它是糖尿病患者死亡的最普遍原因。具体来说，与非糖尿病患者相比，成年糖尿病患者的 CVD 发病率和死亡率的相对风险在男性中为 1 到 3，女性中为 2 到 5。

三、翻译下面一则科技摘要。

目标：提供 2019 年全球糖尿病患病率的估计值以及 2030 年和 2045 年的预测。

方法：从 1990 年到 2018 年共公布了 255 个高质量数据源，代表 138 个国家。对于没有高质量国内数据的国家，估计数是从经济、种族、地理和语言相匹配的类似国家推断出来的。Logistic 回归用于产生 20-79 岁成人中平滑的年龄特异性糖尿病患病率估计（包括以前未诊断的糖尿病）。

结果：2019 年全球糖尿病患病率估计为 9.3%（4.63 亿人），到 2030 年上升到 10.2%（5.78 亿人），到 2045 年上升到 10.9%（7 亿人）。城市（10.8%）的患病率高于农村（7.2%），高收入国家（10.4%）的患病率高于低收入国家（4.0%）。1/2（50.1%）的糖尿病患者不知道自己患有糖尿病。据估计，2019 年全球糖耐量受损患病率为 7.5%（3.74 亿），预计到 2030 年达到 8.0%（4.54 亿），2045 年达到 8.6%（5.48 亿）。

结论：全世界有不到 5 亿人患有糖尿病，预计 2030 年和 2045 年这一数字将分别增加 25% 和 51%。

四、翻译下面一则科普文章。

石油

我们现在开汽车、开飞机使用的油是怎样形成的呢？科学家确知煤是怎样形成的，但若问题到石油怎样形成的，他们似乎就不那么有把握了。他们认为地下的石油在远古时期就已经开始形成，而且是由海中生物形成的。亿万个数不清的微小生物和植物在海水中生长并沉入海底，上面覆盖着大量沉积的泥沙，由于化学变化、压力和温度等因素，经过漫长的岁月，变成了现在我们所说的石油。这些小动物必须在一层层岩石之间密封起来，经过极长的一段时间才能变成石油。石油是在海里形成的，这种说法，只要看一下世界主要油田分布图，就可以得到证实；大油田离开今日的海洋很远的极少。有些地方，天然气和石油从海底浮上水面。含有石油的岩层也是在海里形成的。这种岩层是沉积岩，是在海水的作用之下沉积在洋底的。在有石油的地方，附近几乎总可以发现贝壳的残片以及海洋生物的其他遗迹。有一种很普通的沉积岩，叫做页岩。这是一种松软的岩石，显然是在海底沉积而成的。凡是有页岩的地方，就可能有石油。

地质学家是研究岩石的科学家，他们可以为钻探石油的人指明哪些地方可能有油。有些地方，根本未经钻探，石油就流出地面，而且已经使用了几百年。在特立尼达岛，石油以沥青的形式出现。沥青是一种可以用来铺路的物质。1595 年，沃尔特雷利爵士参参观过特立尼达有名的沥青湖。据说湖里有沥青90亿吨。表层下面很可能储藏着极为丰富的原油。

钻探石油有很大的偶然性。钻透可能到了离油很近的地方而没有碰到油；另一方面，也可能在相当浅的地方打出油来。钻头下去的时候，便把泥土送上来。从不同深度取出土样以后，便进行检验，看是否有含油的迹象钻探石油的人如果在一个地方得不到预期的结果，便道另外一个地方去钻探。在石油勘探方面，已经花了大笔的钱，比如在埃及的沙漠里进行的勘探工作就是如此。有时收效甚微。因此，当我们为自己的小汽车买几加仑汽油的时候，我们所付的不只是汽油本身的费用，而且还有不断进行找油功过的一部分费用。

油田打出原油之后，便送到炼油厂去处理。最普通的处理办法是加热。石油经过家热，最先冒出来的蒸汽冷却后就是质量最高的汽油。汽油的沸点低，倒一点在手上，很快就挥发了。随后从石油分离出来的气体可以浓缩成煤油。最后产生的是各种等级的润滑油。剩下的便是重油，可以用作燃料。

附录一　全国翻译专业资格（水平）考试介绍

一、考试的背景

全国翻译专业资格（水平）考试（以下简称"翻译资格考试"）是受中国国家人力资源和社会保障部委托，由中国外文局负责实施与管理的一项国家级职业资格考试，已纳入中国国务院职业资格目录清单，是一项在全国实行的、统一的、面向全社会的翻译专业资格认证，是对参试人员口译或笔译双语互译能力和水平的评价与认定。

设立这一考试的目的是为加强翻译行业管理，规范翻译就业市场，促进翻译行业人才队伍建设，科学、客观、公正地评价翻译专业人才水平和能力，使中国翻译行业更好地与国际接轨，为中国与世界各国政治、经济、文化、教育等领域的交流合作提供翻译人才资源。

二、考试的效用

翻译资格证书由中国国家人力资源和社会保障部和中国外文局联合颁发，在就业市场具有很高的含金量。

1. 唯一纳入中国国家职业资格制度的语言类考试。2017年，翻译资格考试作为唯一的语言类考试被纳入中国国务院职业资格目录清单。

2. 中国最具含金量的十大证书之一。2016年，《人民日报》等中国主流媒体，将翻译资格证书列入中国最具含金量的十大证书之一。

3. 与中国职称制度完全对应的职业资格证书。翻译资格证书是中国翻译从业人员的职称证书，三级翻译是初级职称（相当于高校职称等级中的"助教"），二级翻译是中级职称（相当于高校职称等级中的"讲师"），一级翻译是副高级职称（相当于高校职称等级中的"副教授"），译审是正高级职称（相当于高校职称等级中的"教授"）。

4. 中国翻译硕士（MTI）必须参加的考试。根据中国教育部有关政策规定："翻译硕士专业学位研究生，入学前未获得二级或二级以上翻译专业资格证书的，在校期间必须参加二级口译或笔译翻译专业资格考试。"翻译资格考试被中国翻译硕士专业教育学位委员会纳入了翻译硕士专业高校教学管理质量监控体系，学生通过二级考试的情况也被列入评估高校翻译专业办学成果的重要指标。

5. 获得翻译资格证书者可申请加入中国翻译协会。根据中国翻译协会有关规定，获得翻译资格考试三级或二级证书者，可申请成为普通会员；获得一级或译审证书者，可申请成为专家会员。

6. 翻译资格证书成为人员招录的必备或优先条件。翻译资格证书已成为评价翻译人才水平的"国家标准",是众多机关、企事业单位,尤其是大型翻译公司招聘翻译人员的必备证书。

7. 翻译资格证书已成为热门城市高端人才引进的重要资质。翻译资格证书已被纳入北京、上海等热门城市高端人才引进、户口申请的资格条件。

8. 翻译资格证书已成为项目招投标的关键资质。翻译资格证书已被联合国和中国政府列入很多大型翻译项目、研究课题申请的必备资质。

9. 国际影响力越来越大的中国职业资格证书。翻译资格考试是全球最大的翻译类考试,是中国第一个在海外设立考点的职业资格考试,正与国际上现有翻译类考试证书推进互认。

三、考试报名条件

翻译资格考试是一项面向全社会的职业资格考试,具有一定外语水平的人员,不分年龄、学历、资历和身份,均可报名参加相应语种二、三级的考试。

翻译资格考试在中国大陆各省、自治区、直辖市均设有考场,考生可在任一考场报考任一语种、级别、类别的考试。

翻译资格考试逐步在海外开设考点,非中国籍人员及中国在外的留学生、从业人员可在开设考点的国家就近报考。

四、考试的语种和专家组成、证书的等级和对应能力

1. 翻译资格考试的语种。开设英语、日语、法语、俄语、德语、西班牙、阿拉伯语、朝鲜语/韩国语、葡萄牙语9个语种。其中,每年上半年举行英、日、法、阿拉伯、葡萄牙语的一、二、三级口笔译考试,下半年举行英语二、三级口笔译、同声传译及俄、德、西班牙、朝鲜语/韩国语的一、二、三级口笔译考试。

2. 翻译资格考试的专家组成。共设有10个专家委员会,包括9个语种专家委员会和1个高校促进委员会,由近300名来自国内外政府机构、高校、企事业单位的权威专家组成。此外,翻译资格考试还建有由近千名专家组成的命审题和阅卷专家组。

3. 翻译资格证书的等级。分为译审、一、二、三级共四个级别,其中译审证书采用评审方式取得,一级证书采用考试和评审结合的方式取得,二、三级证书采用考试方式取得。

4. 翻译资格证书对应的能力要求。

译审对应的能力要求:知识广博,熟悉中国和相关语言国家的文化背景,中外文语言功底深厚;胜任高难度的翻译专业工作,能够解决翻译专业工作中的重大疑难问题,具有

较强的审定重要事项翻译稿件的能力，或者承担重要谈判、国际会议的口译工作能力；译风严谨，译文能表达原作的风格；对翻译专业理论有深入研究，组织、指导翻译专业人员出色完成各项翻译任务，在翻译人才培养方面卓有成效。

一级翻译对应的能力要求：熟悉中国和相关语言国家的文化背景，中外文语言功底扎实；胜任范围较广、难度较大的翻译专业工作，能够承担重要场合的口译或者译文定稿工作，解决翻译工作中的疑难问题；对翻译实践或者理论有所研究，对原文有较强的理解能力，具有较强的中外文表达能力，有正式出版的译著或者公开发表的译文；翻译业绩突出，能够组织、指导三级翻译、二级翻译等翻译专业人员完成各项翻译任务。

二级翻译对应的能力要求：具有比较系统的外语基础知识和翻译理论知识；能够独立承担本专业具有一定难度的口译或笔译工作，语言流畅、译文准确。

三级翻译对应的能力要求：能完成一般性口译或笔译工作。从事口译者应能够基本表达交谈各方原意，语音、语调基本正确；从事笔译者应能够表达一般难度的原文内容，语法基本正确、文字比较通顺。

五、考试科目、方式和时间

笔译资格考试设《笔译综合能力》和《笔译实务》2个科目，《笔译综合能力》考试时间为120分钟，《笔译实务》考试时间为180分钟。

口译资格考试设《口译综合能力》和《口译实务》2个科目。三级《口译实务》科目考试时间为30分钟，其他科目为60分钟。

翻译资格考试在中国国内已实现全部通过计算机作答，海外考点根据情况选择使用计算机作答或纸笔作答。

六、考试发展历程

2003年英语试点考试推出；

2004年法、日语考试推出；

2005年英语同声传译考试推出；全年报考人数首次超过1万人；

2006年俄、德、西班牙、阿拉伯语考试推出；

2008年翻译资格证书与翻译硕士学位实现接轨；

2012年一级考试推出；

2016年翻译资格证书被中国主流媒体评为中国含金量最高的十大证书之一，全年报考人数首次超过10万人；

2017年作为唯一的外语类考试被列入中国国家职业资格目录清单；

2018年全年报考人数首次超过20万人；

2019年成为第一个在海外开设考点的中国职业资格考试；

2020年朝鲜语/韩国语考试推出；

2021年葡萄牙语考试推出。

七、考试的国际化

2019年起，翻译资格考试在海外开考，白俄罗斯国立大学是第一个海外考点。目前，已在俄罗斯莫斯科、圣彼得堡，白俄罗斯明斯克等地开设考点，2020年还将在新加坡、马来西亚、泰国、加拿大等多个国家开设考点。

2020年起，翻译资格考试还将逐步推进与国际上现有翻译类考试的证书互认工作。

翻译资格考试正受到全球翻译界的广泛关注，通过考试官网关注考试的国家和地区超过160个。

附录二　全国翻译专业资格（水平）考试英语笔译三级考试大纲（2020版）

一、总论

全国翻译专业资格（水平）考试英语笔译三级考试设置"笔译综合能力"和"笔译实务"两个科目。

应试人员须：

1. 遵守中华人民共和国宪法和法律法规，贯彻落实党和国家方针政策。

2. 具有良好的职业道德，具有推动翻译行业发展的职业使命感，具备相应的翻译专业能力和业务技能。

3. 具备较强的敬业精神，热爱本职工作，认真履行岗位职责。

二、考试目的

检验应试人员能否独立完成中等难度的笔译工作。

三、基本要求

1. 具备较扎实的语言基础，具备较好的双语表达能力，熟练掌握5000个以上英语单词。

2. 了解中国、涉英语国家和地区的社会、历史、文化等背景情况；掌握较广泛、多领域的相关专业知识。

3. 了解常规翻译理论，较熟练运用一般翻译方法。

4. 能够翻译中等难度文章，把握文章主旨，较准确传递源语的事实和细节，语法正确，文字较通顺。

四、笔译综合

（一）考试目的检验应试人员对英语语法和词汇的掌握程度和运用能力，以及阅读理解、推理与释义能力，语言表达能力。

（二）基本要求

1. 较快速阅读、理解中等难度英语文章的主要内容。

2. 较正确获取与处理相关信息。

3. 较熟练运用语言技巧，及时做出较准确判断和正确选择，无明显错漏。

五、笔译实务

（一）考试目的检验应试人员中英双语互译的能力。

（二）基本要求

1. 较快速阅读、理解中等难度英语文章的主要内容。
2. 较熟练运用翻译策略与技巧，较准确、完整地进行双语互译，无明显错译、漏译。
3. 译文忠实原文，语言较规范，用词正确，译文通顺，无过多语法错误。
4. 英译汉速度为每小时 300—400 个英语单词；汉译英速度为每小时 200—300 个汉字。

英语笔译三级考试模块设置一览表

《笔译综合能力》

序号	题型	题量	分值	时间（分钟）
1	词汇和语法	60 道选择题	60	
2	阅读理解	30 道选择题	30	120
3	完形填空	20 空	10	
总计	—	—	100	

《笔译实务》

序号	题型		题量	分值	时间（分钟）
1	翻译	英译汉	两段或一篇文章，约 600 个单词	50	180
		汉译英	两段或一篇文章，约 400 个汉字	50	
总计	—	—	—	100	

参考书目

Appiah, K. 1993. Thick translation. *Callaloo* (4): 808-819.

Catford, J.C. 1965. *A linguistic theory of translation*. London: Oxford University Press.

Hsien-yung, Pai. 2000. *Taipei People*. (Pai Hsien-yung & Patia Yasin. Trans.). Hong Kong: The Chinese University Press.

Newmark, P. 2001. *A textbook of translation*. Shanghai: Shanghai Foreign Language Education Press.

Nida, E. A. 2004. *Toward a science of translating*. Shanghai: Shanghai Foreign Language Education Press.

Nida, E. A. & Taber, C. R. 2004. *The theory and practice of translation*. Shanghai: Shanghai Foreign Language Education Press.

Wells, W.&Burnet, J. 1999. *Advertising: principles and practice* (Fourth edition). Beijing: Tsinghua University Press.

巴尔胡达罗夫. 1985. 语言与翻译 [M]. 北京：中国对外翻译出版公司.

曹明伦. 2019. 英汉翻译二十讲 [M]. 北京：商务印书馆.

常玉田. 2009. 大学英语翻译教程 [M]. 北京：外语教学与研究出版社.

陈大亮. 2019. 文学翻译的境界：译意·译味·译境 [M]. 北京：商务印书馆.

陈培爱. 2003. 广告学原理 [M] 上海：复旦大学出版社.

刁晏斌. 2019. 汉语的欧化与欧化的汉语—百年汉语历史回顾之一 [J]. 云南师范大学学报 (1): 27-38.

方梦之. 2004. 译学词典 [M]. 上海：上海外语教育出版社.

冯庆华. 2002. 文体翻译论 [M]. 上海：上海外语教育出版社.

冯伟年. 2012. 新编实用英汉翻译实例评析（第2版）[M]. 北京：清华大学出版社.

符蓉, 李延林. 2020. 计算机英语中的it评价型主位及其翻译 [J]. 中国科技翻译 (4):11-13.

顾维勇. 2005. 实用文体翻译 [M]. 北京：国防工业出版社.

金圣华. 2011. 齐向译道行 [M]. 北京：商务印书馆.

李青. 2003. 新编英汉汉英翻译教程 [M]. 北京：北京大学出版社.

连淑能. 1993. 英汉对比研究 [M]. 北京：高等教育出版社.

连淑能. 2002. 论中西思维方式 [J]. 外语与外语教学 (2): 40-46, 63-64.

连淑能 . 2006. 英译汉教程 [M]. 北京：高等教育出版社 .

刘宓庆 . 2006. 新编汉英对比与翻译 [M]. 北京：中国对外翻译出版公司 .

刘宓庆 . 2015. 文体与翻译（第二版）[M]. 北京：中译出版社 .

刘其中 . 2018. 英汉新闻翻译 [M]. 北京：清华大学出版社 .

刘士聪 . 2019. 文学翻译与语言审美 [M]. 天津：南开大学出版社 .

陆谷孙 . 2007. 英汉大词典（第 2 版）[M]. 上海：上海译文出版社 .

马永堂 , 华英 . (2005). 英文广告阅读 [M]. 北京：经济管理出版社 .

蒙兴灿 . 2003. 实用英汉翻译 [M]. 成都：四川大学出版社 .

欧阳昱 2013. 译心雕虫一个奥华作家的翻译笔记 [M]. 台北市：创智文化有限公司 .

潘文国 . 2019. 英汉语对比研究的基本方法与创新 [J]. 外语教学 (1): 1-6.

彭朝忠 . 2019. 广告翻译与翻译中的广告视野 [M]. 北京：化学工业出版社 .

邵志洪 . 2010. 英汉微观对比研究 30 年（1977~2007）综述 [J]. 外国语文 (5): 47-52.

宋洪波 , 朱明炬 . 2020. 实用文体翻译教程 [M]. 北京：清华大学出版社 .

孙迎春 . 2004. 张谷若翻译艺术研究 [M]. 北京：中国对外翻译出版公司 .

谭载喜 . 2002. 新编奈达论翻译 [M]. 北京：中国对外翻译出版公司 .

童元芳 . 2015. 译心与译艺：文学翻译的究竟 [M]. 北京：外语教学与研究出版社 .

王恩冕 . 2009. 大学英汉翻译教程 (第 3 版) [M]. 北京：对外经济贸易大学出版社 .

王力 . 2019. 中国现代语法 [M]. 北京：北京联合出版公司 .

夏济安 (译). 2000. 美国名家散文选读 [M]. 上海：复旦大学出版社 .

夏政 . 2003. 英文广告实用手册 [M]. 成都：西南财经大学出版社 .

徐晓晔 , 马智傲 , 尚余祥等 . 2019. 工业工程英语翻译的研究 [J]. 中国科技翻译 (2):11-13.

杨荣琦 , 陈玉红 . 1995. 英文广告文体与欣赏 [M]. 武汉：华中理工大学出版社 .

余光中 . 2004. 余光中谈翻译 [M]. 北京：中国对外翻译出版公司 .

岳峰 . 2015. 职场笔译：理论与实践 [M]. 厦门：厦门大学出版社 .

张道真 . 现代英语用法词典 [M].

张建 . 1994. 新闻英语文体与范文评析 [M]. 上海：上海外语教育出版社 .

张培基 . 1980. 英汉翻译教程 . 上海：上海外语教育出版社 .

赵刚 , 杜振东 . 2019. 突破汉英翻译二十讲 [M]. 上海：华东理工大学出版社 .

赵静 . 1997. 广告英语 [M]. 北京：外语与外语教学出版社 .

赵萱 , 郑仰成 . 2018. 科技英语翻译 [M]. 外语教学与研究出版社 .

郑玉琪 , 郭艳红 . 2005. 浅谈英文化妆品说明书之美学翻译 [J]. 中国翻译 (2)：72-74.

周邦友 . 2015. 翻译基础教程 [M]. 上海：东华大学出版社 .

周振峰 . 2010. 英汉语言研究对比综述 . 现代语文 [J].

祝吉芳 . 2004. 英汉翻译：方法与试笔 [M]. 北京：北京大学出版社 .

Guidere, M. The Translation of Advertisement: from Adaptation to Localization [EB/OL]http://www.translationdirectory.com/article60.htm, 2003-10-3.